T0375112

Islam

Translated

SOUTH ASIA ACROSS THE DISCIPLINES

A series edited by Muzaffar Alam,
Robert Goldman, and Gauri Viswanathan
Dipesh Chakrabarty, Sheldon Pollock, and
Sanjay Subrahmanyam, founding editors

Funded by a grant from the Andrew W. Mellon Foundation and jointly published by the University of California Press, the University of Chicago Press, and Columbia University Press.

Recent South Asia Across the Disciplines titles:

The Place of Devotion: Siting and Experiencing Divinity in Bengal-Vaishnavism
by Sukanya Sarabadhikary (California)

We Were Adivasis: Aspiration in an Indian Scheduled Tribe
by Megan Moodie (Chicago)

I Too Have Some Dreams: N. M. Rashed and Modernism in Urdu Poetry
by A. Sean Pue (California)

Wombs in Labor: Transnational Commercial Surrogacy in India
by Amrita Pande (Columbia)

Writing Resistance: The Rhetorical Imagination of Hindi Dalit Literature
by Laura R. Brueck (Columbia)

Democracy Against Development: Lower Caste Politics and Political Modernity in Postcolonial India
by Jeffery Witsoe (Chicago)

South Asia Across the Disciplines is a series devoted to publishing first books across a wide range of South Asian studies, including art, history, philology or textual studies, philosophy, religion, and the interpretive social sciences. Series authors all share the goal of opening up new archives and suggesting new methods and approaches, while demonstrating that South Asian scholarship can be at once deep in expertise and broad in appeal.

Islam *Translated*

Literature, Conversion, and the Arabic Cosmopolis of South and Southeast Asia

Ronit Ricci

THE UNIVERSITY OF CHICAGO PRESS
CHICAGO AND LONDON

THE UNIVERSITY OF CHICAGO PRESS, Chicago 60637
THE UNIVERSITY OF CHICAGO PRESS, Ltd., London

Paperback edition 2016
Printed and bound by CPI Group (UK) Ltd, Croydon, CR0 4YY

25 24 23 22 21 20 19 18 17 16 3 4 5 6 7

ISBN-13: 978-0-226-71088-4 (cloth)
ISBN-13: 978-0-226-38053-7 (paper)
ISBN-13: 978-0-226-71090-7 (e-book)
DOI: 10.7208/chicago/9780226710907.001.0001

Library of Congress Cataloging-in-Publication Data

Ricci, Ronit.
Islam translated : literature, conversion, and the Arabic cosmopolis of South and Southeast Asia / Ronit Ricci.
p. cm. — (South Asia across the disciplines)
Includes bibliographical references and index.
ISBN-13: 978-0-226-71088-4 (hardcover : alk. paper)
1. Book of one thousand questions—Translations—History and criticism. 2. Islamic literature—Southeast Asia—Translations—History and criticism. 3. Kitab masa'il 'Abd Allah ibn Salam lil-Nabi. 4. Serat Samud. 5. Ayira macala. 6. Hikayat seribu masalah. 7. Southeast Asian literature—Islamic influences. 8. Muslim converts from Judaism—Early works to 1800—Translations—History and criticism.
I. Title. II. Series: South Asia across the disciplines.
PJ813.R533 2011
809'.9338297—dc22

2010041701

⊗ This paper meets the requirements of ANSI/NISO Z39.48-1992 (Permanence of Paper).

For my parents

Contents

Illustrations

Maps

Figures

Preface

Terminology, Transliteration, and Citation

The discussion in this study of a textual tradition, recounted across languages, regions, and time, has given rise to complications resulting from the diverging ways in which names and terms are written and pronounced in Arabic, Javanese, Tamil, and Malay, as well as within the latter three literary traditions across time, authors, and scripts. Although most such words derive from Arabic, employing their standard Arabic form would privilege that language over the other Islamic languages discussed here and imply that the expressions of concepts and names in the latter languages are somehow less valid. This is an especially vexed point in a book that emphasizes the importance of cultural and historical contextualization when thinking about translation. Therefore, as much as possible, I reproduce the original orthography of names and terminologies as they appear in the particular print edition or manuscript under discussion. For example, the archangel known as Gabriel in English is referred to as Jibrīl when citing Arabic sources but Jipuṟayīl and Jibrail when citing Tamil and Javanese sources, respectively. In certain cases, when repeated shifts in spelling were unfeasible, I have made a choice and remained with it throughout for the sake of clarity and simplicity. I ask for the reader's indulgence for any minor inconsistencies that may remain.

In this book Javanese, Tamil, Arabic, Malay, and Sanskrit words follow currently accepted systems of transliteration, employing the following in-text system for denoting original languages:

A. Arabic
D. Dutch
H. Hebrew
I. Indonesian
J. Javanese
M. Malay
P. Persian
Por. Portuguese
T. Tamil

Widely known names and words are spelled in their Anglicized forms; for example, Ramadan, Nagore, hadith, Mahabharata, and Muhammad. All dates follow the common era unless noted otherwise (A.H. for the Islamic era; Saka for the Javanese era).

Due to space considerations, it was not possible to include all original passages along with their translations. I cite original passages when they are particularly important to my argument and closely analyzed.

Manuscripts Cited in This Book

Many of these manuscripts are anonymous, and the dates and places of their composition and inscription are unknown. The term "inscription" refers to the text being put down in writing, often as a copy or adaptation of an earlier exemplar. Therefore dates of composition and inscription may vary widely, and often, if a manuscript is dated, only the latter is available. When a manuscript is mentioned for the first time, a footnote appears with as complete a bibliographic entry as possible, given the information available. Subsequent mentions are abbreviated and include the title, date (if known), and an abbreviated manuscript location and a catalogue number.

Citations from Javanese manuscripts indicate page numbers. Citations from transliterated Javanese versions indicate canto and verse number, as the page numbers no longer correspond with the original manuscript. For Malay manuscripts I follow the same practice and cite page numbers for my major Malay source, the published *Hikayat Seribu Masalah*. For the single Tamil *Āyira Macalā* I cite verse numbers, as they can be easily followed throughout the print edition.

Acknowledgments

Many individuals and various institutions have assisted me in the course of researching and writing this book, and it is my pleasure to offer my sincere and heartfelt thanks.

I am grateful to my teachers and mentors for their support, guidance, and intellectual inspiration: David Shulman, for first introducing me to Tamil literature in a way that made it irresistible, then sparking my initial interest in Java and offering encouragement and intellectual input for many years since; Nancy Florida, for sharing with me her deep knowledge of, and insight into, Javanese history and literature and for providing a model of superb scholarship; Anton Shammas, for his support, assistance in locating and interpreting Arabic sources, translator's and storyteller's sensibilities, and friendship; Pete Becker, for the pleasures of reading old texts together, and for discussing with me his fascinating ideas on language, translation, and Southeast Asia; Barbara Metcalf, for her thought-provoking questions and insightful comments on earlier versions of my writing; Yopie Prins, for introducing me to the field of comparative literature and remaining a source of guidance and optimism.

In Yogyakarta I thank Wasim Bilal for graciously sharing his knowledge of Javanese literature with me; B. R. M. H. Hariyo Seno for permission to use the Pura Pakualaman manuscript library; Sri Ratna Saktimulya for her help and instruction; and my teachers at the Alam Bahasa language school, especially Budi Sih Rumanti, for their efforts to teach me Javanese.

In Madras I owe a great debt of gratitude to Takkalai M. S. Basheer, a scholar of Tamil Islamic literature and history who discussed Tamil texts with me with expertise and humor and went out of his way many times to find answers to my questions. I also thank Dr. Tayka Shu'ayb 'Alim for answering my queries about his important book, the late Jafar Muhideen of Nagore for introducing me to the sites and history of the town, and the late M. Saiyitu Muhammatu, "Hasan," of Madras who, although bedridden when I visited, received me in his home and shared with me his knowledge of Tamil Islam. Special thanks to the staff at the Islamic Research and Cultural Center on Anna Calai Road, where I always felt welcome.

Upon returning to Ann Arbor, I was fortunate to spend a year at the University of Michigan's Institute for the Humanities. That year is a cherished memory for which I would like particularly to thank the institute's director, Danny Herwitz; fellows' coordinator, Eliza Woodford; the institute's staff; and all members of the 2004–5 fellows' cohort.

A semester spent at the Institute for Comparative Literature and Society at Columbia University in 2007 allowed me to begin thinking about how to write this book. I thank the ICLS staff for their assistance, and my students in the seminar "Translation and Culture" for their ideas and enthusiasm.

The two years I spent as a postdoctoral fellow at the Asia Research Institute, National University of Singapore, allowed me the time, space, and peace of mind to complete this book, as well as the opportunity to take several research trips to Indonesia. I thank ARI's director, Lily Kong, for her ongoing support and kindness, Michael Feener for offering guidance and advice on numerous occasions, and Yasuko Kobayashi, Liew Kai Khiun, and Lai Ah Eng for their encouragement and friendship.

I have been fortunate to cross paths with scholars who are truly generous with their knowledge: I thank Torsten Tschacher for sharing his deep understanding of Islamic Tamil culture with me and offering advice and information whenever I asked. I am most grateful to B. A. Hussainmiya, the pioneering historian of the Malay community in Sri Lanka, for introducing me to its remarkable story and for sharing with me his contacts, manuscripts, and personal knowledge of the community.

Each of the following colleagues, friends, teachers, and mentors have supported me and contributed in various ways that I regret I do not have the space to elaborate on: the Aditomo family, Ben Arps, Teuku Cut Mahmud Aziz, Yigal Bronner, Betty Chandra, Muhammad Hannan Hassan, Tom Hunter, Muhammad Iqbal, P. R. Kumaraswamy, Nuniek Mardiarini, Jan van der Putten, Tony Reid, Paula Richman, Eddy Pursubaryanto and family, Margaretha Sudarsih, the Sumantri family, Budi Susanto, Alef Theria Wasim, Niesdri Welsh, Amrih Widodo, and John Wolff.

Scattered around the world are several special individuals whom I would like to thank for their lasting friendship: Sylwia Ejmont, Jesse Grayman, Priya Hart, George Hoffmann, Orit Kulka, Kobi Meiri, and Mirjana Vajic.

I am grateful to all those who helped me prepare this book for publication: David Shulman and Yigal Bronner offered important advice about the book's structure; a generous 2009 Book Fellowship from the Social Science Research Council provided me with invaluable editorial assistance from Mary Murrell; Mark Oliver reviewed the manuscript with care and insight; Tom Butler contributed the maps; and Iik Idayanti assisted with producing the images. I thank two anonymous reviewers for their many useful comments and suggestions, and Richard Allen, Sandy Hazel, Randy Petilos, Alan Thomas, and the excellent editorial team at South Asia Across the Disciplines and the University of Chicago Press.

I am deeply grateful for the generous support I have received over the years from the United States Department of Education/Fulbright-Hays, the Social Science Research Council, and the US Foreign Language and Area Studies Fellowship Program; the Program in Comparative Literature, the Rackham Graduate School, and the Institute for the Humanities, all at the University of Michigan; the US-Indonesia Society; and the Florence Tan Moeson Fellowship Program at the Library of Congress.

Romo Budi Susanto of Lembaga Studi Realinon in Yogyakarta and Dr. V. Kameswari of the Kuppuswami Sastri Research Institute in Madras kindly agreed to function as my academic sponsors. The Indonesian Council for Arts and Sciences (LIPI) and the American Educational Foundation in Indonesia (AMINEF) and India (USEFI) assisted me in various ways during my stay in these countries.

Several sections of this book first appeared elsewhere: a section of chapter 2 appeared in "On the Untranslatability of 'Translation': Considerations from Java, Indonesia," *Translation Studies* 3.3 (2010): 287–301; parts of chapter 4 were included in "Saving Tamil Muslims from the Torments of Hell," in *Islam in South Asia in Practice*, edited by Barbara Metcalf, 190–200 (Princeton, NJ: Princeton University Press, 2009); a section of chapter 7 appeared in "Conversion to Islam on Java and the 'Book of One Thousand Questions,'" *Bijdragen tot de Taal-, Land en Volkenkunde* 165.1 (April 2009): 8–31; parts of chapter 8 first appeared in "A Jew on Java, a Tamil Torah Scholar, and a Model Malay Rabbi: Representations of Abdullah Ibnu Salam in the 'Book of One Thousand Questions,'" *Journal of the Royal Asiatic Society* 18.4 (October 2008): 481–95; a portion of chapter 9 appeared in "Islamic Literary Networks in South and Southeast Asia," *Journal of Islamic Studies* 21.1 (January 2010):

1–28. I thank these journals and publishers for kindly granting me permission to reprint these materials.

Many books have at their core a personal quest, riddle, or journey. That I found myself writing about a textual tradition depicting a Jew and a Muslim in dialogue is, I think, not a coincidence. And when I consider the time I spent studying and working on what eventually became this book in Jerusalem, Ithaca, Ann Arbor, Yogyakarta, Madras, Singapore, and Canberra, it seems that the travels, translations, and networks that I explore in the following pages echo with the ways my own life has unfolded in recent years. I wish to take this opportunity to thank the friends, neighbors, and kind strangers in all these places—too numerous to mention by name—who offered advice, support, and companionship.

Most of all I wish to express my deep gratitude for my family. I thank my parents and my sisters Anat and Tali, for supporting me in countless ways and for remaining close even while living half a world away; Tamir, without whom writing this book would not have been even remotely possible; and our children, Tom, Yasmin, and Adam, for sharing many adventures and travels and filling life with a special kind of love and wonder.

Abbreviations

AM	Vaṇṇapparimaḷappulavar, *Āyira Macalā*
BKI	*Bijdragen tot de Taal-, Land- en Volkenkunde*
HSM	Edwar Djamaris, *Hikayat Seribu Masalah*
FSUI	Fakultas Sastra Universitas Indonesia, Jakarta
ISEAS	Institute for Southeast Asian Studies, Singapore
JMBRAS	*Journal of the Malaysian Branch of the Royal Asiatic Society*
JSEAH	*Journal of Southeast Asian History*
JSEAS	*Journal of Southeast Asian Studies*
KS	Karaton Surakarta, Surakarta
MN	Mangkunagaran, Surakarta
MSB	Museum Sonobudyo, Yogyakarta
PNRI	Perpustakaan Nasional Republik Indonesia, Jakarta
PP	Pura Pakualaman, Yogyakarta
TBG	*Tijdschrift van het Bataviaasch Genootschap*
VKI	*Verhandelingen van het Koninklijk Instituut voor Taal-, Land- en Volkenkunde*

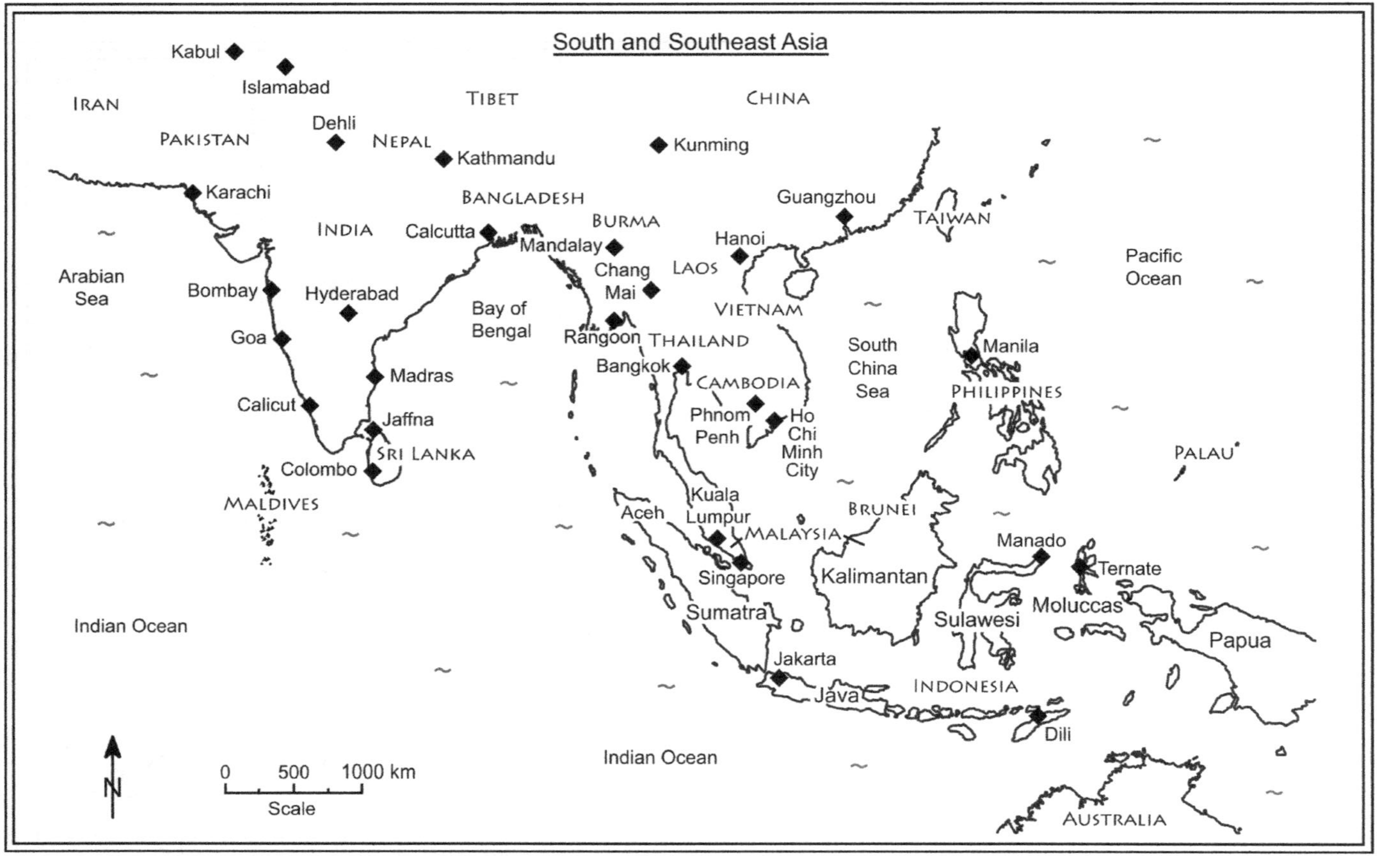

Map 1. South and Southeast Asia. Map by Tom Butler. Reproduced with permission from Tom Butler Maps.

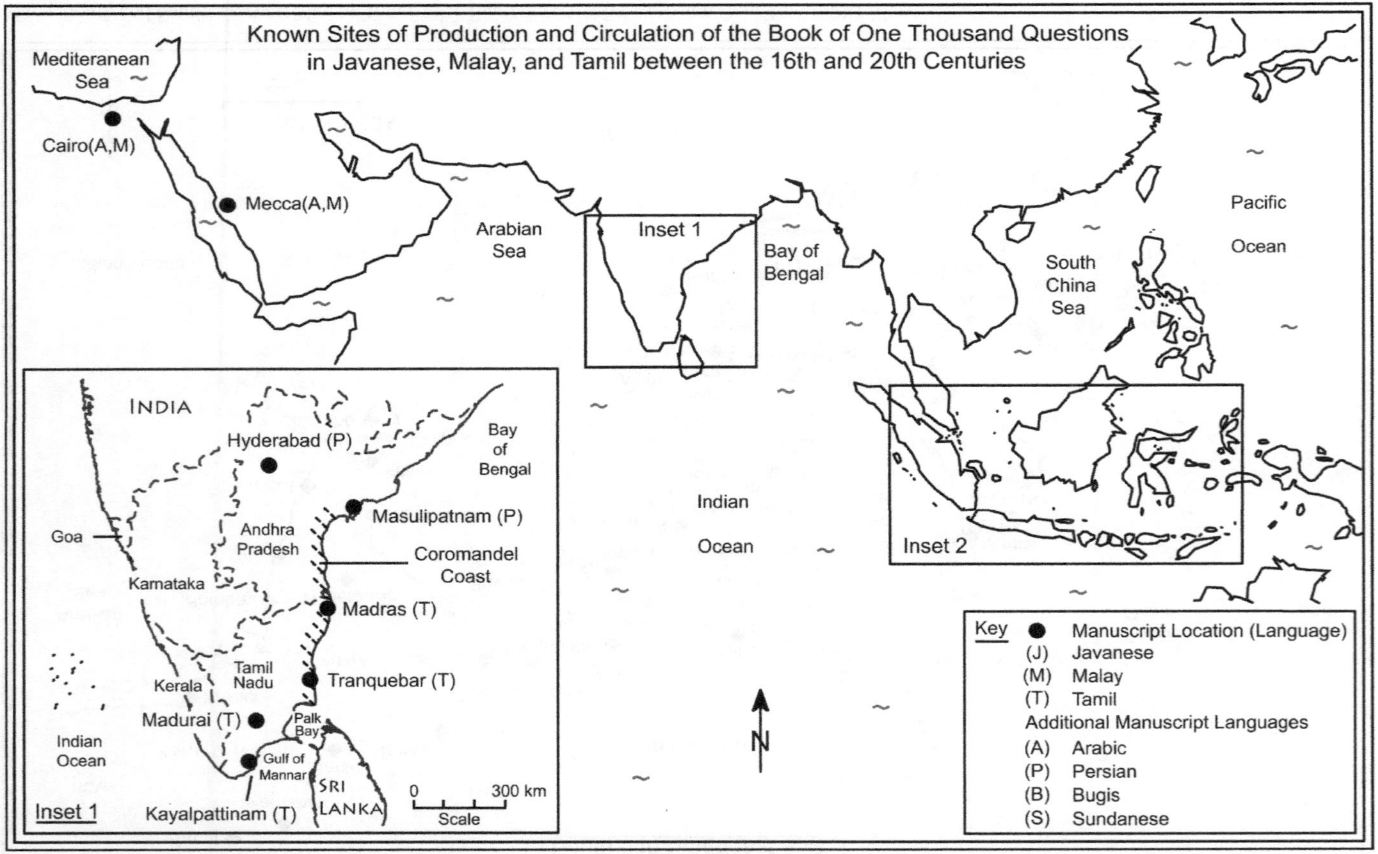

Map 2. Known sites of the production and circulation of the *Book of One Thousand Questions* in Javanese, Malay, and Tamil between the sixteenth and twentieth centuries (with detail of south India). Map by Tom Butler. Reproduced with permission from Tom Butler Maps.

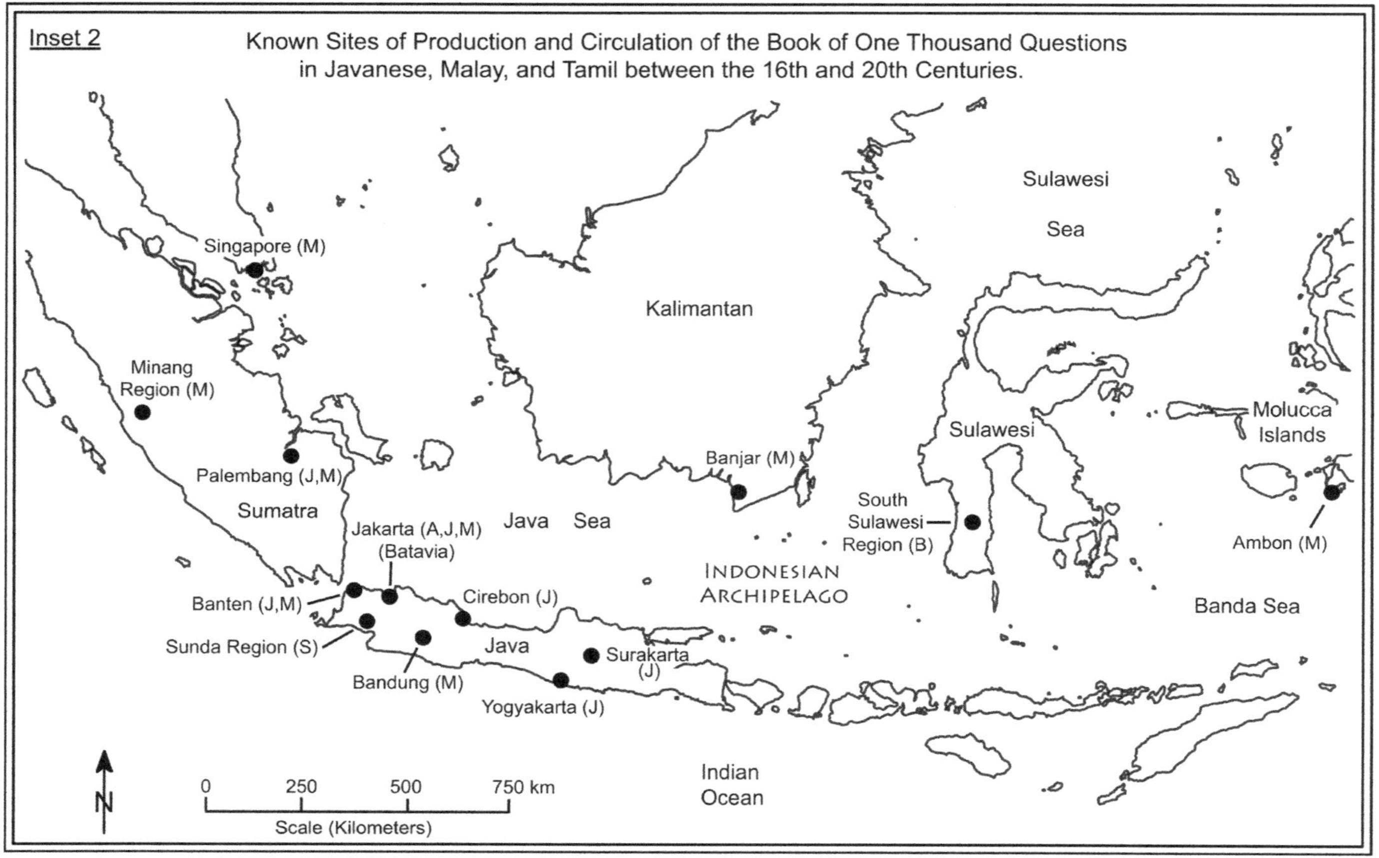

Map 3. Known sites of the production and circulation of the *Book of One Thousand Questions* in Javanese, Malay, and Tamil between the sixteenth and twentieth centuries (with detail of the Indonesian-Malay Archipelago). Map by Tom Butler. Reproduced with permission from Tom Butler Maps.

1

Introduction: An Arabic Cosmopolis?

The spread of Islam eastward into South and Southeast Asia represents one of the most important cultural shifts in world history. When Islam expanded into these regions, it encountered cultures vastly distant and different from those of the Middle East, and it incorporated them into a premodern globalized community of great geographical, linguistic, and social diversity. Long before print and mass communications became widespread, written texts played a key role in spreading ideas and beliefs within this Islamic universe. Texts of many kinds—the Qur'an above all, but also hagiography, poetry, jurisprudence, scientific writing, and more—were the bearers of the new religion and way of life both in Arabic or in vernacular translation. In this study I examine the circulation of Islamic texts, ideas, and literary forms within South and Southeast Asia, the regions where the world's largest Muslim populations reside today. I explore processes of literary transmission, translation, and religious conversion, and how these processes were historically interconnected, mutually dependent, and creatively reformulated in an important area of a transregional Muslim world.

Literary Networks

Different kinds of networks, often intertwined, traversed these regions, forging connections between and among individuals and communities. To the networks of travel, trade, and Sufi brotherhoods, commonly presented as the paths by which Islam spread and flourished, I propose adding the *literary* networks. Literary networks connected Muslims across boundaries of space and culture, and they helped introduce and sustain a complex web of prior texts and new interpretations that were crucial to the establishment of both local and global Islamic identities. Literary networks were comprised of shared texts, including stories, poems, genealogies, histories, and treatises on a broad range of topics, as well as the readers, listeners, authors, patrons, translators, and scribes who created, translated, supported, and transmitted them. Beyond attention to particular texts and individuals, thinking about literary networks also requires exploring the multilayered histories of contacts, selection, interpretation, and serendipity that shaped the networks in particular ways.

Across South and Southeast Asia orally transmitted materials as well as performative traditions complemented and enriched written literatures through a complex ongoing matrix of interaction and exchange. Large numbers of people could be considered as highly literate in their traditions, despite being illiterate by modern day standards, since they lived in environments where texts were recited out loud for various occasions and familiar stories were performed through puppetry, dance, and theater.

In Sumatra, for example, singers memorized large numbers of Malay *pantun* poems and *wayang* tales. Public manuscript readings drew large, enthusiastic, and engaged crowds where "men and women, youth and coolies, slid off their mats, and drawing near, with swaying heads, and moving hands, kept pace with limb and sympathetic look to the songs of their land, the sagas of Sumatra."[1] In Java, where an 1891 survey found that only an estimated one percent of the population was literate in Javanese, rulers regularly commissioned and collected manuscripts.[2] These same rulers were often important patrons of the performing arts through which the stories and lessons put forth in the manuscripts were expressed in music or drama. Such overlap and interaction between written and oral forms of production mean that any discussion of cultural or religious transmission in South and Southeast Asia must remain keenly aware of its non-inscribed aspects. My own focus here, however, is on the circulation of *written* works.

In largely illiterate societies, those capable of reading such works possessed a special kind of authority. Texts written in metrical verse and meant to be recited, often in public, were central to conveying and shaping cultural codes, religious doctrines, and political agendas. Public recitation of a manu-

1. Walter M. Gibson, *The Prison of Weltevreden; and a Glance at the East Indian Archipelago* (New York: J. C. Riker, 1855), 174.

2. For survey results see Merle Calvin Ricklefs, *Polarising Javanese Society: Islamic and Other Visions (C. 1830–1930)* (Singapore: National University of Singapore Press, 2007), 49–51.

script meant that its message reached many listeners simultaneously. In this manner its impact far exceeded that of the book as we imagine it today, read silently by an individual reader. Public readings were commonplace and had important social and political functions in ritual events taking place in court cities, villages, and Islamic educational institutions. It is this particular relationship between written works and their consumption that has, throughout this book, made me favor "audiences" over "readers" when I discuss the impact of literature on those who engaged with it.

The realm of the written word in local Muslim communities was vast and encompassed many themes, genres, and linguistic forms. I use "literature" to refer to a wide range of forms of production, in which often easy boundaries cannot be drawn between the theological, philosophical, legal, political, or belletristic writing.

Generically, too, our categorizations often fail, as the same poetic meters were employed in Java for mystical and political tracts, while the Malay genre of *hikayat* seems to have encompassed almost every possible topic, from romance to history. This is not to say that these literary cultures themselves did not distinguish between various forms of writing, telling, and creative expression. They certainly did. In my discussion of particular traditions and examples I attend to specific categories—like *masalah*, *suluk*, or *purāṇam*—rather than impose an outsider's definition of what "literature" was or was not. The definition of "text" or "literary work" is no simple matter either. In Javanese and Malay especially, histories, biographies, stories, and various compilations were copied repeatedly over time, with authors and scribes often taking lesser or greater license in the way they rewrote the text under the old title (sometimes that changed as well). These practices, which defy ready definitions, are pertinent to the arguments I put forth and will be discussed throughout the book.

The texts, or works, I examine herein (referring to diverse genres of literature as they appeared in both handwritten manuscripts and printed books) were written and rewritten in local languages that were profoundly influenced and shaped by the influx of Arabic. Arabic throughout this study possesses an expanded definition and is understood as the bearer of new stories, ideas, beliefs, scripts, and linguistic and literary forms. Muslims from across linguistically and culturally diverse regions shared inscribed texts as well as oral sources, poetics, and genres derived from or inspired by Arabic models. These shared texts formed a common repository of images, memories, and meanings that in turn fostered a consciousness of belonging to a translocal community. The two-way connections many literary works had—both to a larger

Islamic world and to very local communities—made them dynamic sites of interaction, contestation, and the negotiation of boundaries. Competing agendas (as, for example, between creative and standardizing impulses) often played out between their pages.

Islamization was an ongoing and uneven process in South and Southeast Asia, as it was in many regions. Literary texts of various kinds played an important role in enhancing and shaping this process by introducing those who converted to Islam to their newly acquired faith, history, practices, and genealogies, as well as by reaffirming the truths of Islam for those who were already members of the universal *umma.* As Muslim societies expanded, additional texts were translated and composed, further enhancing Islamization. Literature produced within local Muslim communities, and the literary networks that extended across and beyond the local—especially when studied comparatively—provide new insights into the history of Islam in these regions, the fluctuating balance between local and global elements privileged by particular Muslim authors and societies, and the roles played by literary transmission and translation in their histories.

I approach particular regions of South and Southeast Asia as interconnected nodal points of material and cultural exchange in the process of Islamization. To draw out and examine their connections, I have chosen one particular literary example, the diverse textual tradition of the *Book of One Thousand Questions*, from its Arabic source to its translations and adaptations into the Javanese, Malay, and Tamil languages between the sixteenth and twentieth centuries. This story, and its afterlives, provide a lens through which to examine the intricate relationships between Islamization and literary and linguistic transformation. The *Book of One Thousand Questions* offers a means for considering literary networks and their importance to historical processes. The *One Thousand Questions* also provides a paradigm for examining what I term, following Sheldon Pollock's work on Sanskrit, the "Arabic cosmopolis" of South and Southeast Asia, a translocal Islamic sphere constituted and defined by language, literature, and religion. This "cosmopolis" spanned a large geographic area through South and Southeast Asia, including much of present day Indonesia and Malaysia, parts of the Philippines and the Indian subcontinent, communities in Sri Lanka and southern Thailand, and beyond. My discussion in this book, however, will pertain specifically to the Tamil-speaking region of southeast India and the Indonesian-Malay Archipelago, with an emphasis on Sumatra and Java. This framework permits my work to be based, first and foremost, on primary sources produced in local languages rather than on derivative literature.

Islamization

The spread of Islam in the Indonesian-Malay region was a complex process that has been much debated by scholars, both local and foreign. Basing their research for the most part on archeological findings, travelers' accounts, and local chronicles, scholars have suggested various theories regarding Islam's arrival and ultimate acceptance by indigenous populations.[3] There was likely an Islamic presence in maritime Southeast Asia from the time of 'Uthmān, the third caliph, in the mid seventh century. Evidence also demonstrates that envoys with Arabic names visited the Sumatran court of Srivijaya between the tenth and twelfth centuries. However, no local Islamic states appear to have been established, and no significant conversion is known to have occurred in these regions until a later date.

The first evidence of Muslims in these parts comes from northern Sumatra, where gravestones demonstrate that in the thirteenth century the area was under Islamic rule, and where both Marco Polo (in 1292) and Ibn Baṭṭūṭa (in 1345) noticed, while passing through the region, that local rulers were followers of Islam. An important series of gravestones was found in the east Javanese cemeteries of Trawulan and Tralaya, marking the burial place of Muslims but using Old Javanese numbers and the Saka rather than Hijri years in their dating. These date from the fourteenth to the seventeenth centuries and strongly suggest the presence of local, rather than foreign, Muslims living on Java at the time. The great trading state of Malacca was founded around the beginning of the fifteenth century, becoming an Islamic center for the Archipelago until its capture by the Portuguese in 1511; late fifteenth- and sixteenth-century graves document the establishment of additional Islamic states in north Sumatra, and Tomé Pires wrote about such states along Java's north coast in the early sixteenth century. Evidence suggests that Islam was

3. See Ismail Hamid, *The Malay Islamic Hikayat*, Monograph Institut Bahasa Kesusastraan Dan Kebudayaan Melayu (Kuala Lumpur: Universiti Kebangsaan Malaysia, 1983), 13–28; G. W. J. Drewes, "New Light on the Coming of Islam to Indonesia?," *BKI* 124.4 (1968), 433–459; Merle Calvin Ricklefs, *A History of Modern Indonesia since C. 1200*, 3d ed. (Basingstoke: Palgrave, 2001), 4–13. All three list many further sources on this issue. Major speculations and controversies have revolved around the possible source of Indonesian Islam (Arabia, North and South India, Persia, China, and Kurdistan have all been suggested), the dating of its arrival, the chronology of the unfolding process, and the reasons for a major Islamization occurring only several centuries after Muslims are known to have been present in the region.

also spreading farther east than the Malay peninsula and Java, all the way to the southern Philippines.

The evidence taken together points to a slow and gradual process: by the end of the thirteenth century Islam was established in north Sumatra; in the fourteenth century in northeast Malaya, Brunei, parts of east Java, and the southern Philippines; in the fifteenth century in Malacca and other areas of the Malay Peninsula; in the sixteenth century the coastal areas of central and east Java were mostly Islamic while its western region and much of the interior were not.

The type of evidence that can be gleaned from tombstones and European accounts provides only a partial picture at best. Answers to the still open questions of why significant conversion in Indonesia (in the thirteenth to fifteenth centuries) began only after the several hundred years during which Muslims were passing through or living in Indonesia, of how Islam spread, and of why it became the dominant religion have been sought by some scholars in local chronicles that attest to Indonesians' multiple understandings of their own conversion history.[4] Such writing includes, for example, several Malay chronicles like the *Hikayat Raja-raja Pasai* ("Book of the Pasai Kings") and the *Sejarah Melayu* ("Malay Annals"), as well as the Javanese *Babad Tanah Jawi* ("History of Java"). Although most surviving editions date from the eighteenth and nineteenth centuries, they likely contain much older stories, and their emphasis on the roles of magic, esoteric learning, trade, and the foreign origins of the first Islamic teachers may well point to some aspects of the historical events. Even while much remains unknown to us about the origins and development of the conversion process—which was happening throughout the Archipelago's multiple islands and among many of its ethnic and religious groups—what is clear is that Islam brought about significant change in the region. From politics, law, social custom, and education to literary production, conversion to Islam altered in fundamental ways previous structures of rule, everyday life, and belief.

Turning to the Tamil region, archeological studies suggest an Islamic presence—rooted in Arab trade—in the Coromandel region since the eighth century of the Common Era, with that presence strengthened by the mid ninth century. Scholarship on Indian Ocean trade points to a continuous and dynamic Islamic presence in the Malabar, Coromandel, and Sri Lankan re-

4. See, for example, C. C. Berg, "The Javanese Picture of the Past," in *An Introduction to Indonesian Historiography*, ed. Mohammad Ali Soedjatmoko, G. J. Resnik and G. McT. Kahin (Ithaca: Cornell University Press, 1965), 87–117; Russel Jones, "Ten Conversion Myths from Indonesia," in *Conversion to Islam*, ed. Nehemia Levtzion (New York and London: Holmes and Meier, 1979), 129–58.

gions from around that time through the Portuguese colonial period, with Coromandel ports forming important trade centers. Such trade, especially in horses, gems, textiles, and pearls, has historically sustained the Muslim coastal communities.[5] Nearby Sri Lanka, with its deep-rooted Muslim-Tamil population, has also long been associated with the important pilgrimage site of Adam's Peak, the place where, since the early days of Islam, Adam was believed to have fallen from paradise to earth, a tradition recounted in several *One Thousand Questions* tellings.

As in the case of the Indonesian-Malay Archipelago, tombstones in the Tamil region provide evidence of, and approximate dating for, an early Islamic presence.[6] Inscriptions on gravestones in the mosque on Kilakkarai's shore attest to the existence of Arab settlements there from the seventh or eighth centuries. Arab traders received permission from local kings (the Cholas, and later the Pandyas) to settle in the area, and were sometimes granted land and the right to create their own communities.

The numbers of such settlers increased as the region began to play a central role in the international textile trade linking South India to the ports of west Asia and the Indonesian Archipelago. One consequence of this process was the rise to prominence of foreign Muslim commercial men in the Tamil country's local courts.[7] Further evidence on the spread of Islam and Muslim life in the region comes from traveler accounts, including those of the above mentioned Marco Polo and Ibn Baṭṭūṭa. Both famous travelers arrived in Tamil Nadu after visiting Sri Lanka and reported landing along the coast called Ma'bar by the Muslims, referring to the Coromandel coast. The port towns along that coast, with their trade links to Arabia and the Indian Ocean, became South Indian Islamic centers with clearly identified Muslim populations by the twelfth or thirteenth century.[8] The towns were dominated by the Maraikkāyar, groups of elite Sunni, Tamil-speaking trading families.

5. Susan Elizabeth Schomburg, "'Reviving Religion': The Qādirī Sufi Order, Popular Devotion to Sufi Saint Muḥyīuddīn 'Abdul Qādir al-Gīlanī, and Processes of 'Islamization' in Tamil Nadu and Sri Lanka" (Ph.D. diss., Harvard University, 2003), 19–20.

6. The summary below is based on Takya Shu'ayb 'Alim, *Arabic, Arwi and Persian in Sarandib and Tamil Nadu* (Madras: Imāmul 'Arūs Trust, 1993), 12–24.

7. Susan Bayly, *Saints, Goddesses and Kings: Muslims and Christians in South Indian Society, 1700–1900* (Cambridge: Cambridge University Press, 1989), 73–74.

8. The following draws on Bayly, *Saints, Goddesses and Kings*, 78–100. Evidence for similarly extensive Muslim-dominated trade between Yemen, the southwestern Indian coast of Malabar, and Southeast Asia in the thirteenth century is discussed in Sebastian R. Prange, "Like Banners on the Sea: Muslim Trade Networks and Islamization in Malabar and Maritime Southeast Asia," in *Islamic Connections: Muslim Societies in South and Southeast Asia*, ed. R. Michael Feener and Terenjit Sevea (Singapore: ISEAS, 2009), 28–31.

All other Tamil-speaking Muslims in the south were known as Lebbais, a population which was probably introduced to Islam by the thirteenth or fourteenth century, and which was also Sunni and included fishermen, pearl divers, and many hinterland cultivators, artisans, and petty traders.[9]

Important events in somewhat later times included the founding of a short-lived Muslim "sultanate" in Madurai in 1334; the period of Portuguese rule (1501–75), which brought much hardship to the Muslim population (to be discussed below); and a period of sustained Muslim rule in the far south in the eighteenth century, which saw the rise of the Nawabs of Arcot as well as successive attempts by various military powers including Hyderabad, the Maratha confederacy, the French, and the British to control the region.

The influence of Sufis has been viewed as central to the spread of Islam in the Archipelago and South India. With their focus on personal devotion, healing, and the charismatic power of teachers and saints, Sufis have provided a bridge between the beliefs of non-Muslims and Muslim worship, as they have in many other regions of South and Southeast Asia. Tomb shrines, often associated with Sufi masters, have given rise to devotional cults that served as critical forces in the expansion of Islam.[10]

Contacts of many kinds provided the foundation for the emergence of Islamic literary networks. The coasts of Southeast India and Indonesia were part of the Indian Ocean's commercial network, through which goods along with shared texts and values crossed the seas carried by Muslim merchants, pilgrims, soldiers, and scholars, and where coastal towns, functioning as important trade centers and ports, developed into major centers of Islamic learning and culture.[11] For example, in the sixteenth and seventeenth centuries the Sultanate of Banten on Java's northern coast had extensive trade contacts with the Chulias, Muslim traders from the Coromandel coast, many of whom settled in the town.[12] Iron, steel, diamonds, and fabrics were exported

9. A third group of Muslims residing in the Tamil region, claiming Dakhni (a southern variant of Urdu) as their mother tongue, lies outside the scope of this study. See Bayly, *Saints, Goddesses and Kings*, 96–101.

10. Bayly, *Saints, Goddesses and Kings*, 74–75. An important study of Sufi influence on the acceptance of Islam in a neighboring region is Richard M. Eaton, *Sufis of Bijapur* (Princeton: Princeton University Press, 1978).

11. On the relationship between trade and Islam in these regions see Andre Wink, "'*Al-Hind*': India and Indonesia in the Islamic World Economy, C. 700–1800 A.D.," in *India and Indonesia During the Ancien Regime*, vol. 3, (Leiden: E. J. Brill, 1989), 48–49; Kenneth McPherson, *The Indian Ocean: A History of People and the Sea* (New Delhi: Oxford University Press, 1993), 76–78.

12. Claude Guillot, "Banten and the Bay of Bengal During the Sixteenth and Seventeenth Centuries," in *Commerce and Culture in the Bay of Bengal, 1500–1800*, ed. Om Prakash and Denys Lombard (New Delhi: Manohar, Indian Council of Historical Research, 1999), 163–81.

to Aceh via Masulipatnam from the Persianized kingdom of Golconda in the seventeenth century, in exchange for benzoin, camphor, and pepper.[13] Shipping records from Malacca and Nagapattinam in the eighteenth century show the continuing strength of trade from Coromandel to Southeast Asia even in the face of growing European competition, pointing to a "remarkable persistence of old forms of trade."[14]

Apart from trade, the Muslims of South India and the Archipelago shared a variety of other relationships: at least as early as the seventeenth century they had a shared set of pilgrimage sites, some of which are still popular today. Well known in South India is the lineage of the seventeenth-century Sufi mystic sheikh Ṣadaqatullāh of Kayalpattinam, whose tomb continues to attract devotees from Malaysia and Indonesia; members of the two communities intermarried, with the Maraikkāyar, claiming descent from Arab seafarers, preferring intermarriage with the Muslims of the Archipelago over marriage with the lower strata of Tamil Muslim society.[15] The school of Islamic law (A. *madh'hab*) followed by Javanese and South Indian Muslims living along the coast was one and then same (Shāfi'ī); contacts in the sphere of Islamic education appear to have been strong, with similar institutions emerging in Tamil Nadu, Sumatra, and Java;[16] Indonesian pilgrims on their way to Arabia used to stop in the Maldives,[17] and in the eighteenth century a Coromandel mosque existed in Batavia. Under colonial auspices contacts—whether through trade or the deployment, employment, or exile of subjects—continued.[18]

Contacts between Southeast India and the Archipelago, as portrayed and understood in literature, are of special interest to my analysis in this book.

13. Denys Lombard, "The Indian World as Seen from Acheh in the Seventeenth Century," in *Commerce and Culture in the Bay of Bengal, 1500–1800*, 186.

14. Sinnappah Arasaratnam, "The Chulia Muslim Merchants in Southeast Asia, 1650–1800," in *Merchant Networks in the Early Modern World*, ed. Sanjay Subrahmanyam (Aldershot: Variorum, 1996), 139.

15. Susan Bayly, "Islam and State Power in Pre-Colonial South India," in *India and Indonesia During the Ancien Regime*, ed. P. J. Marshall and R. van Niel (Leiden: E. J. Brill, 1989), 145.

16. For example, 'Umar Wali, an eighteenth-century Tamil scholar of Arabic and Islamic law who had a large following, went to Sumatra in 1763 and spent fourteen years there. According to Tamil sources he established a number of *madrasah* schools called *pasenthiran* in the region. Shu'ayb 'Alim, *Arabic, Arwi and Persian in Sarandib and Tamil Nadu*. 502.

17. Ibid., 26.

18. Raffles noted that native soldiers often served first in India, then Java. He mentioned the quarters of Javanese soldiers in Calcutta and the fact that such neighborhoods existed in several Indian cities. Thomas Stamford Raffles, *The History of Java in Two Volumes with Maps and Plates*, 2 vols. (1817. London and New York: Oxford in Asia Historical Reprints, Oxford University Press, 1965), 202.

Early Sanskrit and Tamil texts mention various localities in the Archipelago.[19] The lands of Indonesia figure in a significant number of South Indian Sufi legends. The presence of sultans and port towns created a tension, familiar in Tamil literature, between the wild, uncivilized sphere (T. *kāṭu*) and the tamed, human world (T. *nāṭu*). India is often mentioned in Javanese and Malay literature as the land "above the winds" (M. *atas angin*) contrasted with the lands "below the winds" (M. *bawah angin*), connoting the Archipelago. Tamils and South Indian religious teachers are mentioned in major Malay literary texts like the *Hikayat Raja-Raja Pasai* (c. 1742), the *Hikayat Hang Tuah* (inscribed in the sixteenth century), and the *Sejarah Melayu*. According to the latter two texts, the ship carrying the apostle of Islam to Malay shores came from Ma'bar, the Arabic name for the Coromandel coast.[20] Bayly notes the similarities between the Javanese tales of the *wali sanga* (nine "saints" credited with bringing Islam to Java) and of Tamil teachers fulfilling the same mission.[21]

The complex patterns of the transmission and circulation of texts, ideas, and beliefs between Muslims in these regions of South and Southeast Asia become especially salient when we consider the Malay community of Sri Lanka. This community, which has its origins in exiles from the Dutch East Indies shipped to Sri Lanka beginning in the seventeenth century, testifies in its very existence, its literary history, and its linguistic peculiarities to the kind of mobility and exchange I highlight in this book. The Sri Lankan Malays have retained much of their original language and culture, while also interacting and mixing with local Muslims, many of whom were Tamils. That the Muslim communities of Sri Lanka and Tamil Nadu were closely related by ties of trade, learning, and family is well known. And indeed, literary works popular among these communities—the Malays, Sri Lankan, and Indian

19. Southeast Asia is mentioned in the second-century Tamil epic the *Cilappatikāram*. Even more pertinent here is the possibility that Maṇimēkalai, heroine of the Tamil epic by that name, was an indigenous Southeast Asian deity. Monius states that "although the details of the transmission of the story of Maṇimēkalai, *whether from South to Southeast Asia or vice versa*, will probably never be known, the presence of the goddess . . . in a variety of languages and literary forms is certainly suggestive of a discrete cultural/literary region extending from South India through mainland and maritime Southeast Asia. . . ." Anne E. Monius, *Imagining a Place for Buddhism: Literary Culture and Religious Community in Tamil-Speaking South India* (Oxford: Oxford University Press, 2001), 112 (my emphasis). On references to Southeast Asia in early Sanskrit literature, see H. B. Sarkar, "A Geographical Introduction to Southeast Asia: The Indian Perspective," *BKI* 137 (1981): 293–323.

20. Stuart Robson, "Java at the Crossroads," *BKI* 137 (1981): 259–92.

21. Bayly, "Islam and State Power in Pre-Colonial South India," 153–54; Bayly, *Saints, Goddesses and Kings*, 74, 117.

Muslim-Tamils—are known to have been exchanged, shared, and locally transformed. In this regard the Sri Lankan Malays may be imagined as a bridge between Muslims in the Archipelago and South India.[22]

The Comparative Study of India and Indonesia

In this book I engage in conversation with a scholarly field with a long past: the comparative study of the regions that today comprise Indonesia and India (with special attention paid to their religious and literary traditions) has a history going back at least two centuries. This legacy is in large part colonial, with a strong emphasis on Hindu-Buddhist traditions and on India as bestowing civilization on its neighbor to the southeast. Such an analytical comparative framework was employed as early as 1784 with the publication of Marsden's *A History of Sumatra*,[23] and it remained intact long after in books like Sarkar's *Indian Influences on the Literature of Java and Bali* (1934), Gonda's *Sanskrit in Indonesia* (1952) or Coedes's *The Indianized States of Southeast Asia* (1964), which portrayed a flow of people and ideas which was almost entirely unidirectional.

Various reasons contributed to the scholarly and popular preoccupation with understanding Indonesia on Indian terms, among them colonial agendas, the high visibility of non-Islamic Indian influences on the popular arts of Indonesia like *wayang*, the many Hindu-Buddhist architectural monuments dotting the landscape, familiarity with Indian culture, and the importance of Sanskrit for the emerging European science of philology, as well as an impression that Islam was but a veneer, mostly superficial, over a more deeply rooted Hindu-Buddhist belief system. An Indian "filter" was sometimes considered to have "diluted" or "corrupted" Islam, or to have "tinted" it with mysticism, when compared with the assumed nature of Arabian Islam. In such debates Indonesia was again seen as being at the receiving end, where by the time Islam had finally arrived there it was much changed, and often seen as less "authentic." Although the dissemination of linguistic, artistic, and literary elements from India toward the southeast was indeed profound, expanding the comparative lens on these contacts to put more emphasis on both Islamic

22. The pioneering studies in this field are B. A. Hussainmiya, *Lost Cousins: The Malays of Sri Lanka* (Bangi: Universiti Kebangsaan Malaysia, 1987), and B. A. Hussainmiya, *Orang Rejimen: The Malays of the Ceylon Rifle Regiment* (Bangi: Universiti Kebangsaan Malaysia, 1990).

23. William Marsden, *The History of Sumatra, containing an Account of the Government, Laws, Customs and Manners of the Native Inhabitants, with a Description of the Natural Productions, and a Relation of the Ancient Political State of That Island* (London: printed for the author and sold by T. Payne and son, 1784).

elements and the interactive rather than unidirectional nature of the process yields a more complicated historical picture.

My intent, therefore, is neither to dismiss the centrality of pre-Islamic contacts and influences nor to posit a clear-cut answer to how Islam came to the Archipelago, a question to which a single, conclusive answer is impossible. Rather, I will highlight contacts among communities that accepted Islam, a powerful force in shaping regional societies and cultures as we know them today. Further, I emphasize contacts, connections, and circulation and insist on seeing literary interaction and transmission as ongoing, dynamic processes rather than one-way trajectories. Such a perspective allows us to see more clearly and precisely the richness, diversity, and depth of a world shared by Muslims across these regions.[24]

The kinds of interactions among individuals and communities and the circulation of texts outlined above were central to the two major processes that I explore in this book: translation and religious conversion. Conversion brings about large translation projects, while widely disseminated translated texts encourage further conversion. When stories and ideas are translated, a familiar language—including its vocabulary, idioms, syntax—is converted in the process into something that is somewhat foreign. A certain balance arises between what is translated and what remains untranslatable. Not only are texts translated and people converted, but it is instructive also to consider the ways converted literary works and translated selves evolve. These processes must be understood within a context in which the spread of Islam in both South and Southeast Asia, however distant these regions are from the Middle East culturally and geographically, cannot be fully understood without seriously considering the role of Arabic, including ideas about its sanctity, its resulting untranslatability, and the range of ideas and stories it carried along as its legacy. Arabic's incorporation—at many levels—into local vernaculars has brought about profound and long-lasting transformations.

I consider the questions of conversion to Islam, the spread of Arabic, and translation within the framework of the Arabic cosmopolis, the discussion of

24. A scholarly tendency to view all movement of importance as going in a single direction (from South to Southeast Asia; from India to Indonesia) is similarly visible in scholarship on contacts between the Middle East and Southeast Asia, in which a unilinear transmission of Islam from Arabia to Indonesia has often been assumed. Such stereotypical assumptions have recently been complicated by the bringing to light of fourteenth-century Arabic sources that present prominent Arab figures as disciples of Muslim scholars hailing from, or associated with, the Indonesian Archipelago. R. Michael Feener, "Introduction: Issues and Ideologies in the Study of Regional Muslim Cultures," *Islamic Connections*, xviii.

which derives inspiration from the theory of an earlier, Sanskrit cosmopolis in South and Southeast Asia.

The Arabic Cosmopolis of South and Southeast Asia

In a groundbreaking series of articles and a subsequent book, *The Language of the Gods in the World of Men: Sanskrit, Culture, and Power in Premodern India*, Sheldon Pollock introduced the concept of the "Sanskrit Cosmopolis" of 300–1300, claiming a unique political and cultural status for that language, which developed almost simultaneously across large parts of India and Southeast Asia. He then charted the history of the transition from the use of the cosmopolitan Sanskrit to the emergence of vernacular literary cultures and compared the process to that which occurred in Europe, where Latin was replaced by vernacular production.[25] Pollock's interest lies, first and foremost, in the relationship between cultural production and political power in premodern South Asia and, further afield, in Southeast Asia. He examines this relationship through a study of what he defines as two key moments of change: the first, around the beginning of the Common Era, marked Sanskrit's move out of the realm of sacred language into that of literature and politics. As the divine Sanskrit entered the world of men, two closely related cultural forms were invented: *kāvya* (an innovative form of written, literary language) and *praśasti* (inscriptions, the medium for political vision), together exemplifying and expressing a massive cultural-political transformation. Sanskrit, as Pollock puts it, "seems to have almost been born transregional; it was at home everywhere—and perhaps, in a sense, at home nowhere," a language not bound by place and in a relationship of extreme superposition—"hyperglossia"—over local languages.[26] In addition to this translocality, the features constituting Sanskrit's power during this period were its transethnicity, aesthetic resources and, crucially, its possession of the "dignity and stability conferred by grammar."[27]

25. Much had been written about the existence of a translocal Sanskrit sphere before Pollock's important theorization of this notion. For example, Gonda in his encyclopedic study *Sanskrit in Indonesia* (1952), traced the linguistic influence of Sanskrit in the Archipelago; Sarkar, in *Indian Influences on the Literatures of Java and Bali* (1934), discussed the spread of Sanskritic literary notions far beyond India; Wales, in *The Making of Greater India* (1961), viewed large parts of South and Southeast Asia as coming historically under Indian—in this case Sanskritic—cultural influence.

26. Sheldon Pollock, *The Language of the Gods in the World of Men: Sanskrit, Culture, and Power in Premodern India* (Berkeley and Los Angeles: University of California Press, 2006), 262, 50.

27. Ibid., 255.

The second moment, a millennium later, signaled the rise of local languages, hitherto only spoken, as literary mediums, languages that challenged Sanskrit's unique authority in the literary and political realms and eventually came to replace it. These changes were accompanied by the emergence of new, more limited power formations. Pollock acknowledges that understanding the precise nature of both Sanskrit imperial power and the later Indian pre-Mughal polities poses serious challenges to scholars. And yet, however fragmentary and challenging the historical record remains, the question Pollock asks—why and how was the South Asian state so closely bound up with Sanskrit—and the wide range of sources and evidence he cites and analyzes in response to his query, constitute immensely important contributions to the field.[28] Pollock's work opens up many new avenues of inquiry that go beyond the particular configurations of the Sanskrit cosmopolis itself. This book, in part, is an attempt to follow such a path, as I argue for the rise of an *Arabic* cosmopolis in parts of the same geographical regions discussed by Pollock, one that came to coexist with, often overlap with, and in some cases inherit the Sanskrit cosmopolis.

In South and Southeast Asia both Sanskrit and Arabic have served, in closely parallel ways, as generative cultural nodes operating historically in conflated multilingual, diglossic, and "hyperglossic" environments. The Sanskrit case is highly instructive, and suggestive, for a comparative study with that of the Arabic. For Muslims worldwide Arabic possesses a unique status among languages. It is considered the perfect tongue, in which God's divine decrees were communicated to His Prophet. Consequently, at least ideally, it is considered untranslatable. The Muslims of South and Southeast Asia proved no exception in their reverence toward the Arabic language, as they set up institutions where it could be studied, adopted its script to their own languages, borrowed its religious terminology and everyday vocabulary, prayed in it, and embraced its literary and historical narratives and forms. As a result, when I consider an Islamic cosmopolitanism in these regions, Arabic features as one of its major elements. Translation, too, emerges as one of its foundational practices.

Several differences stand out between the cosmopolis discussed by Pollock and that which I outline. The first among them is that Sanskrit was not diffused by a single, scripture-based religion, a condition which was clearly central to the spread of Arabic.[29] Although kāvya and the earlier liturgical Veda did share certain traits, and some scholars have viewed the former as

28. Ibid., 1, 251.

29. Sheldon Pollock, "The Cosmopolitan Vernacular," *The Journal of Asian Studies* 57.1 (1998): 12.

the inheritor of the Vedic mantra, kāvya inaugurated a new phase in Indian cultural history which was not bound to any particular religious tradition.[30] The major rationale for Arabic's ascendance in these regions, on the contrary, was its status as being inextricably bound within Islam. Despite this substantial difference, both languages resembled one another in that no organized political power, colonial enterprise, military conquest, or large migration was involved in their diffusion. In both cases, moreover, literature was often produced under the patronage of royal courts. In the case of Sanskrit this condition embodied the link between culture and power; in the case of Arabic, between cultural production and forms of power often intertwined with the religious.

The analyses of the two cosmopoleis differ too in that a comparison strictly correlating to Pollock's example would entail comparing the role of Arabic in the region to that of Sanskrit, and the role of languages like Malay, Tamil, and Javanese with other vernaculars, whether in India or in the surrounding regions. Arabic per se certainly possessed an authoritative status, and a broad range of texts written in it were produced and circulated in the Tamil area as well as the Indonesian Archipelago. Although the use of Arabic for inscriptions has not been studied as widely as for Sanskrit and is only gradually coming to light, recent work, such as Guillot and Kalus's book on the inscriptions of Pasai, clearly shows that it was significant.[31] Chapter 6 is dedicated to the dissemination of Arabic in these regions. The main emphasis of my discussion, however, lies elsewhere.

Within the Arabic cosmopolis, I focus on Arabicized, rather than Arabic, language and literary cultures between the sixteenth and twentieth centuries. By "Arabicized" I refer to the wide range of instances in which Arabic influenced local languages, most often by combining with them rather than by replacing them. Evidence suggests this phenomenon is strongly linked to that discussed by Pollock for an earlier period. Throughout South India and Java during the Sanskrit cosmopolis era (300–1300), local languages absorbed Sanskrit vocabulary, literary conventions, genres, and themes. Works were written, very consciously, in hybrid forms of language. Compositions in maṇippiravāḷam, a metaphorical and linguistic stringing together of Sanskrit "pearls" (S. *maṇi*) and Tamil "coral" (T. *piravāḷam*) on a single necklace, highlighted the beauty and expressiveness of both while maintaining a line of distinction. On Java the Kawi language combined an old form of Javanese with

30. Pollock, *Language of the Gods in the World of Men*, 75–76.

31. Claude Guillot and Ludvik Kalus, *Les Monuments Funéraires et L'histoire du Sultanat de Pasai à Sumatra* (Paris: Archipel, 2008).

Sanskrit, enabling the production of literary works considered to this day to be among the most intricate and captivating of Javanese literature.

Thus the tendency to adopt an initially foreign vocabulary, along with themes, styles, ideas, and stories, was not at all new in this region. A long history—not only of lexical exchange but of such combined literary production—was already in place when traders, theologians, travelers, and translated works carried Arabic to these regions. The processes that produced Kawi, for example, prepared the ground in an important way for the elaborate and deep adaptation of Muslim textual models into Javanese. Linguistic change and borrowing are of course not in any way unique to this case, but the extent to which they took place—first with Sanskrit, later with Arabic, providing historical continuity—is far-ranging and impressive. In both cases, the combinations emerging from the use of a cosmopolitan language alongside a local tongue opened up new and intriguing possibilities.

An additional way to think about the Arabicized languages is to consider language primarily as a "mode of discourse that draws on a particular cultural and religious tradition," as Zaman does in his discussion of the language of the *'ulamā*, the traditional Muslim religious scholars.[32] Beginning with Ibn Baṭṭūṭa but focusing his study on scholars of the early twentieth century and their "language," he notes the "existence and efficacy of a shared and longstanding language of discourse and learning, of shared ideas about what constituted valuable knowledge and how such knowledge was articulated, preserved, and transmitted."[33] The adoption and use of so much Arabic—in both strictly linguistic and broader ways—by Muslim speakers of Tamil, Malay, and Javanese can be understood similarly as a shared metamode of discourse.

Pollock coined the term "cosmopolitan vernaculars" to label emergent regional literary languages like Kannada or Marathi that conformed to a superimposed model established in the cosmopolitan Sanskrit tradition in everything from lexicon and versification to figures, genres, and themes.[34] As will be discussed in the following chapters, vernacular writing and literary texts were already in existence in Javanese and Tamil long before the arrival of Islam (a result, in part, of the Sanskrit cosmopolis epoch), and Malay too has recently been shown to possess local systems of writing which preceded the use of the

32. Muhammad Qasim Zaman, "The Scope and Limits of Islamic Cosmopolitanism and the Discursive Language of the 'Ulama," *Muslim Networks from Hajj to Hip Hop*, ed. miriam cook and Bruce B. Lawrence (Chapel Hill: University of North Carolina Press, 2005), 103.

33. Ibid., 84.

34. Pollock, *Language of the Gods in the World of Men*, 322.

modified Arabic script known as jawi.[35] For Javanese and Tamil especially (in which, as compared with Malay, more evidence of the early literary traditions survives), no claim can be made that a vernacular literary tradition first arose in the shadow of Arabic, as Pollock claims for Kannada as influenced by Sanskrit. However, there is no doubt that Arabic deeply affected and reshaped linguistic and literary practices, making these languages—as used by Muslim authors and audiences—into vernaculars linked to a different cosmopolitan order than that to which they had previously belonged.

Arabic, then, inaugurated not just a new cosmopolitan age but a new vernacular age as well. In terms of the comparison drawn here, its diffusion and impact resemble most closely the developments Pollock describes for the early vernacular age. At that time Sanskrit provided the ultimate code for local literary cultures that, through emulation, competition, and imaginative selection, were developing in their own, independent directions. The later interactions between Arabic and vernaculars like Tamil or Malay provide an example of "a strong tendency with wider application, perhaps even a law: it is only in response to a superposed and prestigious form of preexistent literature that a new vernacular literature develops."[36] Such developments, in turn, are closely related to Pollock's aim of examining not only how the vernacular reconfigures the cosmopolitan or vice versa but how the two produce each other in the course of their interaction.[37]

Rather than thinking, as has been the common practice, of the ways in which, for example, Javanese has been *Arabicized* by the contact with speakers and writers of Arabic and Islamic sources, we may think of how Arabic itself, in such a setting, was *vernacularized*. The spelling, pronunciation, and often also the meaning of Arabic words changed markedly when adopted into Javanese, and Arabic literary genres and themes also took on a local twist. For audiences who were unfamiliar with the vocabulary as well as grammatical and syntactical elements of "real" Arabic, this form of the language *was* Arabic. Such audiences across South and Southeast Asia were by no means negligible in size and importance, and they—along with their forms of vernacularized Arabic—formed a significant component of the cosmopolis.

In addition, many Muslims from these regions participated in networks of sheikhs, Sufi gurus, theologians, reformers, and disciples from across the

35. Uli Kozok, *The Tanjung Tanah Code of Law: The Oldest Extant Malay Manuscript* (Cambridge: St. Catharine's College and the University Press, 2004).

36. Pollock, *Language of the Gods in the World of Men*, 328.

37. Pollock, "The Cosmopolitan Vernacular," 6–8.

Muslim world who converged on Mecca for the hajj pilgrimage and often for longer periods of residence and study. Well known is the fact that the neighborhood of Southeast Asians in the sacred city, known as *Kampong Jawah*, was the largest of any visiting groups in the mid nineteenth century, and no language besides Arabic was as widely understood there at the time as Malay.[38] From this we may deduce that Arabic was being influenced by the various vernaculars as it was in turn transforming them, not only in their own lands but also in Islam's historical heartland.

Pollock focuses much of his attention on the political dimension of Sanskrit: on its changing relationship to power and polity in premodern South and Southeast Asia. In the analysis of the Arabic cosmopolis I offer, these questions do not take center stage in the same way, yet they are certainly worthy of mention. Pollock points out that in contrast to the widely held view of vernacularization as a popular, anti-establishment kind of movement, it was in fact often initiated and propagated from the center, patronized by courts and kings. In the case of the Arabic cosmopolis many of the texts written in Arabicized forms of language received royal patronage, a fact that can be gleaned from the number and proportion of such texts within court library collections. For example, in the Karaton Surakarta library, only a single "Indic classic" (rendered from Kawi into modern Javanese verse) is found for every approximately thirty manuscripts that are obviously Islamic in character. This is in clear contrast to the prevailing perception among nineteenth-century Dutch scholars (later inherited by Western and Indonesian scholars) that "traditional Javanese literature" was to a large degree derivative of Indian, non-Islamic sources.[39] The poets of the major works of the Tamil Islamic tradition named and praised the patrons who supported their writing.[40] In the sultanate of Malacca in 1511, on the eve of the Portuguese conquest, young princes listened to the adventures of the Prophet's famed uncle Amir Hamza read aloud from a Malay manuscript, so that their hearts would be filled with

38. On *Kampong Jawah* see Snouck C. Hurgronje, *Mekka in the Latter Part of the Nineteenth Century*, trans. J. H. Monahan, reprint ed. (Leiden: E. J. Brill, 1931), 215–92. On the prevalence of Malay in Mecca, see Martin van Bruinessen, *Kitab Kuning, Pesantren dan Tarekat: Tradisi-Tradisi Islam di Indonesia* (Bandung: Mizan, 1995), 41; on contacts between religious scholars in the Middle East and the Indonesian Archipelago in the seventeenth and eighteenth centuries, see Azyumardi Azra, *Jaringan Ulama: Timur Tengah dan Kepulauan Nusantara Abad XVII dan XVIII* (Bandung: Mizan, 1999). Some of the leading scholars residing in Arabia at the time were from India.

39. Nancy K. Florida, "Writing Traditions in Colonial Java: The Question of Islam," in *Cultures of Scholarship*, ed. S. C. Humphreyes (Ann Arbor: University of Michigan Press, 1997), 203–4.

40. On the patronage of Cītakkāti, chief minister to the king of Ramnad, of the seventeenth century poet Umaṟuppulavar, see Schomburg, "Reviving Religion," 273–74.

courage. Such texts had special resonance within an Islamic culture that was, by definition, a culture of the Book, centered around the Qur'an as inscribed divine revelation. Written volumes dictated and preserved the authority of God, and that of human rulers, and these works were treated as sacred heirlooms, deserving of the utmost respect and deference. This importance of the literary idiom to royal courts in the Indonesian-Malay world and in India points to an intertwining of the political and cultural. It also highlights an overlap of the religious and political that is characteristic of Islamic thought.

In the case of Sanskrit, the epics, especially the Mahabharata, were crucial in creating a shared political vision that circulated across the cosmopolis, with its geocultural landscape that had multiple centers or none at all, as exemplified by the many mount Merus and Ganges rivers encountered repeatedly from north India all the way to Cambodia. During a later period vernacular epics developed everywhere, drawing on that greatest of cosmopolitan epics, in which "the boundless universalizing Sanskrit tale was refitted onto the perceptible, traversable, indeed governable world of regional political practice."[41] In the case of the Arabic cosmopolis, a similar refitting occurred from the distant Arab lands. In addition to the many Arabic legal, theological, and mystical texts that circulated in South and Southeast Asia, texts written in local, Arabicized forms of language retold the narratives of the Prophet's life and of the lives of his companions and earlier Muslim prophets, recounted early histories of Islam, and preached particular codes of (often gendered) conduct. Such works, which were often performed, conveyed a political message recast for a new context. Ideals of leadership, authority, hierarchy, devotion, and community were introduced in a familiar idiom that resounded with the cosmopolitan.

An attempt to define the socio-textual communities I discuss in this book must be made despite the difficulty of categorizing them neatly. Although I address the literary production and the literary networks of Javanese-, Malay-, and Tamil-speaking Muslims, the Arabicized forms of these languages were not spoken and written by Muslims alone. Although in the early stages of Islamization and contact with Arabic it is likely that Arabic was incorporated for strictly religious purposes into Malay and Javanese, a point was later reached when much of the influx of Arabic was assimilated to a degree that made it "invisible," no longer employed for specifically Islamic expression, or at least not exclusively in that context. The case of Tamil seems to differ on this account, as a highly Arabicized form of the language, known as Arwi (see chapter 4), was used primarily by the Muslim community. Concurrently,

41. Pollock, *Language of the Gods in the World of Men*, 397.

Tamil Muslims contributed to the broader landscape of literary production in Tamil by introducing new genres and expanding old ones, appreciated by Muslims and non-Muslims alike. Clearly in the multilingual, multiethnic, and otherwise culturally diverse regions at issue here it is impossible to claim that only Muslims used a particular language or a particular mode of expression. Nonetheless, we may consider the fact that prior to the mid nineteenth century being Javanese meant, quite exclusively, being Muslim.[42] And in Malay the common expression *masuk jawi* or *masuk Melayu*—to "enter Malayness"—enmeshed linguistic, ethnic, and religious identities, as it was often equated with *masuk Islam* (to enter Islam, become a Muslim) or meant, simply, to be circumcised.

The Book of One Thousand Questions

In the following chapters I examine the Arabic cosmopolis, its literary networks, and the processes of translation and conversion to Islam within it, through the example of a textual tradition, the *Book of One Thousand Questions*, as it appeared in Javanese, Malay, and Tamil. The *Book of One Thousand Questions* (hence, the *One Thousand Questions*) narrates a conversion from Judaism to Islam set in seventh-century Arabia. In it the Prophet Muhammad replies to many questions spanning ritual, history, belief, and mysticism posed to him by a Jewish leader and scholar by the name of Abdullah Ibnu Salam. The latter, convinced by the Prophet's wisdom and divine inspiration, embraces Islam. The reasons for selecting this corpus are three, and they often overlap: my study is, in a sense, a biography of this important, widely disseminated Muslim text, which has traveled, circulated across continents, and been translated into multiple languages beginning in the tenth century. Concurrently, I employ the *One Thousand Questions* as a paradigm for considering how translation and conversion have been historically intertwined and how the circulation of such Islamic, Arabicized texts helped shape and maintain an Arabic cosmopolitan sphere in South and Southeast Asia.

With its roots in Qur'anic passages and early hadith literature discussing the Prophet's encounters with the Jews, and its elaboration into a separate text in Arabic circa the tenth century, the narrative of this catechistic dialogue developed into an important source that exemplified Muhammad's discursive powers and provided a model of Islam's ability to overshadow and overcome its religious predecessors by persuasion and peaceful means. The *One Thousand*

42. Ricklefs, *Polarising Javanese Society*, 109.

Questions was translated and adapted into various languages, and it circulated across vast geographical and cultural terrains. Among translations, those in Persian are of special interest, as they may very well be directly or indirectly the source of the texts I discuss. Pijper believed at least several such Persian manuscripts were produced in southern India, including a 1615 copy from Hyderabad.[43]

In addition, from the sixteenth century onward, translations were made into Turkish, Urdu, Tamil, Malay, Javanese, Sundanese, and Buginese, among other languages. The *One Thousand Questions* remained an important text within an expanding, and highly diverse, Muslim world.

In my discussion of the *One Thousand Questions* across languages, periods, and places, I have come to prefer, following A. K Ramanujan, the word "tellings" to the terms "versions" and "variants" because the latter terms can, and typically do, imply that there is an original, invariant Ur-text.[44] In most of the examples I bring forth there is no definitive answer to the question of textual genealogy, and, in any case, it is to the particular and diverse contexts in which the different tellings were produced and circulated that I wish to draw attention. The word "telling," invoking orality and conversation, resonates with the conversations between the figures of the Prophet and Ibnu Salam in the multiple *One Thousand Questions*, and with the series of "conversations" and exchanges between and within cultures in the cosmopolis I explore in this book.

The choice of "conversion" is also worthy of mention, as several scholars have viewed it as simplistic or restrictive in its scope when compared with "Islamization."[45] Conversion is often understood to connote an individual choice of one religion over another on theological grounds, whereas Islamization is seen as gradual and complex, referring to a variety of processes influenced by social, cultural, and historical contexts. Although the latter term is certainly useful and I employ it throughout, conversion—especially as the process and rite at the heart of the *One Thousand Questions*—is a central topic of my inquiry.

43. Guillaume Frederic Pijper, *Het boek der duizend vragen* (Leiden: E. J. Brill, 1924), 57.
44. A. K. Ramanujan, "Three Hundred Ramayanas: Five Examples and Three Thoughts on Translation," in *Many Ramayanas: The Diversity of a Narrative Tradition in South Asia*, ed. Paula Richman (Berkeley and Los Angeles: University of California Press, 1991), 25.
45. Anthony H. Johns, "Sufism in Southeast Asia: Reflections and Reconsiderations," *JSEAS* 26.1 (1995): 169–83; W. Cummings, "Scripting Islamization: Arabic Texts in Early Modern Makassar," *Ethnohistory* 48.8 (2001): 559–86; Schomburg, "Reviving Religion," 555–58.

Outline of Chapters

Chapter 2 traces the long and complex translation history of the *One Thousand Questions* during the course of its broad dissemination. I also explore differing notions of "translation" through particular attention to Javanese, Malay, and Tamil literary cultures. This exploration shows that "translation" is not a universal. Rather, its diverse meanings and circumstances of production have, to a large degree, shaped particular transmission and circulation histories. In this mapping of the *One Thousand Questions*' circulation, I foreground the ways in which the spread of religious ideas and practices is intimately linked with translation. The narrative of the multidirectional movement of the *One Thousand Questions* sets the stage for further examinations of the story and its significance in particular contexts within the Arabic cosmopolis.

Chapters 3 through 5 introduce and expand on the transmission, transformation, and dissemination of the *One Thousand Questions* in Javanese, Tamil, and Malay, respectively. I describe the three languages' particular textures of translation and the common themes and vocabularies they share. Another goal of these chapters is to provide introductions to literary cultures still all-too-neglected by scholars of comparative literature.

In these later retellings of the *One Thousand Questions* in communities distant from the birthplace of Islam, the old narrative retained its significance, yet a different story also emerged. The translated tellings still presented their audiences with the tale of an early and significant conversion that was facilitated long ago by the Prophet himself, guided in every step by revelations from the archangel Jibrail (A. Jibrīl). However, as the *One Thousand Questions* absorbed elements more specific to the receiving culture, it became a commentary on local notions of conversion, suggesting through the long and winding path of questions and replies preceding the story's climax of embracing Islam what a particular community, at a particular historical moment, may have viewed as the most crucial elements of belief and practice that justified a religious transformation. I show how the *One Thousand Questions*—as well as similar literary productions—enfolded audiences within a geographically and culturally diverse Muslim world by introducing stories, dialogues, questions, historical and mythic characters, Arabic/Islamic terminology and vocabulary, Qur'anic quotations, and a gallery of shared images. The *One Thousand Questions* was especially well suited to this role through its wide scope: its links to other scriptures, texts, translations, and oral traditions; its appeal both to converts and long-time Muslims; the authority of the Prophet lying at its center; and its dissemination across many cultures and languages.

Together, chapters 2 through 5 (Part One of the book) establish the paradigmatic status of *One Thousand Questions*. In Part Two, I return to the broad questions of an Arabic cosmopolis, Islamic literary networks, and religious conversion that I have raised in this Introduction. Chapter 6 explores how the cosmopolitan Arabic interacted with South and Southeast Asian vernaculars in ways that significantly transformed local religious and cultural landscapes. In chapter 7 I analyze the *One Thousand Questions* as a little-studied source for considering how conversion to Islam was remembered and understood by Javanese, Malay, and Tamil Muslims. Chapter 8 examines the two figures of the *One Thousand Questions*: the questioning Jew and the Prophet. Specifically, I examine the appearance of a Jewish protagonist in the literature of societies where Jews were rarely encountered, in addition to the figure of the Prophet as understood from different linguistic and cultural perspectives. Finally, chapter 9 centers on the creation of new histories for societies in transition—as is the case when conversion is widespread—that seek to make sense of a past only recently adopted. This chapter goes beyond the paradigm of the *One Thousand Questions* to address some telling details and far-reaching contours of the Arabic cosmopolis.

The scope of what this study strives to cover—temporally, culturally, and geographically—is immensely broad and cannot possibly be achieved by an individual scholar or a single methodology. In order to call attention to, and underscore, the complexities and interconnectedness inherent in the Arabic cosmopolis phenomenon, I have chosen to explore and analyze relevant materials produced in three major languages of South and Southeast Asia. Although the extent of my discussion of these diverse primary materials varies, depending in large part on the availability of sources, it is the comparative examination of Javanese, Malay, and Tamil sources, not hitherto undertaken in a single study, that can make a significant contribution to our understanding of the dynamics of the cosmopolis. In the spirit of Abdullah Ibnu Salam's inquisitiveness and search for knowledge, I have raised many questions, a host of which remain as yet unanswered. It is my hope that further research in the various regions, languages, and literary cultures of the Arabic cosmopolis of South and Southeast Asia will complement, complicate, and challenge the findings presented here.

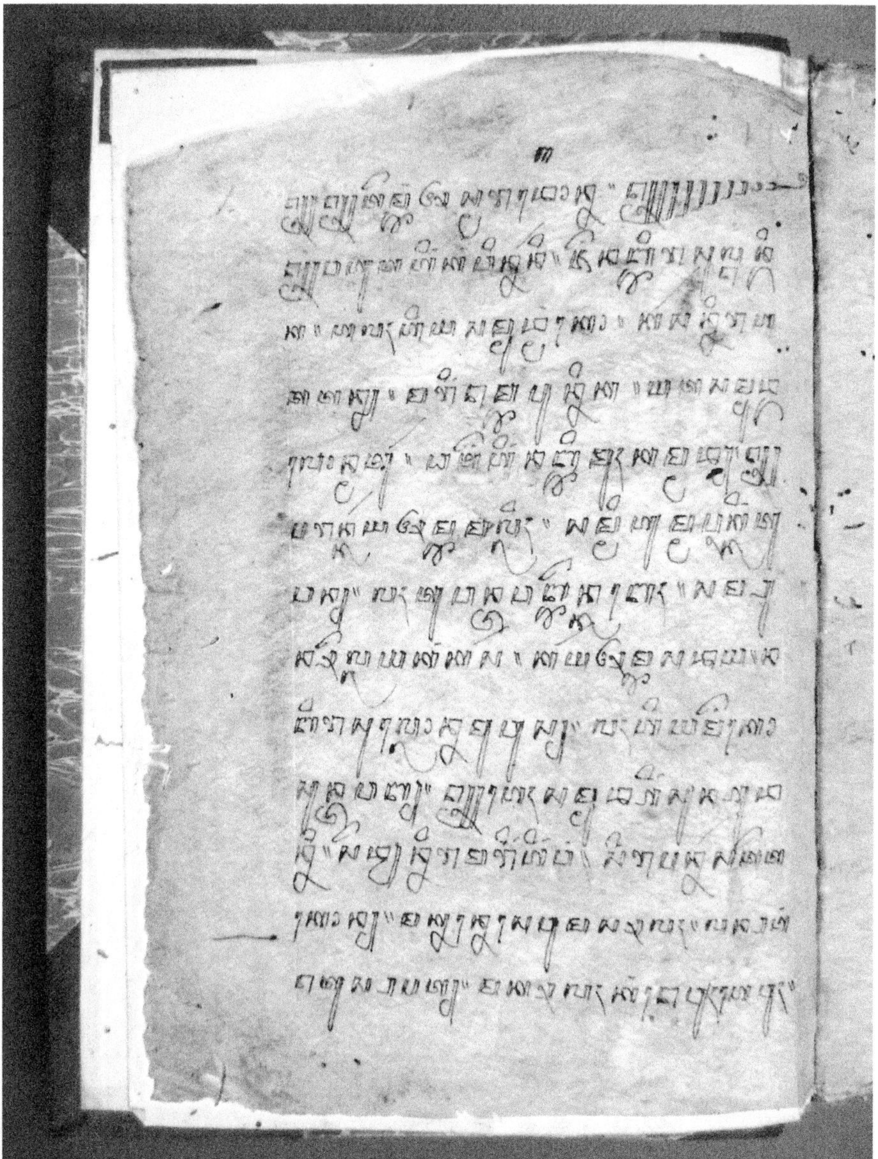

Fig 1. Opening page of *Serat Samud*. Javanese. MS. FSUI CI 109. Courtesy Fakultas Sastra Universitas Indonesia. Reproduced with permission.

Fig 2. Opening page of *Serat Samud.* Javanese, pégon script. MS. FSUI CI 110. Courtesy Fakultas Sastra Universitas Indonesia. Reproduced with permission.

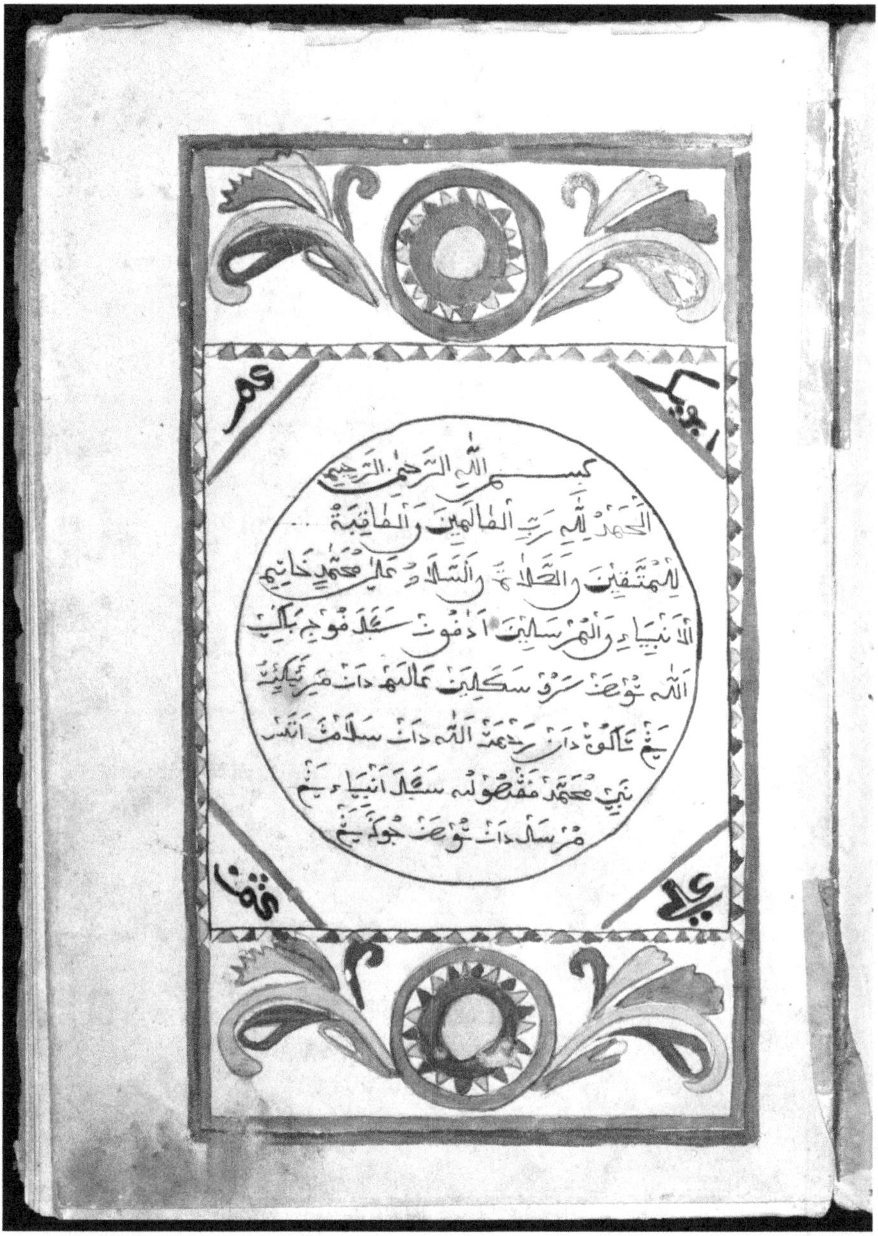

Fig 3. *Kitab Seribu Masa'il.* Malay, jawi script. 1910. MS. ML 442. Courtesy Perpustakaan Nasional Republik Indonesia. Reproduced with permission.

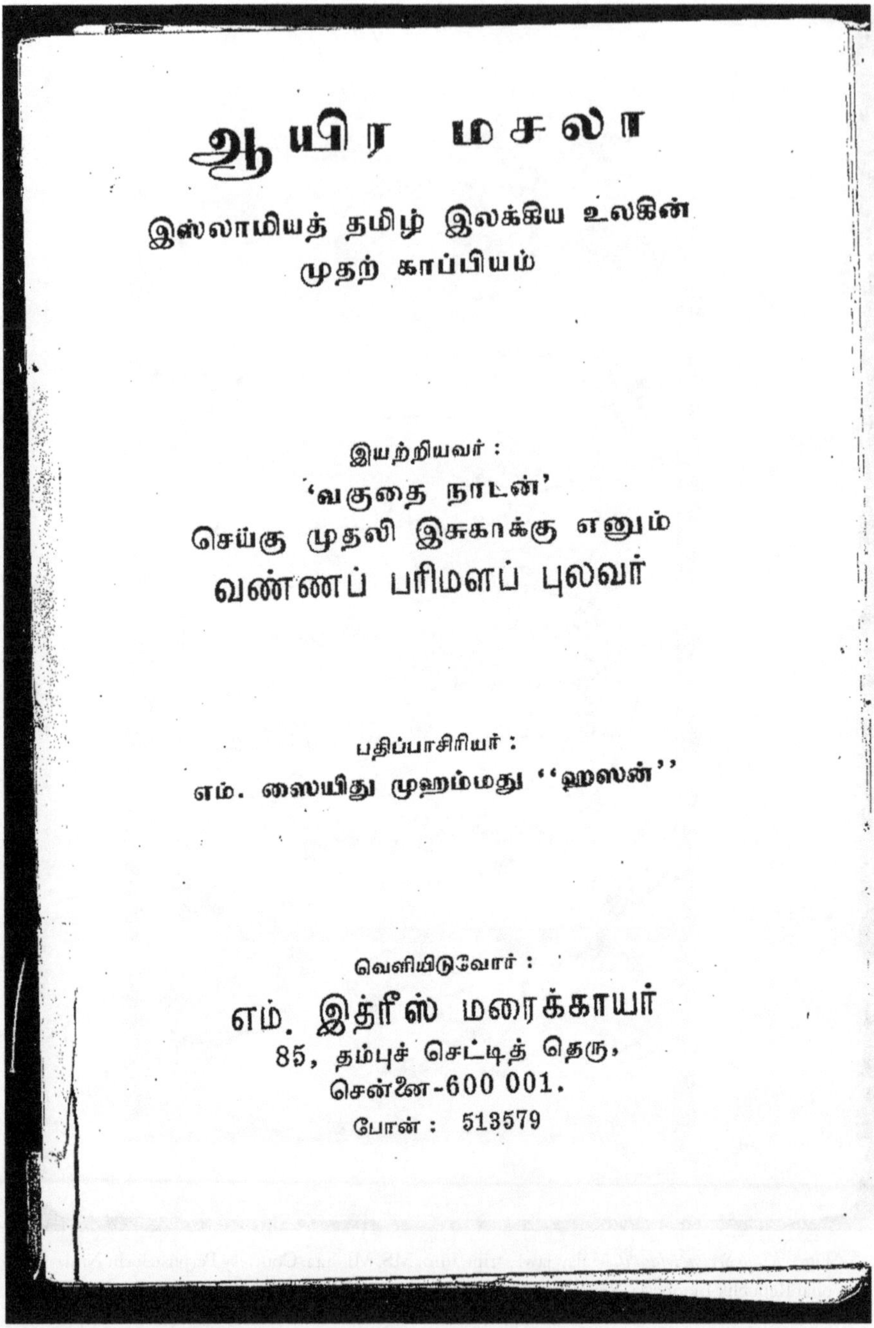

ஆயிர மசலா

இஸ்லாமியத் தமிழ் இலக்கிய உலகின்
முதற் காப்பியம்

இயற்றியவர் :
'வகுதை நாடன்'
செய்கு முதலி இசுகாக்கு எனும்
வண்ணப் பரிமளப் புலவர்

பதிப்பாசிரியர் :
எம். ஸையிது முஹம்மது ''ஹஸன்''

வெளியிடுவோர் :
எம். இத்ரீஸ் மரைக்காயர்
85, தம்புச் செட்டித் தெரு,
சென்னை-600 001.
போன் : 513579

Fig 4. *Āyira Macalā*. Tamil. From Vaṇṇapparimaappuḷavar, *Āyira Macalā* (1572), M. Saiyitu Muhammatu, "Hasan" (Madras: M. Itrīs Maraikkāyar, 1984). Reproduced with permission from Ahamed Rifai.

Part One *Translation*

2

On "Translation" and Its Untranslatability

Rendering texts from one language into another, what we conventionally refer to as "translation," has no doubt been a powerful force throughout human history for as long as it has been practiced, allowing for the circulation and diffusion of scientific, technological, linguistic, and literary knowledge across great geographical and cultural distances. In the realm of religion its force has been particularly evident, with the translation of scriptures and related works initiating and sustaining the spread of religions far from their places of origin, and altering societies' ways of life and understandings of the human and divine. Translation was a key factor in the Islamization of South and Southeast Asia, and the Arabic cosmopolis in these regions was, to a large degree, produced by translation.

Despite the certainty that circulating translated materials played a major role in the spread of Islam, it remains less clear what exactly translation meant in contexts distant in place and time. What was the meaning of the rendering of a text from one language into another, and how were such transformations articulated, implemented, resisted, and practiced? What were the goals and challenges faced by translators in the past? It is to particular translation traditions and their histories that we must look in order to better understand the literary cultures of South and Southeast Asia, developed through constant contact and exchange.

The difficulty of seeking answers to such questions begins with the English word "translation," which itself possesses no synonyms and which is not easily translated or correlated with "equivalent" terminology in other languages. Many cultures exhibit diverse ways of addressing and defining the meanings of rewording or rewriting a text from another language, ways that only partly overlap with "translation" or defy its meaning altogether. To highlight differences in assumptions about translation, its meanings and definitions, I explore local terminologies when discussing ideals and practices of rewriting across cultures. My point is that the very word "translation," with the cultural connotations and expectations it carries, is untranslatable—and the philosophies and practices it implies all the more so.

The histories of translation into and from Tamil, Javanese, and Malay are long and complex. Addressing even some of their elements—ideas about translation and the practices followed—offers a better understanding of the translation movements that have had profound effects on the societies concerned and allows a more nuanced theorizing of translation as a culturally specific practice. In addition, studying the multiple meanings of translation points us to similarities and continuities between the Sanskrit cosmopolis and the Arabic one and between the ways these two cosmopolitan languages were combined with local languages through a kind of assimilation of meaning and sound. For example, recent studies have pointed to the ways in which the rich commentary tradition of Sanskrit was incorporated into Old Javanese and Balinese texts alongside the translation, with its often interlinear mode of alternating between languages. The intratextual commentary thus became a gloss, an interpretation and expansion of the prior text, replacing the older form of exegesis.[1] This practice was later followed also in the translation and adaptation of Arabic sources with Arabic phrases and often single words translated and interpreted within the Javanese narratives.

Early Western scholarship on Malay and Javanese literature was mainly written by Dutch scholars in the nineteenth and twentieth centuries. Such works, including those of van Ronkel, Brakel, Pigeaud, Pijper, and Drewes especially, laid the foundation for future scholarly investigations by providing detailed historical accounts of the creation of certain literary texts, by analyzing their content and structure, by translating them into Dutch or English, and by noting elements of the texts' earlier translations from Sanskrit, Arabic, or Persian. More recent scholarship on translation in South and Southeast Asia has, for example, critically engaged with some of the challenges inherent in translating Javanese history (Florida 1995), Burmese proverbs (Becker 1995), and Tamil and Kannada poetry (Ramanujan 1973; 1981) into English. Such work has raised a host of issues related to the ways in which translation was understood and carried out in these cultures, all of which remain at present relatively unknown among literary scholars and critics.

1. Thomas Hunter, "Translation in a World of Diglossia," Unpublished paper, 2009.

In the context of the numerous still-open questions regarding translation traditions in South and Southeast Asia, it is tempting to attempt to posit a "non-Western" or Asian model of translation in opposition to "Western translation." That is not, however, my intent. The goal of this chapter, rather, is to highlight major features of translation as conceived and practiced in Javanese, Malay, and Tamil. I then briefly compare these traditions to a Western translation tradition so as to more clearly show where some differences lie. I am not suggesting a replacement of one set of universalizing principles about translation with another, but rather an expansion of our understanding of what translation has meant historically through an examination of its theories and practices in additional languages and geographical regions.

Since I do not compare the *One Thousand Questions* tellings in Malay, Tamil, and Javanese with an "original," prototypical text to which they can all be traced, it might be reasonable to ask what my justification is for employing "translation" as an analytical category. Is the focus of my discussion indeed *translation*? Might some other term, such as "transmission," "diffusion," or "dissemination," be more apt? My argument is that, in order to understand a significant historical process through which Islam—as a belief system and way of life—spread far and wide and was adopted in South and Southeast Asia, we must attend to translation in its narrowest sense—the rendering of the words of one language into another. Discussing conversion and the formation of the Arabic cosmopolis without affording centrality to the crucial role played by translation would present a partial and misleading picture.

And so translation is used here both in the strictly defined (however utopian) sense of conveying a text of one language in another and in a wider, more flexible sense of striving for an "equivalence" of meaning. In the case of the *One Thousand Questions*, previous Arabic and Persian texts served as the basis for those I will be examining in this book. As I will show, many details of the narrative's long history suggest a common foundation. It is in fact quite striking to what extent certain elements of the story remain little changed despite the great temporal and spatial distances between the various tellings. This documentable history of textual affinities is what I mean by "translation" in its commonsense meaning.

In another sense, however, "translation" is less a textual genealogy and more a set of cultural practices that vary from place to place as well as over time. I look for textual evidence of these multidimensional practices in individual words, narrative, style, and genre. Translation in this broader sense incorporates elements of transmission, a process which continues to occur long after a story is first introduced into new linguistic and cultural surroundings, and through which a story takes on unique local characteristics in addition to the elements common to it across languages. I hence broaden the use of the term "translation" to include practices for which different designations may now exist but which within the cultures I study were forms of translation. My prevailing assumption throughout is that it is problematic if not impossible to speak universally about "translation" without emphasizing the particular context in which it takes place.

The Book of One Thousand Questions—*A Brief History*

The frame story of the text is straightforward: an important Jewish leader in seventh-century Arabia, known in most tellings as Abdullah Ibnu Salam, challenges the Prophet Muhammad with a series of questions, is convinced by the answers, and then converts to Islam. The tenth century Arabic work known as *Kitāb Masā'il 'Abdallāh Bin Salām* (or a variation thereof) grew out of several centuries of prior texts, circulating in the form of hadith traditions and Qur'anic commentaries.[2]

The tradition of encounters between Muhammad and the Jews goes back to Qur'anic passages in which the Prophet is informed about questions he might be asked and told their correct replies. Muslim commentators have interpreted the questions as being posed by challenging Jews, and a reference to a Jewish convert to Islam has been taken to allude to Ibnu Salam, the protagonist of the *One Thousand Questions*.[3] The Qur'anic citations were later elaborated by some of the earliest writers of Islamic history, including Ibn Hishām, Muslim, and al-Ṭabarī. These hadith writings typically relate that Ibnu Salam heard of the Prophet's coming while he was picking dates, and that he went to meet him and asked three questions which he believed only a prophet could answer. When Muhammad replied correctly, Ibnu Salam converted on the spot.[4]

Another tradition holds that the Prophet never told anyone except the convert Ibnu Salam with certainty that they would inhabit paradise in the future.[5] Yet another hadith relates a case in which a Jewish man and woman, both married to others, have committed adultery. The Jews are portrayed as attempting to shield the couple from a punishment by stoning, as com-

2. *Kitāb Masā'il Sayyidī 'Abdallāh Bin Salām Lin-Nabī* (Cairo: Al-Yusufiya, ca. 1920).

3. For an example of the questions, see Qur'an 17: 85; on the Jewish convert see Qur'an 46:10.

4. Muhammad ibn 'Abd Allah al-Khaṭīb Tibrīzī, *Mishkāt al-Maṣābiḥ*, trans. James D. Robson, 4 vols. (Lahore: Sh. Muhammad Ashraf, 1963), 1272.

5. Imām Muslim, *Ṣaḥīḥ Muslim: Being Traditions of the Sayings and Doings of the Prophet Muhammad as Narrated by His Companions and Compiled under the Title Al-Jāmi' al-Ṣaḥīḥ by Imām Muslim*, trans. Abdul Hamid Siddiqi, 4 vols. (New Delhi: Kitab Bhavan, 1977), 1323.

manded in the Torah. A rabbi places his hand over the verse specifying the punishment, trying to hide it from view. Abdullah Ibnu Salam then strikes his hand and proclaims the verse to the Prophet.[6] And so, although the Arabic text of the *One Thousand Questions* dates from the tenth century, hadith tradition locates the germ of the story in the very early and formative period of Islam, and in the context of its most sacred scripture.

With time, the Ibnu Salam accounts acquired an element central to the *One Thousand Questions*, that of questioning the Prophet and viewing his replies as a sign of his Truth. Whereas in the ninth century Ṣaḥīḥ al-Bukhārī collection only three questions by Ibnu Salam are mentioned, gradually their number multiplied until no less than a thousand were said to have been posed. No longer relegated to brief hadith narratives, the tale of Ibnu Salam had evolved into a full-fledged textual tradition. Since all tellings of the *One Thousand Questions* derive their existence, however indirectly, from the early Arabic narrative of Ibnu Salam's debate with the Prophet, I will briefly summarize the history of this Arabic corpus.

The Questions of 'Abdallah bin Salām in Arabic

An Arabic work depicting the dialogue between the Prophet and Ibnu Salam was first mentioned in the year 963, when the Samanid vizier al-Bal'ami drew on it for his Persian version of al-Ṭabarī's *Annals of Apostles and Kings* (A. *Tārīkh-ur-Rusul wa al-Mulūk*).[7] The Arabic text appears to have survived in two forms: as a self-standing work, available in manuscripts and in print, and as a part of the well-known cosmography compilation by Ibn al-Wardi, *The Pearl of Wonders* (A. *Kharidat al 'Aja'ib*). Numerous manuscripts of the latter are found in libraries across Europe with the earliest dated from the mid sixteenth century. Many Arabic tellings of the text as a self-standing work survive in manuscript form, preserved in Algiers, Berlin, Oxford, Paris, and elsewhere. Those dated range from the fifteenth to the eighteenth centuries, with many produced in unknown locales and frequently bearing no title or missing their introductory and/or concluding sections. Of special note is a manuscript found in Jakarta: the *One Thousand Questions* telling within it is undated, but another work appearing in the same volume and written by the

6. 'Abdul Mālik Ibn Hishām, *Al-Sīrat al-Nabawīyya*, ed. Muṣṭfā al-Saqqā, Ibrahīm al-Ibyari, and 'Abd al-Ḥafiz Shalabi (Cairo: Maktabat wa-Maṭba'at al-Bābī al-Ḥalabī, 1955), 1:564–66.

7. For this summary I draw on Guillaume Frederic Pijper, *Het boek der duizend vragen* (Leiden: E. J. Brill, 1924), 35–54.

same hand is dated 1711, strongly suggesting that the *One Thousand Questions*, in Arabic, was known already at this early date in the Archipelago.[8]

Three print editions were published in the nineteenth and early twentieth centuries. The first was published in Cairo in 1867. The second—which is the Arabic source I use in this book—was also printed in Cairo and, though undated, was probably published in the 1920s or earlier. The third, obtained by Pijper in 1923, does not note its place or year of publication. In the edition I have used, titled *Kitāb Masā'il Sayyidī 'Abdallāh Bin Salām Lin-nabī*, the work is written in simple, short-sentence prose.[9] Based on the style and lack of any punctuation, it seems to hark back to an older manuscript, published without significant change.[10]

A Latin translation of an Arabic *One Thousand Questions* completed in 1143 (see below) allows access to a very early Arabic source.[11] Guillaume Pijper, the Dutch scholar who studied the *One Thousand Questions* with an emphasis on its Malay tellings, found in that translation a scheme that holds for all later tellings in its main points, attesting to the accuracy of the translation. This scheme included an introduction telling of how Abdullah came to ask Muhammad a series of questions and of their meeting in Medina; the main body of the book, including the questions and replies; and the resolution, Abdullah's conversion. Later, post-1143 Arabic editions exhibit various changes, some of which are commonly found. For example, in them Ibnu Salam possesses prior knowledge of Muhammad's impending appearance, Muhammad knows Ibnu Salam's queries even before he speaks, and the number of questions remains constant at 1404.[12]

Although it is impossible to compare all variations in the extant tellings, some consistent features characterize the tradition. In the 1143 text, the first question concerns whether Muhammad is a messenger or prophet (A. *rasūl* or *nabī*), with his reply being "both." This question is the first asked in all subsequent tellings. A series of questions on the meaning of Islam and faith (A. *imān*) follow, with later tellings providing more detailed definitions of these terms (Islam, faith), perhaps reflecting theological developments. Then follow

8. MS. Nr 553. Referenced in Ph. S. van Ronkel, ed., *Supplement to the Catalogue of the Arabic Manuscripts Preserved in the Museum of the Batavia Society of Arts and Sciences* (Batavia and the Hague: Albrecht and Co. and Martinus Nijhoff, 1913), 323.

9. Pijper, *Het boek der duizend vragen*, 39.

10. *Kitāb Masā'il Sayyidī 'Abdallāh Bin Salām Lin-Nabī.*

11. Pijper, *Het boek der duizend vragen*, 40.

12. All these examples appear in *Kitāb Masā'il Sayyidī 'Abdallāh Bin Salām Lin-Nabī*, 1–2. The number one thousand, or any number for that matter, does not appear in the title of the Arabic tellings.

more questions on a great range of topics, some based on very old materials: letter mysticism, number aphorisms, mystical elements including the bird that touches neither earth nor sky, cosmology (including the teaching that Jerusalem, not Mecca, is the navel of the earth), creation of the world and the first Man, including the notion that the world was first created from a gem or pearl, and eschatology. Although post-1143 tellings change, shorten, omit, and add some elements, many of the themes remain common across time. The conclusions of Arabic tellings yield some variation in terms of the level of detail supplied, but, in all, Abdullah converts to Islam.[13]

Beyond Arabic

Interestingly, the first translation of the Arabic text was not into another Muslim language but into Latin, as part of Peter the Venerable's twelfth-century translation project. His project encouraged acquaintance with and study of Muslim religious doctrine and literature in Christian Europe, which was engaged in the Crusades at the time. The project, known today as the "Toledo Collection," included five texts, among them the Qur'an (in its first complete translation ever) and the *One Thousand Questions*, translated by Herman of Dalmatia in 1143 as *Doctrina Mahumet*. The Arabic text used for this translation—now at a library in Paris—has been identified by Kritzeck as *Masa'il Abi-al Ḥāriṯ 'Abdallah bin Salām* and is apparently identical with one of the texts printed in Cairo.[14] The Latin version of the text was then translated into several European languages. Pijper mentions translations into Portuguese and Dutch, while Bobzin found a Dutch edition printed in Amsterdam in 1658 as well as Italian (n.d.), German (1540), and French (1625) translations.

Significantly, in several cases, the *Doctrina Mahumet* was bound in a single volume with the Qur'an, as had been done originally in Peter the Venerable's project. Bibliander printed the Latin text with the Qur'an in Basel in 1543. Dutch and German editions were printed in the same manner. This strongly suggests that the text was viewed and used in Christian Europe as a supplement

13. An internal critique provides little contribution to understanding the text's external history. With its origin an important concern for Pijper, he suggested some evidence for viewing Bukhara's Samanid court in the ninth or tenth century as the text's place of composition, but this remains highly speculative. Pijper, *Het boek der duizend vragen*, 54.

14. James Kritzeck, *Peter the Venerable and Islam* (Princeton: Princeton University Press, 1964.) The Arabic manuscript is listed as Paris BN MS. Ar. 1973 and 1974. Charles Burnett, "Arabic into Latin in Twelfth Century Spain: The Works of Hermann of Carinthia," *Mittellateinisches Jahrbuch* 13 (1978): 129.

to, or commentary on, the Qur'an, according *Doctrina Mahumet* great authority. Its categorization as *doctrina* in the Latin title points to its important status as well. And indeed Bobzin views the text as influential in shaping European conceptions of Islam.[15]

Also significant, in a similar vein, is the fact that sections of the Latin *One Thousand Questions* were added as a supplement to a 1598 Dutch travel account of the Moluccas. Depicted in the travelogue are a local funeral, circumcision, and other rituals. The editors used sections of the Latin translation to attempt a better understanding of the culture described.[16] This reliance on the Latin version—by the Dutch—to explain Islam in Indonesia points once more to this text being viewed as authoritative and comprehensive. This example also shows the nonlinear, roundabout ways in which the story traveled and was used and understood. Over a century before Valentijn, a minister for the Dutch Reformed Church in the Dutch East Indies, reported a familiarity with the Malay *One Thousand Questions* in the Moluccas (the "Spice Islands"), its Latin version was incorporated into a Dutch book on that same region.

The only known English translation was based not on the *One Thousand Questions* in Latin but on a North African Arabic text and was produced by the Reverend N. Davis, a missionary of the Church of Scotland. His translation, suggestively titled *The Errors of Mohammedanism Exposed: or, A Dialogue Between the Arabian Prophet and a Jew*, was published in Malta in 1847.[17] The remarkable status of the Arabic text was indicated by Davis in his preface:

> Excepting the Koran, there is hardly a production in Barbary, so universally known and so commonly to be met with as the one I now beg to offer to the English reader.
>
> Even at Torzar, a city in the deserts of Gereed, a copy of it was shown to me by the Kaid of the Dreed tribe, and of its contents I heard it said that a Mohammedan might as well deny the Koran as the "questions of Abdallah Ben Sallaam."[18]

Persian tellings, including those produced in South India, are important links in the history of the *One Thousand Questions*. The Persian texts include several additions when compared with the Arabic, most prominent among

15. Hartmut Bobzin, *Der Koran im Zeitalter der Reformation* (Stuttgart: Steiner, 1995), 334–35.
16. Karel A. Steenbrink, *Dutch Colonialism and Indonesian Islam: Contacts and Conflicts, 1596–1950*, trans. Jan Steenbrink and Henry Jansen (Amsterdam: Rodopi, 1993), 31–33.
17. N. Davis, *The Errors of Mohammedanism Exposed or, a Dialogue between the Arabian Prophet and a Jew* (Malta: G. Muir, 1847).
18. Ibid., 1.

them the setting of the number of questions as one thousand, a feature that was transmitted in many translations. The Persian word *hazār* means not only "one thousand" but, generally, a great number, which may be what the translator wished to emphasize. In addition, the three pre-Qur'anic scriptures—*Taurāh* (also referred to as *Taurāt*, from H. *Torah*), *Sabur* (Psalms), and *Injil* (the Gospels)—are listed, and Abdullah is accompanied to the debate by seven hundred Jewish followers. The Persian translations appear under the titles, in literal English rendering, *The Book of 'Abdullah's Questions*, *One Thousand Questions*, and *The Book of Twenty-Eight Questions*. A Turkish manuscript from 1559, known as *Kerk Sual* ("Forty Questions"), may be based on a Persian telling.[19] In it Muhammad begins his replies to the Jews by saying "if you ask . . . then the answer is . . ."—probably harking back to and echoing the Qur'anic questions mentioned above.

Besides translations into Persian that were produced in India, the text was also translated into Urdu (titled *Hazār Mas'ala* and *'Aqā'id Nāma*), whereby it gained popularity throughout the nineteenth century. The Urdu text—*Hazār Mas'ala* ("One Thousand Questions")—is mentioned in the *Bihishti Zewar*, an early twentieth-century guide for respectable Muslim women in the Indian subcontinent written by the reformist Maulana Ashraf 'Ali Thanawi, who included it within a list of over twenty-five books that he considered "harmful." Other "harmful" types of books included lyric poetry, miraculous tales of the prophets, works on divination and dreams, and works with a Shi'i element.[20] In the Indonesian Archipelago, the text appeared also in Sundanese (spoken in West Java) and Buginese (spoken in Sulawesi) in addition to the tellings in Javanese and Malay.[21]

I now come to the translations that are the focus of this book. Below I briefly introduce them, as they will be discussed in detail in subsequent chapters. Drawing a link between early Arabic tellings and those in Tamil, Javanese, and Malay is important if we are to consider such later tellings as translations—however broadly defined—of an Arabic source. Continuity within the tradition between Arabic tellings and those in the other three languages is evident in various themes and dimensions of the texts: the Jews' coming to Medina to discuss their questions with the Prophet frames

19. Pijper, *Het boek der duizend vragen*, 64–67.

20. Barbara Daly Metcalf, *Perfecting Women: Maulana Ashraf 'Ali Thanawi's "Bihishti Zewar": A Partial Translation with Commentary* (Berkely and Los Angeles: University of California Press, 1990), 379.

21. E. P. Wieringa, Joan de Lijster-Streef, and Jan Just Witkam, eds., *Catalogue of Malay and Minangkabau Manuscripts in the Library of Leiden University and Other Collections in the Netherlands*, vol. 1 (Leiden: Legatum Warnerianum in Leiden University Library, 1998), 188.

Muhammad and Abdullah Ibnu Salam's dialogue; the Prophet greets the Jews and converses with Abdullah until the latter is convinced and converts by reciting the Muslim profession of faith; Qur'anic quotations are used to support Muhammad's replies; and Abdullah utters a phrase of assent after each of his questions is answered. In addition, common topics raised include prior prophets, God's unity, the book sent to the Muslims, letter mysticism, the role of Gabriel, the tablet on which all events and fates are inscribed, the plights of Adam and Eve, Jerusalem as the navel of the earth, the Day of Judgment and the bridge all must pass, and the joys of paradise. Several riddles appear, including one about the spot on earth touched just once by the sun, the son who is stronger than his father, and the symbolic meaning of the numerals from one to one hundred.

The single Tamil telling, *Āyira Macalā*, was composed by Vaṇṇapparimaḷappulavar, known also by his Muslim name Ceyku Mutali Icukākku. It is considered the earliest complete Muslim text that is extant in Tamil today, and it has been held in high esteem for several centuries. The Tamil text was based on a Persian telling, a likely development in the South Indian context where Persian was widely used as a literary language. It was first read in public in a traditional introductory ceremony in the Madurai court in 1572.

The earliest extant Javanese *One Thousand Questions* is titled *Samud*, Ibnu Salam's name in Java; housed in Leiden, *Samud* (MS. LOr 4001) exhibits orthographic and metrical features that date it to the late seventeenth or early eighteenth century. It briefly notes an Arabic source (see chapter 3), and the number of questions, 1404, is also consistent with Arabic tellings. Many of the topics appearing in this earliest text reappear in the later extant texts, including the profession of God's unity, Adam's fall, mention of many rituals like prayer, fasting, and ritual bathing, and descriptions of paradise and hell. At least two dozen additional Javanese *One Thousand Questions* manuscripts reside in Indonesian manuscript collections. Sometimes the Samud story is found as an independent manuscript, and at others it is included within a collection of several prose or *suluk* poetry works, its length thus varying considerably. Later texts in which Ibnu Salam is presented as teacher rather than disciple no longer employ the name Samud but are rather titled *Suluk Ngabdulsalam*.

Malay poses no less of a complex picture. When Valentijn visited Ambon in the Moluccas as early as 1726, he found there a copy of the Malay text. Over thirty Malay manuscripts are housed in libraries around the world, with written and published tellings appearing from Cairo to Palembang. Several tellings explicitly claim Persian origin. The story was composed in different genres, including *syair*, *kitab*, and *hikayat*. The Malay texts have titles that employ variations on *Seribu Masalah*—"One Thousand Questions"—including *Hikayat Seribu Masa'il*, *Hikayat Masalah Seribu*, *Kitab Seribu Masa'il*, and *Seribu Sual*.

Possible shared sites of production for Malay and Javanese tellings—like Palembang or Banten—hint at interactions between authors and translators working in the two languages. A shared claim to a Persian ancestry of Malay and Tamil tellings likely accounts for some of the striking similarities between them.

This brief translation history of the *One Thousand Questions* has brought us across western Asia and Europe to South Asia and the Indonesian Archipelago. I now go on to consider ideas about translation, and its practice, prevalent in the literary cultures of these latter regions. Terminologies of translation—whether a text has been considered a "translation" or "adaptation" for example—are not simply descriptive. Such terms play a role in defining, categorizing, and assessing phenomena and have consequences for the way texts are studied, described, presented, and judged. As several scholars have noted, translation is not a universal concept but is historically and culturally determined.[22] Therefore, in this discussion, I pay close attention to how transmission across languages and cultures was approached and defined in the particular contexts of Javanese, Tamil, and Malay, attempting to avoid the pitfalls of irrelevant and misplaced assumptions.

The Javanese Context

Many Islamic texts translated in the Indonesian Archipelago between the sixteenth and early twentieth centuries do not explicitly acknowledge a source text or language, leaving much room for speculation about the translation process and about the perceived significance of the translation act. Catalogue entries such as "Muslim romance from the Middle East" or "adaptation of a Muslim tale originally composed in Arabic" abound. This is testimony not only to the difficulty scholars face in their attempt to classify and define these "translations" but also, and more importantly, to the disinclination of authors, translators, or scribes to include an explicit "translation statement" in their works. Neither did translators stress their personal achievement. A pervasive

22. A. Pistor Hatam, "The Art of Translation: Rewriting Persian Texts from the Seljuks to the Ottomans," in *XII Congress of the Comité International d'Études Pre-Ottomanes et Ottomanes* (Prague: Academy of Sciences of the Czech Republic Oriental Institute, 1996), 305–16; Gottfried Hagen, "Translations and Translators in a Multilingual Society: A Case Study of Persian-Ottoman Translations, Late Fifteenth Century to Early Seventeenth Century," *Eurasian Studies* 2.1 (2003): 95–134.

cultural code prescribed humility and self-deprecation. Authors and translators regularly apologized for their failings: lack of style, dearth of knowledge of the languages involved (including their own), and for presumed errors throughout their work.[23] Texts—translated or otherwise—tended to remain anonymous.

Why translate? Why tell a particular story? Javanese texts do not always offer an explicit answer and often pass over this question in silence. In some cases, however, a motive is mentioned. Most commonly the translation of a text is said to bestow blessings, merit, and good fortune on the person translating as well as on those who read the text or listen to it being read aloud. It is difficult, if not impossible, to distinguish here between the motives for translation and those for composing or for copying an existing text, as they are often identical, implying that translation was not necessarily viewed as a separate literary endeavor or a distinct undertaking worthy of mention.

Didactic goals are explicit in many theological, hagiographical, and ritualistic texts. Another motive for telling a story, a more personal one, can be found in the *Serat Mikrad*, produced in the Pakualam court and recounting the Prophet's nocturnal ascension to heaven, his journey through the hells and paradise, and his meeting with God. The text, written for the ill Pakualam III, was selected for its content, to be told to a dying ruler, offering him comfort and compassion before his final journey.[24]

Although many texts do not mention the language they were translated from, there are instances of Javanese texts that do. Such texts allow us to begin mapping the cultural contacts taking place at particular periods between Javanese and outsiders, contacts that led to acquaintance with new ideas, stories, and literary forms. In the centuries during and following the Islamization process on Java, materials written in Persian, Arabic, and Malay provided major sources for literary and religious translations.

It is easiest to see the source language in interlinear translations. In the traditional teaching method in religious schools, a teacher would explain a treatise in Arabic and provide Javanese glosses to the students. Such an ex-

23. Such an apology appears already in the oldest Javanese work preserved, the *Ramayana Kakawin* (c. 9th century). In the *Kitab Patahulrahman* the author, acknowledging he is "turning an Arabic work into Javanese verse," says of himself: "But though playing the poet I have no command of the language / I cannot find the right words" (J. *kumawi tan wruh basané / tan wruh ing tindak-tanduk*). G. W. J. Drewes, *Directions for Travellers on the Mystic Path: Zakariyyā al-Anṣārī's "Kitāb Fatḥ al-Raḥmān" and Its Indonesian Adaptations*, VKI, vol. 81 (The Hague: Martinus Nijhoff, 1977), 52–53.

24. Harya Surya Amisena, *Serat Kadis Serta Mikrad*, Pura Pakualaman Library, Yogyakarta. MS. PP Is. 9.

ample is found in a 1623 handwritten copy of the Arabic *Masa'il al-ta'līm*, a text on Islamic jurisprudence, in which the Javanese notes appear beneath the Arabic lines, which were purposely written with large spaces between them and wide margins. Due to the resulting layout of text and glosses such books were referred to as "bearded books" (J. *kitab jenggotan*).[25]

A possible reference to explicit translation appears, in a less explicit manner, in the opening lines of the *Serat Jaka Semangun*, a text relating the deeds of the young hero Semangun, a defender of the Prophet: the story "originates from *Ngarab*," which could mean either that the story originates from Arabia or from the Arabic language (or both), and here "was told in Javanese." This reference—although possibly mentioning Arabic as the source for translation—is still quite ambiguous and more likely refers to the Arab lands.[26] Raslan al-Dimashqi's *Risālat al-tawḥīd* exists not only with an interlinear translation but also in a Javanese adaptation. The author introduces it as an Arabic work rendered in Javanese verse, although it is a loose adaptation of several of the text's themes rather than the same text written in a different language.[27]

At other times a text that is clearly an adaptation of an Arabic work—although it could have reached Java via a different language—is simply told by the Javanese author without any reference whatsoever to an earlier text or to his composing a specifically Javanese telling. Such is the case with *Serat Mikrad*, a text which, as already mentioned, relates one of the crucial events in the Prophet's life. After a brief—and conventional— apology to his readers for writing in an insufficiently proper idiom, the author begins recounting the story without further ado. This is probably testimony that the story—at least in this manuscript telling inscribed in the 1920s—had become thoroughly familiar. Although it had its roots in Arabia during Islam's initial years, its actual translation was perceived as a thing of the distant past, no longer worthy of mention.[28]

Some texts, such as the one translated into English by G. W. J. Drewes as *An Early Javanese Code of Muslim Ethics*, claim explicitly to be compilations of source materials from earlier texts. Those earlier texts—al-Ghazālī's *Bidāya*, and the books titled (in a Javanized manner) *Masabeh Mafateh* and

25. Annabel Teh Gallop and Bernard Arps, *Golden Letters: Writing Traditions of Indonesia / Surat Emas: Budaya Tulis di Indonesia* (London: The British Library, 1991), 100.

26. *Saking Ngarab pinangkané / wus binasakaken Jawi.* M. Syakir Ali, *Serat Jaka Semangun: Studi Tentang Pengaruh Bahasa Arab Terhadap Bahasa Jawa* (Yogyakarta: Departemen Pendidikan dan Kebudayaan: Proyek Penelitian dan Pengkajian Kebudayaan Nusantara, 1986), 19.

27. *Nembangaken kitab Arabi.* Drewes, *Directions for Travellers on the Mystic Path*, 52.

28. *Serat Mikrad Nabi Muhammad*, Museum Sonobudoyo Library, Yogyakarta, 1920s. MS. MSB I23.

Rawdatululama, among others—were written in Arabic, and their integration into the *Code* implies either direct translation from Arabic or reliance on prior translation into Javanese.

Translations and adaptations into Javanese from Malay are also assumed to have been quite popular, although it is often difficult to say definitively whether a Malay telling preceded a Javanese telling or vice versa. Since Persian was an important language of Muslim learning, it appears that many texts written in Persian were translated first into Malay—possibly in Aceh, which was an important Malay kingdom and cosmopolitan center in the sixteenth and seventeenth centuries—and then from Malay into Javanese. The Persian texts had by no means to originate in distant Persia, as Persian was widely used by Indian Muslims, including those of the subcontinent's far south. Indian traders and travelers, abundant in the coastal towns of Aceh and the Malay Peninsula, could have transmitted such texts and stories.

Terminologies of "Translation"

In the traditions I am analyzing here, various terms describe the rewriting of a text in a different language. In eighteenth- and nineteenth-century Javanese manuscripts, authors employed the verb *njawakaken* to indicate translation. This verb means literally "to Javanize, [or] to render Javanese," emphasizing not the source language—the language from which the text is being translated—nor the process of carrying a story across, but the language it is being rendered into anew. The focus on the specificity of the resulting text, on its Javanese-ness, which becomes its central feature, is striking. The use of *njawakaken* was not limited to descriptions of the translation process from foreign languages into Javanese. It was also used for texts written in Kawi, a form of Javanese with a large component of Sanskrit, in which a body of literature was created between the ninth and fourteenth centuries. When such texts were rewritten in modern Javanese, authors often referred to their practice as "Javanizing" the Kawi, even though the latter was an older form of Javanese. We might say then that "to Javanize" referred to the adaptation of a text to a contemporary Javanese idiom.

A similar notion is expressed in the phrase *binasakaken Jawa*, deriving from *basa*, "language" or "speech," often referring more specifically to the *krama* speech level.[29] The verb *mbasakaken* can mean to say something in

29. There are three basic speech levels in Javanese, defined principally by the use of particular vocabulary sets and the choice of affixes. Speech levels are used to indicate degrees of politeness, formality, and intimacy. Very briefly and schematically, the three basic levels are as fol-

krama or to express something in the form of a saying. In the passive, with the designation "Java" added, it means to "render into the language of Java," "to express in Javanese." This term can appear with or without mention of the source now being rendered in Javanese. An interesting example—where the term *Jawi* (Java, Javanese language, a Javanese) finds double use—is found in the early *Samud*, where the author uses the term *binasakaken Jawi* to refer to his translation act and the term *wong tan Jawi* (non-Javanese) to refer to his own identity.[30] We are left to marvel at the abilities of a nonlocal, nonnative speaker who is able to retell the story in a cultural idiom that is not his own. This is therefore another example—first and foremost—of the idea of bringing a story *into* Javanese.

Less explicit but still quite similar is the way some texts may define themselves as translations or retellings from Kawi. In these instances we find a stress on the transmission from ancient times, supposedly from a previous form of Javanese, as noted above. Since many Kawi texts were based on or inspired by non-Muslim Indian works, or were pre-Islamic Javanese creations, the notion that Islamic tales were indeed derived from Kawi tellings is questionable. It seems that the use of the idiom *kang ing panurwa kawi* indicates the status of the story as ancient and authoritative. *Purwa* as a verb, as found here, means to begin, to originate, to create. Since *kawi* also means "poet," the phrase could refer to a work being created by the revered poets [of the past].[31] Explicitly, the emphasis is here put on a text's poetic source and where it is coming *from*, at least in a temporal sense, and—more implicitly—on its incorporation, from now on, *into* Javanese.

An additional example of the particular attitude found in Javanese translation terminology is that of making a foreign story accessible not just because it has been linguistically converted but because it has been made Javanese. In Java, texts were written in verse, to be sung, and, most commonly since the eighteenth century, according to the *macapat* meters. Such classical verse is

lows: *ngoko*, considered unrefined and informal, is used to address children, subordinates, and intimates; *krama*, the polite and formal level, is used to speak to those one knows only slightly or to whom one shows deference; *madya* (literally "middle") is semi-polite and semi-formal, used with people one knows well but with whom one is not truly intimate or with those who are close but still deserving of respect, such as older relatives.

30. *Samud*, MS LOr 4001.

31. This example is from *Samud*, Perpustakaan Nasional Republik Indonesia, Jakarta, MS. PNRI KBG 413. An example from Amisena, *Serat Kadis Serta Mikrad*, better illustrates the motif of rewriting Kawi works, describing itself as: *lapel kawi dèn maknani basa Jawa* ("a Kawi text explained in Javanese"). *Maknani Jawa*, "to explain the meaning, significance of a term in Javanese," is yet another way translation is addressed in the literature.

referred to as *tembang*. Sometimes the derived verb *nembangaken*—to sing a classical song, to sing for one's pleasure—is employed by translators to indicate producing a work in which a source was rewritten in Javanese verse. Emphasized here is a central component of the Javanese writing tradition; it, too, was a significant element of the translation process through which texts became localized in Java.[32]

In the realm of story production, the term *winarni* (narrated, told) blends the processes and practices of narrating, transmitting, and translating stories. It may appear in an introduction such as *wonten cerita winarni* . . . *saking kitab metunèka* (there is a story that is told . . . its source is a *kitab*), with *kitab* most likely referring to an Arabic, or Arabic-derived book, or simply as *wau ta ingkang winarni* (thus it was told . . .).[33] Although this is no doubt a more general, generic term, its derivation from *warna* (form, appearance, color, kind) hints at ways in which, again, a story finds a shape and hue—however figuratively—that make it a part of its new, Javanese, surroundings.

Several additional terms are common. *Salin/santun* is one, implying a change, a replacement, as in a change of clothes, name, or living place. This bespeaks not a repetition in another language but exchanging the text in one language for another—potentially very different—just as one acquires a completely new name after falling ill or changes clothes for a special occasion. *Njarwani/njarwakaken* means to explain or assign meaning, and was often used (like the above-mentioned *njawakaken*) for the process of retelling in modern Javanese an earlier, Old Javanese text which was no longer widely understood.

Is it possible to attribute the differential use of particular translation concepts to certain places or historical periods? For such a purpose, the explanatory sample presented here may well be too small. The problem is further confounded by uncertainty regarding the date of composition and inscription of many works. In a preliminary manner I suggest, however, that the earliest Javanese Islamic texts we have, the *Tuhfa* (early seventeenth century) and *Early Javanese Code* (sixteenth century?), both translations from Arabic sources, employ the term *nembangaken* (versify in Javanese). A somewhat

32. Examples of this term are found in the Javanese translation of the *Tuhfa* (*Nembang basa ing Tuhfa*) and in the *Kitab Patahulrahman* (*Nembangaken kitab Arabi*); see, respectively, Anthony H. Johns, *The Gift Addressed to the Spirit of the Prophet* (Canberra: Australian National University, 1965), 28, and Drewes, *Directions for Travellers on the Mystic Path*, 52. Interestingly, in both these cases the term is used for translations which are explicitly from Arabic.

33. These examples are taken from the following two manuscripts, respectively: *Samud*, Perpustakaan Nasional Republik Indonesia, Jakarta, MS. PNRI Br. 504; *Serat Samud*, Fakultas Sastra Universitas Indonesia, Jakarta, MS. FSUI CI 109.

later text, the early *Samud* (late seventeenth or early eighteenth century), uses *binasakaken Jawi* (to render into Javanese). In an 1823 *Samud* fragment copied in Surakarta we find *jinawakaken* (to Javanize), whereas *panurwa kawi* (as told by the poets of old, or: as told previously in Kawi) appears in the somewhat later mid to late nineteenth-century *Samud* and the 1884 Pakualam *Serat Samud*.[34] These findings provisionally suggest a distancing from the more Java-centered terminology as time went by and as such stories were perhaps seen less as translations than simply Javanese stories told anew.

In this context we might expect that the more general *winarni* (narrated) would come into focus at a relatively late stage, but that does not appear to be the case.[35] Furthermore, when Malay terminology is discussed below it will become apparent that a general "storytelling" term for a translated work can be quite old. Therefore, I presently avoid any firm conclusions on this issue, but it is likely that different translation terms—with their nuances of meaning—circulated concurrently. These variegated terms—some of which are found in the *One Thousand Questions* corpus manuscripts—rather than dictating or even suggesting a sameness of source and translation, or a carrying across (as the English term implies) of a single, authoritative version from one place or linguistic code to another, express an openness to change and to the culturally specific.

I now turn to examine more closely the appearance of a translation discourse in the Javanese *One Thousand Questions*. The 1884 Pakualam *Serat Samud* mentions a poet telling the story of the learned Samud, but no additional source or authorship is expressed. Although it may be that by the late nineteenth century this text was thought of as Javanese—rather than a translated work—this is probably also the author's following in the footsteps of predecessors who did not explicitly mention the act of translation. As will be discussed, this text is very similar in verse form and content to several others and was most likely copied (with some variation) from an older, circulating text. The motive for this telling of the *One Thousand Questions* is found at the very end of the text, immediately after Samud's conversion and his departure are described:

34. Respectively, *Samud* fragment in *Para Nabi Nerangaken Bab Rijal Saha Sanès-Sanèsipun*, Karaton Surakarta Library, Surakarta, 1823 [?], MS. KS 339.1; *Samud*, Perpustakaan Nasional Republik Indonesia, Jakarta. MS. PNRI KBG 413; *Serat Samud*, Pura Pakualaman Library, Yogyakarta, 1884, MS. PP St. 80.

35. For example, *winarni* is used in *Serat Samud*, MS. FSUI CI 109, which, being written on *dhluwang* bark-paper, appears to have been inscribed in the early nineteenth century at the latest.

All those who read [or] listen
Are granted great mercy
The one who writes and the one who stores [the text]
May they also be granted
Love from great God
And the blessings of the Prophet Muhammad
In this world and the next guarded day and night
By the angels.

For [taking part in this text] is equal to visiting
The Ka'abah and reading
The Qur'an for all of you
And it is the same as
Giving as alms a mountain of gold
And all your descendents
Granted forgiveness
Of all their sins
Guarded by a million angels
And [gaining] all that is in this world.[36]

This is a common invocation of blessings to be incurred on all participants in the creation and use of the text who, by taking part in writing, storing, and listening, are likened to those visiting the holiest shrine of Islam or reading its sacred scripture. The rewards promised are immense, making an association with the text most attractive.

A second telling, the 1898 *Serat Suluk Samud Ibnu Salam*—belonging to the same textual family as the *Serat Samud*—does not mention translation or adaptation into Javanese either.[37] It makes no mention of an author, translator, or scribe, nor of a place of inscription. It does, however, mention 1898 as its inscription date. In contrast to the Pakualam text, which introduces the frame for the Samud story in its opening lines, this telling glosses over the narrative structure that is common to most tellings. In the initial canto the author—addressing the listener as "my child" (J. *kulup*)—explains that this text will elaborate on mystical teachings regarding the nature of the body, the soul, and the relationship between Man and God. In the second canto the author mentions that it will be through the teachings of the Prophet that these truths

36. *Serat Samud*, 1884, MS. PP St. 80, c. 20, vv. 33–34.
37. *Serat Suluk Samud Ibnu Salam*, Museum Sonobudoyo Library, Yogyakarta, 1898, transcribed 1932, MS. MSB P173a.

will be revealed. There is no further mention of why or how the text was composed.

These two texts of the *One Thousand Questions*, both inscribed in the late nineteenth century, exemplify some major elements, previously discussed, regarding translation practices in Javanese which are often—along with the translator's identity—entirely implicit. Although a variety of terms refer to translation and transmission across the larger *One Thousand Questions* corpus, more than a dozen Javanese tellings I examined do not mention a prior source. Acknowledgment of an earlier author, language, or title is highly unusual—providing the exception, not the rule.

One possible such exception is found in the earliest extant manuscript, the Leiden *Samud*, which mentions that the story was rendered into Javanese from *Ngarbi*.[38] It is unclear whether Ngarbi refers specifically to the Arabic language or more generally, and vaguely, to a distant Arab or Arab-influenced source. If indeed the Arabic language is emphasized, this mention may be an indication that at the relatively early period at which the manuscript was compiled or copied, the link between the *One Thousand Questions* story and its foreign source was still seen as more concrete and significant than in the later tellings, which omit any mention of source. However, especially when compared with how Malay *One Thousand Questions* texts typically stress that translation took place from *bahasa* Parsi—the *language* of Persia, rather than simply "Persia"—the Javanese mention seems likely to refer to "Arab" as an important source of Islamic teachings and stories rather than to Arabic itself. A second exception is found in a mid to late nineteenth-century *Serat Samud* manuscript written in pégon script (modified Arabic, to be discussed below), in which Muhammad's uncle 'Abbās is mentioned as the source of the story.[39] This reference may point to a Malay connection for this particular telling. Interestingly, this text too belongs to the same textual family as both the Pakualam *Serat Samud* (with which it shares all twenty cantos in terms of verse form and sequence) and the *Serat Suluk Samud Ibnu Salam*.

Both the terminology used (or not used) in these works and the silence on earlier sources point to a certain distancing from the act of "translation" or retelling, and a stress on the Javanese-ness of the texts. Since in Islamic tradition generally sources and genealogies of transmission are crucial to the reliability and authority of textual materials, this omission of prior sources highlights a cultural element which was apparently not adopted—at least not consistently—along with the literary materials and religious doctrine.

38. *Samud*, Leiden Oriental Manuscripts Collection, MS. LOr 4001, p. 108.
39. *Serat Samud*, MS. FSUI CI 110.

The Malay Context

Of the three language contexts I explore in this book, Malay was the one that became, to the greatest extent, the language of Islam in the region. Beginning in the second half of the fourteenth century but especially between the sixteenth and mid nineteenth centuries, a vast number of texts from Arabic and Persian sources were translated into Malay, and many later works were further based on such early translations. In addition, there exists an older layer of Malay literature with many surviving texts, especially of the hikayat genre, originating in the pre-Islamic period (between the seventh and first half of the fourteenth centuries), as they retell in Malay episodes or entire narratives based on the Ramayana and Mahabharata epics.[40] Translation of such pre-Islamic works was not done directly from Indian sources but rather, in most cases, from Old Javanese tellings circulating well beyond the borders of Java. A form of translation within Malay was the rewriting of older Hindu tales, adapted to Islamic notions. In such tellings names were changed, Islamic titles like *maulana* or sultan were given to heroes, and chapters had descriptive headings following Persian custom. According to Windstedt, such stories "exhibit traces of the Sanskrit epics, of Javanese shadow-play tales and of Tamil influence, a combination to be found in a port like Malacca of the fifteenth century."[41] In such texts an earlier, familiar story was reworked—at times superficially, at others more substantially—to fit a new cultural matrix. Such translations allow us to see quite subtle processes occurring within a language and culture during a time of significant transition.

With the spread of Islam one of the first types of texts to be translated for Malay audiences were stories of the Prophet Muhammad, his companions, other prophets of Islam, and depictions of major events in early Islamic history.[42] Since Islam reached the Malay world after being established for centuries in the Middle East and parts of India, the literature brought by traders and teachers included stories told first in Turkish, Urdu, and other languages. Such stories were used to entertain, instruct, and condition their audiences,

40. On the periodization of Malay literature, see Vladimir Braginsky, *The Heritage of Traditional Malay Literature: A Historical Survey of Genres, Writings and Literary Views* (Singapore: ISEAS, 2004), 35.

41. Richard O. Winstedt, *A History of Classical Malay Literature* (Kuala Lumpur: Oxford University Press, 1969), 74.

42. Harun Mat Piah, Ismail Hamid, Siti Hawa Salleh, Abu Hassan Sham, Abdul Rahman Kaeh, and Jamillah Haji Ahmad, *Traditional Malay Literature*, trans. Harry Aveling, 2nd ed. (Kuala Lumpur: Dewan Bahasa dan Pustaka, 2002), 316.

which at an early stage would likely have included new converts. After the initial introduction of prophetic tales and tracts on elementary beliefs and practices, additional, well-known works were translated from Arabic and Persian, including, among others, the eleventh-century Persian *Shāhnāmé*, the twelfth-century Persian adaptation of *Layla wa Majnūn*, and the Arabic *Alf Layla wa Layla* (M. *Hikayat Seribu Satu Malam*, Arabian Nights).[43]

Much historical information about the development of Islam in the region can be gleaned from translated texts. For example, some of the abovementioned stories of the prophets display a strong Shi'i element which, although no longer dominant in the Archipelago, was significant in the sixteenth and seventeenth centuries, probably due to ongoing contact with Muslim persons and texts from Persia and India. Among such works in Malay are the *Hikayat Fatimah*, *Hikayat Ali Khawin*, *Hikayat Abu Bakar*, and the *Hikayat Muhammad Hanafiyyah*.[44]

If we examine how not only content but also genre were translated into Malay, we find that types of Arabic verse were introduced into Malay poetry and found a place in its tradition. Most famous among such genres is the Malay *syair*, thought to derive from a form of Arabic poetry and to have first been formulated in Malay by the Sufi writer Hamzah Fansuri in the sixteenth century. This form, which as a Malay translation from Arabic was early on closely linked to religion (perhaps influenced by Ibn al-'Arabī's Sufi poetry), later came to be used in all categories of Malay literature. Other Arabic-derived poetic forms in Malay include the *qasidah*, *marhaban*, *berzanji*, *hadrah* and *dabus*, all coming under the general term *dikir*, devotional songs, evoking God and recounting His greatness. Many features of the hikayat, which became the most widely used genre in Malay, can be traced back to the Middle East and Persia.[45]

In Malay, as we have seen for the most part for Javanese, there was a widespread lack of interest in writers', including translators', specific, individual identities. Generally speaking, Malay authors and translators tended to remain anonymous. In the case of theological texts the unusual step of identifying both the source and the Malay translator was sometimes taken. For example, we find explicit mention of 'Abdul Samad al-Palimbani as the

43. Ibid., 154–57.

44. Ibid., 341. Marcinkowski is convinced that Shi'ite elements entered Malay-Indonesian Islam by way of southern India. M. Ismail Marcinkowski, "Shi'ites in Southeast Asia," *Encyclopaedia Iranica Online*. http://www.iranica.com.Ismail.

45. Mat Piah et al., *Traditional Malay Literature*, 154.

translator of Imām Ghazāli's *Bidāyat al-Hidāya* and *Iḥya' 'Ulum al-Dīn* into Malay in 1778.[46]

The motives for writing and translating, when stated, seem to resonate with those in Javanese as well: gaining merit, acquiring blessings, praising the prophets, saving the writer and his audience from the torments of the grave. Some texts, including the Malay *One Thousand Questions* I discuss, titled *Hikayat Seribu Masalah* and edited by Djamaris, include a warning that the audience should not make light of the content of the work, claiming that its authority lies with God, thus any disrespect toward it would be equal to treachery toward both God and His Prophet.[47]

A third element common to both Malay and Javanese is the frequent lack of addressing the act of translation, including any mention of the language from which the Malay translation was made. An example of this tendency is found in the above-mentioned *Hikayat Muhammad Hanafiyya*: although scholars have concluded that it was a direct translation from Persian—based on its large Persian vocabulary, Persian verse forms, and a narrative familiar from Persian literature—this fact is not noted anywhere in the Malay text itself.[48]

Beyond such silences, how did particular terms in Malay texts give voice to particular understandings of translation? To answer this question I now return to the *One Thousand Questions*. Djamaris's edition of the *Hikayat Seribu Masalah* opens with the following words:

> Adapun bahwa kitab ini seribu masalah didalamnya ceritera Abdullah Ibn Samud daripada bahasa Parsi, maka dipindahkan oleh faqir yang hina kepada bahasa Jawi.
>
> (This is the book of one thousand questions, which contains the story of Abdullah ibn Samud. From Persian it was "moved" by a humble *faqir* into the Jawi language.)[49]

These lines provide a straightforward—albeit brief—statement about the transmission of the text into Malay, referred to here as Jawi, Malay written

46. Ibid., 382.
47. *Hikayat Seribu Masalah*, ed. Edwar Djamaris (Jakarta: Pusat Pembinaan dan Pengembangan Bahasa Departemen Pendidikan dan Kebudayaan, 1994), 87. Hereafter, *HSM*.
48. L. F. Brakel, *Hikayat Muhammad Hanafiyyah: A Medieval Muslim-Malay Romance* (The Hague: Martinus Nijhoff, 1975), 112.
49. *Faqir*, which has also entered English, means in Malay "poor, destitute," but can also refer to a religious mendicant, either Hindu or Muslim. *HSM*, 18.

in a modified form of the Arabic script.[50] *Bahasa*, translated as "language," in fact has a wider semantic field that includes ideas about appropriate behavior and the relevant manners which allow a group of people to live together.[51] Thinking of the translation not only in linguistic terms (from Persian to Malay) but also in social terms, as targeting a particular community, is suggestive of how such a work was perceived by its author and audience.[52]

An interesting exception within the general tendency to ascribe a Persian source to Malay *One Thousand Questions* manuscripts is found in a 1910 *Kitab Seribu Masa'il* of unknown place and authorship. In the first place, it explicitly mentions the word *asal* (origin, place of origin, source); in addition, it names what may be Javanese (*bahasa Jawah*) as its source language. The full citation reads: "The origin of this text is from Javanese, the one who first 'owned' it was 'Abbās, may God be pleased with him, then it was told by the one who 'owns this telling' now."[53] Since *Jawah* may refer to *Jawi*, that is Malay rather than Javanese, we cannot be completely certain that this particular telling is based on a Javanese one, but the probability seems high. This unusual mention points to the production of the *One Thousand Questions* in the Archipelago being far from homogenous.

50. Jawi can refer to Javanese (as above), to Southeast Asian Muslims, the Malay language, or to Malay written in Arabic script. Throughout this book I use Jawi when discussing a language or community and jawi when referring to the script.

51. On the significance of *bahasa* see Henk Maier, *We Are Playing Relatives: A Survey of Malay Writing* (Leiden: KITLV, 2004), 6–8.

52. In his introduction (*HSM*, 6) Djamaris mentions that the manuscript he was working from stated the text originated in *bahasa Quarisy*—and that other manuscript tellings claim it originated in Persian—but in his transliterated edition he disregarded that earlier mention. *Quarisy* is in all likelihood a mistake. The scribe, using jawi script, could have easily written *Quarisy* instead of *Farsi*, *Farisi*, or *Parsi* by adding or leaving out a diacritical mark. Another interesting aspect of this statement is that it uses the name Ibn Samud—rather than the more common Ibn (or Ibnu) Salam—as the protagonist's name. This cited introductory section follows a previous paragraph in which the text is introduced without reference to translation, and in which the name Ibn Salam, not Ibn Samud, is mentioned: based on this fact it is probable that the author was working from two editions and attempting to combine them into one. Further testimony for this assertion is found in a repetition of the scene of Ibn Salam receiving the letter from Muhammad and announcing it to the Jews (*HSM*, 19).

53. *Asalnya caritra ini daripada bahasa Jawah, bermula yang ampunya caritra ini baginda 'Abas radi Allah anhu kemudian diceritakan oleh orang yang empunya carita ini. Kitab Seribu Masa'il*, Perpustakaan Nasional Republik Indonesia, Jakarta, 1910, MS. PNRI ML 442. The term *empunya caritra*, "to own, to possess a story," is common in Malay literature and refers to the storyteller, the person passing on the story, its guardian. *Mpu* or *empu* (in Malay and Javanese) refers also to a master craftsman and is a title for an outstanding artist, poet, or *keris*-maker. The storyteller possesses something of these artistic, creative, even magical abilities connoted by his title.

The verb used in several *One Thousand Questions* manuscripts to describe what happened to the story as it came to be told in Malay is *dipindahkan*, literally to move, relocate, or to transfer something, with a wider semantic range of changing, moving from place to place, spreading (like disease), and translating. The image is one of something—an object—being taken and carried in a physical manner to another, new, location. This is similar to one of the definitions for English "translation," which in its formal or technical use means "the process of moving something from one place to another."[54] In this sense the Malay would imply a quite different sense from *njawakaken*, with its emphasis on Javanese at the receiving end of the translation process. However, if we think of *dipindahkan* in terms of the transport of a story to a new place, a sense of a new, and perhaps different, beginning for the text is part of the image evoked.

Related to these images is the use of the verb *menyalin*, already mentioned for Javanese, that is used in Malay as well. It refers to changing (as of clothes), copying, or translating. In addition, in its form *bersalin*, it means to give birth, thus adding the apt images of newness, creation, and the combination of the past and the future's potential to the translation process. The Arabic-derived *menterjemahkan*, "to translate," is also sometimes used. An example is found in an 1822 copy of Kemas Fakhruddin of Palembang's untitled text usually known as *Kitab Mukhtasar: Maka adalah aku menterjemahkan kitab ini dengan bahasa Jawi* (Thus I translate this book into Malay).[55] This wording may be related to this being a direct translation of an Arabic work in which each phrase of the original is followed by a Malay translation, with the choice of terminology implying a distinction between such a literal, interlinear type of translation and a more culturally specific one.

Another term that is often employed for telling a story is *diceriterakan* or *diperkatakan*, "was told, was narrated," similar to the Javanese *winarni*. The stress of this term seems to be not on the translation *from* a particular language, nor *into* another, but on the narrative itself, the narrating process, and the narrator, who may be mentioned by name or as the story's guardian. The term does not appear to be specifically linked to a particular type of literature and is found in works as diverse as the Islamic Persian-inspired *Hikayat Muhammad Hanafiyya* and the early, Hindu-derived Malay Ramayana, known as *Hikayat Seri Rama*.

Although the use of such general terms—"narrating," "transferring"—may imply that it is the story which holds the utmost importance, such that its

54. *The Concise Oxford Dictionary*, 9th ed. (New York: Oxford University Press, 1995), 1532.
55. Drewes, *Directions for Travellers on the Mystic Path*, 106.

prior source is relegated to the margins, when we examine Malay *One Thousand Questions* manuscripts we find almost all mention a source. Most striking is the consistent attribution of the story to the Prophet's uncle 'Abbās, an ancient, Arab, authoritative source that places the beginning of the story's transmission squarely during the Prophet's lifetime, soon after the events depicted.[56] The mention of 'Abbās as the one who first told the story, followed by mention of the storyteller who is now telling it anew, implies a line of transmission (A. *silsilah*) that stretches from seventh-century Arabia to the contemporary Malay setting in which the story is again being narrated. The frequent mention of Persian as the language from which Malay *One Thousand Questions* tellings were derived is another indication of the importance—in the eyes of those retelling it—of the story's past and its path into Malay. Both Persian and Jawi are categorized as languages (M. *bahasa*), rather than as general adjectives that could imply anything Persian or Malay, emphasizing the linguistic dimension of the translation act.

The Malay *One Thousand Questions* texts present themselves as more strongly connected to roots elsewhere than do the Javanese texts. They point to their retelling in Malay but make certain to note their transmission and translation history, if briefly. The use of words signifying "telling" for presenting the way the story is told may well be yet another element in this strategy: such words are likely, especially in the context of the *One Thousand Questions*' story, to be translations of the Arabic terminology employed in hadith literature, in which genealogies of transmission are crucial marks of authority and truth. Every hadith opens with the words "so and so reported," or "so and so said (A. *ḥaddaṭa, qāla*) that . . . ," then describes the sayings or actions of the Prophet either as witnessed by the speaker or accompanied by a meticulous listing of the names of those who passed down the tradition. In using such language the Malay *One Thousand Questions* further strengthens the impression that, although a translation, it is bound by history and tradition to authoritative, authentic sources.

The Tamil Context

In the Tamil literary tradition, mention of translation in the sense of an adaptation of an original work goes back to the *Tolkāppiyam*, the ancient and authoritative Tamil grammar that probably dates from the early centuries B.C. and is a detailed guide on the makeup and uses of language and literature. In the context of discussing two types of writing—*mutal* and *vali*—it states

56. The story is also attributed to 'Abbās in Arabic and Tamil tellings.

that *mutal* is an original work whereas *vali* is "one which is adapted from the original work." *Vali* is further divided into four types: works that are abridged, expanded, abridged as well as expanded, and "translated in accordance with the tradition of Tamil."[57]

The word used for the fourth type of *vali* is *moḻipeyar*, a word that in modern Tamil has assumed the meaning "to translate." However, it has the wider semantic range of "to give meaning in another language," "to interpret, explain in other words," and "to move from one place to another, to transfer, to convert." It is unclear in the *Tolkāppiyam* reference whether the stress is on rewriting in Tamil a text of another language or on a retelling in Tamil that remains within the limits of the known traditional models. Whether *moḻipeyar* assumed the meaning of translation in the more modern, precision-oriented sense much later or not, it is clear that it includes shades of meaning which are very similar to the translation vocabulary we have examined in Javanese and Malay: the focus is first and foremost on making a text Tamil, in accordance with local ideas about writing; it is an interpretation, an explanation, a meaningful expression, rather than an equivalent using a different language; and it hints at a change, a move, a conversion.[58]

Several types of translation are found in Tamil Muslim literature. I begin with those made to fit existing models of literature, expanded to include Islamic materials. There are the poems of the *piḷḷaitamiḻ* genre, devotional hymns in which the poet takes on the voice of a mother, recounts the childhood days of a famous king, a god, or a saint, and offers praise and veneration to that infant or child. Several such poems were composed in honor of the infant Muhammad. Other Tamil forms that Muslim authors expanded to include their literary materials were *mālai* (literally "garland," a number of verses on a theme joined together), *antāti* (poems in which the last letter or metrical syllable of the previous stanza becomes the first of the succeeding stanza), *kalampakam* (eulogies), *kōvai* (expressing divine devotion using love themes), *catakam* (poems containing one hundred verses), *kīrttaṉai* (poems set to music), *tālāttu* (lullabies), and *kummi* (poems composed in a meter adapted to the kummi dance).[59] It is evident from this long (and not exhaustive) list that Muslim writers were very much a part of the Tamil literary sphere.

57. Sutras 650–52. S. Ilakkuvanar, *Tolkappiyam (in English) with Critical Studies* (Madurai: Kural Neri Publishing, 1964), 260.

58. The use of *moḻipeyar* is also encountered in the early Tamil literature, including poems of the caṅkam age and the well-known epic *Cilappatikāram*.

59. Examples can be found in M. M. Uwise, *Muslim Contribution to Tamil Literature* (Kilakkarai: Fifth International Islamic Tamil Literary Conference, 1990), 151–64.

Another type of translation combines a Tamil form with a non-Tamil, Muslim form. The most well known and revered Muslim text in Tamil is the Prophet's life history as told by Umaṟuppulavar. With the composition of his *Cīṟāppurāṇam*, Umaṟu incorporated the Arabic genre of *sīra*, biographies of the Prophet, into Tamil literature; the work is both a translation of earlier works on this topic from Arabic and a very local creation.

Although the work itself includes no internal evidence on the year of its composition and Umaṟu's life, traditional accounts relate that he was born in the mid seventeenth century and was court poet at Eṭṭaiyāpuram, in southeastern Tamil Nadu.[60] His patron Cīttakāti, advisor to the Ramnad ruler, commissioned the work. He wished for a Tamil work on Muhammad, concerned that Muslims were too often reading the Hindu epics. Since Umaṟu did not know at first what to write and needed someone to translate Arabic sources for him, he was sent to a teacher who refused to help because Umaṟu came dressed in Hindu garb. While despairing, the Prophet appeared to him in a dream and sent him back to the teacher, who, having had a similar dream, then arranged for him to study. As Shulman notes, this story "may reflect a consciousness of the complex nature of this work: like the Muslim poet draped in Hindu costume, the *Cīṟāppurāṇam* is a Muslim creation in Hindu form."[61]

The *Cīṟā*, divided into three parts relating the Prophet's early life, his prophethood, and the *hijra*, combined Tamil literary images, landscapes, vocabularies of praise, and devotional elements common to both Muslims and non-Muslims at the time. Especially notable is the affinity between this work and the earlier, ninth-century *Irāmāvatāram*, Kampaṉ's great Tamil Ramayana. Thus Ali's procession through Medina parallels Rama's march through Mithilā; like Kampaṉ, who described Ayodhya in terms of the caṅkam literature's Tamil landscapes, so Umaṟu describes the Prophet's Arabia as the Tamil land, with its monsoon clouds, flora and fauna, mountains and waterfalls. Phrases, similes, and the arrangement of chapters in the *Cīṟā* follow Kampaṉ as well.[62] Nonetheless, Umaṟu did not adopt the Hindu *purāṇam* form wholesale but appropriated the Prophet into the Tamil world via a generic use of language and convention, allowing Tamil Muslims to remain within their cultural sphere but with that sphere expanded to include their Prophet's

60. Ibid., 51. The town has a burial shrine (T. *tarkā*) dedicated to Umaṟuppulavar.

61. David Shulman, "Muslim Popular Literature in Tamil: The Tamimaṉcāri Mālai," in *Islam in Asia*, ed. Y. Friedmann, vol. 1 (Jerusalem: Magnes, 1984), 175.

62. V. Narayan, "Religious Vocabulary and Regional Identity: A Study of the Tamil *Cīrappurāṇam*," in *Beyond Turk and Hindu*, ed. D. Gilmartin and and B. Lawrence (Gainesville: University of Florida Press, 2001), 74–97.

biography through the use of Arabic sources translated into a Tamil idiom.[63] Thus Umaruppulavar's *Cīṟā* introduced an Arabic genre and combined it with the earlier Sanskritic-Tamil genre of *purāṇam*, while other Tamil Muslims accommodated existing literary forms and combined old with new.

A third type of translated works included Muslim literary forms in Tamil that do not have parallels in non-Muslim Tamil literature. Through such works not only content but form was translated into a new setting. Besides the newly introduced *macalā* literature, to be discussed in chapter 4, we find, for example, the *paṭaippōr*, "war poems." These typically depict the heroic wars of Muslim fighters. The earliest example of this genre, *Cakkuṉ Paṭaippōr*, was composed by Variccai Mukiyittīṉ pulavar in 1686 and tells of Cakkuṉ, ruler of Iraq and leader of the non-Muslims, who was defeated by the Prophet, was converted along with his followers, and who continued to reign over Iraq.[64] Another well-known work of this type is Acaṉalippulavar's 1738 *Aintupaṭaippōr*, a series of five war poems describing the exploits of 'Alī bin Abi Ṭālib.[65] Other Islamic literary genres adopted include *kisah* (narration of stories), *munājāt* (invoking blessings), and *nāmā* (P. *nāmé*, a "story," "chronicle," or "book"). Using literary forms newly introduced into Tamil allowed writers not only to convey the Islamic stories and teachings in their own language—as was done in works employing non-Muslim genres like the *purāṇam* or *mālai*—but also to retain the structure and narrative strategies of the earlier Muslim works.

Many translations from Arabic were produced as well, among them works of *tafsīr* (Qur'anic exegesis), hadith, *'aqāid* (creed), *fiqh* (jurisprudence), and hagiography. Some such works were direct translations, of al-Ghazāli and Ibn al-'Arabī for example, as well as biographies of "saint" Mukiyittīn, as the very popular 'Abdul Q̱ādir Jilāni is known in Tamil Nadu. Others were—as already noted—Tamil works heavily drawing on their Arabic sources. Some major Tamil works, mostly moralistic poems like the *Tirukkuṟal*, were translated from Tamil into Arabic by local Muslim authors.[66]

If we consider the aspects of translation practices examined for Javanese and Malay in the Tamil context, we find very similar expressions of humility by authors and translators, always deferring to generations of past teachers and scholars and expressing anxiety about their own writing abilities and

63. V. Narayan, "The Ramayana and Its Muslim Interpreters," in *Questioning Ramayanas*, ed. Paula Richman (New Delhi: Oxford University Press, 2000), 265–81.

64. Uwise, *Muslim Contribution to Tamil Literature*, 28–29.

65. Shulman, "Muslim Popular Literature in Tamil," 201.

66. Takya Shu'ayb 'Alim, *Arabic, Arwi and Persian in Sarandib and Tamil Nadu* (Madras: Imāmul 'Arūs Trust, 1993), 264–300.

their acknowledged mistakes. As we have seen in the case of the Tamil *Cīṟa*, Umaṟuppulavar—although he recast "prior text" (a concept I will explore further later in this book) in an innovative way—showed respect and reverence to prior authority, and deference to a long and esteemed tradition, by relying on existing models and on the example of the famed Kampaṉ.

In the *One Thousand Questions* the author Vaṇṇapparimaḷappulavar mentions he is anxious about writing. His concern is rooted in the fact that in order to write well he must master many domains: grammatical rules (*eḻuttuviti*), the particles of speech (*cōl*), meaning (*poruḷ*), prosody (*yāppu*), rhetorical ornamentation (*alankāram*), the great number of poetic meters (*cir*), and rhyming (*toṭai*). He explicitly says he fears the reproach and rejection of all good people.[67] As part of a tradition of belittling oneself, expressing modesty, and making no claims to knowledge or ability, he asks forgiveness for any fault or mistake in the book. He professes he is "afraid of the speakers of true Tamil, knowers of the Vedas, exalted ones," who will surely recognize his ignorance. He proclaims that he is singing, or telling, this story without expecting reward (T. *payaṉ*).[68]

Despite his misgivings the poet is sure of one thing: his wish to tell this story in Tamil. He does not use a word which corresponds to "translation," and in Tamil there is no single verb which implies to "Tamilize," as was the case for Javanese and Malay. But the stress is quite similar to the latter languages when the poet expresses his resolve to recite in Tamil the story as it unfolds.[69]

I have noted that most translations into Javanese and Malay do not explicitly address the choice of works deemed appropriate for translation, the translation process, and even the language of the source text, the time of translation, and the translator's identity. According to Uwise, who has published the best study of Muslim Tamil literature to date,[70] many of the Tamil works can be traced to an author, although often nothing is known of the person beyond his or her name and hometown. Author names usually include a single name with the title *pulavar* (poet) appended to them, as we have seen in the case of Umaṟu (A. 'Umar). Often Arabic names were given to poets (and others) in addition to a Tamil name. Thus the author of the *One Thousand Questions*, as mentioned, was known both as Vaṇṇapparimaḷappulavar and by his Arabic name Ceyku Mutali Icukkāku. Some works mention a date of writing or first

67. Vaṇṇapparimaḷappulavar, *Āyira Macalā*, ed. M. Saiyitu Muhammatu, "Hasan" (Madras: M. Itrīs Maraikkāyar, 1984), Invocation, v. 26. Henceforth, *AM*. Citations are to verse.

68. *AM*, Invocation, v. 28.

69. *Virikkum tamiḻaip paṭikkuḷ yāṉ / viḷambat tuṇinta vēḷmatamē*. *AM*, Invocation, v. 27.

70. M. M. Uwise, ed., *Tamiḻilakkiya Aṟapuccol Akarāti* (Madurai: Kamaraj University, 1983).

public reading; the language of a source used is sometimes related, although there is not always a direct link between that language and the Tamil work produced.[71]

In brief mentions of the translation process in Muslim Tamil texts, we find that a work could be based—and perhaps *had* to be based to some extent—on a non-Tamil, usually Arabic or Persian source, but that it was not directly translated from that source. Certain texts declare explicitly that, rather than offering a "direct" translation, they are based on an author consulting earlier materials, then setting about to write his own innovative and localized Tamil creation. This often meant that an intermediary participated in the process, supplying the Arabic material and explaining it to the author, so that he became capable of producing his own work.

We have seen that Umaṟuppulavar's patron sent him to study with an important teacher, the famed sheikh Ṣadaqatullāh, who then commissioned a translation of the most important of Arabic *sīras*—Ibn Hishām's *Sīrat Rasūlullah*—into Tamil, which Umaṟu would later use for his writing.[72] Another poet, Alippulavar, who wished to compose a Tamil account of the Prophet's ascension to heaven (A. *mi'rāj*), traveled to the coastal town of Kayalpattinam and obtained from scholars there a copy of the original Arabic work as well as a Tamil commentary on it, both of which he consulted in writing his *Mi'raj Mālai*, completed in 1589.[73] Similarly, the *One Thousand Questions* mentions in its introduction that Vaṇṇapparimaḷappulavar received assistance from one Mullāmiyā Cayitu Makutum from the town of Culaiyumānakar, south of Madurai.[74] Mullāmiyā is said to have supplied the poet with a Tamil commentary on, or translation of, Persian materials.[75]

Schomburg lists twelve additional Tamil Muslim works, written between the seventeenth and late nineteenth centuries, in which the author explicitly acknowledged the assistance of others, whether in supplying source materials in Arabic, offering a Tamil commentary on the original work, or in a more

71. In a recent intriguing study Torsten Tschacher has shown that among Tamil Islamic literary works only the *kāppiyams* consistently mention authors, dates, and patrons. Torsten Tschacher, "Commenting Translation: Concepts and Practices of Translation in Islamic Tamil Literature." Unpublished paper, 2009.

72. The translation from Arabic into Tamil was made by Sheikh Ṣadaqatullāh's disciple Mahmud Tibi. Shu'ayb 'Alim, *Arabic, Arwi and Persian in Sarandib and Tamil Nadu*, 286.

73. Susan Elizabeth Schomburg, "'Reviving Religion': The Qādirī Sufi Order, Popular Devotion to Sufi Saint Muḥyīuddīn 'Abdul Qādir al-Gīlanī, and Processes Of 'Islamization' in Tamil Nadu and Sri Lanka" (Ph.D. diss., Harvard University, 2003), 261.

74. *AM*, Introduction on author, p. 4.

75. *AM*, v. 29.

unspecified sense advising the poet as he wrote his work.[76] Although by no means universal, this practice of consultation, mediation, and collaboration was widely followed and is evident in the works considered of the highest quality within the tradition.

Translation therefore could proceed without direct knowledge of the source language but rather with the help of a scholar who passed on the necessary information to the translator writing in Tamil. Such accounts appear both in traditions external to the text (as in the case of *Cīṟāppurāṇam*) and within the text itself (as in the *One Thousand Questions*), where the person providing the assistance is explicitly acknowledged as a partner in the text's creation and highly praised by the poet.[77] This practice is further testimony to the ways in which translation was perceived not as an individual endeavor but rather as a collective effort and accomplishment which drew heavily on prior tellings and literary conventions as well as on a form of joint production.

Multiple Models of Translation

Having looked at ideas about, and practices of, translation—some explicitly expressed, others more circumstantial—in Javanese, Malay, and Tamil texts, we can clearly see that despite their differences they possess important common features. To emphasize these features I now turn briefly to a particular translation context in medieval Europe—twelfth-century Spain—and compare it with the tendencies of the Javanese, Malay and Tamil ones examined above. The point of this comparison is not to generalize in any way about "Europe" or "The West." Rather, through the connecting link of a common narrative translated in two very different periods and parts of the globe, I wish to reiterate the idea that acts of translation and their accompanying narratives have had, and still possess, multiple meanings.

Similar to the case of South and Southeast Asia, many anonymously translated texts can be found in European traditions. However, there is also evidence of individual translators, of their names and their motives for translating a particular text. Prefaces to twelfth- and thirteenth-century translations, typically from Arabic to Latin, often explained a translator's aims

76. Schomburg, "Reviving Religion," 650–64.

77. Although the poet, Vaṇṇapparimaḷappulavar, is most modest about his own abilities, he holds Mullāmiyā in high esteem and describes him using a powerful poetic metaphor: he sails his boat in the ocean of Arabic and Persian, spreading the sail of the five daily prayers with God's grace as the anchor, in the water passages of Malaiyāḷa, arriving in Culaiyumānakar untouched by fatigue, like nabi Nuh (Noah) traveling in his ship from the lands of the north. *AM*, Invocation, v. 29.

and provided details on the circumstances under which he worked.[78] Greek science, for centuries kept alive largely in Arabic, along with the Arabs' own knowledge of mathematics, astronomy, and medicine, was conveyed into Latin by translators conscious of their role in the recovery of such critical materials.

In a pertinent example, Peter the Venerable, initiator of the translation project in Toledo that produced the *One Thousand Questions*' translation into Latin, stated his motive for translating Muslim texts into Latin as supplying his fellow Christians—typically ignorant of the Muslim religion—with trustworthy information about Islam. Possessing such information would, according to Peter, enable Christians to refute elements which they would consider false in Muslim doctrine and create a powerful resistance to Islam.[79]

In prefaces made by some of the translators Peter employed, even more detailed—and telling—testimony is found. In his dedicatory letter to the first translation in the collection, the *Fabulae Saracenorum*—a compendium of Muslim cosmology and history which cannot be traced to its Arabic source in part because the translator intentionally omitted its chain of authority (A. *isnād*)—Robert of Ketton explicitly outlined his actions: "I exposed the law of the aforementioned [Muhammad] by my own hand, and brought it into the treasury of the Roman tongue, in order that, once its baseness became known, the Cornerstone [Christ; cf. Eph. 2:20], the most precious Redemption of the human race, might send forth His splendors farther and wider."[80]

In his prefatory letter to the translation of the Qur'an—its first ever complete edition in a language other than Arabic—Robert writes, addressing his letter to Peter: "Selecting nothing, altering nothing in the sense except for the sake of intelligibility . . . I have uncovered Muhammad's smoke so that it may be extinguished by your bellows."[81] The very title he awarded the translation of the text on Muhammad and the early caliphs ("The stories of the Saracens: The faulty and ridiculous chronicle of the Saracens") and the mocking and contemptuous tone he used in his introductory letter meant that Robert framed the translation in a particular, very negative manner, influencing readers' concept of the content even before having seen the first page. In Gerard

78. Marie-Therese d'Alverny, "Translations and Translators," in *Renaissance and Renewal in the Twelfth Century*, ed. R. L. Benson, G. Constable, and C. D. Lanham (Cambridge, Mass.: Harvard University Press, 1982), 421.

79. James Kritzeck, *Peter the Venerable and Islam* (Princeton: Princeton University Press, 1964), 42.

80. Ibid., 62–63.

81. Ibid., 65. It is ironic that Robert stresses his faithfulness to the original since he took many liberties in translation, including a redivision of the Qur'an's chapters.

Genette's terms (and in a manner common to many published translations at present) his inserted paratexts—the title and introduction—accorded the translator a powerful sway over readers' minds.[82] The same, although to a lesser degree, can be said of the title chosen for Herman of Dalmatia's Latin translation of the *One Thousand Questions* as part of the same project. Giving it the title *Doctrina Mahumet* framed the translation in a way that accorded it the legitimacy of official teachings which, according to Herman, meant the work possessed great authority among the Muslims.

Lastly, an additional striking feature of this early translation project has to do with notions of faithfulness to an original text. Peter deemed important the employment of a Muslim translator, known as Mohammed, who was responsible for supplying the other translators with exact meanings of Arabic words and background on Islamic doctrine. Peter stated explicitly that the translations "should not lack the fullest fidelity, nor anything be taken away by deceit."[83] This statement, while it may not tell us much about the actual texture of the resulting translations, conveys a conviction that equivalence in translation is both desirable and possible, a belief that would later be echoed by generations of Christian missionaries striving to translate the Bible into a vast number of languages. This kind of declaration, on the contrary, appears nowhere in the Javanese, Malay, and Tamil materials discussed.

Looking to another instance—the 1847 translation of the *One Thousand Questions* from Arabic to English—seven centuries after the translators of Toledo completed their work, a similar ideological approach is evident. Framing the translation with a provocative title implying an exposition of Muslim errors, an introductory quote from Luke ("Out of thine own mouth will I judge thee"), a dedication to a fellow clergyman ("The following attempt to expose the errors of Mohammedanism is most respectfully inscribed, by his most obliged pupil, the Translator"), and an introduction that brands the Prophet "the Imposter," the Reverend Davis left no doubt regarding his motives and strategies of translation.[84]

The Toledo Collection translation project is not representative of medieval European translation models, which were often quite similar to the ones described for Indonesia and India in terms of translators' apologetic stance and their anonymity. However, it does call our attention to the existence of an alternative trend, one that does not find a parallel in Javanese, Malay, and

82. Gerard Genette, *Paratexts: Thresholds of Interpretation*, trans. Jane E. Lewin (Cambridge: Cambridge University Press, 1997).

83. Kritzeck, *Peter the Venerable and Islam*, 68.

84. Davis, *The Errors of Mohammedanism Exposed*, 1–6.

Tamil sources and that also differs from other currents in European medieval translation: The Toledan translators—and Davis—did not express humility nor regret their shortcomings. Their names appeared clearly on the translations, and they expressed a clear goal for their undertaking, a religious one in the cases mentioned. The translator's introduction tended to frame the text in a way complementing the translator's—or his patron's—agenda. Fidelity to the source text was viewed as an important principle, at least ideally, although it was not always followed in practice.

In contrast, Tamil, Malay, and Javanese translators and authors regularly included apologies for their ignorance and dearth of skills. However conventional and formulaic, these words of humbleness express a deference to prior authority and a sense that the contemporary individual is always lacking in comparison with earlier generations of teachers and scholars. That translations were often anonymous is further testimony to a particular individual's contribution being deemed unimportant in the larger endeavor, in which translations were understood as collective works. Motives for translation were often absent. When present, they had typically to do with producing merit and good fortune, invoking blessings, or offering advice, comfort, or knowledge, and they expressed these aims briefly and succinctly. When appearing in a text's opening lines, such justifications framed the text in a similar way to the Latin translations. When appearing at the end, as was often the case, they had less of an impact in this respect.

The question of fidelity is a significant one. This is not to say that translators working in Javanese or Tamil could not tell precision from vagueness, or lacked sufficient skills—linguistic and poetic—to reproduce a "faithful," relatively precise rendering of a source text. The dominant ideal, however, seemed to be that to "translate" or—as we have seen in the case of Javanese—to "Javanize" (J. *njawakaken*) meant to retell or rewrite a text in ways that were often both culturally appropriate and impressively creative. Using one's imaginative powers and literary skills in making a story Javanese was considered the appropriate thing to do, a creative act that would contribute to a specifically Javanese audience. Mediated, collaborative translation, as in the case of Tamil, was a way to draw on more than a single person's knowledge and expressive powers, merging the older Arabic or Persian text with a new creation and placing the poet and his craft at the heart of the translation process.

In this brief comparison, meant to highlight significant assumptions about the meaning and practice of translation in different traditions, two major points emerge: in the particular twelfth-century European example presented, a stress on the individual translator went hand in hand with a preoccupation with fidelity in translation, whereas in the Tamil, Javanese, and Malay materials, and especially the latter two, anonymity—the effacing of the individual—was coupled with creativity and change. Related to this point and perhaps even more striking is the paradox in the relationship between fidelity to a source text and propagating its content. In the Toledo project translations, the stress on accuracy and precision was explicitly employed as part of an effort to undermine and discredit the teachings offered in the Arabic texts; in the Javanese, Malay, and Tamil translations a distancing from the source in the form of creativity and poetic freedom was part of a powerful array of tools used to accredit earlier sources and present them as legitimate.

3

The *Book of Samud*: A Javanese Literary Tradition

The *Book of One Thousand Questions* is named in Javanese for its Jewish protagonist Samud Ibnu Salam. Known in most cases as *Serat Samud* or *Suluk Samud*, it tells a story of both continuity and change. As in other tellings, Samud's identity within the narrative changes markedly following his encounter with the Prophet Muhammad and his subsequent conversion. In addition the story itself, as told in Java, was dramatically transformed both across time and in relation to its tellings in other, neighboring cultures.

Such transformations of the *One Thousand Questions*' in Java, to be explored in this chapter, point to the ways in which Javanese Muslims, as members of larger communities in their region and beyond, were shaping and reshaping their literary works in accordance with developments in the religious and cultural spheres both at home and in Islam's distant lands.

Authors continued to present their audiences with a story famous across the Muslim world, thus connecting them to many others familiar with Ibnu Salam's dialogue with the Prophet. Concurrently, and to an increasing degree throughout the nineteenth century, they formulated a message relevant for the particular period and place in which they lived. The shifts in the Ibnu Salam narrative in Java exemplify a broader trend through which Islamic texts were often reconfigured in order to emphasize the local forms of a global religion. Ongoing tensions related to the depth of engagement with Arabic or Arabic-derived sources and their thought-world, as well as to a continuing involvement with pre-Islamic practices central to Javanese life of the kind apparent in the Samud texts and other Javanese works, underscore the complexities and ambiguities that pervaded the Arabic cosmopolis of South and Southeast Asia.

Attesting to its popularity, the *Samud* corpus survives in at least two dozen manuscripts, but there are likely to be many more not yet available to scholars. These manuscripts date from the late seventeenth century to the 1930s.[1] Most texts in the corpus share the following elements: a Jew named Samud Ibnu Salam questions the Prophet Muhammad on many topics that relate to Islam; the Prophet replies to all questions, at times at length, at others very briefly; central themes raised in the dialogue include God's unity, teachings of the "seven grades of being" (J. *martabat pitu*), cosmology, rituals, genealogies of the prophets and segments of their histories, death and its aftermath, and parallel mappings of prophets, days of the week, and the letters of the alphabet on the human body. The language is quite consistent across the corpus and includes many repetitive phrases as Samud and Muhammad address each other. Titles of these manuscripts vary somewhat, but the name Samud is an important identifying marker.

The earliest manuscript extant is the Leiden *Samud* (MS. LOr 4001), dating from the late seventeenth or early eighteenth centuries. Its production site may well have been along Java's north coast.[2] In the footsteps of this early manuscript came others, several of which mention the date of their copying, including a 1823 *Samud* fragment from the Karaton Surakarta that is a copy of a manuscript belonging to a man of Palembang in southern Sumatra and that attributes its teachings to a famous teacher in east Java, and the 1835 *Serat Suluk Samud*, likely produced in west Java.[3] Additional Samud texts were inscribed in Java throughout the nineteenth and early twentieth centuries, with the story of *Sèh Ngabdulsalam* published by Albert Rusche and Co. in

1. The texts comprising the Javanese corpus are found in national, academic, and court libraries in Jakarta, Yogyakarta, and Surakarta in Java, and in the Netherlands. In the Surakarta and Yogyakarta courts the texts belong to the once-ruling families. In the case of the other libraries, texts were collected, commissioned, and purchased over time, often by Dutch scholars and administrators, in different regions of Java. *The One Thousand Questions* was inscribed on palm leaves, bark paper known as *dhluwang*, and European paper, before appearing in print in 1913, in Surakarta; it was written in both Arabic and Javanese scripts.

2. G. W. J. Drewes, "Javanese Versions of The 'Questions of 'Abdallah B. Salam,'" *BKI* 142 (1986): 326; Theodore G. T. Pigeaud, *Literature of Java*, 3 vols. (The Hague: Martinus Nijhoff, 1967–70), 2:118.

3. *Samud* fragment in *Para Nabi Nerangaken Bab Rijal Saha Sanès-Sanèsipun*, Karaton Surakarta Library, Surakarta, 1823 [?], MS. KS 339.1, and *Serat Suluk Samud*, Museum Sonobudoyo Library, Yogyakarta, 1835, MS. MSB P 207, respectively.

Surakarta in 1913, introducing it through the print medium to a much larger potential audience than it had previously enjoyed.

From the little information—explicit and implicit—found in these manuscripts, we can begin mapping the circulation of the *One Thousand Questions* in Java over the course of at least two centuries: most extant copies were produced in central Java, most notably in Surakarta, but the story was known also along the northern coast and in Cirebon to the west. The *One Thousand Questions* had a relatively wide geographic circulation, an impression that will be further strengthened when its Malay tellings—some of which may have been produced in Java—are discussed in chapter 5.

Despite the questions still surrounding the precise translation history of the *One Thousand Questions* into Javanese, it is very likely that at least some of its tellings, including the earliest extant, were translated directly from an Arabic source rather than a Persian or Malay one. An eighteenth-century Arabic manuscript of the *One Thousand Questions* found in Batavia testifies to an acquaintance in the Archipelago with the story in Arabic at that early date. In terms of content, the number of questions in Arabic tellings since at least the twelfth century has remained at one thousand four hundred and four, whereas in Persian, Malay, and Tamil it is consistently mentioned as one thousand. Ali, who in early Arabic tellings is depicted as greeting the Jews, often appears as the bearer of Muhammad's letter in Javanese tellings but is only rarely mentioned in Malay ones. The question about why some children resemble their father while others resemble their mother is common to the *One Thousand Questions* in Arabic and Javanese, but not in Tamil and Malay. On the final page of the Javanese Leiden manuscript we find a statement of a type that is unusual in Javanese works, most often silent regarding matters of authorship and translation. The statement relates to the text's translation history, indicating it was translated into Javanese from Arabic or that it originated in the Arab lands (J. *saka Ngarabi*)—but the former possibility is much more likely. A suggestive and curious detail appears at the very end, where, after the author's formulaic apologies for his deficient language abilities, he explains that he is not Javanese but does not elaborate on his origins.[4]

An examination of dates and place names reveals something of the geographical and temporal extent of familiarity with the *One Thousand Questions*. The question persists, however, as to what in fact was transmitted under the title *Samud* (and its variants), as it is not unusual for manuscripts bearing the same or similar title to be far from identical. They can, indeed, be rather strik-

4. *Samud*, Leiden Oriental Manuscripts Collection, MS. LOr 4001, p. 108.

ingly different, challenging familiar notions of the meanings of authorship and narrative consistency. Since there is no archetypical Javanese text and no definitive translation path linking Javanese tellings to another language, I am concerned here not with how similar each telling is to such a hypothetical prototype, but rather with the existence of clusters of related texts within the larger corpus and the ways in which different authors chose to convey the story and its message.

Despite the variation apparent within the Javanese corpus and the creativity shown by authors and scribes in relating the story, a certain thematic and narrative consistency is apparent for at least part of the corpus. Such tellings are not word-for-word copies of one another; rather, they contain very similar sequences of questions and replies and use similar language, at times employing parallel vocabulary at the word, sentence, or stanza levels. The most direct path to identifying such similarities is through an examination of the texts' *tembang macapat*, metrical verse forms in which most eighteenth and nineteenth century Javanese poetry—meant to be recited aloud—was composed. A comparison of these metrical forms and of the first line of each new canto across texts reveals much about how similar or different the works are. Through such an analysis of the Javanese corpus I have identified two textual families. Defining the texts by a familial relation means here that, for the most part, they possess an identical tembang sequence (although not all include the entire sequence) and the same topic appears at the beginning of each new canto, suggesting that the question-and-answer debates they contain follow very similar lines.

The familial metaphor that captures the relationships between similar tellings or copies of texts implies that such texts share some common elements, in terms of content and structure, resembling one another to various degrees, as relatives may share certain traits but not others. It also implies a continuity through time and a branching out in space as generations of a reproduced story are born, mature, and give birth to their own literary offspring. The first family includes seven of the older *One Thousand Questions* manuscripts in which Ibnu Salam is the disciple, not teacher. These texts do not refer to each other and none mention a prior source for their composition, making it difficult to ascertain the connection between them, if and how such connections transpired, or where and when. Dates of inscription are suggestive—but not definitive—in providing information on the texts' histories. The second family includes two texts of the more recent *Sèh Ngabdulsalam* variant, one in manuscript form and the other—likely based on the former—in print.

Even though uncertainty remains as to many of the details regarding composition and inscription of Javanese works, such textual families reveal that it is possible to say with assurance that some texts were copied with high degrees of continuity and consistency over at least several decades, and likely longer. This means that audiences in different places and settings could be familiar with the same text, or with very similar texts, enabling them to draw on a common source. This fact was especially significant for a work like the *One Thousand Questions*, introducing as it did a broad array of Islamic rites and traditions. Such thematic and stylistic continuity was common within the Arabic cosmopolis of South and Southeast Asia, the context in which the Javanese *One Thousand Questions* was produced and transmitted.

The story itself was, of course, derived either directly or indirectly from Arabic; on Java it circulated in Javanese, Arabic, and Malay, three important Islamic languages; and it introduced many Arabic words, expressions, and citations to its audiences, at times accompanying these by translation or interpretation. Arabic-derived concepts thus shaped the religious lessons learned and connected Javanese Muslims to the wider, shared networks of learning and belief that stretched across their region and beyond.

One area in which an Arabicized culture can be assessed concretely is in the realm of writing. Some *One Thousand Questions* tellings were written in Javanese script, while other scribes used *pégon*, Javanese written in Arabic script. An early example of a third option—presenting a combination, or compromise—is found in the *Samud* manuscript. In a kind of mirror image of the common practice of adding diacritics to Arabic letters, thus modifying them to allow for unrepresented Javanese sounds, the text, written in Javanese script, employs a pattern of diacritics to indicate the use and sound of Arabic letters not represented in Javanese. For example, a small mark above the Javanese letter *ng* signifies an Arabic *ain*: thus Javanese *Ngibrani* should read *'Ibrani* (Hebrew).

Such examples indicate that a certain system for "transcribing" Arabic was already developed by the late seventeenth or early eighteenth century, when the manuscript was inscribed. Although this system was not by any means universally employed, it points to an awareness of Arabic vocabulary and its "authentic" spelling. Examining the pattern shows that some words that would become "naturalized" in Javanese during a later period and, therefore, did not merit any special marking may have still been viewed as foreign in earlier times, and deserving of special indication. Though it is uncertain how such words were in fact pronounced during this early period, it is likely that the marks were used as a way to remind and encourage reciters to resort to the authoritative Arabic sounds. The fact that an identical mark is used for all cases indicating a shift from Javanese to Arabic strengthens the assumption of familiarity with what were considered Javanese and Arabic "equivalents."

I will discuss several of the Javanese *One Thousand Questions* manuscripts available today in depth in this chapter and throughout the book.

The Leiden Samud *Manuscript*

The Leiden *Samud* manuscript, the earliest extant, serves as a "baseline" of sorts to assess the processes of change evident in the Javanese *One Thousand Questions* tradition, allowing a view of those elements remaining relatively constant as well as those that were radically transformed over time.

The manuscript has no title or colophon and its beginning is missing, but based on linguistic, orthographic, and metric evidence it was most likely produced in the early eighteenth century or earlier, along Java's northern *pasisir* coast.[5] Despite the difficulty of assigning it a definitive date, several of its features testify to its age: inscribed on bark paper, it exhibits no metric divisions within individual stanzas (J. *pada lingsa*), an unusual element found also in an early seventeenth-century *Menak* manuscript; the *tengahan* meters (marked by metrical variation within one and the same canto), appearing in cantos four and seven, are also typically associated with older manuscripts; words in *Samud* are connected in a kind of *sandhi*, without repeating a consonant or adding a vowel, but rather having the same letter as both consonant at word's end and vowel at another's beginning. This feature, known as *sastra lampahan*, is typical of Old Javanese, where adding a letter disrupted metrical considerations by making a short syllable long.[6]

In *Samud*'s initial lines the Prophet is in the midst of dictating to Ali a letter to the Jews that will soon be carried to their leader Samud Ibnu Salam. In the following scene the Jews consult with Ibnu Salam, depicted as wise and knowledgeable, about the meaning of the letter and the appropriate response. Already here it is mentioned that Muhammad's coming was prophesied in the Torèt, the Jewish scripture, establishing it as the supreme prior text that is henceforth referred to regarding many important matters.[7] Ibnu Salam declares that, to clarify whether the sender of the letter is indeed the long-expected Prophet, he will assemble a list of challenging questions based on the Torèt and then put them to Muhammad. The description of the questions as *gaib-gaib* defines them as embodying secret, esoteric knowledge, rather

5. Guillaume Frederic Pijper, *Het boek der duizend vragen* (Leiden: E. J. Brill, 1924), 67–71.

6. I thank Ben Arps for his input on the metrical characteristics of the manuscript.

7. *Samud*, MS. LOr 4001, p. 5. *Torèt* is a translation of Hebrew *Torah*. However, the Torah refers only to the first of three parts of the Hebrew Bible whereas *torèt*, as used throughout these Muslim texts, is a generic title that encompasses the entire Jewish scripture.

than obvious matters or simple interpretation, and highlights the inherent difficulty of providing correct replies. If Muhammad is able to answer the questions correctly, says Ibnu Salam, it will be fitting that he and his people will follow Muhammad's path.

The questions, numbering 1404, are then arranged in a book, and Samud leaves for Mecca, flanked by scholars and disciples. With an air of great confidence they arrive and, having been announced by a messenger, find the Prophet seated at the mosque's front porch (J. *surambi*) surrounded by his companions, relatives, and followers. To the question "who might you be?" Samud replies with a brief exposition, offering a definition of Judaism, highly unusual in Javanese literature:

> Yes my name is Samud
> I am Ibnu Salam
> Indeed I follow
> The religion of the prophets of Israel
> Of the descendents of Jacob
> I am exalted
> Granted an authority in reading
> The Torah scripture
> By Him who sent
> The prophets [bearing it] to me
> Indeed that which is
> Followed by all Jews
> And Christians.[8]

Samud then tells the Prophet he is prepared to question him, and Muhammad replies that he knows Samud has come with 1404 difficult questions derived from the Torèt. This prior knowledge shocks Samud into silence, and he then weeps, deeply moved.

This scene fills the first canto and is typical of this early *One Thousand Questions* as a whole in its relative descriptiveness and in its attendance to detail and emotion. It sets the stage for several themes of the story as told throughout the work, including the tension between Samud as strict examiner and as awed devotee; Muhammad as the replier whose knowledge is tested *and* the one who knows the questions well in advance; the Torèt as a joint point of reference for both religious leaders; the Prophet's mosque as the

8. *Samud*, MS. LOr 4001, p. 5. The final lines could also read "followed by the Jews and Christians all," emphasizing their conflation into a single group, not a rare occurrence.

single, static site of the unfolding drama; and the promise of transformation that propels the story forward from the start.

In terms of content the Leiden manuscript already includes many of the themes that reappear, abbreviated or in full, in later Javanese tellings. For example, the relationship between the prophet Adam's biography, the human body, and Muslim rituals is laid out in detail. Samud asks why Muslims fast during Ramadan and receives the reply: We fast because the *kuldi*—the forbidden fruit of paradise—remained in Adam's stomach for thirty days during which he did not eat nor drink. Therefore, God has commanded that during the fasting month one should only eat at night.[9] Asking about the five daily prayers Muslims perform, Samud received a reply relating two of these prayers to Adam: *asar* commemorates the time of day when Adam violated God's prohibition and ate the forbidden kuldi fruit. For this transgression all of Adam's children in future generations will have to face the Day of Judgment; *mahrib*, the evening prayer, recalls the time of day when Adam repented and was pardoned by God for his mistake.[10]

What are the four parts of the body that are exalted above all others? The Prophet offers a long reply: when nabi Adam was tempted, seeing the kuldi tree and desiring it, all light disappeared from his face and it was no longer bright, but filthy. His hand picked the fruit, he ate it and thus angered God. He then had to depart from paradise. Crushed by grief, repenting, he begged forgiveness until God pardoned him. This is the reason Adam's descendents must wash away the four sins of seeing, touching, walking, and eating before performing the prayers. They must begin by washing the face that saw and desired the forbidden fruit, then the hands that touched it, next the feet that walked toward the kuldi, and finally the mouth that ate it. They must also wash both ears so as not to hear the sound of those tortured in hell's fire, and the throat so as not to be fettered in hell.[11]

The recurring references to Adam's actions and plight allow the author to repeat this important story several times throughout the text, always mentioning the details anew: the forbidden yet tempting fruit on the tree, disobeying God, the banishment from paradise, the regret, the pardon, and ensuing human life on earth through which all of Adam's children still pay the price for that original error. The ritual purification is related very concretely to the story's plot and to Adam's gradual distancing of himself from what he did: the glance, the steps taken, the hand raised toward the fruit. The rewards

9. *Samud*, MS. LOr 4001, pp. 95–96.
10. Ibid., p. 80.
11. Ibid., pp. 85–86.

for cleansing (among Samud's following questions) are just as concrete, related again to the story and the aforementioned body parts: for example, from washing the face one gains a light emanating in this world and the next; from washing the hands, the embraces of heavenly *widadari*.[12]

Connecting this fundamental story with the daily ritual of prayer and the annual fasting month is a constant reminder of human weaknesses. It is also a reminder of God's grace and compassion for forgiving Adam his transgression. Thirdly, it reminds the person performing the ritual of the consequence of Adam's deed and the future encounter and judgment of *kiyamat* (Judgment Day). The concrete explanations resonate with other, similar modes of interpretation throughout the Javanese texts, among them analogies that are often employed to present abstract ideas.

In the context of the early *Samud*, as well as in later tellings, the reiteration of the story with its stress on the personality and actions of Adam—first human and prophet—is always appropriate anew: Adam represents all human beginnings and is a model for how humans should and should not behave, how they should relate to God, and how and why memory and retelling are crucial elements for the Muslim individual and community.

Among other questions appearing in the Leiden manuscript that resonate with later Javanese tellings are those about the four hellish lands on earth and the lands that will be spared on Judgment Day; the angel of death who, after taking away the breath of every living being, will take his own life; the fate of *kapir* children on Judgment Day, as their parents are sent to hell while their youth and innocence may save them from damnation. There are questions that call for explanations of various categories: of oceans, heavens, deeds, rewards and punishments. Many of these questions and their replies touch upon stories, beliefs, and classifications fundamental to Islamic tradition, by this time firmly established in Javanese literature.

A theme that recurs in many Javanese tellings of the *One Thousand Questions* but seems to be most highly elaborated in the early *Samud* is the resemblance, or lack thereof, of parents and their children. Whereas in later tellings the question typically addresses how and why a child may resemble his or her mother or father, we find here an extended discussion that involves also a child's grandparents, aunts, uncles, and cousins. For example, Muhammad states that if the woman's desire is stronger, the child will resemble her; if the man's is stronger, the child will resemble him; if both lack desire the child

12. Ibid., pp, 86–87.

will resemble an aunt or uncle. Intense female desire will result in a daughter who is prone to ill deeds and looks like the mother's niece, while intense male passion foretells the birth of a God-fearing son resembling his elders who is destined to become a learned sage.[13] This discussion presents its audience not only with a certain form of genetic speculation but also with a mapping of appropriate gender relations and the results of their abuse.

The encounter and dialogue between Samud and Muhammad, as depicted in the Leiden manuscript, emphasizes Samud's religious identity which, according to the story's own logic, provides the raison d'être for the debate. This is noteworthy because Samud's clear-cut identity and religious affiliation gradually blurred as the narrative was passed down to subsequent generations.

Within the context of their dialogue both the Jews and Muhammad are in agreement regarding the appearance of prophetic verses in the Torèt that foretell the arrival of Muhammad, "seal of the prophets." Incorporated here is the Muslim notion that Muhammad's coming was predicted in the Torah, from which it follows that accepting and embracing him as a prophet, and consequently embracing Islam as his disciples, was a natural and necessary step for the Jews.[14] Throughout the Leiden manuscript Muhammad and Samud both refer often to the Torèt: it is the source of Samud's many questions and his testing of the Prophet as well as the foundation of the Prophet's legitimacy and ability to prove his true prophethood.

At a point in the dialogue when many questions have already been asked and answered, Muhammad turns directly to the Jews and Christians, to the scholars present and to Samud himself, and demands to know whether they put their trust in his words. They all (*yahudi*, *nasarani*, and *wong kupar*, the infidels) acknowledge that they do. Then Muhammad again invokes the Torèt as the supreme prior text and source of Truth and reminds them that his name was inscribed in it in the distant past, appearing in the Hebrew language and recited by Moses. Next he cites an Arabic phrase and explains it in Javanese as referring to the "closing" or "sealing" of the Torèt, Sabur (Psalms), and Injil (the Gospel)—the three ancient scriptures—that was destined to occur upon his arrival and the emergence of Islam. In the final scene, after

13. Ibid., pp. 44–45.

14. On these traditions see Arent Jan Wensinck, *Muhammad and the Jews of Medina*, trans. Wolfgang Behn (Freiburg: Klaus Schwarz, 1975), 39–44. Passages in the Hebrew Bible viewed as anticipating Muhammad include Isaiah 42:1–7; Zechariah 9:9; Genesis 49:10–12. On this notion see Camilla Adang, *Muslim Writers on Judaism and the Hebrew Bible from Ibn Rabban to Ibn Hazm* (Leiden: E. J. Brill, 1996), 141–44.

Samud and his people convert, Samud justifies their decision by saying that all of Muhammad's words had been in harmony with those of the Jewish scripture.[15]

The reliance on the Torèt as a crucial source of legitimacy is not unique to the Leiden manuscript and appears in additional Javanese tellings as well as in other languages. However, among Javanese tellings this theme is most pronounced here, being raised repetitively and forcefully on both sides of the debate. Although the Qur'an is certainly also an important source of moral codes and divine inspiration cited by the Prophet, the Torèt holds a special position as a bridge between the Jews' old faith and the one they are about to embrace. The idea that Muhammad was in fact to be expected and awaited by Jewish communities who would recognize him by the signs portended in their scripture deepened the sense that Ibnu Salam's commitment to the Prophet in *One Thousand Questions* tellings reaffirmed the anticipated outcome of such a meeting. This contrasted with the way the Jews—according to this interpretation—had historically misunderstood the signs, refused to accept them, or rejected them outright.

Examining the contours of the earliest *One Thousand Questions* manuscript available in Javanese highlights the themes and emphases that later reappeared in other tellings and that constitute a common ground for discussing some of the ways in which the story was told on Java. However, reading additional manuscripts and glancing back in time also clarifies themes that make no appearance in the older telling, but which gradually became central when a major shift took place in the Javanese Samud tradition. I now introduce two such later manuscripts and discuss them in terms of this shift, texts that offer insight into significant religious and social change.

The *Serat Suluk Samud Ibnu Salam*, housed in the Sonobudoyo library in Yogyakarta, provides no explicit details of its creation beyond the year of inscription, 1898, possibly in Surakarta. The text lacks the typical frame story of Samud's meeting with the Prophet as well as a depiction of his conversion to Islam at the end of the dialogue. It is comprised of a long series of questions and answers that read rather like technical lists, almost entirely devoid of descriptive or figurative language. The theme of listing is not limited to the form of the questioning sequence but is also apparent in sections of the content itself, in which the Prophet supplies Samud with various lists—for example, the number of spirit types and their various natures, the types of

15. *Samud*, MS. LOr 4001, pp. 92 and 100, respectively.

desires and hearts—which at times make the text resemble a catalogue more than a poetic work.

Certain mistakes within the text—incorrect references to pagination and verse forms—make it clear that the manuscript is an imperfect copy of a previously inscribed text. The fact that pagination references exist at all is highly unusual in a manuscript of this type, and these, the fact that the text refers to itself as *buku* (from D., "book"), and the general lack of the traditional verse markers that predict and dictate the mood and content of the different cantos, all indicate that it was inscribed on the verge of—or during—a period of significant change. The *Serat Suluk Samud* seems to represent an encounter of "traditional" Javanese literature with modernity at a moment when the ancient practice of manuscript production was drawing to a close, printed books were becoming more numerous, and the notion of questioning—of the religious, the political, the national—was acquiring a new urgency on Java.

The second text that serves as the basis for this discussion was inscribed at the Pakualam court in Yogyakarta in 1884 (*Serat Samud*, Pura Pakualaman Library, MS. PP St. 80). There is no mention of authorship or of whether this work is a copy of an earlier one, although, as noted, the results of a comparative textual analysis point to it being closely linked to at least six other texts.[16]

Apart from its value as a product of this particular court, which produced a line of rulers highly committed to literature as well as to additional art forms, the Pakualam *Serat Samud* forms an interesting comparative bridge between other Javanese tellings, on the one hand, and the Tamil and Malay texts, on the other. While it presents and addresses many of the themes common to Javanese tellings—especially mystical teachings—it also retains a story frame which is at times surprisingly similar to the Tamil and Malay tellings, whether explicitly or via more subtle cues.

The relationship between the two manuscripts is noteworthy. As mentioned, the 1884 Pakualam *Serat Samud* and the 1898 *Serat Suluk Samud Ibnu Salam* belong to the same textual family, with eight of the *Suluk*'s fifteen

16. The Pakualam "minor court" (J. *kadipatèn*) was the last court to emerge in central Java following the division of the Mataram kingdom in 1755. It was founded in 1813 during the brief British rule of Java. On the history of this court, see Soedarisman Poerwokoesoemo, *Kadipatèn Pakualaman* (Yogyakarta: Gadjah Mada University Press, 1985). Since I was not granted permission to scan the manuscript at the library and there are no microfilm copies available, I copied and transliterated the manuscript for my research purposes. In citing the manuscript I indicate the canto and verse numbers based on my transliteration.

cantos corresponding in their metrical verse and their themes to cantos in the *Serat Samud*.[17] Furthermore, of the *Serat Suluk Samud*'s 3,535 lines, 2,214 lines—almost two thirds—correspond to those of the *Serat Samud* in order and content. In such lines either identical or very similar language is employed, with synonyms—rather than word repetition—appearing often. For example, we find the corresponding *miyos* and *mijil* (to emerge), *jeneng* and *nama* (name), *muwus* and *ngandika* (to speak).

Interestingly, in the two texts some cantos present the same topic while employing different meters. For example, the theme of God's creative utterance *kun* is discussed in *gambuh* meter in the *Serat Suluk Samud* but in *pangkur* meter in *Serat Samud*; the colors seen at death are addressed in *megatruh* meter in the *Serat Suluk Samud* but in *asmaradana* meter in *Serat Samud*. These examples present a form of poetic translation in which a topic remains the same while its appearance in differing meters makes for a change in mood, emphasis, or association.

The similarities between these two tellings are quite striking, all the more so because—on some counts—the tellings also differ markedly. As mentioned, they diverge in the ways in which they are framed, a significant matter. In the *Serat Samud* Ibnu Salam travels to meet the Prophet, and their dialogue ends in conversion. It is noteworthy that already in the opening pages, as Ibnu Salam presents Muhammad's challenge to his people, he is convinced of the new prophet's truth. In this respect Ibnu Salam is a convert even before setting off to ask his questions. At the same time, since he selects difficult questions based on the scriptures with which to test Muhammad, he is the teacher, the examiner, rather than an obedient disciple. However, as Ibnu Salam finds out at the meeting (as was the case in the early *Samud* manuscript), Muhammad is aware not only of all the answers but also of the questions he will be asked, and he knows Ibnu Salam's intentions. This beginning underscores the complexity of the encounter and the many levels at which it unfolds concurrently.

The *Suluk Samud Ibnu Salam*, on the other hand, does not relate any of these details. Its first canto explains that this text will elaborate on mystical teachings regarding the relationship between Man and God. The disciple, addressed fondly as *kulup* (child), is urged to concentrate on the teachings and to avoid hesitation as he ponders his origins, the true nature of his being, and his unity with God. In the second canto the author states that it will be

17. These are cantos 3 (Sinom), 5 (Asmaradana), 6 (Dhandhanggula), 7 (Kinanthi), 8 (Durma), 10 (Pangkur), 12 (Dhandhanggula), and 13 (Durma), corresponding to cantos 14, 15, 16, 17, 18, 19, 20 and 12 in *Serat Samud*, respectively.

through the teachings of the Prophet that the truths presented—the "signs of esoteric knowledge" (J. *sasmitaning ngèlmu kang sejati*)—will be revealed. Although in the following pages the *Serat Suluk Samud* and *Serat Samud* do converge on many issues, these divergent introductions frame them very differently and make it seem, at least initially, as though they follow different trajectories.

In the terminology of familial relations I employ to analyze how such texts may relate to each other, these two can be viewed as possessing different genealogical roles. The 1884 *Serat Samud* was likely a copy of an older, perhaps circulating *One Thousand Questions* telling that may have inspired the additional texts mentioned above that shared both metrical and thematic sequences with it. In this sense it can be imagined as a son or daughter of a previous generation. The 1898 *Serat Suluk Samud Ibnu Salam* appears to be a copy of an earlier telling, but in terms of its relationship to the available textual family it moves onto unfamiliar ground and presents its own "take" on certain themes, including a self-reflexive stance on being a book in the modern sense of the word. It can thus be thought of more as a grandson or younger cousin of the older tellings, still very much a part of the family but cultivating its own thoughts and ideas, looking toward a future of writing and reading practices on Java that was unknown to its forefathers.

A Changing Story

Whereas the early *Samud* emphasized narrative detail, stories, rituals, and the central role of the Prophet, later tellings like the *Serat Suluk Samud Ibnu Salam* and *Serat Samud* took on a different emphasis and tone as the *One Thousand Questions* evolved into a work focused on mystical teachings that were central to Javanese Islam.

At the core of the *One Thousand Questions* in many of its Javanese variants are the teachings of *waḥdat al-wujūd* or Unity of Being, teachings that were elaborated by Ibn al-'Arabī in the thirteenth century and introduced to Indonesia in the latter part of the sixteenth century in the Malay poems of Hamzah Fansuri. Most broadly, these teachings attempted to grapple with the ontological relationship between God and the world (and Man in particular) and address the question of whether they are one and the same, distinct from each another, or both.

Central to debates over this matter in Indonesia was the formulation of the mystical doctrine of the "seven grades of being." Adapted from Ibn al-'Arabī via several channels, these were probably developed by Shamsuddīn al-Sumatrāni (d. 1630) from the *Tuḥfa*, an important Arabic work composed by the Indian author ibn Faḍlillāh of Gujarat (d. 1620) and retold in Malay and Javanese. At their heart was the idea that God is Being, and that "this Being proceeds to the visible world through six stages of emanation but is involved in no change thereby."[18] The most well-known and well-documented example of the doctrine's diverse interpretations in the Archipelago is Nūruddīn ar-Rāniri's criticism of Hamzah Fansuri's mystical Malay poetry in seventeenth-century Aceh, which the former viewed as *wujudiya yang sesat* (a deviant wujūdiya).[19] Nūruddīn's favor with the king brought disaster upon Hamzah's followers, led to the burning of his books, and guaranteed that secrecy and allegory—already important elements of the teachings—would be even more strongly associated with them in the attempt to avoid danger.

Despite criticism surrounding the concept of waḥdat al-wujūd, it is a fundamental and central doctrine of various schools of Sufism. Scholars in the Malay-Indonesian world continued to embrace and debate it throughout the eighteenth and into the nineteenth centuries. Controversies about waḥdat al-wujūd most often centered on the risk of it being misunderstood, misinterpreted, and spread among those likely to take it, mistakenly, at face value, leading to pantheistic beliefs.

The popularity of wujudiya teachings as well as other doctrines and rituals adopted by Muslims in the Archipelago was closely associated with the introduction of some of the great Sufi orders (J. *tarékat*, from Arabic *ṭarīqa*) into the region. This process accelerated from the seventeenth century on as men from Java and Sumatra traveled to the holy cities of Islam to seek knowledge, some returning after initiation into one or more of the orders, at times attaining the title of *khalīfa*. Their teachers in Mecca or Medina were often of Indian origin. In this way the Indian Shattariya order—by way of 'Abd al-Ra'uf of Singkel, who introduced it to Sumatra in 1661, and his many disciples and followers—became firmly established in Sumatra and Java. The Shattariya accommodated itself with relative ease to local tradition, and it became the most "indigenized" of the orders.[20] It was thus through the Shattariya that Sufi metaphysical ideas and symbolic classifications based on the *martabat pitu* doctrine and wujudiya teachings became part of Javanese popular beliefs.

18. Anthony H. Johns, *The Gift Addressed to the Spirit of the Prophet* (Canberra: Australian National University, 1965), 6.

19. Syed Muhammad Naguib Al-Attas, *Raniri and the Wujudiyyah of 17th Century Acheh*, Monographs of the Malaysian Branch of the Royal Asiatic Society (Singapore: Malaysia Printers, 1966).

20. Martin van Bruinessen, "Origins and Development of the Sufi Orders (Tarékat) in Southeast Asia," *Studia Islamika* 1.1 (1994): 1–23.

Although there is no explicit indication in the Javanese *One Thousand Questions* tradition that it was associated directly with this order, it is highly probable that such was the case.

One of the avenues by which these teachings were expressed, explored, and disseminated in Javanese was by way of the literary genre of *suluk*. With time the Javanese *One Thousand Questions* was gradually transformed into one such suluk among many.

Suluk (from Arabic *sulūk*, "traversing the Sufi path") are mystical Javanese-Islamic poems that typically address God's relationship to His creation, death and life, and the path to perfected knowledge. Strongly influenced by Ibn al-ʿArabī's writings as they found their way to the Archipelago, as well as by doctrines of several dominant Sufi orders in the region and local mystical teachings, their appearance in numerous Javanese manuscripts attests to their central cultural role. In one of the more popular suluk formats, a major topic or an array of issues are tackled by means of a series of questions and replies. Bonds of authority and intimacy often connect the pair engaged in dialogue, most often as husband and wife, guru and disciple, or master and slave.[21]

For example, in some tellings of the *Suluk Sujinah* the dialogue takes place between Princess Sujinah of Mecca, who agrees to marry whomever will answer all her questions about Islam and mysticism, and the man who succeeds, the Javanese Purwadaksina.[22] In *Suluk Dhudha* a speculative dialogue on Islamic mysticism unfolds between a widower (J. *dhudha*) and a widow.[23] In *Suluk Abesi* (or *Besi*), Bilal, the Abyssinian slave of the Prophet's time, enters a debate with a Muslim leader.[24]

21. Following a path to transformation through speaking with a teacher or several teachers was not unknown in central Java at the time when Islam arrived. Such a journey was perhaps most visibly inscribed on the stone galleries of the ninth-century Buddhist monument of Borobudur. Depicting scenes from the Sanskrit text of the *Gaṇḍavyūha*, it shows the young pilgrim Sudhana going from teacher to teacher (S. *kalyāṇamitra*) progressing on his path to enlightenment.

22. *Suluk Sujinah*. Place and date of composition unknown, inscribed Surakarta, 1908, by Soma Sukarsa. Museum Sonobudoyo Library, Yogyakarta, MS. MSB P195. See T. E. Behrend, ed., *Katalog Induk Naskah-Naskah Nusantara: Museum Sonobudoyo Yogyakarta* (Jakarta: Jembatan, 1990), 536.

23. Pakubuwana IV, *Suluk Dhudha*. Composed Surakarta, ca. 1788; inscribed Surakarta, 1885/6, by Madyasuwara. Karaton Surakarta Library, Surakarta, MS. KS482.5. See Nancy K. Florida, *Javanese Literature in Surakarta Manuscripts*, vol. 1: *Introduction and Manuscripts of the Karaton Surakarta* (Ithaca: Cornell University Press, 1993), 265.

24. For an example see the anonymous *Suluk Besi*; place and date of composition and inscription unknown. Fakultas Sastra Universitas Indonesia, Jakarta, MS. FSUI PW 125, 160–71. T. E. Behrend and Titik Pudjiastutu, eds., *Katalog Induk Naskah Naskah Nusantara: Fakultas Sastra Universitas Indonesia* (Jakarta: Yayasan Obor Indonesia/École Française D'Extrême Orient, 1997), 740.

The Ibnu Salam story is defined as a suluk by its title in several Javanese tellings, including the *Serat Suluk Samud Ibnu Salam*. It is easy to see why its frame story fits so well with the suluk genre in Javanese: the question and answer format was integral to the story when it came to Java; the pair in dialogue is in a relationship of teacher and disciple, however atypical as it involves the Prophet himself and a respected leader of another faith; and the issues raised and discussed are Islamic—and mystical—in nature. It remains an open question whether this story was imposed perfectly onto an existing Javanese model or whether it—or similar stories—provided the models for early dialogic forms of suluk.

Wujudiya Teachings and the Javanese One Thousand Questions

In its opening canto the *Serat Suluk Samud Ibnu Salam* offers an introduction to the mystical teachings it propounds. The central metaphor employed to introduce the topic of God's relationship to man is that of the body, from the stage prior to its creation, before it became manifest through the unity of a man and woman, through its existence in this world, to death. Reflection on the true nature of being and unity with God is pivotal to an understanding—however initial—of the doctrine. Of the Javanese *One Thousand Questions* manuscripts I have examined, this text provides the most pronounced example of the incorporation of the waḥdat al-wujūd teachings into the Samud story, to the point where it focuses almost exclusively on them. It exemplifies the way in which Javanese tellings came to distance themselves from the older frame story and its narrative detail and became centered on the teachings as such.

Unity is only one aspect of God, an understanding of which proves insufficient to knowing Him. The other aspect is the multiplicity that coexists with oneness. These two aspects were presented by Ibn al-ʻArabī as a "unity of contradictions," forming the gist of his philosophy.[25] This topic, appearing in various forms and accompanied by the relevant terminology, became a central theme of the Javanese texts. God and Man, *roh* and *jisim* (soul and body), the dwelling and the dweller, the one bowed to and the one bowing, all are in

25. Javanese works do not present a "purely" Ibn al-ʻArabī worldview. Rather, terminologies and ideas from other sources are combined to form the teachings presented. In the case of the *One Thousand Questions* and other famous works like the *Centhini*, *Hidayat Wirid Jati*, and *Serat Wulang Rèh*, a strong influence of al-Ghazāli is clear. Simuh, "Pengaruh Tasawuf dalam Kesusastraan Jawa Abad 19," undated photocopy, 54–56.

truth one, since ultimately only a single *wujud*—God's—exists. The attempt to grasp how this multiplicity, the endless variety of species, phenomena, and perceptions known from daily human life, arises from a single source yet also remains differentiated within it, forms Samud's greatest challenge. The seemingly contradictory ideas of the teachings are difficult to grapple with, calling for a more concrete way to make them accessible to the disciple.

This way is found in a series of analogies presented in the texts, a common and preferred means of teaching in Javanese literature. For example, the relationship—in which not all difference between Creator and created is denied, nor is complete identification achieved—is depicted in the negative; one without the other would be like a lotus without a lake, a sea without its shore, a board without writing or writing without a board, as well as a *keris* sheath entering a *keris*.[26] All these possibilities suggest an underlying unity whose disruption or disintegration evokes paradoxical conditions.

Other metaphors that introduce the unity in concrete form include the stars that, although hidden from view by the sun's light at noon, have not in reality disappeared. A further analogy on the same theme of unity—one of the most commonly used both by Ibn al-ʿArabī and in Javanese suluk—is that of a mirror, in which Man is understood as the mirror image of God.[27] This also relates to the idea of "dependent, relative being" (J. *wujud ilapi*) by which everything present in the world is dependent on God in the sense that it emanates from, and also remains a part of, Him. This important concept appears again in the analogy of the many lights of the stars emerging from wind.[28] Another type of analogy purposefully uses irrational metaphors that are difficult to picture and cannot be grasped by the intellect. They serve not to clarify a concept but to prove how immune it is to clarification. These analogies relate to *ilmu rasa*—mystical, esoteric knowledge—and suggest this form of knowledge lies beyond the grasp of most. It is like a fish swallowing an ocean, like a horse galloping inside a stable, or a wasp making a hole in the sky.[29] In explaining the origin of Samud's being—that was hidden within God's knowledge long before it took actual form—the Prophet uses the popular tree metaphor: a complete tree with branches, leaves, and roots resides

26. *Serat Suluk Samud Ibnu Salam*, Museum Sonobudoyo Library, Yogyakarta, 1898, transcribed 1932. MS. MSB P173a, p. 26, v. 37. For this text I use the reference system in the transliterated version, based on the page and verse in the original manuscript.

27. Ibid., p. 100, v. 25.

28. Ibid., p. 70, vv. 21–24.

29. Ibid., p. 85, v. 21.

within a single tiny seed. The tree cannot be perceived, but we know that it is indeed there—as potential—like God's creations waiting to materialize.[30]

Not everything in the text is elucidated by way of analogies, and even what is explained thusly requires further understanding, to be attained by both intellectual and practical means. As is true for many suluk, the teachings offered in the text are not meant for all. They include esoteric elements that, falling on the wrong ears, could be dangerous and harmful. The idea that man and God are one might be wrongly interpreted, leading to disastrous personal and social consequences. Therefore the text was intended to be read or listened to with a guru. Even with a guru, and even with the Prophet himself as guru as in the *One Thousand Questions*, some questions are not to be asked. Several times within the text, in reply to Samud's questions about God's essence, the spirit's (J. *roh*) whereabouts, and death, the Prophet says he cannot answer: Samud has ventured into a territory that is not his to enter. In the *Serat Suluk Samud* this emphasis on secrecy is clear from the start, as the text ventures to reveal that which is hidden or obscure (J. *samar*). The text proclaims itself as meant for those of a clear mind, and even they must approach this doctrine cautiously. On several occasions the text explicitly juxtaposes certain common beliefs with those of the *ahlullah*, or Sufi followers of these teachings, delineating the community for whom this text is most relevant.[31]

A Transformed Book of One Thousand Questions

In emphasizing the waḥdat al-wujūd perception of reality and aspects of hidden meaning and secrecy, the dialogue between the Prophet and the Jew in Javanese took a direction different from its Tamil and Malay counterparts. The story of Ibnu Salam was connected, however implicitly, with teachings of a particular school, associated with those taught by the *wali* Siti Jenar. This independent-minded and charismatic teacher is said to have been executed by the council of Islamic leaders on Java in the sixteenth century for spreading such dangerous ideas to the uninitiated, his teachings and death episodes echoing those of the martyred al-Ḥallāj in tenth-century Baghdad.[32]

30. Ibid., p. 26, v. 34; *Serat Samud*, 1884, MS. PP St.80, c. 15, v. 52.

31. *Serat Suluk Samud Ibnu Salam*, 1898, MS. MSB P173a, pp. 89–90. vv. 9–12, in which Sufi (*ahlullah*) views regarding the body are juxtaposed with those of the *santri* (also referred to as *ahlul sarak*).

32. On his resemblance to al-Ḥallāj, see A. Muchlis, *Dari Walisongo Hingga Sunan Bungkul* (Surabaya: Penerbit SIC, 1996), 37–41.

Although these teachings formed a dominant strain within Javanese literary traditions in the eighteenth and the first half of the nineteenth centuries and were widely popular, they were controversial, considered by some as inappropriate or even illegitimate. By the end of the nineteenth century, when the *Serat Suluk Samud Ibnu Salam* manuscript was inscribed, a major shift was occurring within Javanese Islam through which a stress on teachings considered more orthodox was well under way.

A comparative examination of *One Thousand Questions* manuscripts from different periods and places in Java reveals how the importance of the wujudiya doctrine increased gradually for those rewriting the text, and how the balance between the frame story and the doctrinal teachings shifted over time, although not in a clearly linear fashion. In the early *Samud* the details of Samud's encounter with his followers and the Prophet all appear. But in the *Serat Suluk Samud Ibnu Salam*, inscribed in 1898, we find all those details missing, and the text, while still employing the figures of Samud and Muhammad and a question and answer format, is entirely focused on the teachings it propounds, to the exclusion of mentioning Samud's Jewish identity, the location of the debate, and the final conversion scene.

Such changes in the text, highlighting the teachings while the centrality of the formulaic story decreased in importance, underscore the profound importance of the particular content stressed in the Javanese. They allow us to see how it differs from the *One Thousand Questions'* content in other languages and how a story—although recognizable as "the same story"—was altered to fit and express a particular doctrine. Combining this thematic emphasis with the traditional frame produced powerful results: by incorporating waḥdat al-wujūd teachings into a famous narrative employing the Prophet himself as guru, this story was used in Java as a means to circulate popular, although increasingly controversial, teachings, and accord them a certain legitimacy.

Another further, no less dramatic, transformation of the story also took place at about the same time.[33] New tellings of the *One Thousand Questions* produced in Java in the final years of the nineteenth century no longer feature the Prophet, the Jew, and conversion to Islam. The rise of these new tellings

33. An earlier version of this discussion appeared in Ronit Ricci, "From Jewish Disciple to Muslim Guru: On Literary and Religious Transformations in Late Nineteenth Century Java," in *Islamic Connections: Muslim Societies in South and Southeast Asia*, ed. R. Michael Feener and Terenjit Sevea (Singapore: ISEAS, 2009), 68–85.

corresponded temporally with a decline—and possible cessation—of production of the older *Samud* story.[34]

Most transformed tellings employ the title "Sèh" (A. *sheikh*) and the name Ngabdulsalam to refer to their protagonist, who bears a name that is almost identical to that of his "ancestor" Abdullah Ibnu Salam. Sèh Ngabdulsalam is a guru whose disciples (who are also referred to as his sons) come to him with questions. Many of the themes Sèh Ngabdulsalam discusses remain the same as before—signifying their ongoing relevance—but the rationale of embracing Islam is no longer what drives the story, since both teacher and disciples are Muslim. I suggest thinking of this text as a *lakon cabang*, or branch story, of the type branching out of the Mahabharata tales in shadow puppet theater performances on Java, both connected to the literary trunk and extending away from it.

A comparison of the two variants of the Ibnu Salam story reveals, first, a continuity of genre: each is a suluk, written in macapat meters, in which the basic format of a question and answer debate remains intact.[35] In both variants a knowledgeable, venerable teacher bestows his teachings upon a person (or group of disciples) who comes to question him. However, in the story of Sèh Ngabdulsalam the questioner of the older tellings has himself become the teacher; he bears the name not of the Jewish Samud but (with small variation) of the Muslim convert Abdullah Ibnu Salam. In terms of content, some topics that consistently appear in the older tellings are absent from the reworked story of Sèh Ngabdulsalam. These include, among others, paradise and hell, God's throne, the angels, the fate of infidel children, the Day of Judgment, the story of Moses and Pharaoh, and the spirit. Topics that carry over from the earlier tellings—specifically, from the *Serat Samud* and the *Serat Suluk Samud Ibnu Salam*—into the story of Sèh Ngabdulsalam include *iman* (from A. "faith") and Islam, the daily prayers, the four stages of the Sufi path, God's names, actions, attributes, and essence, God's unity, God's light, the prophets, grades of being, and the relationship between the world and the human body.

34. The latest *Serat Samud*—in which Samud is the disciple—I am aware of is the 1898 *Serat Suluk Samud Ibnu Salam*, 1898, MS. MSB P173a. The first *Sèh Ngabdulsalam* text, in which the disciple turns guru, is dated that same year. From the 1890s on and into the 1930s the latter story was copied several times.

35. This comparison is based on *Sèh Samud* and *Suluk Ngabdulsalam*, the two textual variants which appear, almost consecutively, in a 1901 anonymous *Piwulang* manuscript compilation from Surakarta, Fakultas Sastra Universitas Indonesia, Jakarta, MS. FSUI PW 56, and on *Soeloek Sheh Ngabdoelsalam*, ed. Sastrawiryana (Surakarta: Albert Rusche and Co., 1913). I refer to the protagonist as Sèh Ngabdulsalam for the sake of consistency.

Themes that are added in Sèh Ngabdulsalam tellings when compared with their predecessors are teachings that relate to Javanese gamelan music and, to a lesser extent, the *wayang* shadow puppet theater. Framing issues are also significant. In the *Soeloek Sheh Ngabdoelsalam*, printed in Javanese script and published in Surakarta in 1913, the text is reframed before beginning the section on gamelan music with the story of Sèh Ngabdulsalam declared completed, a new set of disciples appearing, and the teacher feeling perplexed and angry at their ongoing adherence to Javanese arts. Another important addition is the consistent mention of Arabic religious books (*kitab*) as prior sources of knowledge that inform the later text, grounding it in a particular type of authority.

Some of the disciples of the guru Sèh Ngabdulsalam who come to him with questions live on Java while others come from afar; their forms of knowledge are defined as expertise in Arabic and the kitabs and/or as Javanese wisdom. In its concluding lines the text seems to favor the latter form of knowledge over the more strictly Islamic one.

The *Soeloek Sheh Ngabdoelsalam* has the following statement on its title page:

> The content of these teachings is diverse, excerpted from Islamic books (J. *kitab*), written by scholars in ancient times. Some of its writings were later rectified by Sastrawiryana, an associate editor for the newspaper *Jawi Kandha*.[36]

This statement provides an important paratext, offering insight to the changing circumstances of transmission. The *One Thousand Questions* now appears in print, as a book by a European publisher, its older telling, "excerpted" from Islamic religious books, "corrected" by a contemporary Javanese editor. The statement uses the Dutch-derived word for "editor" (J. *redaktur*), signaling a modern, Western-oriented professional affiliation. It adds that Sastrawiryana worked as associate editor for the *Jawi Kandha*, a Malay-Javanese thrice-weekly newspaper that first appeared in 1891 from the printing press of A. Schultz in Surakarta and was one of the first newspapers to recruit an Indonesian editor.[37]

36. "Isi piwulang warni-warni. Petikan saking kitab. Inggitanipun sarjana ing jaman kina. Ing mangké kaleresaken kasusastranipun sawatawis dhateng Mas Sastrawiryana. Médhe redaktur serat kabar Jawi Kandha." *Soeloek Sheh Ngabdoelsalam*, ed. Sastrawiryana, title page.

37. Ahmat B. Adam, *The Vernacular Press and the Emergence of Modern Indonesian Consciousness* (Ithaca: Cornell University Press, 1995), 89.

Thus in this particular telling of *Sèh Ngabdulsalam* the Samud story was altered in terms both of content and of the forms of its authorship, appearance, and potential circulation. Moreover, in light of these changes, the *Serat Suluk Samud Ibnu Salam*, with its loss of the story frame relating to Arabia and a Jewish Samud, its references to page numbers, and its self-reflexivity in declaring itself as a book—rather than a Javanese serat, suluk, or kitab—now appears to have anticipated the *Soeloek Sheh Ngabdoelsalam*: in the latter the narrative was also recast in a more immediately relevant context, and its printed form made it visibly a book in the modern sense, with its pages numbered, its editor named, and its year of publication definitively stated. All these elements again point in the direction of the social, religious, and technological changes taking place on Java and accelerating in the late nineteenth century and the first decades of the twentieth, when most of the *Sèh Ngabdulsalam* tellings were printed or inscribed.

Sèh Ngabdulsalam's story presents some interesting new additions, including discussion of the gamelan ensemble, the art of accompanying the gamelan with vocal music (*nyindhen*), the Javanese *tlèdhèk* and *tayuban* dances, and the wayang shadow puppet theater. Also discussed are the origin and destination of creation (J. *sankanparan*), a topic that is central to many Javanese works. The inclusion of all these among Sèh Ngabdulsalam's teachings gives the text a flavor much different from the more translocal *Sèh Samud*.

The *Sèh Ngabdulsalam* branch emerging from the old *One Thousand Questions'* textual trunk raises the question of why a story long told about a Jewish leader conversing with the Prophet and embracing Islam mutated to one of a Javanese guru replying to the questions of his disciples, all of whom were Muslim from the start. In particular it calls attention to the way the conversion element, central to the earlier story, may have been reworked under changing circumstances or dismissed of altogether.

I see the transformed story as presenting an alternative, or rearticulated, discussion of conversion, understood here in a broad sense that implies significant change. No longer a story portraying the historical competition between Judaism and Islam, conversion to Islam was removed as its driving rationale. Interreligious competition and conversion were reconceptualized as the narrative emphasis shifted to intra-Muslim—and intra-Javanese—concerns, tensions, and debates.

Conditions on Java in the mid to late nineteenth century—when many of the existing *Serat Samud, Serat Suluk Samud*, and *Suluk Sèh Ngabdulsalam* manuscripts were produced—offer potential explanations for the shifting emphasis of the *One Thousand Questions*. Economic and social upheaval brought about by the Cultivation System, the disappearance of structures of traditional authority as the colonial government usurped the power of local elites, the opening of the first railway lines, and easier access to Arabia and to Europe, via the newly opened Suez Canal, were all among developments signaling that profound change was under way. Three processes, in particular, stand out in their centrality: the Islamic revival, the rising importance of the tarékat (Sufi "order," brotherhood), and the increasing Dutch presence on the island.

As was true for many places around the Muslim world in the latter part of the nineteenth century, Indonesia witnessed a wave of Islamic religious revivalism, which manifested itself in a stricter observance of religious rules and rites and calls for intensifying the power of Islam. Mecca-trained or -inspired teachers and pilgrims championed the revival movements in various regions of the Archipelago. On Java the movement first arose in the 1870s in Banten, where it was connected mainly with the Qadiriya tarékat. Indeed, such groups and their teachings were so central to developments on Java that Kartodirdjo viewed the revival of Islamic mysticism as embodied in the tarékat as the most vital aspect of the religious movement at the time.[38]

The three tarékat of greatest significance in nineteenth-century Java, all revitalized at the time, were the old and well-established Naqshbandiya, Qadiriya, and Shattariya. The Shattariya, with its strong speculative tendencies and association with wujudiya teachings, had been the dominant Sufi order in Southeast Asia in the seventeenth and eighteenth centuries and into the nineteenth, but it was now being replaced in popularity in some areas by the Qadiriya-Naqshbandiya with its stronger emphasis on Islamic law.

Each Sufi tarékat had its following, its rites and traditions. Such forms of exclusive internal loyalty and community enhanced inter-tarékat competition and tensions, as the groups competed for followers and influence, so much so that Kartodirdjo saw the rivalry between the tarékat as "one of the striking aspects of the brotherhood movement."[39] For example, as Steenbrink has written, a strong enmity arose between the Naqshbandiya and the Shattariya orders in Western Sumatra. The former charged that the latter's *kiblat*—orientation toward Mecca at prayer time—was incorrect; that their Arabic recitations were wrong; and that their method of determining the onset of the fasting month was questionable. Some Shattariya mosques were deemed

38. Sartono Kartodirdjo, *The Peasants' Revolt of Banten in 1888*, VKI, vol. 50 (The Hague: Martinus Nijhoff, 1966), 149.
39. Ibid., 162.

unacceptable by Naqshbandiya imams.[40] Such accusations ring of deep theological divisions, and they are not unlike those directed at non-Muslims. They suggest that a change from one tarékat to another could have been viewed in terms analogous to religious conversion.[41]

More broadly, Muslim-Javanese society was undergoing a process of polarization into two major factions. Whereas throughout the eighteenth and early nineteenth centuries Javanese society attained what Ricklefs has termed a "mystical synthesis," defined by a strong sense of Islamic identity, the fulfillment of the five pillars of Islamic ritual life, and the acceptance of an array of local spiritual forces like the Goddess of the Southern Ocean, as the nineteenth century progressed divisions became increasingly apparent.[42] On the one hand were those, known as the *putihan* (white people), who viewed themselves as devout Muslims and the bearers of true Islamic identity; on the other were those known as *abangan* (red people), in whose lives Islam played a less central role.[43] Such developments certainly contributed to the rise of competing identities and affiliations, manifested in educational choices, observance or neglect of particular rituals, and, at times, attitudes of mutual animosity and contempt. All these factors are central in considering the shifting story of the *One Thousand Questions* in Javanese, from a narrative emphasizing interreligious conversion to one engaging with, and foregrounding, competing Muslim allegiances. Also in the background to changing notions of conversion was the pervasive Dutch presence on Java that brought in its wake an ongoing, and gradually increasing, exposure to Western ideas and practices. The *Soeloek Sheh Ngabdoelsalam*'s focus on a very local form of Islam that had been typically tolerant of the elaborate Javanese arts of music, theater, and dance that outsiders—like Dutch scholars—or revivalists may have viewed as

40. Karel A. Steenbrink, *Beberapa Aspek Tentang Islam di Indonesia Abad Ke-19* (Jakarta: Bulan Bintang, 1984), 178–79.

41. Although initiation into more than a single order was not uncommon, once initiated by a particular teacher complete loyalty and obedience toward him were expected. Van Bruinessen, writing of conflicts involving Sufi orders in Indonesia in the twentieth century, states that "some of the most severe conflicts were, in fact, not between Sufis and anti-tasawwuf reformists but between rival *tarékat* shayks." Martin van Bruinessen, "Controversies and Polemics Involving the Sufi Orders in Twentieth Century Indonesia," in *Islamic Mysticism Contested: Thirteen Centuries of Controversies and Polemics*, ed. Frederick De Jong and Bernd Radtke (Leiden: Brill, 1999), 728.

42. Merle Calvin Ricklefs, *Mystic Synthesis in Java: A History of Islamization from the Fourteenth to the Early Nineteenth Centuries* (Norwalk: EastBridge, 2006). For a summary, see 221–24.

43. Merle Calvin Ricklefs, *Polarising Javanese Society: Islamic and Other Visions (C. 1830–1930)* (Singapore: National University of Singapore Press, 2007). On the *abangan–putihan* divide, see 84–104.

"un-Islamic," points to a felt need to restate the importance of its place within Javanese society.

Transformed Teacher, Disciples, and Challenges

At the center of the *One Thousand Questions* is the figure of the Prophet, who bestows his knowledge and grace on a formidable challenger who is eager to learn and quick to grasp the extraordinary aspects of the Prophet's nature and teachings. The Prophet's figure is absent from the *Soeloek Sheh Ngabdoelsalam*, replaced by a Javanese guru who, although capable and wise, cannot be likened to Muhammad. In fact, Sèh Ngabdulsalam is depicted as resembling the disciple Ibnu Salam much more closely than he does the guru Muhammad as he appeared in earlier tellings. Whereas the Prophet draws inspiration from the archangel Jibrail to reply swiftly and correctly to all of Ibnu Salam's questions, Sèh Ngabdulsalam receives no such divine assistance; the Prophet sits in the mosque, where Ibnu Salam meets him and where the entire narrative unfolds, in a single location. Sèh Ngabdulsalam also receives his disciples, but they come and go continuously, supplying the narrative with some sense of mobility; whereas the debate with the Prophet seems to be taking place almost outside of time—with no mention of its passing despite the hundreds of questions asked—Sèh Ngabdulsalam's followers punctuate the cycles of day and night with their visits.[44]

The sons not only come from various places, including India, Singapore, and several locales on Java, but they are also defined as possessing one of two different types of knowledge: Arab or Javanese. Whereas the disciple Ibnu Salam was described as a great scholar of the ancient scriptures—referring above all to the Torèt—the sons are depicted as *wènèh alim* or *wènèh Jawa*: some are *alims*—Islamic religious scholars—and some are endowed with Javanese wisdom. These designations are defined in the text: *kang ngalim kitabé luwih*—the alims are experts on kitabs, the largely theological manuals derived from Arabic; *kang Jawa sugih kawignyan*—the Javanese posses a wealth of wisdom.[45] The distinction seems both to run along the lines of language per se—Arabic and Javanese—but even more so to relate to broader cultural spheres, juxtaposing two perspectives, forms of practice, and repertoires of symbols and references.

The initial part of the book emphasizes the Arab, or Arabic, forms of knowledge as exemplified by several of the disciples citing prior sources when

44. The discussion and examples below are based on *Soeloek Sheh Ngabdoelsalam*, ed. Sastrawiryana.
45. Ibid., 1.

posing their questions. They mention either coming across these sources themselves or hearing others quote them at the mosque, and they express a desire to understand their meaning. The father too resorts to such books occasionally. Whereas in the earlier *One Thousand Questions* tellings in Javanese it is rare to find mention of any prior source besides the Torah, Psalms, and Gospels, here we find seven titles mentioned, among them *Kitab Sanusi*, *Kitab Tapsir*, *Kitab Juwahir*, *Kitab Sittin*, and *Kitab Usul.*

Citing a kitab accords authority to a particular type of religious knowledge, as seen in the following example:[46]

The meaning of Islam
As discussed in *Kitab Juwahir*
Al Islam so goes the Arabic
An taslimu illahi
This means that
Islam is
Truly surrendering soul
Yes and your body my child
To Allah the Ruler the Almighty

Such a passage clearly acknowledges the centrality and authority of the *kitab* tradition—the type of knowledge and belief system it represents—as it connects a common definition of Islam to a well-known textual source in the Arabic language. The references to textual sources provide important information as to the Arabic religious literature read on Java at the time. Indeed, the titles cited in *Soeloek Sheh Ngabdoelsalam*—including the *Kitab Juwahir* appearing in the verse above—corroborate with several of those mentioned in *Serat Centhini*, the early nineteenth-century encyclopedic Javanese text about a wandering *santri*'s search for knowledge.[47]

After more than forty pages a transition occurs in the narrative. The tale of the disciples who were depicted as *ahli kitab* ends and four others who are

46. Tegesé kang aran Islam / wicara Kitab Juwahir / al Islamu lapal ira / an taslimu illahi / déné maknané kuwi / utawa ta Islam iku / sayekti pasrah jiwa / iya raga nira kaki / marang Allah kang Ngamurba kang Misésa. The verse is written in the Dhandhanggula meter. *Soeloek Sheh Ngabdoelsalam*, ed. Sastrawiryana, 14. In the translation into English, Arabic quotations within the Javanese are left as such and italicized, so as to reproduce the language combination of the original.

47. The Arabic texts mentioned in *Serat Centhini* are discussed in Soebardi, "Santri-Religious Elements as Reflected in the Book of Tjentini," *BKI* 127.3 (1971): 331–49. *Santri* here refers to a wandering student of Islam.

known as *ahlul sasmita Jawi*—experts in the subtle signs of Javanese teachings—come to the fore. There are themes in this section of the text that do not appear in the older *One Thousand Questions* in Javanese, themes that take the localization of the text on Java a step further. These include the gamelan ensemble and its music, the wayang shadow puppet theater, and forms of Javanese dance and song.

If there is a tension here, in the distinction consistently made between "Arab" and "Java," it is clearly not one between different religions but rather between perceptions of what it meant to be a Javanese Muslim. The two designations have the potential for opposing one another, overlapping, or, possibly, engaging in dialogue.[48] Within the text the followers of both are brothers, disciples of a single guru who accepts them all. And yet the division carries a certain significance: beyond the questions and answers explicitly presented lies a debate about competing interpretations, identities, and affiliations.

In the closing pages of the text Sèh Ngabdulsalam struggles with the way in which the four "Javanese" disciples are unable to detach themselves from their involvement with traditional Javanese art forms.[49] He is angered by this attachment, which he deems frivolous and even verging on the religiously forbidden, and tries to change their minds by way of threat and persuasion. Unsuccessful, he retires to his home to meditate and emerges with a vision and goal: to clarify the origins of wayang and gamelan to his sons so that they understand a deeper meaning inherent in them, one they have missed due to their worldly preoccupations.

In the pages that follow Sèh Ngabdulsalam develops an interpretation of the gamelan instruments and music in which he uses the gamelan as a metaphor for Islamic teachings. He begins by discussing several types of gamelan, as, for example, the *gangsa monggang*, an archaic three-tone gamelan kept in the courts of Yogyakarta and Surakarta and played on solemn occasions, and the *cara balèn*, played to greet guests and accompany the arrival of bride and groom during marriage ceremonies. However, he reminds his disciples that even though they are engaged with the gamelan they should not forget—or disregard—the four stages of the Sufi path: *saréngat*, *tarérkat*, *kakékat*, and *makripat*.

The guru offers an interpretation of several gamelan instruments and scales. For example, the twenty *bonangs* of the *sléndro* gamelan are connected

48. The dialogue element, or an attempt to transcend the two categories, is evident in the figure of the disciple Radèn Sabdasampurna, whose name means "perfected speech" and who is, accordingly, said to possess excellent skills in both Javanese and Arabic.

49. *Soeloek Sheh Ngabdoelsalam*, ed. Sastrawiryana, 44–52.

with the twenty *sipat*, God's attributes; the *gong*, *kethuk*, *kenong*, and *kempul* are equated with the fourfold division of the attributes and with the four letters of God's name; the *kendhang* drum is described as a leader, giving the music a beat and direction. A person aspiring to higher knowledge but still interested in state matters is likened to a gamelan without a kendhang, suggesting a situation that is not right and that cannot bring about desired results.

Although some details within this section remain obscure, the comparison establishes a relationship between the gamelan ensemble and Islamic teachings. The Sèh's metaphorical interpretation suggests that the gamelan is not only as it seems and, therefore, that the disciples' inability to separate from it should neither upset him, as it did initially, nor mean that they are frivolous. On the contrary, they are deeply connected to that which in fact represents and embodies Islam. In this sense there is no contradiction between "Javanese" and "Arab," but rather they can be understood as one and the same. However, the use of the gamelan as metaphor is in itself indicative, as its music was shunned by strictly Islamic circles and would likely not be appreciated within them as a symbol of deeper Muslim truths.

The *One Thousand Questions* was strikingly transformed on Java in the late nineteenth century from a story relating the historical antagonism between Judaism and Islam narrated through a dialogue between Samud Ibnu Salam and the Prophet and ending in conversion, to one depicting a Javanese Muslim guru in dialogue with his disciples who come in search of knowledge, defined broadly as "Arab" or "Javanese." The closing lines of a traditional *One Thousand Questions* and those of *Soeloek Sheh Ngabdoelsalam* prove emblematic of both the literary and religious changes—or conversions—that the story underwent.

In most Javanese tellings Ibnu Salam, after many questions, decides he has sufficient proof of Muhammad's genuine prophethood to embrace the new religion. He acknowledges Muhammad, who accepts him as a follower. In several tellings he recites the *shahāda*, is given a new name, and is blessed by the Prophet. The *Soeloek Sheh Ngabdoelsalam*, in contrast, draws to a close with the above-mentioned discussion of the gamelan. The Sèh is asked about the difference between the pélog and sléndro gamelans, or musical scales. Sléndro, considered the basic scale, with equal intervals and pentatonic, is explained in terms of Islamic terminology. When, at last, the Sèh addresses the pélog scale, he defines it as *sumbang*: somewhat out of tune, shifted, using a word that can also mean "offensive to sight, hearing or moral sense." The pélog *bonang*, *saron* and *demung* are all out of tune, as are the other instruments. Nevertheless, the pélog's content, or meaning (J. *surasa*), is pleasing to the senses, delicious (J. *éca*), its music sweet and satisfying to the ear. Immediately following this passage the text concludes with these lines that, in the comparison I am suggesting, offer an alternative, or substitute, to a scene of conversion from Judaism to Islam:

If you discuss
The fine knowledge of *rasa*
That emerges from suluk
Without using any Islamic textbooks
That is good
Not opening the great screen
Of secrets
Its symbols are not far
Surely it is delightful insofar as you have not opened the screen[50]

Coming at the heels of the pélog interpretation and employing the same word used to describe it—*éca*, delightful, tasty—the text suggests a comparison between the delicious flavor of the pélog and that of suluk poetry and the hidden, true knowledge—*ngèlmu rasa*—it expounds. It also hints at a similarity between the seemingly discordant yet gratifying pélog and the mystery or secrecy of the suluk. More broadly still, a comparison is suggested between the gamelan and suluk, both veiling and concealing a truth hidden from view, one all the more sweet because of its subtle, unapparent nature.

The passage explicitly counterposes the kitab, Islamic textbooks, with the Javanese mystical poetry of suluk. According to the author, the refined knowledge, having to do with insight, inner feeling, and true meaning emerges from the suluk, implying that the type of knowledge found in the kitab, which is more formalized and theologically minded, cannot touch upon the deeper significance expressed in the suluk. This contrast is common in Javanese literature of the late nineteenth and early twentieth centuries, reflecting the tensions between those dedicated more strictly to Islamic law and those following a more mystical interpretation of Islam.[51]

50. The verse is written in the Sinom meter: Lamun sira amicara / ngèlmu rasa ingkang luwih / kang teka suluk wetunya / tan nganggo kitab sathithik / iku rupané becik / nora biyak waran agung / marang ing wadénira / pralambangé nora tebih / pasthi éca déné nora biyak wrana. *Soeloek Sheh Ngabdoelsalam*, ed. Sastrawiryana, 53. *Rasa* has a range of meaning which encompasses taste, sensation, meaning, connotation, sense, experience, insight, mysticism.

51. In suluk there is often an expression of a special delight, or deliciousness, found in veiling, in keeping something secret—through analogy, allegory, or multiplicity of meaning—in order for it to be revealed, as it is near at hand already.

The contrast between kitab and suluk reiterates what we have seen all along: the two literary forms represent different types of knowledge, different perspectives on Islam. The distinction between them—and the communities they represented—was reflected also in contemporary educational systems and their curriculums: in the *pesantren* religious schools mystical works were virtually absent from the curriculum in the late nineteenth century, and the stress was on kitabs of Islamic law and Arabic grammar. The suluk-type works were passed through initiation from guru to disciple and were popular among followers of tarékat.[52]

The Jewish and Muslim protagonists of older tellings were here replaced with representatives of the categories "Arab" and "Java." Just as Judaism and Islam shared much that is common in terms of beliefs, practices, and stories, so the Sèh's disciples were all brothers, descended from a common father. Very likely it was precisely this proximity, this closeness and familial relationship—between Islam and Judaism, "Arab" and "Java" forms of Islam—that created the tension that propelled the story forward in its two incarnations, since, despite the affinities, something fundamental separated the faiths of Ibnu Salam and the Prophet as it did the forms of Islam represented by kitabs and suluk. The parallel between the two sides of the debate in the older *Samud* texts and the *Soeloek Sheh Ngabdoelsalam* is imperfect. And yet in both *One Thousand Questions* branches there is an emphasis on the importance of two competing views, contested with respect, through persuasion, using references common to both but—ultimately—differing in interpretation. From two religions engaged in a dialogue that ends in one overcoming the other, the story shifts to a dialogue between two perspectives on Islam, embodied in the designations "Arab" and "Java," the pélog and sléndro scales, suluk and kitab. An embrace of—or conversion to—the Javanese perspective is deemed the correct choice in the end.

The earlier transformation of the story from a traditional, translocal narrative to a suluk centered on mystical teachings was a step in the direction of further change, occurring in the closing years of the nineteenth century. That later change, which quite radically transformed Samud Ibnu Salam from a Jewish disciple to a Muslim guru, should be read in light of religious and cultural developments in late nineteenth-century Java. Although the *One Thousand Questions* contains no explicit statement of tarékat-affiliation, it was

52. Steenbrink, *Beberapa Aspek Tentang Islam di Indonesia Abad Ke-19*, 157. Some of the kitab mentioned and cited in *Soeloek Sheh Ngabdoelsalam* (*Kitab Sitin*, *Kitab Usul*, and *Kitab Sanusi*) are known to have been taught in nineteenth-century pesantren, further validating the claim that the *Soeloek* is engaged in a contemporary debate over Muslim affiliations.

likely associated with the Shattariya, with its speculative teachings and employment of Javanese arts in metaphorical ways. As the Shattariya was being replaced as the most popular Sufi order on Java by tarékat that more strongly emphasized ritual and Islamic law, the *Soeloek Sheh Ngabdoelsalam* maintained the ongoing relevance of its teachings to Javanese society.

The *Soeloek Sheh Ngabdoelsalam* is not alone among literary works of this era in its emphasis on a Javanese-oriented Islam. Although within the *One Thousand Questions'* global history its shifting narrative represents a significant change, within the sphere of Javanese writings it is one among several important works responding to outside pressure and changing circumstances. Such works cover a range of nuanced perspectives: from those, like the *Serat Dermagandhul*, that present Islam as foreign to Java, through those, like the *Serat Wedhatama*, that emphasize Javanese spirituality as the paramount path, to the *Soeloek*, that reaffirms an Islam deeply rooted in Javanese soil. Just as earlier the *One Thousand Questions* was adapted as one suluk among many, so its newer telling became embedded within the larger literary picture. In both cases the story found a place within Javanese literary production of the period while concurrently invoking a broader Islamic tradition. As Azra has amply demonstrated in his study of Islamic reformism in Southeast Asia, Javanese Islam had long been connected with, and informed by, transnational networks of scholars and pilgrims. The ideas and teachings of the kind that appeared in the Javanese *One Thousand Questions* traditions reflect this connectivity to wider circles.

The *One Thousand Questions'* transformations in Java point, above all, to the creative energies of poets and scribes writing in Javanese between the seventeenth and twentieth centuries. Ambivalence and ambiguity were certainly apparent in these creative endeavors, well illustrated in the tension between two forms of Islam presented in the *Soeloek Sheh Ngabdoelsalam*. The move from according great authority to the ancient scriptures in the *One Thousand Questions* to according it to commentaries in Arabic kitabs and mystical suluk, and Abdullah Ibnu Salam's journey from Jewish disciple to Muslim guru, parallel the transition—spatial and temporal—from a depiction of conversion in seventh-century Arabia to a discussion of forms of conversion and change in contemporary Java. In the internal dialogue defining the contours of what it meant to be Muslim and Javanese was implicit also the question of belonging, or modes of belonging to the wider, Islamic-Arabic cosmopolis.

4

The Tamil *Āyira Macalā*: Questions and Marvels

The *Āyira Macalā*, the Tamil [*Book of*] *One Thousand Questions*, dates from the sixteenth century and is widely considered the earliest complete Muslim Tamil text extant.[1] Translated and adapted from Persian and drawing on familiar Tamil conventions, as well as expanding them in innovative ways, it offers a poetic adaptation of the Prophet's dialogue with Ibnu Salam. The author and initial audience of the Tamil *One Thousand Questions* lived in a period that was defined in part by the challenges of Portuguese conquest, as well as by the Muslim minority position among Tamils. These factors contributed to the shaping of a work that dwells at length on the boundaries of Muslim and non-Muslim, forging that dichotomy into a central theme.

Despite these dimensions, the work is very much a product of the Arabic cosmopolis and its diverse yet common literary cultures. Self-identifying as a *macalā* book, incorporating Arabic-derived conventions, vocabulary, and images, and expressing poetically and lucidly why accepting Islam and practicing it means choosing truth and righteousness, the Tamil *One Thousand Questions* was a foundational text that contributed to connecting Tamil Muslims with others across the region who read Ibnu Salam's story of awakening and

1. Vaṇṇapparimaḷappulavar, *Āyira Macalā*, ed. M. Saiyitu Muhammatu, "Hasan" (1572; Madras: M. Itrīs Maraikkāyar/Millat Publishers, 1984); hereafter, *AM*. Citations are to verse. Only fragments remain from two earlier works, *Palccanta Mālai* ("A Garland of Many Verse Forms," a pre-12th century treatise on love themes) and an untitled medical treatise by Yakup Cittār (13th C.?). M. M. Uwise, *Muslim Contribution to Tamil Literature* (Kilakkarai: Fifth International Islamic Tamil Literary Conference, 1990), 1–15.

transformation, and to fostering a common repository of customs, stories, and beliefs.

The Tamil One Thousand Questions: *An Introduction*

The Tamil text was composed in 980 A.H (1572) by Vaṇṇapparimaḷappulavar, known also by his Muslim name Ceyku Mutali Icukākku. The poet hailed from Vakutai Nāṭu, a settlement in the deep Tamil south that most likely refers to Kayalpattinam. The Tamil *One Thousand Questions* was first read aloud in the traditional ceremony of araṅkeṟṟam, the public introduction of a new work, in the Madurai court. As mentioned in chapter 2, the poet was assisted by one Mullāmiyā Cayitu Makutum, who is said to have been a great expert in both Arabic and Persian. Mullāmiyā bears two important titles: *cayitu* (A. *sayyid*), indicating descent from the Prophet Muhammad, especially via his grandsons Ḥasan and Ḥusayn, and *makutum* (A. *makhdūm*) a Sufi title common in South Asia, indicating descent from Muhammad's maternal uncle 'Abbās. Taken together these titles point to the prestige of the one possessing them, coming as he does from a long line of Arab forbearers going back to the Prophet's closest kin. This association, along with Mullāmiyā's expertise in Arabic and Persian traditions, suggest that upon setting out to create the Tamil *One Thousand Questions* Vaṇṇapparimaḷappulavar was drawing on respectable and authentic sources.

A likely reference to the reigning Nāyaka king at the time, Kumāra Kṛṣṇappā (r. 1563–73), son of the Madurai Nāyaka dynasty's founder, appears in the final line of the stanza dedicated to this ceremony. The reference to "the protector whose nature is blackness" (*kaṟuppāṟu kāvalavarē*), a Tamil translation of *kṛṣṇa* (S. "black"), may refer to the ruler having a patron's role in the composition of the poem and express acknowledgment of his power.[2] Either way it is significant. This acknowledgment of a patron, along with the explicit dating of the work, the indication that it was based on a Persian source, and the long introductory section all echo introductions to Persian *mathnawi* poems, and these features may well point to the latter as providing the model for Tamil Muslim poets as they composed the opening stanzas of their works.

The Tamil *One Thousand Questions* contains the following major narrative elements: the archangel Jipuṟayīl tells Muhammad to send a letter to the Jews; the scribe Cātu Ipunu Ukkācu writes the letter and carries it to their land; Ibnu Salam's (T. Aputullā Ipuṉu Calām) discusses Muhammad's message with the Jews and decides to go to Medina with seven hundred of

2. *AM*, Invocation, v. 35.

his followers to challenge the Prophet; Ibnu Salam asks, and Muhammad answers, a long series of questions; and the Jewish leader converts to Islam.

While retaining these common, story-like motifs of the *One Thousand Questions* tradition, the Tamil text employs poetic language throughout. It is written in metrical verse, meant to be recited, and includes many descriptive passages, instances of sound play, and allusions to contemporary practices, from childbirth to fortune-telling. The language is difficult and at times obscure, due to errors made as the text was recopied, to the use of concepts no longer readily understood, and to condensed references to events or textual sources that were part of a larger cultural literacy. An additional difficulty arises from the fact that very few Arabic-derived words (abundant in the text) appear in standard (or any) Tamil dictionaries.

The work belongs officially to the *kāppiyam* genre of long narrative poetic works (S. *kāvya*, sometimes erroneously referred to as "epics"). The designation appears in the invocation, where the *One Thousand Questions* is defined as a "narrative poem that speaks the glory of Allah's Prophet."[3] Its foundational status as "the first Muslim Tamil *kāppiyam*" is declared on the cover of the text's published version. Although it lacks some of the literary elements of later Islamic *kāppiyam*s and its story is atypical of them, it does contain several formal structural elements common to all works of this genre. These include the introductory *kāppu* section invoking divine protection, and the invocatory *kaṭavuḷ vāḻttu* in which praise is offered to God, the Prophet, the four caliphs, the Prophet's companions, his grandsons Acaṉ and Ucaiṉ, the prophets, the saints (*avuliyā*), the religious scholars, and the imams that founded the four schools of law. Local saints are not invoked, a practice that is common in later works.[4] In his preface M. Aptul Karīm notes that much of the *One Thousand Questions*' invocatory section was consistently adapted by future generations of authors composing Islamic works in Tamil, who viewed it as an exemplary prototype.[5]

It is significant that the text is defined as a *kāppiyam*. Internal evidence points to the work being viewed also as a *purāṇam*, a genre typically recounting the legendary exploits and lives of Hindu gods, but which word could also

3. *Ālanapi pukaḻcūṟu kāviyam. AM*, Invocation, v. 35.

4. These include, most typically, saint Mukiyittīṉ 'Abdul Qādir Jīlānī and Shāhūl Hamītu. Although the Tamil and Malay *One Thousand Question* tellings are similar in many of the narrative details, this type of invocation is entirely absent in Malay, which begins with the traditional Arabic *bismillah*.

5. *AM*, vii.

refer to "story," "book," or "history." This reference is found in verse 25 of the invocation, where the work is given, in addition to the title *Āyira Macalā*—no doubt a translation of its Persian source's title—an additional, Tamil title: *Aticaya Purāṇam*, "The Book of Wonders."[6] The use of *purāṇam* in the sense of "book, story" was perhaps more appropriate than the rule-bound *kāppiyam*, and it may have been an attempt to render the Arabic or Persian *hikayat*, *kitab*, or *nāmé* in the text's title into Tamil. But the category of *kāppiyam* may have carried more prestige in view of the tremendous popularity of "epics" in Indian society, and its use could have been seen as a way to attract an audience. In addition, the reason the work was not simply designated as *macalā* (as later works were, see below) may have been that this genre was yet unfamiliar, with the *One Thousand Questions* being the first of its kind to be produced in Tamil. The confluence of three generic definitions—*macalā*, *purāṇam*, and *kāppiyam*—offered for this single work testifies to Tamil Muslim literary production being in a certain mode of flux at the time, with authors exploring different possibilities and frameworks of expression.

The *One Thousand Questions*, written in verse in its entirety, begins with the invocations, already mentioned, the *araṅkeṟṟam*, depicting the circumstances of the work's initial public presentation, and an introduction (T. *patika varalāṟu*) listing all the sections of the work, each with a title reflecting its central theme. Such a "table of contents" is not typical of Muslim Tamil literature.

The work, made up of a total of 1,095 verses, is divided into many sections, twenty-seven in all if the various introductions are excluded. They vary in length from several, to several dozen, stanzas. The Tamil word *varalāṟu* ("history," in modern use, but referring more widely in the past to "origin," "details," "circumstances") is appended to a theme in each section—thus *Iṟacūl vaḷamai varalāṟu* ("On The Messenger's Greatness"). The topics covered include God's throne, the heavens, paradise, hell, women's sins, Adam's story, the netherworlds, Mt. Kopukkā (A. *jabal Qāf*), Judgment Day, eschatology, Jesus, the children of infidels, death, and Ibnu Salam's conversion.

It is difficult to ascertain whether the text represents a particular viewpoint within the Muslim community, one standing in opposition to rival ideologies. What is clearly drawn by it, however, are some of the lines dividing Muslims and non-Muslims in their everyday practices and beliefs. As for an affiliation with a particular Sufi brotherhood, Schomburg believes that further study

6. *AM*, Invocation, v. 25.

will reveal historical connections with the Tamil Qadiri order, whose members produced many important literary and devotional works in Tamil.[7]

Evidence of the work's status is found in the writings of the German missionary Ziegenbalg, who lived in the Danish colony of Tranquebar in the early eighteenth century. In his *Bibliotheca Malabarica* he described his manuscript collection as including eleven Muslim works. When discussing the "*Ayromuschala*" he commented on the high regard the Muslims of the region had for this text, so much so that children were supposed to commit it to memory.[8]

The *One Thousand Questions*' most recent edition was published in Madras in 1984 as part of a concerted effort on the part of several Muslim scholars, including the publisher M. Itrīs Maraikkāyar of Kilakkarai, to reintroduce texts that had been neglected and forgotten over time. The *One Thousand Questions*—referred to as "first among *kāppiyams*" (T. *talaikkāppiyam*)—was among the works the initiators of the project were most interested in publishing, because of its status and historical significance. In his introduction to the edition M. Saiyitu Muhammatu, "Hasan," discusses the obstacles of obtaining a legible and complete copy of the work. An old *ōlai*—a text written on palm leaves, strung together as a book—was finally located. Working with this copy, a copy of the first printed edition predating 1856, which was also found at the time, and an Urdu telling (*Hazar Masa'il*), Muhammatu was able to produce this latest edition.[9]

The reconstruction of the sixteenth-century text enables an engagement with the questions of Muslim life in the Tamil region at that time and with the kinds of challenges faced by that community. The discovery of the sea route around the Cape of Good Hope by Vasco de Gama allowed the Portuguese to set foot in India in 1498, arriving in its southern regions shortly afterwards. Thus began over seventy years of Portuguese political and economic expan-

7. Susan Elizabeth Schomburg, "'Reviving Religion': The Qādirī Sufi Order, Popular Devotion to Sufi Saint Muḥyīuddīn 'Abdul Qādir al-Gīlanī, and Processes of 'Islamization' in Tamil Nadu and Sri Lanka" (Ph.D. diss., Harvard University, 2003), 260.

8. Bartholomäus Ziegenbalg's *Bibliotheca Malabarica* was sent to Germany in 1708 where parts of it were published in 1710. The section including the list of Muslim Tamil books was published in 1880 by Wilhelm Germann; see his "Ziegenbalgs Bibliotheca Malabarica" (part 1), in *Missionsnachrichten der Ostindischen Missionsanstalt zu Halle* 32.1 (1880), pp. 16–17. For a partial English translation and discussion see Albertine Gaur, "Bartholomäus Ziegenbalg's *Verzeichnis der Malabarischen Bücher*," *JRAS* 3/4 (October 1967): 63-95. The Tamil *One Thousand Questions* is mentioned on page 91.

9. *AM*, xx–xxiii.

sion in the Tamil area accompanied by a vehement anti-Muslim campaign.[10] Taking control of the seas, the Portuguese deemed any ship sailing without their permission to be subject to plunder, a decree that deeply affected seafaring coastal Muslim communities. Property loss, physical hardships, and the confiscation of mosques were not uncommon. Some evidence points to Coromandel fishing communities being forced to convert to Christianity.

However, Muslim life was not entirely stifled during this period. Shu'ayb, who has written an extensive study on the Muslims of Tamil Nadu and Sri Lanka and their literary production, discusses resistance to the Portuguese presence and policies by Muslim military leaders in Kerala, Tamil Nadu, and Sri Lanka. Emphasizing more than the physical force of these leaders, he gives credit in the struggle to religious and spiritual figures, most noteworthy among them the great "saint" Shāhūl Hamītu (1504–70), whose life coincided almost exactly with the Portuguese threat. The sixteenth century also witnessed the life of Ṣadaq Ibrahīm Maraikkāyar (1547–1618), a disciple of Shāhūl Hamītu and the ancestor of a family whose sons were among the most influential Islamic religious reformers, revivalists, and saints of Islamic Tamil history.[11] In discussing Muslim life of the period and region that produced the *Āyira Macalā*, mention should also be made of an important Qadiri mosque and shrine (T. *tarkā*) in Madurai, built at an unknown date, but which, according to its officials interviewed in the 1990s, may have been erected by the Nawabs of Arcot in the late sixteenth century.[12]

Since Muslims were present in the Tamil region long before the sixteenth century, the question arises as to why, apart from two fragments, no works older than the *One Thousand Questions* have survived. Such a longstanding and literate Muslim community must have produced written works, an assumption that is strengthened by the complexity of the Tamil *One Thousand Questions*, which was unlikely to have been the inaugurating work of the community. It is probable that many pre-Portuguese works were destroyed during Portuguese rule. The *Āyira Macalā* is a remnant, a reminder of a line of Muslim poets who had been creating literary works in Tamil, works that have been lost to subsequent generations.

10. The following summary of this period is based on Shu'ayb 'Alim, *Arabic, Arwi and Persian in Sarandib and Tamil Nadu* (Madras: Imāmul 'Arūs Trust, 1993), 24–39. Shu'ayb is unrelenting in his criticism of the Portuguese attitude toward the Muslims. For a more nuanced view see C. R. de Silva, "Muslim Traders in the Indian Ocean in the Sixteenth Century and the Portuguese Impact," in *Muslims of Sri Lanka: Avenues to Antiquity*, ed. M. A. M. Shukri (Beruwala: Jamiah Naleemia, 1986), 147–65.

11. Schomburg, "Reviving Religion," 255.

12. Ibid., 42.

In this context the choice of the *One Thousand Questions* for translation into Tamil for local consumption during the final days of Portuguese power is instructive. A comprehensive work on Islamic teachings must have been deemed necessary, following the loss of many works and the trials of Portuguese conquest. Training new leaders and educators was likely a high priority, a task that could be accomplished in part through the dissemination of such a text. At a time when Muslims were threatened from without and needed to regroup around common ideals, the *One Thousand Questions* highlighted many doctrines and rituals central to Islam and offered ways to address the challenges facing the community.

The Āyira Macalā *and Islamic Literature in Tamil*

In addition to situating the *One Thousand Questions* temporally, the work needs to be viewed in the broad context of Islamic literature produced in the Tamil region. Islamic-Tamil literary culture connected and overlapped with other literary cultures within the Arabic cosmopolis (Persian, Arabic, Urdu, Malay), but it has received little scholarly attention, and therefore many of the links and similarities remain obscure. This is a literature that covers a wide spectrum of genres, styles, and themes. As was the case for Javanese literature, written in both the Javanese and Arabic scripts (pégon), so Muslims writing in Tamil employed either the Tamil script or Araputtamiḻ—Tamil written in Arabic script and commonly known as arwi—or both.[13]

The literature produced by Muslims in Tamil can be divided into several categories. In some cases existing literary genres were expanded to include explicitly Islamic themes and stories. Such was the case, for example, with the *piḷḷaitamiḻ* genre, already mentioned, devotional poems in which the poet takes on the voice of a mother who recounts the childhood days of a famous king, god, or saint, and who offers praise and veneration to that infant or child. Writing such poems to the Prophet in accordance with the genre's conventions meant shaping the Prophet's portrayal in particular ways; concurrently, the influence of Muslim theology—with its prohibitions against regarding God as a baby and addressing Muhammad as a divine being—subtly trans-

13. Similar to the case of jawi, discussed in chapter 2, I use Arwi when referring to the heavily Arabicized language of Tamil Muslims, and arwi when referring to the modified form of the Arabic script used for writing Tamil.

formed certain parts of the formulaic depiction and helped the piḷḷaitamiḻ develop in new directions.[14]

A second category of Islamic Tamil works included those that combined Tamil conventions with non-Tamil ones, often incorporating stylistic and poetic devices, as well as content, from Arabic, Persian or Sanskritic traditions. Most famous among such literary works is the beloved *Cīṟāppurāṇam*, the Prophet's biography composed in the seventeenth century by Umaṟuppulavar. Relying on translated Arabic sources but remaining within a familiar Tamil world of convention and idiom (as when the Prophet's Arabia is depicted in terms of the Tamil land, with its monsoon clouds and waterfalls), the *Cīṟā* combined old and new, and foreign and familiar.

A third category of works were those that had no parallels in non-Muslim Tamil literature, through which both content and form were translated into a new setting. Among these newly introduced genres were the *paṭaippōr* "war poems," depicting the heroic wars of Muslim fighters, and *kisah* narrative tales. Also included among such works, and constituting an important contribution of Muslim authors to Tamil literature, was the genre of *macalā*, to which the *One Thousand Questions* prominently belongs.

This popular dialogic genre, based on a series of questions and replies, was adopted—as we have seen in the case of Javanese—by Muslims beyond the Arabic-speaking world. In Tamil *macalā* (question, problem) was introduced as a new literary form in the sixteenth century with the composition of *Āyira Macalā*, which provided a model for future efforts. In 1613 an additional work of this genre, *Tiru Neri Nītam* ("Rules of Good Conduct") was composed by Pīr Muhammad. As in the earlier prototype established by the *One Thousand Questions*, here too a group of Jews ask questions of the Prophet, at times supplemented by additional queries by his companions, and he replies. The work is divided into four main sections and contains subjects—like marriage rites and property law—not generally found in other Tamil works on Islamic ethics. The author adopted themes from the works of Rūmi and Al-Ghazāli. He presented his work as a Tamil version of the sacred scriptures passed from Allah to His Prophet.[15]

Two additional *macalā* works are famous in Tamil literature, both appearing at a much later date. The first was Aptul Kātiru Leppai's *Tavattutu Veḷḷāṭṭi*

14. The earliest known Muslim *piḷḷaitamiḻ* poems date from the eighteenth century; see Paula Richman, *Extraordinary Child: Poems from a South Indian Devotional Genre* (Honolulu: University of Hawai'i Press, 1997), 130–57.

15. Uwise, *Muslim Contribution to Tamil Literature*, 25.

Macalā ("The Questions of the Servant Tavattutu"), composed in Kayalpattinam in 1865 and republished several times between 1884 and 1953, attesting to its continuing popularity.

The story tells of a rich, childless merchant living in Baghdad who after many years fathers a son, Paturucamān, whom Tavattutu was hired to care for. When the son grows up and loses all his wealth, Tavattutu convinces him to sell her to the sultan Harun al-Rashid and live off the money. At the court she asks the great sultan to test her knowledge, and he calls upon four of his most learned *'ulamā* to perform the task. Tavattutu, a woman of low birth but an expert in many fields of Islamic learning, manages to answer the 'ulamā's six hundred and sixty-nine questions correctly, receives the payment, and marries Paturucamān. Given that the Tamil of the text is interspersed with much Arabic and Persian, Uwise concluded that the author was familiar with sources written in these two languages, including the Qur'an and hadith literature.

The second famous *macalā* is *Nūṟu Macalā* ("One Hundred Questions"), of unknown authorship, published in 1876 by Muhammatu Kācip and republished several times thereafter. Similar to *Tavattutu Veḷḷāṭṭi Macalā*, this story too begins with a childless king to whom a son, Appās, is finally born. In his youth he sips an alcoholic drink, is banished to the forest for this un-Islamic deed, and meets princess Mekarpān, who will marry any man who can answer all her clever questions. Appās is able to stand up to the challenge, winning the princess's hand in marriage.[16] This motif of questioning followed by marriage appeared also in Javanese *suluk*.

These two works, *Tavattutu Veḷḷāṭṭi Macalā* and *Nūṟu Macalā*, combine typical Indian "folktale" elements (a childless king, retreat to the forest, riddles and enigmas) with Islamic teachings, incorporating the *macalā* form into larger, familiar narratives.

Drawing Boundaries: Muslim and non-Muslim in the Tamil Text

The *One Thousand Questions* addresses themes that are central to Muslim life including, prominently, descriptions of the afterlife—both the pleasures of paradise and the torments of hell. Such scenes allow for a mapping of the permissible and forbidden according to mainstream Muslim tradition while also underscoring specific boundaries espoused by an author in a particular society, time, and place. The depictions of hell in the *Āyira Macalā* open a

16. M. M. Uwise and B. M. Ajmalkāṉ, *Islāmiyat Tamiḻ Ilakkiya Varalāṟu*, 4 vols. (Maturai: Kāmāracar Palkalai Kaḻakam, 1994), 3:208–225.

window for viewing the ways in which the text accords with broader Muslim agendas and with the particularities of its Tamil context. These scenes highlight the emphasis in the Tamil *One Thousand Questions* on a differentiation between those who are and are not devoted to Islam.

The longest and most detailed sections devoted to descriptions of hell (*narakam*) in the *One Thousand Questions* traditions examined in this study appear in the Tamil telling, which has two separate chapters on this topic: the "Hell Chapter" (*narakattiṉ varalāṟu*) followed by "The Faults of Women" (*piḻai mātar*), together amounting to a total of 135 verses (*AM*, vv. 524–659). Opening with mention of the seven burning hells and a depiction of great raging fires, the text continues with Ibnu Salam expressing fear and anxiety as he asks the Prophet who will be sent to suffer their heat. The Prophet enumerates many groups, including some that are expected on any Islamic list: those who neglect to pray, who practice usury, who lie, who do not give alms to the poor, and who harm orphans; slanderers, thieves, deniers of the Prophet's role, and those who find fault in the Qur'an. An additional typical category is that of women disobeying their husbands' commands, dressing in improper ways, or speaking words of love to another.

Side by side with those categorized as hell-deserving sinners for such prevalent reasons are included people who commit different kinds of sins:

> Weeping, slapping [their bodies], falling down,
> Letting loose their long hair, beating [themselves]
> They stand
> Calling God and scolding Him.
> These sinners will go to hell.
> Ladies assemble, collapsing on the body, weeping,
> Clasping hands, they cry.
> Those surrounding the deceased, those watching,
> Along with the dead
> Will assemble in hell.
> (*AM*, vv. 538–39)

These lines depict non-Muslim mourning customs. Weeping loudly, beating the chest, and falling down to the ground with little regard for hair or dress were all common practices that were forbidden, according to the text's author, to Muslims. Those following them will accrue harsh punishment for themselves as well as for the person whom they are mourning. In another example, Muhammad is speaking:

The sinners
Have no escape.
Everyday, always
Roasting, melting, sinking.
Praising as God idols of copper and stone,
In vain infidelity
Perished those *kāpirs*,
He said.
(*AM*, v. 555)

Here, as in other instances throughout the text, care was taken to stress the great sin of idol worship, the prism through which Muslims perceived the daily rituals in homes and temples of the surrounding non-Muslim communities. Statues of the Hindu deities were highly visible, and Muslims must be on guard against adopting their neighbors' view that these images are anything but lumps of steel and stone.

In the second chapter, dedicated to the question of who is destined for hell, Ibnu Salam focuses his interest on women and the punishments they will encounter for specific sins. In this section the text again delineates what is socially permissible or forbidden, with the underlying message that women have more opportunities to take the wrong path and later regret it, in part because of their assumed nature and tendencies. Once again the more general feminine sins and their appropriate punishments are encountered, punishments that fit the crime: women who lied to their husbands will have their tongues pulled out; those who bear children through immoral relationships will have their bellies rise like mountains; the tongues of those who gossip and speak ill of others will be crushed like gravel; and those who collect interest will have their bodies squeezed like the *puṉṉai* fruit, as they have figuratively squeezed their clients into difficulty by imposing the forbidden interest.

Restrictions imposed for women that are more culturally specific are interwoven within this long list of sins and punishments. For example, they are forbidden to listen to music, a crime for which hot lead will be poured into their ears. This prohibition is repeated, and in the second instance expanded to include different kinds of songs and even lullabies; those who adorn themselves with anklets, tiny bells, and tinkling ankle rings, whose sound attracts the eye and ear, will have their bodies "adorned" with chains as they melt and burn (*AM*, v. 595).

In a later section of this chapter, as the Prophet goes on enumerating more and more examples, he no longer restricts himself to women. An interesting point is made in his reference to homosexual relationships:

Man with man embrace in lust
Committing *canā*
Shameless,
Like dogs.
They are tossed into the water then,
Their bodies bloated
Blood and pus flow
. . . .
They cry.
(*AM*, v. 611)[17]

As earlier, the text addresses the concerns of Muslims living among a non-Muslim majority. Employing the powerful word *canā* (A. *zinā*, premarital and extramarital sex), the author clearly places homosexuality beyond the pale.[18] The complete prohibitions against music were a reaction to the wide prevalence of music in Tamil culture, including its prominence in most temple rituals. Accepting "superstitions" and adorning the body in an attractive way were similarly viewed as vile imitation and a threat to the "good" Muslim woman.

A category about which Ibnu Salam specifically inquires in a follow-up question is the *muṉāpik*, the hypocrites, residents of Medina who ostensibly converted to Islam but did not adhere to the Prophet. This category is mentioned in all tellings of the story, as it is linked with some of the Prophet's worst enemies during his early years of preaching:

Seemingly Muslim,
Knowing all about religion,
Prayer and fasting.
But in his heart a *kāpir*
Wholly opposed to *dīn*.
Such is the *muṉāpik*.
(*AM*, v. 627)[19]

17. The seventh line is obscure and is therefore left untranslated.

18. On the shifting and understudied perceptions of male homosexuality in the Muslim world, see E. K. Rowson, "Homosexuality in Islamic Law," *Encyclopaedia Iranica*, www.iranicaonline.org (accessed December 15, 2004).

19. *AM*, v. 627. The Arabic terms for hypocrite, infidel (T. *kāpir*; A. *kāfir*) and Islam (T. *tīn*, A. *dīn*) are left untranslated.

Stressing the inner realms of faith as opposed to outer piety and religious knowledge, the text again points, however subtly, to a distinction with the surrounding culture, with its abundance of colorful and sensuous rituals. It is not relegating Islamic rituals of prayer and fasting to the margins, but it does imply that external expressions are insufficient. Whether a Muslim is a true believer or is only pretending (possibly eyeing infidel convictions) will be clearly known to God, who will destine the hypocrite to hell.

Some scholars have suggested that Indian Muslims and Hindus shared many customs, rituals, and attitudes in the past, and that their consolidation into distinct and often opposing communities took place in large part during British colonial rule, introducing as it did censuses and other bureaucratic impositions that forced people to identify with a specific, narrow, and religiously defined category.[20] It is also the case however, even today, that Muslims and Hindus in South India share customs and sacred sites, especially in regard to pilgrimages to the tombs of holy men. Significantly, the category "Hindus" (or "Siva worshippers," "Goddess worshippers") appears nowhere in these *One Thousand Questions* descriptions, thus denying us the ability of pointing to a concrete and unified identity—symbolized by a name—for these non-Muslims. And yet an examination of the topics presented—a list of acts and attitudes sharply separating Muslim from non-Muslim—as well as the use of "Islam" and "*tīn*" to refer to the Muslims' allegiance, points to the existence of complex, perhaps contradictory attitudes. Customs which in the nineteenth and twentieth centuries were associated with reformist Islam were already a part—at least ideally—of Tamil Muslim culture.

Opposing music and physical adornment, rejecting superstitions, fortunetelling, and folk magic, embracing the covering of women's hair and their housebound etiquette as well as a prohibition on homosexuality were presented as the pillars of a strong community of the faithful that must continuously struggle to differentiate itself from the majority culture. The fact that followers of these customs were threatened with such terrifying consequences indicates that these were precisely the customs at the nexus of common temptation in this particular locale, which needed to be monitored and rejected most urgently.

The hell scenes are not the only ground on which the boundaries between Muslim and non-Muslim are drawn. Throughout the *One Thousand Questions* many of the central rites and rituals of Muslim life are mentioned, either in

20. See Peter Hardy, "Modern European and Muslim Explanations of Conversion to Islam in South Asia: A Preliminary Survey of the Literature," in *Conversion to Islam*, ed. Nehemia Levtzion (New York: Holmes and Meier, 1979), 69, for the introduction of the census.

detail or in passing, among them the pilgrimage, circumcision, prayer, recitation of the profession of faith, marriage, and the giving of alms. Some rituals are contrasted, either explicitly or subtly, with local customs viewed as un-Islamic.

The theme of death and the rites surrounding burial are a case in point. The depiction of unacceptable funeral customs and their impending punishment provides one example. The cremation ground is mentioned in passing in one of the hell scenes, as a fearsome site of foul odors. In contrast, the text mentions Jesus as having been wrapped upon his death in *kapaṉ*, the shrouds in which all Muslims are buried. More notable still in this regard is Muhammad's answer to Ibnu Salam's question about the crow messenger, in which Muhammad relates the story of Kāpīl and Āpīl (Cain and Abel) and the strife kindled by Ipulīs, who persuaded Kāpīl to kill his own brother. After he did so Kāpīl stood motionless and confused, not knowing what to do with his brother's corpse. By God's decree two crows then appeared before him, fighting and pecking one another fiercely until one killed the other. The surviving crow dug a small pit in the ground with its beak, placed the corpse within it, and covered it with sand, providing an example for Kāpīl—and all future generations—of the burial practices that must be followed.

The question Ibnu Salam asks about the fate of the angel of death (T. Icurāpīl, also mentioned as Kālaṉ, the god of death) and its corresponding reply address the heart of a pivotal Islamic notion: no one, not even an archangel, is above death, and Icurāpīl therefore is commanded by God to pluck out his own breath of life, as he has done to all other creatures. This emphasis on the end of death—in the larger context of this telling—may well have been meant to highlight the contrast with the belief in a cycle of death and rebirth, prevalent among followers of neighboring religions.

Two categories of hell-goers stand out in their absence from the Tamil text: Jews and Christians. In Malay and Javanese tellings these two categories consistently appear, always listed by their Arabic names, *Yahudi* and *Nasrani*, respectively. Their absence may stem from the Tamil text directing more of its focus on negating the practices and beliefs of its audience's immediate neighbors rather than those of religious groups who had a relatively marginal or nonexistent local following at the time. Still, it is a curious point, since Christians and Jews were even less likely to be encountered in the Indonesian Archipelago than in the Tamil region, and yet they are repeatedly mentioned in the texts originating there. The absence of Christians as a group destined for hell is especially noteworthy because of the strong Portuguese affiliation with Christianity, with their religious beliefs as a major cause for anti-Muslim sentiment. It may have been risky to explicitly denounce Christianity in a literary work of the period, and it is also possible that the sources used by the poet failed to mention Christians and Jews. The most persuasive rationale remains, however, that the Tamil author was most preoccupied with denouncing the surrounding culture in an attempt to remind Muslims of their faith and practices and to revitalize the community following a difficult period.

The descriptions of sin and punishment in all three traditions—Javanese, Tamil, and Malay—reveal much about the social worlds in which the texts were read, making them into complex sources of cultural and historical knowledge. Many of the customs the texts oppose were shared between Muslims and non-Muslims, or were at least deemed acceptable during a non-Muslim past, like certain forms of asceticism, music, dress codes, and "folk beliefs." In the case of the Tamil *One Thousand Questions*, it is likely that the minority position of the Muslims and their struggle to reassert themselves following the Portuguese period contributed to this emphasis on maintaining distinct boundaries between Muslims and non-Muslims.[21]

Explaining the Inexplicable?

One of the ways in which the *One Thousand Questions* offered comfort and strength to its Tamil audiences was through the particular references it makes to the unique capacities of the Prophet. The questions in the Tamil text are phrased differently from those in Javanese and rarely touch explicitly upon waḥdat al-wujūd teachings, although those were known in Tamil Muslim literature from as early as the sixteenth century. Without a questioning of those teachings by Abdullah, the Prophet does not seem to need to resort to analogies in the replies. The text does, however, consistently employ its own strategy to remind its audience of mysterious, unexplained events and to invoke a sense of wonder at the Prophet's knowledge and powers. As the Javanese texts use analogies to explain difficult concepts and to enhance a sense of how human understanding of such concepts is limited, so the Tamil text resorts to consistent references to miracles performed by the Prophet in order to evoke a similar message. In this Tamil case references to these miracles appear not so much in the replies to the questions asked but rather in the epithets used to describe the Prophet when he is addressed or is about to speak.

21. For comparison, toward the end of the Leiden *Samud* manuscript there is a discussion of hell that differentiates starkly between Muslims and others. The ensuing acceptance of Islam by Ibnu Salam—following upon the heels of this statement—impresses upon the reader that a Muslim/non-Muslim boundary in this particular, fearsome context signals to Ibnu Salam that conversion is, indeed, desirable. Nonetheless, this is a rather unusual episode in Javanese, whereas in Tamil delineating the communities is central.

According to Newby, early writings on the Prophet were divided into two types shortly after the Prophet's death.[22] There were collections of Muhammad's sayings and deeds for personal edification, as well as collections expanding on the miraculous and fabulous tales that proved the validity of his prophecy. The Tamil text seems to draw on earlier sources, in which such miraculous stories had been elaborated at length. Some of these miracles are well known and have themselves become the topics of separate literary works in various languages, such as the story of the Prophet's splitting of the moon, mentioned three times within the *One Thousand Questions* alone.[23] Other miracles are less famous and appear only once, but they clearly contribute—especially as they add up throughout the text—to the image of the Prophet's suprahuman abilities and his special relationship with God. The centrality of miracles in this particular telling is also expressed in the Tamil title of the work, *Aticaya Purāṇam*—"The Book of Wonders" or "The Miraculous History"—appended as it is to the more Islamic, conventional title of *Āyira Macalā*.[24]

I will mention only some examples of many such miracles alluded to in the text, in which humans, animals, and even stones participate and provide a backdrop for the Prophet's deeds. These events are almost always presented as epithets of the Prophet, in vocative or descriptive form: "famed one [who suckled] Alimā's [dry] breasts" (*AM*, v. 242) points to a miraculous event when Muhammad was still just a baby, who by suckling caused the nursemaid's dry breasts to produce abundant milk; "he who allowed the mute to speak" refers to the time when the Prophet sat with his companions, picking up seven pebbles that, while in his hand, began reciting God's name;[25] "he who spoke with the deer" relates the time a captured doe asked the Prophet for help so she could go and suckle her young;[26] "he who rescued the thirsty" relates the tradition that Hassan and Hussain were once weeping from thirst when the Prophet put his tongue in their mouth. They sucked it and their thirst was quenched.[27]

22. Gordon Darnell Newby, *The Making of the Last Prophet: A Reconstruction of the Earliest Biography of Muhammad* (Columbia: University of South Carolina Press, 1989), 14.

23. *AM*, vv. 119, 318, 229. This miracle, in which the king of Mecca challenged Muhammad to split the moon and then return it whole to the sky as a sign of true prophecy, is quite popular in Muslim literature. The story is probably based on Qur'an 52:1–2.

24. *Āyira Macalā eṉṉum Aticaya Purāṇam*, *AM*, Invocation, v. 25.

25. Mohammad Inayat Ahmad, *The Authenticated Miracles of Mohammad* (New Delhi: Award Publishing, 1982), 111.

26. Ibid., 124.

27. *AM*, v. 242; Ahmad, *Authenticated Miracles of Mohammad*, 68.

It is important to distinguish here between these and a different type of epithet—and type of title in general—accorded the Prophet in this and other texts: referring to Muhammad as Prophet (*nabī*) and God's Messenger (*rasūlullah*) by using the Arabic titles occurs across languages; local titles such as *gusti* (Lord) in Javanese are common as well; Tamil especially tends to employ both the more general and the locally colored epithets, such as "the prophet emitting the fragrance of musk" or "the prophet adored by the kings of all directions" (*AM*, vv. 9 and 750, respectively). All epithets have an important role to play within the texts, but here I emphasize those epithets bearing miraculous references, and distinguish them from the rest, because the Tamil text consistently evokes this particular type of epithet, a tendency that appears significant neither in Malay nor in Javanese.

The use of epithets in Tamil poetry—in addition to such uses in other, related South Indian Dravidian languages such as Telugu and Kannada—has a long history going back as far as the caṅkam poetry of the first centuries A.D. In those poems, depicting both private and public worlds and employing the landscapes, flora, fauna, seasons, and cultural rituals of the Tamil region in a complex poetic language, mention is made of, for example, "the lord whose rage destroyed the triple forts," referring to Śiva and his destruction of the demons' cities in the sky; "the child of the daughter of great Himavat," evoking the Tamil god of war and love, Murukaṉ, the son of Pārvatī, the Himalaya's daughter; and "the one whose throat like blue gems shines with light," again a reference to Śiva, who by swallowing the *halāhalā* poison saved the world and had his throat turn eternally blue.[28]

Continuing in a similar vein, in the devotional poetry of later centuries (sixth to ninth centuries) dedicated to the gods Śiva and Viṣṇu and to the Goddess in many of their localized forms, epithets are regularly used in a way that not only enriches the poet's repository of metric and poetic possibilities but also constantly reiterates certain attributes of each god, committing them forcefully to the consciousnesses of listeners. These attributes are further linked, in many cases, to a larger narrative that the epithet might evoke with very few words.

Some epithets were local—or could be seen as either local or transregional—whereas others clearly traversed the boundaries of a particular location. In his poems the famous ninth-century Tamil Vaiṣṇava poet and saint Nammāḻvār often used epithets evoking widely known Puranic traditions. When he referred to Viṣṇu as "our Kaṇṇaṉ dark as the rain cloud," he spoke

28. Somasundaram J. M. Pillai, *Two Thousand Years of Tamil Literature: An Anthology with Studies and Translations* (Madras: J. M. Somasundaram Pillai, 1959), 75, 79, 160 respectively.

to the god's typical portrayal as dark, black-blue in color;[29] and when he addressed him as "our lord fast asleep on the five headed serpent," he was evoking in his listener's mind the image of Viṣṇu lying sleeping on the coiled Adiśeṣa in the midst of the ocean of milk.[30] The use of such images was common in South and Southeast Asian literary cultures during the period defined by Pollock as the vernacular millennium. When the Javanese author of the *Ramayana Kakawin*, for example, refers to Hanuman as the "son of the wind" or depicts the love god Kama as accompanying Rama and Sita at the time of their reunion, he is drawing on the circulating repository of images and epithets common across the Sanskrit cosmopolis.[31] In later periods Muslim poets adopted a similar strategy.

Following a long line of predecessors who used epithets in both formulaic and creative ways, the Tamil Muslim poets could easily incorporate this tradition into their writing. For one thing, it was a familiar technique for both poets and audience: when Vaṇṇapparimaḷappulavar invoked the Prophet as "the messenger with the lotus feet," the image must have resonated with his listeners. For another, the technique served the poets' metrical and stylistic goals as they embellished their literary creations. However, and no less important, this old technique facilitated the entry of new and unfamiliar material into the text in the guise of a familiar form. A connection to prior tradition, that of Arabic, was thereby used, through literary conventions, to begin creating allusions to prior Islamic texts only briefly hinted at by the epithets. By addressing and describing the Prophet throughout the text as the performer of various miracles—known to the author from other sources but not necessarily to his audience—the listeners learned of Muhammad's exceptional powers and could gradually internalize and memorize the events commemorated through the text.

Interwoven into the narrative of the one thousand questions and their answers are what we might imagine as small capsules, each containing a condensed form of a miraculous tale, to be encountered time and again as the narrative unfolds. These quick encounters within the flow of the story provide consistent reminders that although a debate seems to be taking place between two men—Ibnu Salam and Muhammad—the Prophet is unique: he has God's guidance and protection at all times, the ability to perform exceptional

29. A. K. Ramanujan, *Hymns for the Drowning: Poems for Viṣṇu by Nammāḻvār* (New Delhi: Penguin, 1993), 34. Kaṇṇaṉ is a Tamil name for Viṣṇu.

30. Ibid., 45.

31. H. Kern, *Ramayana Kakawin, Oudjavaansch Heldendicht* (The Hague: 1900), canto 26, verses 8 and 30.

feats, combined with an understanding of—and ability to bring about—the unexplainable.

It is at this point—explaining the unexplainable—that the Javanese and Tamil narrative strategies, seemingly so different in other aspects, converge. The Javanese text uses mundane, everyday examples such as trees and mirrors to introduce and explain difficult religious concepts by analogy, whereas the Tamil text employs material from traditional histories originating in Arabia to introduce the Prophet, his companions, and adversaries, by recalling the Prophet's miracles via the use of epithets. In some ways the two models remain distinct, as they engage with different concepts and have different goals for their audiences. And yet they also share the common ground of providing culturally specific means for listeners to contemplate that which is beyond simple human grasp: both strategies allow the listener to relate to familiar objects and situations, and yet to realize that these can be traversed to other planes; the familiar can become unknown, and even the most mundane things and experiences, like a rice field or the sensation of thirst, can be viewed in a new light when God's power is introduced. Each of these rich literary traditions draws on its own past and strategies, familiar to poets and audience, to forcefully convey this message.

Particularities of the Tamil One Thousand Questions

The Tamil *One Thousand Questions* exhibits its own character in a variety of ways. Questions of gender are prominent. Ibnu Salam asks the Prophet about God's gender, should He be worshipped and praised as a male or as a youthful female? The reply includes two elements: God is within us, dwelling everywhere; He is the Creator, male.

The question is raised in an environment of worship recognizing both male and female divine manifestations. A powerful and popular image in South India is that of *ardhanārīśvara*, Śiva in his half-male, half-female form; worship of the Goddess in her various manifestations was also highly popular in the Tamil region. Anthropomorphic images of the gods and goddesses portray their gender clearly through bodily form, dress, hair styles, and jewelry, all external markers that Islam strictly forbids, with its uncompromising ban on any divine representation. The gendered, palpable images of the iconography are unnecessary—so the text implicitly argues—since God, albeit invisibly, dwells in all things.

In contrast, perhaps, to the avoidance of any depiction of God, we find a rich portrayal of the archangel Jipuṟayīl, who is described at more length in Tamil than in the other tellings. As in Malay tellings his face is shining, emitting light. His body is compared to the moon; he is fragrant as camphor, and more beautiful and compassionate than any creature. His 24,000 feathers are divided into three rows, made up of rubies, pearls, and emeralds. If he spreads even a small portion of his feathers while soaring the entire world will be hidden in darkness. There is a sense in which this detailed and sensual verbal iconography serves as substitute for the above, forbidden type.

We have already seen the detailed questions and answers relating specific feminine sins and their punishments in hell, highlighting women's major role in setting cultural boundaries, as well as the attitude toward homosexuality. An additional aspect comes to light when Ibnu Salam asks the Prophet about the *hurliṅkaḷ*, the heavenly nymphs who welcome pious Muslim men upon their arrival in paradise.[32] These are described in verse after verse depicting their appearance and grace, which fit perfectly with classical Tamil standards of beauty. Following the tradition of *kesātipatam* (from head to toe), the poet includes a description of women mandatory in all epic works. Women with eyes like lotuses, palms of pearl, bodies of musk, hair like the rain cloud, and a swan's gait await the men with fragrant garlands, ready to introduce them to a life of pleasure.

The conventional description is followed by a conversation, or rather argument, between the hurliṅkaḷ and the human wives of the men entering paradise. The women complain that their husbands have been unjustly taken away. They have shared joy and sorrow with their husbands in this world, but now are expected to part. The nymphs retort by saying there is impurity on earth, whereas in heaven all are pure; this purity justifies their new position as heavenly wives to the pious men.

In this brief passage the text gives voice to a contradiction: men with the moral values deemed correct attain paradise and are rewarded with beautiful and submissive companions who replace their earthly—and often pious—wives. Women are separated from their long-time partners whom they served on earth and, in addition, are offered no replacement or alternative. Allowing the wives' protest to surface underscores the problematic inherent in this differentiated attitude toward men and women, and questions it. The text in this instance and others does not shy away from presenting the conventional narrative, then questioning it through the expression of a very human voice. Although the women's trials are not solved and the section draws to a close soon after this fraught encounter, the inclusion of their voices is significant. As is the case for so much in the *One Thousand Questions* narrative, making

32. From A. *ḥur al-'ain*, the "black-eyed ones," women of paradise, described in the Qur'an; see 52:20 and 54:72.

allowances for questioning of the existing order, and for doubt thereof, is an important technique in its own right.

There is a tendency in the text to incorporate Tamil proverbs as a way of explaining particular situations in a familiar, perhaps clichéd way. Somewhat similar to the use of analogies in Javanese, such old sayings must have echoed for their audiences in a manner that made the topics discussed more accessible. The women carrying children born of adultery will suffer in hell, their bodies torn apart like "a sari spread over thorns"; if men of this world had but a glimpse of the heavenly nymphs' beautiful hands, they would "faint like a peacock upon hearing thunder"; when the sinners in hell bemoan their fate and regret their earthly alienation from Islam, they say they were "like a neem tree" toward Islam and *imān*, alluding to the bitterness of the neem leaves; the dead in their graves will be resurrected, with God's grace raising them to life "like rain pouring over thirsty paddy fields."

The Tamil telling of the text is deeply sensual. When those in paradise enjoy a feast, a cloud of sweet scents and perfume hangs over them; the scents of musk, fragrant oils, pollen, and flower garlands appear often; colors shine brilliantly, as when Puṟāk (A. Burāq) is depicted with his red-gold head, green hooves, and diamond-blue eyes; the *tūpā* tree of paradise has roots of silver, branches of gold, and shining, pearly leaves. Taste is evoked as well: the tūpā tree is described as bearing dates, pomegranates, cashew nuts, and twenty-one other types of fruit, all delicious as milk, honey, and butter.

Sounds appear aplenty in the frequent instances of onomatopoeia, repetitive vocative forms, and representations of exclamations, as when those in hell cry *aiyō*, expressing their grief. Lastly, the sense of touch is evoked in descriptions of couples caressing in paradise and of women there touching the blind who immediately regain their sight.[33]

The sensual images are powerful tools in attracting an audience and committing it to imagining the sensations depicted. The flavors of fruit, the glimmer of gold, and the scent of garlands were all familiar, allowing both a sense of proximity to the rewards promised in paradise and an impression that things familiar will be transformed and improved. The images of paradise's beauties can only tap the imagination, creating anticipation and desire. Many of the images—women's beauty, scents of musk, and colorful flowers—are quite common in Tamil works. Further examples of cultural specificity can be easily found in the text: Ibnu Salam mentions the typical Tamil division of the world into *kāṭu* (uncultivated land, forest, desert) and *nāṭu* (kingdom,

33. For the scents, see *AM*, vv. 423, 463–64; for Puṟāk's colors, vv. 441–43; for the fruits of the *tūpā*, vv. 497–505; the women awakening the blind, vv. 520–22.

agricultural, inhabited land); the angels are described in terms befitting the Hindu deities, with eyes that never blink; the Prophet's tongue flows with sweet *amṛta*, the ancient nectar of the gods; Ibnu Salam uses the Tamil *aṭiyēṉ*, an expression of servitude employed by non-Muslim poets addressing their gods.[34] As was evident in the hell scenes, many non-Muslim images and idioms prevalent in the wider society have entered the text and provide evidence of contemporary, often meta-religious literary conventions.

Certain particularities of Tamil culture and language-use shape and enhance these unique features of how the *One Thousand Questions* story is told—and experienced—in Tamil. I stress the experience of reading aloud or listening to the text, since this telling of it offers an aesthetic journey that propounds the power of the teachings the *One Thousand Questions* sets out to offer.

Tamil is rich in sound play, repetition, onomatopoeia, and other forms of poetic speech. A section on the descriptions of hell exemplifies this tendency (onomatopoeia italicized):

> Above the bellies of those women
> Drunk with wine
> *Kotu kotu kotu* water boils
> *Kata kata kata* it is poured
> On their bowels, liver and all
> *Motu motu motu* forcefully,
> As fainting [or drunken] they fall.
> (*AM*, v. 597)

The first sound can either represent incoherent speech, the "mumbo jumbo" of the women who have sinned by drinking the forbidden wine, or it can represent the sound of water boiling; the second mimics the sound of a boiling liquid being poured, in this case over the women's bodies; the third is the noise of swallowing or sucking up thick liquid as the water comes in contact with the women's inner organs, or as they forcefully emerge from the body as a result of the ordeal. Although forms of onomatopoeia are in part culturally based, the simmering, bubbling, boiling, close-to-explosion heat of the water is quite palpable for all. The word translated here as "fainting" (T. *muraṇṭu*) can also mean drunken, not sober, obstinate, or insane, and could well refer once more to a punishment befitting the crime: drunken women are then

34. *AM*, vv. 63, 24, 216 and 80 respectively.

subjected to torture that makes them speak incoherently and lose control over their bodies, as happens under the influence of alcohol.

An especially beautiful example of onomatopoeia is found in the depiction of Pur̲āk, the Prophet Muhammad's winged horse, with the sound of his hooves galloping through paradise. In addition, in the story of the small bug who entered the nose of the great bull bearing the earth on its horns, only to reach its brain and eat away at it, the sound *muku muku* represents the bug's constant buzzing or movement, torturing the bull.[35]

Another major feature of Tamil is that it is a "left branching" language, in which the verb is always placed in a sentence's final position. This creates difficulty for literal translation but can offer a powerful narrative effect. For example, when Muhammad decides to send a letter to Ibnu Salam inviting him to a debate, he calls for a scribe and dictates the letter. The following verse describes the content of the message and the writing process, and is translated quite literally to emphasize the effect of the verb's position:

> The entire letter without error he wrote
> Leave the sins, he wrote
> The wise deserve fame, he wrote
> Two are God's [worlds], he wrote
> The Messenger is great, he wrote
> Quickly that letter he wrote
> An envoy of peace he dispatched.
> (*AM*, v. 19)

The importance of the actual writing is brought out in this passage, in which every line but the last ends with "he wrote." The form used in Tamil (T. *viṉai eccam*) is a nonfinite form implying that the action is still taking place and is not yet in the realm of the definite past. Only with the finite verb "he

35. *AM*, v. 758. This story is part of an entire canto the Tamil *One Thousand Questions* devotes to the bull, said to carry the world upon its horns (c. 18, vv. 744–67). Ipulīcu (the Devil, from A. Iblīs) tempted the bull to drop the world by telling him how carefree he would then be, released from his heavy burden. The bull was convinced and only by God's grace was the world saved from destruction. The bull was then punished when a small bug was sent to enter his nose and eat through to his brain. This element finds a parallel in the story, appearing in Ibn Isḥāq's biography of the Prophet, of the lowly gnat that entered king Nebuchadnezzar's brain via his nose and brought about his tormented death because, in his arrogance, he wished to rule the heavens. A similar story, in rabbinic literature, has a gnat with a one-day lifespan killing the emperor Titus. Newby, *The Making of the Last Prophet*, 189, 191. In this particular context the elaboration on the bull's weakness and moral deficiency may also be linked to the prominent status of cows, and the role of the bull as Siva's vehicle, in Indian society.

dispatched, he sent" is the action completed. The importance of writing the letter is stressed: it will bring not only an invitation to Ibnu Salam but also set the stage for the debate by informing him in advance of the various points emphasized in the letter: God's omnipresence in the worlds, the Prophet's greatness, the need to leave behind false beliefs, prove one's wisdom, and gain fame. The writing may have also been brought to the fore as Muhammad himself was illiterate, a fact only further highlighting the uniqueness of his accomplishments. The final line, which does not conform to the pattern of the rest—standing out for readers and listeners alike—sums up the writing and the letter's content by stating what in fact the overarching tone and intention of the mission was: a message of peace (T. *celāmiku*, from A. *salām*). The position of this element within the verse, at the start of the final line, follows the classical Tamil convention of placing the gist of a verse at that particular point.

Another example points to the repetitive use of the vocative, placed similarly at the end of every line. Each time a different vocative is used by Ibnu Salam when addressing the Prophet, but all vocatives end in the Tamil long vowel *ē*, used for emphasis and as a poetic expletive. Tamil and Arabic epithets for the Prophet are used in the same manner:

> *Kāraṇarē*—O Source [of all creation]!
> *Maṉṉavarē*—O king!
> *Iṟacūlē*—O messenger! (A. *rasūl*)
> *Nāyakamē*—O king!
> *Kattīpē*—O preacher! (A. *ḫātib*)
> *Tamaṉiyamē*—O blood vessel [for the Muslims]!
> *Calavātullāvē*—O the one on whom God's blessings [and peace]are bestowed! (From A. *salawatullah 'alaihi wa salām*)

The entire verse reads:

> "You who split the moon, O Source!
> O king!
> Forever youthful, O messenger!
> Elevated over men, O king!
> Versed in Islamic law, O preacher!
> For Muslims a lifeline!
> May God bless you and grant you peace!
> Your words are true. I will ask further, he [Ibnu Salam] said.
> (*AM*, v. 318)

The English, especially in a literal translation, has little of the Tamil's force. But in Tamil the repetitive, emphatic sound combined with a listing of various aspects of the Prophet's personality and deeds creates a powerful combination: at the end of each description (ruler of men, expert of legal teachings) the listener is reminded—several times in this single verse, without ever mentioning Muhammad's name—of his Prophet's greatness.

Poetic Tamil tends to place verbs and vocatives at the end of lines and verses. In the following verse is found an additional, playful way in which important elements are placed at the verse's end, creating and playing with tension and curiosity, resolved only when each verse has been read to its completion. Again, there is an awkwardness in adhering to this format in English, but in this way the Tamil tendency is retained:

Like lotuses, fish,
[even] Kālaṉ rejects their blue-darkness
Poisonous, overflowing with nectar
Slightly red within. Those who have faith,
Who follow the right path with dedication [shall possess them]
More pointed even than the sword
In Ali's fair hand
Are their eyes.
(*AM*, v. 374)

The entire verse leads, slowly and enticingly, to the final line and word, which is the subject of all previous descriptions: the eyes of the women of paradise. The author uses highly conventional language but also engages the listener in a scaled down tour of Tamil culture: He describes the eyes conventionally as lotus- and fish-like, both poisonous and sweet with nectar, so dark that even Kālaṉ, the god of death, retreats upon seeing them; he conforms to the local standards of feminine beauty by depicting them as slightly red, and then reminds the listeners of the rewards of faith (A. imān) and even manages to insert mention of the Prophet's beloved son-in-law Ali, the famed warrior, and his mythical sword. By using this sentence structure the author is able to create an expectation which—when finally resolved—allows the listener to assess how this expectation is either fulfilled or denied, and how the solution offered at the end, in this case presenting the eyes as the verse's subject, lends new meaning to what has been heard.

The Tamilizing of the text occurs in part at the level of single words. One such word is the Tamil rendering of the Arabic *al-lawḥ al-maḥfūẓ*, usually translated as "the safely preserved tablet" or "the imperishable tablet."[36] The *lawḥ*, meaning board, plank, or tablet, has been understood by Muslim commentators to refer to the original, heavenly Qur'an, as well as to the site upon which all divine decisions and the archetypes of all things—past, present, and future—are inscribed. It sometimes refers to the slate on which all deeds throughout one's lifetime are recorded, to be reviewed as the basis for judgment at the end of days. The lawḥ has an important place in Sufi mysticism and in esoteric philosophy and cosmology, in which various forms of the tablet have been identified with the universal soul and the material board that receives the forms of the supersensory world. The mystically inspired may have glimpses of God's decrees on the tablet, which are denied to ordinary humans.[37]

In the Tamil *One Thousand Questions* the phrase first appears when Ibnu Salam questions Muhammad's ability to reply to his many queries: how does he know what to say? The Prophet then describes the transmission of knowledge, beginning with God and ending with himself, passing through several archangels on the way. The knowledge is described as having been inscribed on the board called, in a Tamilized form, *ilavuku makupūlu*.

The Tamil word used for "plank, board" is *palakai*. It is repeated twice more—without the Arabic phrase—in the following verses that are still describing the inscription upon it. In the context of Tamil literary production *palakai* is a significant word: it evokes its earlier use in the traditional accounts of the ancient *caṅkam*, or academy of scholar- poets, which is believed to have existed in Madurai long ago. The history of the three consecutive academies, the first two of which were eventually swallowed by the sea, is shrouded in mystery. But Nakkīraṉār's grammar of the love poetry genre (circa ninth century) elaborates on their location, duration, and activities. A fuller account appears in Parañcōti Muṉivar's seventeenth-century Śaiva text, the *Tiruviḷaiyāṭal*, which includes a retelling of the story.[38]

According to the latter text, the poets of the original caṅkam were created as phonemes making up the body of the Goddess of Speech. Traveling widely, they came finally to Madurai, where they were greeted by Śiva, who

36. The *lawḥ maḥfuẓ* is mentioned in Qur'an 85:22.

37. Arent Jan Wensinck, "Lawḥ," *Encyclopaedia of Islam*, 2d ed., ed. P. Bearman et al. (Leiden and Boston: Brill, 2010), 5:698. The Hebrew word corresponding to Arabic *lawḥ* (*luaḥ*) is used for the tablets inscribed with ten commandments brought down by Moses from Mt. Sinai (Exodus 32:15).

38. Nakkīraṉār's work is the earliest Tamil text extant offering a full account of literary origins. David Shulman, "First Grammarian, First Poet: A South Indian Vision of Cultural Origins," *Indian Economic and Social History Review* 38.4 (2001): 359–61.

had taken the form of a learned poet. The Pandya king granted them seats of their own in the temple. Other local poets envied their special status and came to contest with them. In their exasperation with these long disputes, the poets ask Śiva for a palakai—a board or slate—that would serve to weigh and measure actual poetic wisdom. Śiva appears with a luminous slate impregnated with mantric power. Although small, it expands indefinitely to make room for true poets to sit on it, no matter their number. It also, while floating in the Madurai temple tank, dumps any pretentious but false poet into the water.[39]

There are significant differences between the caṅkam palakai and the palakai as al-lawḥ al-maḥfūz invoked by the Muslim poet of the *One Thousand Questions*. However, in both instances the board functions as a source or parameter for a special kind of knowledge; it provides an instrument to measure, calculate, and assess a person's deeds, whether they are the entirety of a human's actions over the course of a life, or the writing of poetry; it represents and embodies a profound creative force, and it is given by, and continually associated with, the divine.

Translating the *ilavuhu* as palakai connects an old and respected poetic tradition with a new and in some ways strikingly different one. It highlights a continuity in the use of ideas and words within Tamil literature, which here, in an important translation of a well-known Muslim work, is employed to both resound with an earlier use and to underscore an innovative context. The word palakai—as in the caṅgam accounts—evokes and connects the act of writing, poetic Truth, and ideas about authority and authorship. Divine inspiration is part of both accounts, as is an element of secrecy and mystery attached to the plank. Both refer to an ancient, venerable tradition. Lastly, the particular word choice firmly plants the translated work on Tamil literary ground. This is further emphasized by the claim that the Tamil *One Thousand Questions* was first publicly introduced at the Madurai caṅgam in 1572.

Another intriguing example of translation at the word level is the use of the Tamil word *maṟai* for scripture in general and the Qur'an in particular. *Maṟai* means a secret, a divine precept, or sacred writing, and is the word commonly used in Tamil to refer to the Sanskrit Vedas. The Vedas—the Sanskrit-Brahmanic "scriptures"—are known collectively as *nāṉmaṟai* (the four Vedas) comprised of the Ṛg, Atharva, Sama, and Yajur Vedas. The term is used in Tamil in various expressions and compounds closely associated with faith and wisdom: *maṟaittalaivi* (the Goddess of Secrets, Lakṣmī), *maṟaipporuḷ* (the deep treasures of the Vedas), *maṟaimuṭivu* (the substance

39. Ibid., 362–66.

of the Vedas, the Vedanta), *maṟaimutal* (the first secret, Śiva), *maṟaimoḻi* (an incantation), *maṟaiyavar* (learned sage, brahman), *maṟaiyilār* (the ignorant).[40] The collection of poems praising Śiva, written by the three celebrated Śaiva "saints" Appar, Campantar, and Cuntarar in the ninth century and collected in the *Tēvāram*, is considered as the Tamil Veda and commonly referred to as *Tirumaṟai*. In the *One Thousand Questions* the words *veda* (T. *vētam*) and *maṟai* are used interchangeably to refer to the four scriptures sacred to Muslims, of which the Qur'an is the seal and perfected version: the Torèt (Torah), Injil (Gospels), Sabur (Psalms), and, finally, the Qur'an. The conventional phrases for all four—either *nālu vēta* or *nāṉmaṟai*—are applied.[41]

The use of *maṟai* to designate the Qur'an offers another example of how a single, significant word takes on new meaning within a literary tradition being shaped in new directions. The authority and power of the *maṟai* within the Tamil cultural context was difficult to rival. Side by side with the use of Arabic words like Qur'an and *furqān*, *maṟai* was deemed appropriate for expressing the profoundness and mystery of the Muslim scripture, which is thus, at the very least, placed on a par with the ancient, sacred teachings and likely made to exceed them.

A third example is evident in the discourse of melting or dissolving, a theme that has been central to certain genres of Tamil literature, most notably to Śaiva bhakti hymns. The devotee praying or worshipping his god, expressing his longing and love, often describes an experience of melting in great heat, of fusion of a self that dissolves and disintegrates. For example, we find the following in Māṇikkavācakar's ninth-century collection of poems, the *Tiruvācakam*:

> Our Lord
> On that day when you looked at me
> You took possession of me
> In grace entered me
> And out of love melted my mind.[42]

Cēkkiḻār, in his *Periya Purāṇam*, depicts the great Tamil Śaiva "saint" Appar as he arrives at Śiva's temple in Viḻimiḻalai:

40. M. Winslow, ed., *A Comprehensive Tamil and English Dictionary* (New Delhi: Asian Educational Services, 1991), 854.

41. *AM*, invocation, v. 3.

42. *Tiruvācakam* [38:7], cited in Glenn E. Yocum, "Māṇīkkavācakar's Image of Śiva," *History of Religions* 16.1 (1976): 7.

. . . He folded his hands in adoration,
And praised the Lord's feet, his
Deep love melted into a
Liquid stream, the flood from
His eyes gushed out
And spread over his body.[43]

The transformative experience of melting is one of closeness to God and therefore extremely powerful; it is also one of suffering: from the heat and energy generated by the encounter, from the gap that cannot be breached, from the distance still remaining between lover and beloved. The number of words to describe the process of melting in Tamil testifies to its importance. The Tamil Lexicon lists forty such words, with many of the definitions referring specifically to a "melting of the heart" or "melting with love" (*aḻital*, *nekkurukutal*, *kacital*, *pocital*), and many having semantic fields that include feeling or inflicting pain, growing emaciated, fading away (*aḻital*, *nekiḻtal*, *kuḻaital*, *ukutal*).[44]

In the Tamil *One Thousand Questions* this common referent is employed often. Several words signifying "to melt, to dissolve" appear throughout, with the verb *uruku* the most frequently used among them. Like many of the other words in this category, *uruku* has a range of meanings: "to dissolve with heat," "to melt," "to liquefy," "to be fused." More figuratively it can mean "to become tender," "to melt as the heart," "to be appeased," "to sympathize," "be kind," and "to glow with love." The noun form, *urukkam*, refers to a "melting of the heart," "tenderness," "pity," "compassion," or "tender or ardent love for a deity." Whereas in other works we find that "to melt" invokes in-depth experiences and emotions of striving toward a loved one—human or divine—its use in the *One Thousand Questions* is to a large degree confined to negative circumstances. On the journey to Medina Ibnu Salam and his followers hear talk of the Prophet everywhere, and people warning that those who do not follow Islam will melt like wax in the fires of hell; in the descriptions of hell provided by Muhammad, time and again sinners are depicted as dissolving in its raging heat, their bodies, brains, and lives melting away:

43. *Periya Purāṇam*, 252–54, cited in Indira Viswanathan Peterson, "Lives of the Wandering Singers: Pilgrimage and Poetry in Tamil Śaivite Hagiography," *History of Religions* 22.4 (1983): 356.

44. "Cologne on-Line Tamil Lexicon," 2003 ed., http://webapps.uni-koeln.de/tamil/.

Many rooms, many fires,
A sea of light, everywhere fire.
Not even a needle-sized space is fire-free.
Decaying, dissolving in fire
Fettered
The sinners of the earth
Can be seen.
(*AM*, v. 530)

Furthermore, molten lead is poured into the ears of those who listened to music; on the Day of Judgment, standing on a great plain in the scorching heat, many will be bathed in sweat, melting "like butter"; the body of the angel of death, as he takes his own life after that of everyone else on earth, is hot and melting; the children of the infidels are told that their parents are melting and tormented in hell; a great mountain of fire melts and traps the infidels; if but a single scorpion of those associated with the mountain would descend to earth and sting another great mountain, that mountain would melt and dissolve like water.

The use of *uruku* and other terms for melting (*urukku*, *vetumpu*) is not restricted to suffering and is used also in discussing creation: for example, the white shiny pearl created by God melted to become a great river, its waters gushing forth and producing foam, from which the seven worlds crystallized. However, it is in the realm of sheer human pain and terror that *uruku* is most commonly employed in the Tamil *One Thousand Questions*.

The discourse of dissolving, which in earlier poetry depicted a transformational experience of melting as a result of love, devotion, possession, and contact with a deity, changed into one in which suffering, punishment, and retribution—most often explained as resulting from defiance toward God's commands—became central. As in the other examples discussed, the terminology remained consistent but was played out in a new and very different context, inviting a reassessment of ideas of attachment, duty, the body, and human relationships with the divine. Along with the play on sounds and images, the evocative play with words, as their use and meaning shifted, constitutes an important aspect of the Tamil *One Thousand Questions*.

The *One Thousand Questions*, as translated into Tamil in the sixteenth century, became an important, authoritative, and popular text. Claimed as central to Tamil Muslim history and identity, it was republished as late as the 1980s so that a new generation may appreciate its stylistic beauty and the Islamic teachings it propounds.

Reading the *One Thousand Questions* in Tamil and thinking about it in context allows us to appreciate the depth of involvement and engagement of Muslims with the literary traditions of their mother tongue. It highlights Tamil Muslims' important contributions to Tamil literature by way of expanding the limits of existing genres, and of introducing novel combinations and entirely new models for literary production. Inhabiting a textual world partly overlapping with and partly diverging from the literary worlds of non-Muslims around them, Muslim authors enriched the language and its possibilities for creative expression beyond what was previously known. The *One Thousand Questions*, as an early work, set an example for the path to be taken by later writers, including the famed Umaṟuppulavar, author of the Prophet's biography, which is considered the greatest of Islamic works in Tamil. Interestingly, Umaṟu is seen not only as a successor to Vaṇṇaparimaḷappulavar in a literary or religious sense but also as his biological descendent. Thus, with the wisdom of hindsight, we can look not only back into the past to understand Vaṇṇaparimaḷappulavar's own world of prior texts, but also forward, to his writing and its role as "precursor" to much of later Tamil Muslim literature.

The next chapter considers the historical and linguistic context of a *Book of One Thousand Questions* tradition that has much in common with the Tamil one: Malay, a major Islamic culture within the Arabic cosmopolis of South and Southeast Asia.

5

Seribu Masalah The Malay *Book of One Thousand Questions*

Malay tellings of the *Book of One Thousand Questions* have long been known in the Archipelago and have circulated across great geographical distances. Their production in various sites is testimony that Malay—in its local forms—was used widely both as a mother tongue and as a language of commerce and Islamic learning. These functions, and especially the latter two, made it a prominent language of the Arabic cosmopolis. The importance of Malay as a conveyor of Islamic stories, assumptions, and beliefs is evident in several particularities of the *One Thousand Questions* as told in this language: Arabic is used often, with the striking feature that many Arabic words and Qur'anic quotations are left untranslated and without commentary, and Arabic script has been consistently employed when committing the story to writing. These features, along with the prose narrative style typically selected and the emphasis on consistent transmission histories, all produced a literary corpus that possessed an aura of authenticity and authority shaped by its multiple contacts with Arabic.

The range of production and circulation sites of *One Thousand Questions* texts becomes evident when the following examples are considered: when Valentijn visited Ambon in the Moluccas as early as 1726, he found there a copy of the text.[1] A manuscript exhibiting Minangkabau linguistic influence

1. Anthony Reid, "Islamization and Christianization in Southeast Asia: The Critical Phase, 1550–1650," in *Southeast Asia in the Early Modern Era*, ed. Anthony Reid (Ithaca: Cornell University Press, 1993), 170.

was copied in 1757, while another was inscribed in Kampung Krutut, Batavia, in 1786. Several others were copied during the nineteenth century. For example, the manuscript on which Pijper's 1924 edition of the *Hikayat Seribu Masa'il* was based was copied by Ki Agus Muhammad Mizan of Palembang in Bandung, in 1856. There is also a text known to have been copied by a Javanese, and yet another belonging to a man of Banjar, either the Javanese town by that name or the town on the southern Kalimantan coast. Traversing the seas to Europe, another *One Thousand Questions*, inscribed on Java in 1812, was presented by Lady Raffles to the Royal Asiatic Society of London in 1830. Pijper listed fifteen manuscripts of the work kept in the libraries of Leiden, Jakarta, and London, to which Drewes added a copy housed in Cambridge, with fragments of the story appearing in van der Tuuk's collection.[2] There are eleven manuscripts in the National Library of Malaysia alone, with additional copies elsewhere in that country and in Singapore. Print editions of the *One Thousand Questions* were published in Singapore (1888–89), Mecca (1911), and Cairo (1921), with the books' circulation to the latter two cities testifying to Malay's status as an Islamic language far beyond Southeast Asia.

Writing of the widely familiar *Hikayat Hang Tuah*, preserved today in some twenty surviving manuscripts, Henk Maier states: "Twenty is a considerable number, and it should serve as an indication that *Hikayat Hang Tuah* was a relatively well-known tale about a well-known hero in the Malay world."[3] More convincing still is the preponderance of the *One Thousand Questions* in Malay, with thirty-one manuscripts, at the very least, preserved at present.

Features of the Malay One Thousand Questions *Corpus*

As noted in chapter 2, the titles of the Malay texts are variations on *Seribu Masalah*—"One Thousand Questions"—including *Hikayat Seribu Masa'il*, *Hikayat Masalah Seribu*, *Kitab Seribu Masa'il*, and *Seribu Sual*. Besides the many hikayat and kitab texts there is a telling, in van der Tuuk's collection, in the form of a syair, the story apparently having been deemed suitable to different Malay genres. The name Samud, or more often Thamud—as it is pronounced in Arabic—appears occasionally, but the protagonist is more often

2. Guillaume Frederic Pijper, *Het boek der duizend vragen* (Leiden: E. J. Brill, 1924), 72–77; G. W. J. Drewes, "Javanese Versions of the 'Questions of 'Abdallah B. Salam,'" *BKI* 142 (1986): 325–27.

3. Henk Maier, *We Are Playing Relatives: A Survey of Malay Writing* (Leiden: KITLV, 2004), 78.

referred to as Abdullah Ibnu Salam. I have come across only a single Malay text specifying his name in the title, *Hikayat Thamud Ibnu al-Salam*.[4]

A notable feature of the prose Malay texts is their narrative consistency, especially in the opening and closing passages, which use much formulaic language (in Arabic and Malay) and very similar descriptions of the protagonists and the events taking place: the story is always credited to ʿAbbās, the Prophet's uncle; Ibnu Salam is depicted as a wise Jewish *pandita* (pundit, sage) who hails from Khaybar, with seven hundred followers; he receives a letter inviting him to meet the Prophet; in the concluding scene he accepts Islam as the true faith, recites the *shahāda*, and takes his leave. The frame remains highly consistent, as do many of the questions and answers, including the final question Ibnu Salam addresses to Muhammad, in which he asks to know the ages of all the prophets. The reply listing the ages ends with Muhammad himself, who acknowledges that he is sixty-three years old, implying to the audience—familiar with his biographies—that the end of his life is nearing. It is at this point that Ibnu Salam converts, underscoring the dramatic timing of the event—in the final days or months of Muhammad's life—making him perhaps the last fortunate person to embrace Islam through direct contact with the seal of the prophets.

Another important feature of the Malay corpus is its frequent incorporation of Arabic, in the form of conventional phrases of praise, vocabulary, Qur'anic citations, and script. For example, it is a rare occurrence when a Malay text fails to begin with the *bismillah* invocation. Although part and parcel of many Muslim texts, it does not feature in its Arabic form in Javanese *One Thousand Questions* manuscripts. Ibnu Salam addresses the Prophet with "ya Muhammad," or "ya rasulullah," as one would do in Arabic; all Malay texts are written in jawi, the modified Arabic script, most often in its typical unvocalized form. Arabic within the text, undifferentiated at first glance from the Malay, is often written in a different ink and is vocalized. In this way a distinction between the languages—apparently deemed important—was maintained.

An additional consistency is found in the large number of texts that explicitly mention Persian as their source. No specific Persian title or author's name appear; only the language generally (*bahasa Parsi*, or *Farsi*) is credited with inspiring these Malay works.

4. *Hikayat Seribu Masa'il*, Perpustakaan Nasional Republik Indonesia, Jakarta. MS. PNRI W 82, p. 99. This title is mentioned at the very end of the story.

The question of the relationship of the text to Persian sources is a significant one, both in terms of the general field of Malay literature and the particular history of the *One Thousand Questions*. As several important studies have demonstrated,[5] some of the earliest translations into Malay and the ones at the core of Malay Islamic literature were based on Persian sources, including the *Hikayat Amir Hamza*, *Hikayat Muhammad Hanafiyya*, *Hikayat Bayan Budiman*, *Taj as-Salatin*, and *Hikayat Bakhtiar*. The *Book of One Thousand Questions*, with its explicit acknowledgment of Persian lineage, thus joins a distinguished list of texts that have had a profound impact on Malay literature and on the dissemination of Islamic culture in the region.

In addition, in the context of the *One Thousand Questions*' translation history, a shared mention of Persian points to a commonality between its Malay and Tamil tellings, both of which claim a Persian source. These claims indeed explain the many similarities in content and sequence the texts in these two languages exhibit. It is very likely that both were translated from Persian texts produced in South India, not Persia itself, as such texts were produced there in the seventeenth century and likely earlier. Relying on a Persian source may also distinguish the Malay texts from Javanese tellings that do not posit such a claim, and that are more likely directly derived from Arabic sources.

A related and somewhat complicating matter touches upon the question of possible Shi'i elements within the *One Thousand Questions* tradition. Such Shi'i elements in Malay literature are often linked to Persian influence, as was discussed by Brakel in his study of the *Hikayat Muhammad Hanafiyya*.[6] Therefore the appearance of Shi'i motifs in the Malay *One Thousand Questions* would not be surprising if it were translated from a Persian text produced in the Hyderabad-Golconda region of South India, where Shi'i influence was strong in the sixteenth century. However, Ali, the Prophet's son-in-law who is revered by Shi'i Muslims, features in Javanese *One Thousand Questions* texts quite regularly (usually as the bearer of the Prophet's letter to Samud), but rarely in Malay ones. Pijper even asserted, and Drewes concurred with him, that a mention of Ali in a Malay *One Thousand Questions* meant that the particular telling was based on a Javanese rather than a Malay work.[7] This assumption requires reevaluation, especially in light of the explicit link to

5. Ph. S. van Ronkel, *De roman van Amir Hamza* (Leiden: E. J. Brill, 1895); L. F. Brakel, *Hikayat Muhammad Hanafiyya: A Medieval Muslim-Malay Romance* (The Hague: Martinus Nijhoff, 1975); Vladimir Braginsky, *The Heritage of Traditional Malay Literature: A Historical Survey of Genres, Writings and Literary Views* (Singapore: ISEAS, 2004).

6. Brakel, *Hikayat Muhammad Hanafiyya*, 5–6, 7–28, 58–63.

7. Pijper, *Het boek der duizend vragen*, 141, 68. Drewes refers here to MS. LOr. 3343. Drewes, "Javanese Versions of the 'Questions of 'Abdallah B. Salam,'" 326.

Persian and the fact that at least one additional Malay *One Thousand Questions* manuscript mentions Ali, along with the other three caliphs, in a decorative introductory page (see fig. 3), while another manuscript praises him and his sons Hassan and Hussain in its final lines.[8] It is very likely the case that "Shi'i" is too restricted a designation for a range of devotional texts and practices in Muslim Southeast Asia that centered on the Prophet's immediate family, the *Ahl al-Bayt*.

However this question is or is not resolved, it raises the issue of possible—and probable—fruitful interactions between authors and translators telling the story in Javanese and Malay, and how they might have spoken to, and perhaps against, each other. Further clues for such interactions are found in the consideration of possible shared production sites for the texts. One likely locale for the production of the early Malay and Javanese texts was Palembang, in eastern Sumatra. The Palembang Sultanate—at its height between 1750 and 1800—was once a meeting place for Malay and Javanese cultures, where the royal library included manuscripts in both languages and Javanese was an official court language. The scribe copying the Malay text on which Pijper's study is based, Ki Agus Muhammad Mizan (in 1856/7–1273 A.H.), called himself a Malay and man of Palembang (M. *al Jawī, Palembanī*). In his study of the Palembang court library collection of the late eighteenth and early nineteenth centuries, Drewes lists an additional *Kitab Seribu Masa'il*.[9] A mention in Florida's catalogue of Javanese manuscripts further strengthens this hypothesis by listing a poem including "the teachings of the Prophet Muhammad in dialogue form with Samad Ibnu Salam" as a Surakarta-inscribed copy of a manuscript belonging to one pun Sabarodin from Pulembang.[10]

Wieringa identifies another potential site of interaction in an article tracing the sources for the *Syair Seribu Masalah*, a versified Malay telling of the *One Thousand Questions*. Based on several elements in the text's content as well as the manuscript's style of the script—which includes dotting the *dal*

8. *Kitab Seribu Masa'il*, Perpustakaan Nasional Republik Indonesia, Jakarta, 1910, MS. PNRI ML 442, and *Hikayat Seribu Masa'il*, Perpustakaan Nasional Republik Indonesia, Jakarta, 1757, MS. PNRI ML 200, respectively.

9. G. W. J. Drewes, *Directions for Travellers on the Mystic Path: Zakariyyā' al-Anṣārī's "Kitāb Fatḥ al-Raḥmān" and Its Indonesian Adaptations*, VKI, vol. 81 (The Hague: Martinus Nijhoff, 1977), 218.

10. *Samud* fragment in *Para Nabi Nerangaken Bab Rijal Saha Sanès-Sanèsipun*. See Nancy K. Florida, *Javanese Literature in Surakarta Manuscripts*, vol. 1: *Introduction and Manuscripts of the Karaton Surakarta* (Ithaca: Cornell University Press, 1993), 192. Note the exchange of *a* and *u*: Samad instead of Samud; Pulembang rather than Palembang.

and indicating the Javanese *pepet* by a *fatḥa* above the consonant and a *hamza* beneath it—he claims a Bantenese origin for the poem.[11]

The Hikayat Seribu Masalah

The text I have selected to represent the Malay *Book of One Thousand Questions* corpus in this study is the *Hikayat Seribu Masalah*, listed as MS. CCCV in Van Ronkel's 1909 catalogue and currently catalogued as MS. PNRI W84 at Indonesia's National Library in Jakarta. Although its dates of composition and inscription are unknown, it was clearly inscribed prior to the year 1873, the year when H. von de Wall, to whose collection it belonged, passed away and his books were donated to the Batavia Society of Arts and Sciences.[12] The text's most recent appearance, in Indonesia, was in a transliterated version, edited by Edwar Djamaris and titled *Hikayat Seribu Masalah*. Djamaris selected the manuscript for transliteration with the highly questionable claim that it "represents all available manuscripts and can be viewed as the best in terms of its content, paper condition and writing" (*HSM*, 3). The text was published in Jakarta by the Pusat Pembinaan dan Pengembangan Bahasa in 1994. This publication was part of the Indonesian Department of Education's efforts to make old texts deemed significant more accessible, although curiously, the book was "not for sale to the public" (I. *tidak diperdagangkan untuk umum*). This transliterated version is the main Malay source I have consulted.

The questions begin with addressing the Prophet's role and his relationship to God, the relationship between God and Islam, and the nature of the archangel Jibrail. These are followed by the "number questions" (see chapter 9), addressing, in an abbreviated manner, an entire range of ritual and historical Islamic themes. The following topics, among others, are subsequently raised and tackled in Ibnu Salam's questions and the Prophet's replies: cosmogony (including the creation of Adam, originating in God's utterance of *kun fayakun*, the skies, the fabled mount Qaf, the different seas, the moon, the stars, and the wind), eschatology (including discussions of hell, the angels, and events to take place on the Day of Judgment), stories related to

11. E. P. Wieringa, "Dotting the Dal and Penetrating the Letters: The Javanese Origin of the Syair Seribu Masalah and Its Bantenese Spelling," *BKI* 159.4 (2003): 499–517.

12. Ph. S. van Ronkel, *Catalogus der Maleische Handschriften in het Museum van het Bataviaasch Genootschap van Kunsten en Wetenschappen* (Batavia and The Hague: Albrecht and Co. and Martinus Nijhoff, 1909), 242, and T. E. Behrend, ed., *Katalog Induk Naskah-Naskah Nusantara: Perpustakaan Nasional Republik Indonesia* (Jakarta: Yayasan Obor Indonesia, 1998), xxii.

the prophet Adam (his creation from multicolored earth and his banishment from Paradise, his shaving and circumcision by Jibrail).

There are several riddle-like questions in this telling, some of which correlate with riddles in the *Āyira Macalā*. Others seem to be additions of the Malay scribe. The latter include, for example, the question of what is stronger than stone (water), what is noble but useless (life in this world), the five who were born parent-less (the reply lists only four: Adam, Hawa [Eve], nabi Saleh, and the goat exchanged for Ismail's sacrifice). Another question engages with the significance of the cock's crow. These riddles have a playful feel to them, when compared with many of the questions focused on more theological or ritual matters, and may have provided some brief entertainment or even distraction to audiences listening to the story.

Additional topics include the resemblance between children and their parents; the lives of Habil, Kabil, Musa, and Nuh (Abel, Cain, Moses, and Noah); the creation of the world from a pearl; the many realms, mountains, and seas comprising the seven worlds; depictions of hell and paradise and the deeds that lead to both; the fate of infidel children; signs that precede the arrival of the Final Hour, including the appearances of the apocalyptic Dajjal, Yajuj, Majuj, and Dabbatul Ard; the resurrection, with Muhammad and then all humans emerging from their graves, and the good going to paradise, the evil to hell; and the prophets' ages, concluding with Muhammad himself. Found here is a remarkably broad range of topics, touching upon history, geography, eschatology, ritual, belief, morality, and hagiography, coming together to present an intricate tapestry of Muslim life.

Despite the fact that details of authorship, date, and place are absent from Djamaris's edited text as well as many other Malay tellings, a certain degree of knowledge about the Malay corpus does emerge from the discussion thus far: Malay *One Thousand Questions* texts were produced in various locales in the Archipelago; they were marked by a high degree of consistency in terms of narrative details and of the content of questions and answers, likely traceable to their Persian sources and an emphasis on relatively strict transmission practices; and the latter tendency allows us to assume with some degree of certainty that undated and relatively late tellings are based on earlier tellings dating back at least to the early eighteenth century. Evidence of this tendency is apparent in the remarkable similarities between the *Hikayat Seribu Masa'il* manuscript produced in 1757 (MS. PNRI ML 200) and the *Kitab Seribu Masa'il* produced in 1910 (MS. PNRI ML 442).

The Malay *Hikayat* includes few questions that are unique to it. What does stand out in this telling is its use of language and the way it incorporates Arabic into the text. However, it does occasionally differ also in thematic emphasis from its Javanese and Tamil counterparts, offering a perspective on some of the topics its author considered worthy of elaboration.

All tellings of the *One Thousand Questions* in Tamil, Javanese, and Malay include discussions of geography—both celestial and earthly. However, the Malay text appears to place more stress on the element of worldly geography than the others, going into more detail, more often. For example, to the question of which lands are paradise-like in our world, the Prophet answers the following: "Rum, Mesir, Qadawiyah that means Syam, and Asfal that refers to Armih."[13] Next, Abdullah inquires a second time about paradise-like lands, but—judging from the reply—seems to be asking about mountains. These are named as "Mt. Andikini in western Arabia, Mt. Qaf, Mt. Anan in the land of Ajam [Persia], and the land of Kabirhurasan." Asked further about paradise-like rivers, the Prophet mentions "Furat near Baghdad, Nil in Egypt, Jihun in the country of Hawariyah, and Sihun [Sindhu?] in India." This is followed by the equivalent in hellish terms: which countries will God place in *neraka* (hell) on *kiyamat*? Qasa, Afsali, Intali, and Malain. Which countries are of *neraka*? "The land of Syam, near the land of Rum called Ruman, Sahrurusi [Russia?], and Gharkhan" (*HSM*, 56).

A particularly interesting example is found in the Prophet's explanation of how and where Adam fell from Paradise to earth. Adam is said to have fallen "in the land (or continent, M. *benua*) of India, near the kingdom of Keling, on Mt. Sailan."[14] This reference reflects the old tradition of Adam falling in the area of southeast India.[15] Sri Lanka (Sailan, Ceylon) as Adam's falling place, occurs in early Arabic sources. The traveler on a pilgrimage to the sacred mountain, Adam's Peak, can there behold Adam's footprint in the rock where he first fell, as Ibn Baṭṭūṭa did in the fourteenth century. Adam's Bridge is, for Muslims, the name of the string of small islands between Sri Lanka and southeastern Tamil Nadu where Adam is supposed to have crossed to India, or Keling (that same "bridge" is considered by Hindus as the site where Rama crossed with his monkey army to Lanka in his attack on the demons' kingdom, as depicted in a central episode of the Ramayana). Through these references we see the Malay telling emphasizing the world's sacred geography,

13. "Rum" can refer to Ottoman Turkey or Byzantium, "Mesir" is Egypt, "Syam" is Syria, and "Armih" may refer to Armenia.

14. *Adapun nabi Allah Adam diturunkan Allah subhanahu wata'ala ke negeri dunia ini benua Hindia hampir negeri Keling di Bukit Sailan. HSM*, 44.

15. "Keling," from Kalinga, a historical kingdom in southeast India and a name referring to Indians, and sometimes specifically to Tamils, in the Archipelago.

mapping the holy lands, rivers, and hills of distant and not-so-distant places for a local readership. Although the Tamil telling includes the same questions on the lands of paradise and hell, it does not elaborate on the location of the places (in the land of . . . near . . .) beyond mentioning their names. This emphasis might very well stem from the culture of trade and travel that carried Malay people to distant shores and ports in India, the Middle East, and beyond, making these sites—or at least their names—familiar and tangible.

Pijper devoted a rather long discussion in his analysis to the ways in which the Arabic in the Malay *One Thousand Questions* was often "corrupted" beyond recognition (D. *hopeloos verbasterd*), including many of the place names that are difficult, if not impossible, to identify. Despite the fact that not all the names are traceable to places known today, there are several that allow us to conjure the map used or imagined by the Malay author: traveling from Egypt with the Nile in the west, the description continues north-east to Turkey, Persia, and central Asia (Kurasan, Armenia?), then south and east to Bagdad, all the way to southern India.

The four earthly places that are mentioned as protected havens in times of disaster—such as when the Antichrist Dajjal descends to earth—are located at the heart of this map: Mecca, Medina, Jerusalem (A. *Baitul Maqdis*), and Mt. Sinai (A. *Tursina*), condensing the sacred space to its utmost center.[16] In an interplay between what may be viewed as center and periphery, but could also be seen on more fluid, shifting terms, the importance of space and place apparent here not only represents a Malay translation or adoption of a Perso-Arabic derived geography but also contains within it—as evident from the mention of Adam's fall to earth in Ceylon, adjacent to South India—an indication of the local region's importance in Arabic sources and the ways in which that region figured prominently in the travels and legends of Muslims from those sacred heartlands themselves.

Differing from other important Malay works like the *Hikayat Iskandar Zulkarnain* and *Hikayat Amir Hamza*, with their abundant depictions of faraway places and peoples visited by their heroes, the spatial contours of developments in the *One Thousand Questions* are for the most part limited

16. It is interesting to compare the physicality of landscapes in the Malay texts with the ones depicted in the Javanese. When discussing the navel of the universe, the *Suluk Samud Ibnu Salam* (1898. MS. MSB 173a) makes no mention of a geographical place. It seems rather removed from an external, physical-historical Muslim world, more focused on an inner one. While other *One Thousand Questions* texts debate lists of rivers, cities, and mountains, this one seems to relate almost exclusively to an "interior landscape" (to borrow A. K. Ramanujan's term).

to the site of Ibnu Salam's dialogue with the Prophet. The minimal movement occurring within the story contrasts with an important geographical dimension of the Arabic cosmopolis narrated through its pages: distant places, some notably sacred, are deemed central to local mappings of belonging. And important locales within the region are marked as both local and global sites of Islamic heritage. The former connected Muslims of the cosmopolis outward with the larger Muslim world, while the latter restated the centrality of the cosmopolis's sphere for the worldwide community.

Two major elements that stand out as distinct to the Malay *One Thousand Questions* when compared with Tamil and Javanese tellings are the use of Arabic and the *One Thousand Questions'* prose narrative style. The story is told in short sentences, in a manner that is straightforward, concrete, and descriptive, especially when compared with the Javanese. It is clearly not as difficult and enigmatic as the latter, lacking its mystical dimension. The frequent repetition of certain phrases is characteristic, reflecting a direct translation of an ultimately Arabic-derived text. For example, Abdullah always precedes his questions with *katakanlah, ya Muhammad* ("tell me, O Muhammad"), which appears in Arabic tellings as *qāl ya Muhammad*, and similarly acknowledges all of the Prophet's replies to him with *sidiq ya Rasulullah* ("you speak truth, O messenger of God"), a localized spelling of the Arabic *ṣadaqta*. Muhammad almost always addresses his listener with *hai Abdullah* at the start of his reply. This constant, identical framing before the question and after the reply encapsulates each topic in the same fashion, with the Prophet's voice within each frame presenting a teaching, gradually touching upon many themes.

The following exchange offers an example (address terms and expressions are italicized):

> Tell me, *ya Muhammad*, what lies beneath the tablet of fate (M. *lauh mahfuz*)?
>
> God's messenger replied: Beneath the tablet is the seventh heaven. Abdullah then said: *sidiq ya rasullulah*. Tell me, *ya Muhammad*, what is that heaven made of?
>
> To that the Prophet replied: That heaven consists of Mt. Qaf, made by God of green emerald, and Mt. Qaf encircles the entire world like a great wall. Abdullah said: *sidiq ya rasulullah*. (*HSM*, 30)

Such recurring phrases that punctuate the narrative give it a kind of musicality, despite its being written in quite straightforward prose. They convey an air of consistency, reliability, and commitment that those listening to the telling, along with an imagined Ibnu Salam, came to associate with the Prophet's message. The repetition of the name "Muhammad" over and over again can be viewed as a form of *dikir* (A. *dhikr*, "remembrance [of God]"; "invocation"), a devotional act typically involving the repetition of God's names, as Muhammad himself has been viewed as the embodiment of God's *dikir* (Qur'an 65:10–11).

The dialogue form typically evokes a conversation, but this element is strengthened further in the Malay telling by the many repetitions, the frequency with which the debaters address each other by name or title, and additional instances evoking orality, as when the Prophet welcomes Abdullah with the greeting *marhaban bika* (from A. "welcome"), or when he asks him "O Abdullah, haven't you heard the ancient story about the time of the prophet Moses, peace be upon him?"[17] in a manner that clearly resembles spoken language.

The title hikayat (A. *ḥikāya*) seems to have been applied over several centuries to almost any conceivable type of work in Malay, making for a very broad category. Despite this diversity it may be said that, typically, authors of Malay hikayat had two major aims when writing, entertainment and instruction, most often on religious themes. Sometimes a plot was lost or compromised in a writing process that resulted in a work that came to resemble a theological treatise, a *kitab*. The *One Thousand Questions* in Malay—with its detailed discussions of ethics, liturgy, eschatology, and the like, no less expansive than those found in formal treatises—is a case in point. Although it retains the frame story intact, it reads more like a kitab than a hikayat, which genre often included scenes of adventure and drama.[18]

That said, the *One Thousand Questions* is not entirely kitab-like. Albeit rarely, in it are found moments when the didactic voice of the author gives way to a more personal tone. Such a moment occurs when those in hell are crying out in regret and pain, begging for help and mercy. The angel torturing them, Zabaniyah, replies that "now even if you cry till your tears turn to blood and your two eyeballs fall out as a result of weeping, it will be of no use" (*HSM*, 66). Although descriptions of hell are often formulaic, this passage stands out as somewhat less conventional than the rest of the text and might have touched listeners more in its personal tone. The *One Thousand Questions*, then, includes many elements of a religious treatise but still maintains a certain flavor of a captivating tale.

17. *Hai Abdullah Ibn Salam, tiadakah engkau dengar hikayat dahulu kala pada zaman nabi Musa alayhi 's-salam? HSM*, 22.

18. And indeed some manuscripts of the text are titled *Kitab Seribu Masalah*. Mat Piah et al., *Traditional Malay Literature*, trans. Harry Aveling, 2d ed. (Kuala Lumpur: Dewan Bahasa dan Pustaka, 2002), 324.

Scholars of Malay writing in the past century have not addressed dialogical texts as a distinct genre. In his exhaustive and authoritative *A History of Classical Malay Literature*, Winstedt did not mention a *masalah*-type genre in Malay. Although he discusses the *One Thousand Questions* in its Malay tellings, he in no way indicates that it forms a part of a larger collection of structurally or thematically similar texts.[19] An additional comprehensive source, Hamid's survey of Malay Islamic hikayats, again mentions the Malay *Kitab Seribu Masalah* but makes no mention of additional dialogic texts.[20] Neither are such texts addressed in *We Are Playing Relatives*, Henk Maier's important study of Malay writing. Snouck Hurgronje, in his classic *The Achehnese* (1906), did not discuss any masalah books nor a local Malay or Achehnese telling of the *One Thousand Questions*.

However, although the case may be that masalah texts were not seen as a distinct genre and did not employ the term in their titles, there are several works in Malay besides the *One Thousand Questions* following a similar format of introducing two leading characters, one of whom is the Prophet Muhammad, the other a person eager to learn about Islam who engages the Prophet in a debate.[21] Examples include *Hikayat Nabi Mengajar Anaknya Fatimah* ("Tale of the Prophet Instructing his Daughter Fatimah") in which Muhammad answers his daughter's questions, instructing her in the duties of the devout Muslim woman and wife; *Hikayat Nabi Mengajar Ali* ("Tale of the Prophet Instructing Ali"), which recounts Muhammad's replies to his son-in law Ali's questions on a range of theological matters; and *Hikayat Nabi dan Iblis* ("Tale of the Prophet and Satan"), which includes a denunciation of Satan's ways and a warning to his followers. In a related example, Braginsky mentions two texts, classified as Sufi hagiography, which emphasize the conversion of infidels to Islam by means of providing answers to difficult questions.[22]

In addition to these works possessing the same structure of question and answer debate as the *One Thousand Questions*, there are many other Malay texts including the term *masalah* (or a close derivative thereof) in their titles. The catalogue of the Indonesian National Library in Jakarta lists—in its Malay section—several manuscripts of *Masa'il al-Mubtadi*. Another example is Sheikh Daud's *Furu'al Masa'il*, a nineteenth-century Malay work on Islamic

19. Richard O. Winstedt, *A History of Classical Malay Literature* (Kuala Lumpur: Oxford University Press, 1969), 148–52.

20. Ismail Hamid, *The Malay Islamic Hikayat* (Kuala Lumpur: Universiti Kebangsaan Malaysia, 1983), 208.

21. Mat Piah et al., *Traditional Malay Literature*, 324–25.

22. Vladimir Braginsky, *The Heritage of Traditional Malay Literature: A Historical Survey of Genres, Writings and Literary Views* (Singapore: ISEAS, 2004), 614.

jurisprudence. In Aceh, where most manuscript collections have yet to be catalogued, similar works in both Arabic and Malay have been identified.[23]

Malay Particularities of the One Thousand Questions

There are several examples of a particularly Malay coloring of the story's details. Dress codes receive attention as a locus of cultural expression: Abdullah asks about what Adam was wearing when he went down to earth. The answer is that Adam was naked, and ran to and fro in great embarrassment, only to find some fig and olive leaves with which he covered his body. Those leaves were made into a kerchief (M. *destar*) and a type of skirt worn by men and women (M. *kain*), both basic local garments. Ibnu Salam asks further about the dress of the inhabitants of paradise, and is told—based on a Qur'anic reference—that they wear a special refined garment called *khullah*, made of silk interwoven with gold. To emphasize the unique nature of this garment, the author adds that even if the believers, who have seventy kinds of clothes with which to cover their bodies, were to assemble together with all the other inhabitants of this world, they would not be able to produce a single piece of *khullah* (*HSM*, 62–63). Abdullah then asks about the jewelry worn in paradise, receiving an answer detailing the types of bangles, necklaces, and rings used for adornment (*HSM*, 63).

In the scene depicting people greeting the "Antichrist" Dajjal (A. ad-Dajjāl), he is said to be riding by with a mountain at his side, bedecked with jewels, *kain sutera* (silks), *dewangga* (a local cloth design), *beludru* (from Por. *beldu*, velvet), and *khatafah* (from A. rug, carpet) (*HSM*, 74). This latter example portrays a combination of local and imported textiles, hinting at the variety of materials available at the time, in a hierarchy of quality and desirability, and at the importance of textiles in the local economy and culture.[24] Interestingly, beautiful textiles are identified both with true paradise and with Dajjal's temptations of a false one.

Another Malay particularity is expressed through the mention of music. The scene is again the coming of Dajjal and his welcome by dancers, singers, and musicians. The latter are loudly playing many different instruments while

23. These include Sheikh Abdurrauf's Malay *Majmū'al-Masā'il* and a fragment of an anonymous Arabic *Soal Jawab Akidah*, in Oman Fathurahman and Holil Munawar, eds., *Catalogue of Aceh Manuscripts: Ali Hasymy Collection* (Tokyo: C-DATS, 2007), 64 and 51, respectively.

24. The use of a Portuguese word is noteworthy. This brief list hints at travel to, or trade with China (silk), the Middle East or Persia (rugs), and Europe (velvet) as well as the production of local goods (dewangga).

surrounding and praising Dajjal. Cooperating with supernatural *jinns* and *syaitans* who assume the forms of deceased mothers and fathers, he deceptively gains the people's trust, and, as they surround him, he goes on to defeat all nations.

The following instruments are played as Dajjal appears: *gong*, *kendang* (small drum), *serunai* (wind instrument with reed), *nafiri* (ceremonial trumpet), *rebab* (two-stringed instrument), *kecapi* (kind of plucked string instrument), *dandi* (kind of drum), *muri* (metal flute), *bangsi* (bamboo lute), *serdam* (bamboo nose flute), and *ceracap* (cymbal, castanets). This list represents a quite extraordinary variety of musical possibilities.

I noted that in the Tamil *One Thousand Questions* music was regarded negatively. In this scene music is associated with *sorga*—the positive, promising hill on Dajjal's right side—but it is a *sorga* bound to a false prophet and to Dajjal's utterly deceitful promise of redemption (*HSM*, 74). And music has already been condemned in an earlier passage in this *One Thousand Questions*, with love for it punished with an afterlife in hell.

As with the detailed descriptions of non-Muslim practices in the Tamil *One Thousand Questions* functioning as reminders of all that is forbidden and yet possibly quite popular at the time of writing, the listing of so many instruments attests to the centrality of music in Malay life and to the challenge facing those who wished to persuade the community that music should be suppressed. Mentioning the combined music of these instruments must have evoked very familiar sounds in the listeners' minds, sounds toward which even the author here expresses some ambivalence, precisely as he is harshly criticizing them. This section stands in interesting contrast with the Javanese text, as many of the same instruments, and similar ones, were central to ritual, entertainment, and public life on Java. And yet no mention of music is made in the older Javanese *One Thousand Questions* tellings, while in the later story of Sèh Ngabdulsalam musical instruments were construed to represent mainstream Islamic notions.

An interesting element appearing in the text is the grouping together of various types of teachers and leaders, including both Islamic religious figures and others to whom the older, pre-Islamic terminology is applied. When Iblis scorns the dwellers of hell, he reminds them that they did not listen to the *mufti* (from A. Muslim jurist), *'alim* (from A. scholar, theologian), *pendeta* (from S. *paṇḍita*, sage; M. Hindu or Buddhist priest), *qadi* (from A. judge), *syeikh* (from A. elder, scholar, leader), *zahid* (from A. ascetic, hermit, dervish) and *orang tua-tua* (M. the elders) (*HSM*, 72). It is evident from this list that titles associated previously with pre-Islamic roles were still in use and relevant, commanding a respect which, if neglected, was considered a major, punishable offense.

Arabic in Malay One Thousand Questions *Tellings*

Although Arabic (its vocabulary, script, and genres) was important to all three linguistic communities discussed in this study and to the ways in which the *One Thousand Questions* was reformulated in each of the three languages, Arabic was employed quite differently, and more often, in the Malay text than in the Javanese and Tamil tellings.

The Malay *One Thousand Questions* opens with the customary Arabic *bismillah*; whenever the Prophet is mentioned his name is followed by the blessing *sallallahu 'alayhi wassalam* (A. "May Allah bless him and give him peace"); he is often referred to by common titles or epithets in Arabic, such as *khatamun nabi* (seal of the prophets), *nabi akhir zaman* (Prophet of the end of time) or *rasulullah* (Allah's messenger, apostle); Ibnu Salam tends to address the Prophet using Arabic phrases as well, most typically by "ya rasulullah" ("O God's messenger").

Most striking, in comparison with the Javanese and Tamil texts, is the way the Malay *One Thousand Questions* is interspersed with untranslated Arabic vocabulary and passages from the Qur'an.

To the question "is Jibrail male or female and what does he look like and how tall does he stand," the Prophet replies (Arabic in italics):

> Hai Abdullah, adapun Jibrail itu *muqarabin* pada Allah ta'ala dan bukan laki-laki dan bukan perempuan dan tiada tinggi dan tiada rendah mukanya bercahaya-cahaya seperti bulan purnama . . .
>
> (O Abdullah, Jibrail is a *muqarabin* of God, and is neither male nor female, neither high nor low, his face glows like the full moon . . .)[25]

The author includes an Arabic word without translating it and without explaining it. He answers all the specifics of Abdullah's question, and so a listener would unlikely guess the meaning of the Arabic addition by searching for a detail left unanswered in Malay.

Another example occurs when Abdullah asks about the elements God used in creating the prophet Adam. The reply includes a list: Adam was created

25. *HSM*, 25. *Muqarrab* in Arabic means "close companion, protégé, favorite."

from earth, earth from a fruit, fruit from water, and so on in a series beginning with hyacinth (*yakut*). Then, relating the final point of origin, Muhammad says:

> ... yakut itu daripada *kun fayakun*, hai Abdullah. Adapun *kun fayakun* itu daripada kudrat Allah ta'ala. (*HSM*, 29)[26]

> (Hyacinth [was created] from *kun fayakun*, O Abdullah. And *kun fayakun* [originated] from Allah's will.)[27]

Again, a central concept remains untranslated. *Kun fayakun* describes the creative process in which God said "be!" (*kun*) and it—anything He wished to create—came into existence (*fayakun*, literally "and it was, it became").[28] As the Malay speaker listens to the genealogy of origins, leading back from Adam to God's all-powerful will, the creative powers of His command and its fulfillment are expressed solely in Arabic.

In the Javanese *One Thousand Questions* tradition, the Muslim profession of faith, when appearing in Arabic, is almost invariably translated into Javanese. Sometimes it appears in the latter only, without the Arabic original. In comparison, in the Malay *One Thousand Questions* Ibnu Salam asks the Prophet whether all Muslims enter paradise on account of their dedicated religious service. The question refers to a debate that began very early in Islamic circles on whether Muslims enter paradise automatically or must act in a certain way to achieve this boon; or, in other words, a question is raised over the importance of faith versus deeds.[29]

The Prophet replies (Arabic in italics):

> Hai Abdullah segala orang yang masuk syurga tiada dengan kebaktian. Barang siapa menyebut *la ilaha illallah Muhammad rasulullah* itulah yang beroleh syurga tiada dengan kebaktian. Jikalau Yahudi dan Nasrani sekali pun jika ia menyebut dua kalimat itu atau orang menyembah berhala sekali pun jika ia masuk Islam syurga baginya.

26. *Allah ta'ala* (A. "God who is most high").

27. *Kodrat* is God's omnipotence, His all-powerful will.

28. "It was He who created the heavens and the earth in all truth; On the day when He says 'Be,' it shall be." Qur'an 6:73.

29. On this debate, see Arent Jan Wensinck, *The Muslim Creed* (1932; Cambridge: Cambridge University Press, 1995), 36–57.

(O Abdullah, all those who enter paradise, it is not due to their religious deeds. Anyone who says *la ilaha illallah Muhammad rasulullah* will gain [entry to] paradise, without practicing their religious duties. Even if a Jew or a Christian says these two sentences, or even if an idolater embraces Islam [by saying the above], he attains paradise. [*HSM*, 24])

Beyond the central doctrinal issue addressed, it is noteworthy that the *shahāda* here appears untranslated. It is clear from the passage that its two sentences are crucial ones, as they allow anyone who says them—including non-Muslims, even those who bow to idols—to enter paradise. But what do they literally mean? Whereas in Javanese texts special care was taken to parse and translate the confession of faith that allows one to embrace—or as expressed here, to "enter"—Islam, in Malay this crucial Arabic phrase is left as it is. Appearing as a mantra with its power unrelated to semantic meaning, it offers salvation to anyone who commits an act of faith by uttering it.

This is not to say that there are no instances of translation within the text. For example, when Abdullah asks whether Muhammad has met God face to face, the Prophet retorts by telling him the story of Musa's encounter. He quotes Musa as saying to God:

Ya Rabbal alamin anzur ilayka
Artinya ya tuhanku aku hendak melihat rupamu. (*HSM*, 22)

The entire first sentence is in Arabic, and the second translates it into Malay:

This means: O my God, I wish to see your form.

The translation does not address the specificity of the address term—*rabbal alamin*, "Lord of the worlds"—and instead translates it simply as "my God." The second part, in Arabic "I will see you," is less specific than the Malay, which expresses the wish to see God's concrete form. Nevertheless the translation is quite accurate.

It is intriguing to consider why Malay tellings employ Arabic so differently from Javanese ones and to explore the assumptions underlying its use and the inconsistencies of its translation. The abundance of Arabic in Malay tellings may be attributed to several factors. From a technical point of view—since the text was written in the jawi script—it was much easier to include Arabic within it, as this did not entail transliteration into a local, and very different, script, as was the case in (non-pégon) Javanese and Tamil tellings. The significant difficulties of writing Arabic words in a non-Arabic script were of no concern to the Malay scribe, who could freely and easily include Arabic in his writing without giving it too much consideration.

Although it is unlikely that a technical matter is at the heart of the differences, how texts were physically inscribed and what materials were used dictated their content to a certain extent. Pigeaud, for example, noted the difficulty of using Arabic script when writing on palm leaves, a difficulty offering an explanation to the fact that no such manuscripts on Java survive.[30]

Some early translations from Arabic into Malay were interlinear.[31] As Islam spread, as more texts were produced and Malay was more widely used as an Islamic language, interlinear works and short tracts in Malay gradually gave way to texts with varying proportions of Malay and Arabic. Malay became infused with an Arabic vocabulary appearing in all literary works, including texts of an explicitly non-Muslim nature like the Ramayana (M. *Hikayat Seri Rama*). Texts with a focus on Islamic religious ideas or practices, such as the *One Thousand Questions*, tended to include Arabic vocabulary as well as quotations from the Qur'an, hadith, and other sources, but did not provide a dual-language version as interlinear translations did.

The point of transition from interlinear to Malay translation was not clear cut, and interlinear translations continued to be produced. Perhaps because many readers of the time were exposed to interlinear translations while studying and to the Arabic of daily life in trading towns—at least to its religious terminology often heard in mosques and Qur'anic recitations—the *One Thousand Questions* in Malay appears to assume a better knowledge of Arabic on the part of its audience than the Javanese telling does. At the very least, concepts and expressions of great importance, including the confession of faith, descriptions of God's creative powers, conventionalized ways of referring to both God and the Prophet, and selected quotations from the Qur'an, were thought to be familiar enough so as not to require translation.

An additional explanation is that understanding—when defined semantically—did not matter much, or at least was not considered the most crucial form of knowledge. As is true in the present among many non-Arab Muslim

30. Theodore G. T. Pigeaud, *Literature of Java*, 3 vols. (The Hague: Martinus Nijhoff, 1967–70), 1:26.

31. The practice of interlinear translation of the Qur'an originated in the early translations from Arabic to Persian, which according to the Hanafi school were permitted only if the Persian was accompanied by the Arabic original, with a word for word translation (A. *tarjamah musawiyah*, equal translation). Later translations by Muslims into other languages tended to follow this pattern. A. L. Tibawi, "Is the Qur'an Translatable?," *The Muslim World* 52 (1962): 16.

communities, a reading knowledge of Arabic among Malay Muslims is quite prevalent, and certain words, phrases, and idioms are used regularly in daily life. Some of this language—and especially where reciting the Qur'an is entailed—would be undecipherable or only vaguely accessible to many readers and speakers had they been asked to explain the literal meaning of single words or complete sentences. Nevertheless, there are important functions to these uses, which are strongly linked to the status of Arabic and to its sanctity—the sanctity of the language itself—and which are independent of its knowledge in a conventional, scholastic, and semantic sense.

If we consider this possibility, the appearance of the untranslated shahāda in the midst of a paragraph promising redemption to anyone at all who will *recite its words* no longer seems surprising. Like the pre-Islamic mantras in Sanskrit, valued for their powers of sound rather than their lexical meaning, Arabic phrases too gained much esteem in a similar fashion. Such phrases were often referred to, in Malay and Javanese, as *lapal* or *rapal*. They consisted most often of formulas, prayers, or spells that exerted power by virtue of their Arabic sound, even while their meaning was foreign, esoteric, or enigmatic.

Arabic, whether understood or not, was clearly a language of power and prestige because of its status as the language in which the Qur'an was revealed to Muhammad. The power of the lapal and quotations from scripture and the hadith tradition exemplify this well when left untranslated, pointing to the authority residing in the use of Arabic even when listeners were often unable to judge its grammatical correctness or the accuracy of a quotation. In this way even an error—an approximated Qur'anic citation for example—was accepted as potent speech.[32] In the specific example of the shahāda, a combination of sacred language and meaning probably played a role, as the message of God's oneness and Muhammad's mission was indeed a crucial one. But in the case of the many other lapal, scattered untranslated in this text and others, Arabic bestowed the text with the authority of God's words. Indeed such words are often preceded by "As God commanded in the Qur'an" (M. *seperti firman Allah ta'ala di dalam Qur'an*), followed by a lapal-type quotation. Reading the Malay *One Thousand Questions* in transliteration with the Arabic quotations italicized and thus "jumping out" of the page is the print

32. The question of "corrupt" or false citation is a loaded one in general, and is also specifically relevant to the *One Thousand Questions*. There are at least two types of "corruption accusations": those (mostly by Muslim scholars) discussing the relationship of the Prophet's words as presented in the text to his "real" words, and those (mostly by Western scholars) discussing spelling, grammatical, and syntactical mistakes. For discussion of these issues, see Hamid, *The Malay Islamic Hikayat*, and Pijper, *Het boek der duizend vragen*, respectively.

equivalent of Arabic words—or more commonly quotations or expressions—appearing in ink of a different color (usually red or grey) among Malay words written in black, as was the case in many manuscripts. These techniques allowed for a differentiation—by scribe, reader, and reciter—of the perceived linguistic identity of certain words and whether the scribe considered them Arabic or Malay, since the two languages were written in scripts that were almost identical. Both methods—in manuscript and print—allow us to examine how many words of Arabic origin appear unobserved, side by side with the highlighted quotations, and hence taken as an integral part of the Malay language by the time the *One Thousand Questions* manuscript was inscribed.

For example, in the quotation cited above in which *kun fayakun* appears as Arabic, we find the words *kodrat* and *Allah ta'ala* as Malay words; when Abdullah asked whether the sun was Muslim or infidel, and was answered that sun and moon were both Muslim and constantly worshipping God, the question and reply do not include any words marked explicitly as Arabic but do, however, include the following as Malay: *kafir*, *Islam*, *mukmin*, *tasbih*, *ibadat*, *Allah ta'ala*, *firman*, and *Qur'an*. Only following the Malay reply does a Qur'anic passage, entirely in Arabic, appear to strengthen the argument about the sun and moon's beliefs (*HSM*, 33). Another method used to differentiate between Arabic and Malay words within manuscripts was by way of vocalizing the words in one language but not the other. Thus in the *Hikayat Seribu Masa'il* inscribed in 1757, Arabic not only appeared in lighter colored ink but was vocalized, whereas the Malay was unvocalized and written in black ink.

Such instances call attention to the question of what was considered Arabic within Malay literature and among its authors, and how this definition shifted over time, with an increasing number of words becoming so familiar that they were integrated into Malay and no longer represented as foreign. As is clear from the above examples, a word or expression—in this case *Allah ta'ala*—could be written as both Arabic and Malay within the same text, pointing to a fluidity in perceiving Arabic and Malay as distinct entities.

An Eschatological Scene

A final example highlighting the Malay particularities of the *One Thousand Questions* concerns its eschatological sections, which although very similar in order and content to those appearing in Tamil, are significantly expanded. The events preceding the Day of Judgment are depicted in sequence, beginning with the signs of approaching *kiyamat*, when the social and physical orders of life on earth will dissolve into chaos. Next Dajjal, the Antichrist, will appear and be killed by Jesus, who will return to the world for a second coming; at that time the *mahdi*, a descendent of Muhammad, will rule, filling the world with justice; after he returns to God Yajuj and Majuj will come forth, to bring destruction and fear to all but the four sacred places protected by God. Finally, after they are eliminated, a strange and terrible beast, *Dabbatul Ard*, will emerge from the earth carrying Musa's staff and Solomon's ring (see Qur'an 27:82) and will rule for three days until God will instruct the archangel Israfil to blow his trumpet, at which time all nonbelievers will perish. In some cases these events are mentioned or hinted at in the Qur'an, while others are described and debated in the hadith traditions.

In the Malay *One Thousand Questions* Dajjal (A. deceiver, imposter) is depicted as climbing to the top of a hill and crying out to all to follow him. Many gather, playing various musical instruments and calling for him. Dajjal, who is blind in one eye, rides a huge white ass and has the words "by Great God, this is an infidel" (A. *wa hātha kafirun bi'llahi 'lazim*) written across his forehead. The unbelievers of different sects and affiliations all bow to him, addressing him as their god. Dajjal rides with a mountain on each side: on his left is one full of torturous elements, fire, and snakes; the one on the right is full of jewels and garments. Depictions of Dajjal possessing these attributes and carrying out these actions appear in major hadith collections like those of Bukhārī, al-Tirmidhī, and Muslim. In a twist that is significant in the context of this study, Dajjal has sometimes been associated with a Jew who lived during the Prophet's lifetime in these very same collections.

Despite Dajjal's clearly eschatological character, he is identified in several hadith narratives with Ibn Ṣayyād or Ibn Ṣa'id, a Jewish boy living in Medina at the time of the Prophet's stay there.[33] He is said to have converted to Islam, and his interactions with Muhammad are depicted as brief dialogues in which the Prophet serves as questioner. Ibn Ṣayyād demands that the Prophet recognize him as the apostle of God, to which Muhammad responds with a surprising indecisiveness. Over time and with the demonization of Ibn Ṣayyād's figure, the question in the hadith was no longer, as it was in an earlier period, whether he was a prophet or not, but whether he was the evil Dajjal. Interestingly, we find here a kind of reverse image of the role applied to Ibnu Salam in the *One Thousand Questions*. Reading the traditions side by side, we find that Ibn Ṣayyād and Ibnu Salam were contemporaries, both living during the Prophet's time, both Jews converted to Islam, and both engaging in dialogue with Muhammad. One, however, was denigrated in traditional narratives as an evil imposter, while the other was put on a pedestal as the

33. On this tradition, see David J. Halperin, "The Ibn Ṣayyād Traditions and the Legend of al-Dajjāl," *Journal of the American Oriental Society* 96.2 (1976): 213–25.

exemplary convert. In the lines from the Malay *One Thousand Questions* in which Ibnu Salam listens to the exploits of Dajjal described by Muhammad, the images of the Prophet's two Jewish contemporaries briefly converge, then diverge.

Having presented the contours of the *Book of One Thousand Questions* in Javanese, Tamil, and Malay, highlighting both the diversity and continuities within this textual tradition as adapted by different Muslim communities in South and Southeast Asia, I return in the following chapters to the broad comparative questions that cut across these languages, literary cultures, and regions, beginning with the role of Arabic.

Part Two *Conversion*

6

Cosmopolitan Arabic's Distant Travels in Translation

The significance of Arabic for Muslim individuals and societies cannot be overstated. The language of the Prophet and the divine Qur'anic revelation, it holds the unique status of sacred language and, in its Qur'anic form, is considered untranslatable. The practical reality in which the Qur'an has been translated into many tongues does not detract from this central ideal that has affected translation practices and ideas about language and expression across the Muslim world.

The Qur'an enjoys a double role as a sacred book and unique literary classic, the embodiment for Muslims of the beliefs that Islam is the superior religion and the Arabic language without peer. No other religious text accords such importance, so often and so explicitly, to the specificity of the language it is written in. This is evident in Qur'anic verses such as "thus we have sent it down, a Qur'an in the Arabic tongue," and "we have revealed the Qur'an in the Arabic tongue so that you may grow in understanding."[1] The ninth-century philologist Ibn Qutayba asserted that since Arabic was superior to all languages—the perfection of human speech—no translator could put the Qur'an in another language, as had been done in translations of the Gospels and Torah. His assertion that translation was impossible "for the languages of the non-Arabs are not as rich as that of the Arabs in metaphor"[2] is questionable, especially in a comparison with languages as rich in sound,

1. Qur'an 20:114 and 12:1, respectively.

2. A. L. Tibawi, "Is the Qur'an Translatable?" *The Muslim World* 52 (1962): 4–16, note 48.

word play, and analogy as Tamil and Javanese, but it represents a deeply held conviction.

In this context of according great importance to Arabic, I consider how the language was viewed, adapted, and adopted in the Islamic cosmopolitan regions of South and Southeast Asia, geographically and linguistically so distant from the Arab lands. Ample evidence points to Arabic's influence running deep, reshaping in many ways the languages of Javanese-, Malay-, and Tamil-speaking Muslims and comprising a defining element of their cosmopolis. The adoption of the Arabic script to write these vernaculars was a key aspect of this transformative process, one that allowed Muslims from diverse cultures to share not just a faith but also the system of writing and the heritage it carried with it. The shifts, or conversions, occurring through the vernaculars' contact with Arabic—with its vocabulary, script, narratives, and echoes of the past—constitute an important form of translation.

Arabic's Travels to South and Southeast Asia

The Arabic language reached different sites in South and Southeast Asia by multiple routes and means. Surviving accounts of Arab geographers written between the ninth and fourteenth centuries attest to a familiarity with many places in India, including its southern regions. In the south are mentioned, for example, the towns of Kilakkarai and Nagapattinam, which became important Islamic centers; Madurai, where the Tamil *Āyira Macalā* was first recited in the sixteenth century; the coasts of Ma'bar and Malabar and, further afield, the islands of Sarandib and Java. The name Fattan or Fātnī, used by Arab writers including Ibn Baṭṭūṭa to refer to different locales, likely derives from the Tamil word for seaport, *paṭṭiṉam*.[3] The knowledge of cities, ports, mountains, and kingdoms as well as the products and peoples of these places points concretely to the ways Arabic was transported, through travel and trade, to these regions.

How Arabic reached the Archipelago is an even more complex question. Noting certain features of Arabic words as they were adapted into Javanese and Malay, van Ronkel believed Arabic did not impact those languages directly but rather through intermediary languages. The most important of these was Persian, long a prominent political and literary language in South India. This Arabic-laden Persian had gradually transformed southern languages like Telugu and Tamil. When merchants of the latter community

3. S. Muhammad Husayn Nainar, *Arab Geographers' Knowledge of Southern India* (Madras: University of Madras, 1942), 36.

reached the Archipelago in great numbers, Arabic was introduced at least in part through their language—with the Arabic component in it having been shaped first by Persian, then by the tendencies of the Dravidian languages themselves—which explains why so many words in Javanese and Malay have final letters or sounds that differ from their Arabic prototypes.[4] More recent scholarship has pointed to direct contacts with speakers of Arabic from the Middle East and especially those reaching Southeast Asia from the Hadramaut. As early as the thirteenth century an association was made in Arabic texts from Yemen between Southeast Asia and exotic aromatics, pointing to a familiarity with the region's spices.[5] Whatever the precise paths taken by Arabic vocabulary, Stuart Campbell in his studies of Arabic and Persian loanwords in Indonesian and Malay has concluded that the introduction of such words has been inextricably linked to Islamization, beginning in the fourteenth century and continuing into the present, with the fields of education, religion, politics, and moral values strongly represented in the borrowed linguistic repertoire.[6]

And indeed, Arabic clearly was not considered a foreign language for many Muslims in India and Indonesia. The range of subjects with which authors and their audiences engaged in Arabic in these regions was broad: it encompassed traditional fields of knowledge such as Qur'anic exegesis, hadith, grammar, jurisprudence, histories of the prophets, and theology, as well as more common, everyday matters, like letter writing, medical tracts, and the composition of lullabies. The range of styles and genres was no less impressive, from the prose of *kitab*s to exquisite mystical poetry, from legal treatises to riddles and charms.

Arabic books were not the preserve of an elite minority or of a community of limited spatial or cultural scope. Van Ronkel, describing the collection of Arabic manuscripts he catalogued at the Museum of the Batavia Society of Arts and Sciences in 1913, and noting that it resembled additional collections across the Dutch East Indies, wrote:

4. Ph. S. van Ronkel, "Over de herkomst van enkele Arabische bastaardwoorden in het Maleich," *TBG* (1904): 189–94. Van Ronkel focuses on the word endings *i* (for example *abdi*, from Arabic *'abd*, slave) and *u* (*waktu*, from *wakt*, time).

5. R. Michael Feener and Michael F. Laffan, "Sufi Scents across the Indian Ocean: Yemeni Hagiography and the Eastern History of Southeast Asian Islam," *Archipel* 70 (2005): 185–208, at 193.

6. Stuart Campbell, "Indonesian/Malay," in *Encyclopaedia of Arabic Language and Linguistics*, ed. Kees Versteegh et al. (Leiden: E. J. Brill, 2007), 2:340–45; cited in Russell Jones, ed., *Loan Words in Indonesian and Malay* (Jakarta: KITLV, 2008), xxiv.

> The significance of the Batavia collection is due to the fact that it contains a number of Muhammadan documents brought together from the whole of the Archipelago, from Aceh to Madura and from Banten to Celebes, and that its composition and numerous annotations give a truthful notion of the Arabic scholarship aimed at by the average Indonesian Muslim student. Thus it is that the number of copies of a very common text may have its importance, if it should only serve to illustrate the history of the study of the sacred science and its propaedeutics in these far away oriental islands.[7]

And indeed, large collections of Arabic manuscripts in India, Indonesia, Malaysia, and the countries of their former colonizers testify to the scope of the production of Arabic texts in South and Southeast Asia. Clearly, these collections are only the tip of the iceberg in that, to a large extent, they represent the collecting impulses of colonial officials and scholars who were working in particular locations and often with particular topics of interest or agendas in mind. Besides collections in academic, private, and national libraries, additional large repositories of Arabic works can be found in educational institutions, including the *madrasa* schools of Tamil Nadu and the *pesantren* of Indonesia, where Arabic books known as *kitab kuning* (yellow books) have long been studied.

Considering Arabic in these regions means acknowledging a continuum and an ongoing process. Such an examination entails looking not only at the scope of materials produced but also at the range of ways in which Arabic's role was played out in particular languages, texts, and scripts. Such an exploration, in turn, leads to a consideration of the shifting relationships between that which was considered local and global, Arabic and vernacular, clichéd and novel. The differentiated use of the Arabic script, for example (discussed below), points to the ways various Muslim communities negotiated questions of expression and identity.

With a continuum in mind, several stages—however fluid—of Arabic production can be discerned. Some works, composed locally or copied from elsewhere, were written solely in Arabic. Such works included, for example, copies of al-Tirmidhī's *Kitāb Shamā'il al-Nabī* or al-Ghazālī's *Bidāyat al-Hidāyah*. They also included virtuoso poetry written by Tamil Muslim poets using only the dotless or dotted Arabic letters rather than the entire alphabet. One such *qaṣīda* using only dotless letters and written in the shape of a leaf,

7. Ph. S. van Ronkel, ed., *Supplement to the Catalogue of the Arabic Manuscripts Preserved in the Museum of the Batavia Society of Arts and Sciences* (Batavia and The Hague: Albrecht and Co. and Martinus Nijhoff, 1913), iii.

was composed by Sheikh Ṣadaqatullah, included in a letter to Aurangzeb, and recited in the emperor's presence in the late seventeenth century.[8]

Some other works were parallel translations, complete or partial, in which the translation of the Arabic text appeared in the margins or line by line, with each line following the one of the original. For example, several copies of Aḥmad al-Marzūqī's *'Aqīdat al-'Awwām* were copied in mid-nineteenth century Aceh. Two contained interlinear translations into Malay while another copy had an interlinear translation into Acehnese. Yet another copy of this Arabic book included a translation into Bugis. The *Talai Fātiḥa*, composed in the mid to late nineteenth century by the great poet Imāmul 'Arūs, contains an Arabic poem with an interlinear Tamil translation. The poem, seeking intercession from all the prophets and their wives, calls on the Muslim women of Sri Lanka to cease their drifting toward the surrounding, non-Muslim culture.[9]

Still other books, rather than presenting an Arabic text and its translation, included sections written in Arabic and others written in Malay or Persian, or sections in more than one language in addition to the Arabic. An untitled collection of anonymous mystical poetry and praise for the prophets and saints, written c. 1800 and used as a textbook for performing *dhikr*, is a case in point. Various copies resembling one another in their make-up and sequence were written in Indonesia: a copy from Banten includes a text in Arabic and Persian; a copy from Aceh contains sections in Arabic, Persian, and a single page in Malay; a third copy has notes in Malay accompanying poems in Arabic and Persian. Yet a fourth copy, the most linguistically diverse, includes many poems in Arabic, some in Persian, and a few in Urdu, Tamil, Malay, and an unidentified (possibly Indian) language.[10]

Finally, much of local production was written in forms of language that I refer to here as Arabicized, the type Pollock termed, in the context of Sanskrit influence, cosmopolitan vernaculars: the languages used by Muslim communities that gradually came to be largely shaped by Arabic's influence, transforming, or translating these languages anew. It is this latter category that I explore, first and foremost, in the following pages and in this book as a whole.

8. Takya Shu'ayb 'Alim, *Arabic, Arwi and Persian in Sarandib and Tamil Nadu* (Madras: Imāmul 'Arūs Trust, 1993), 305.
9. Ibid., 613.
10. Petrus Voorhoeve, ed., *Handlist of Arabic Manuscripts in the Library of the University of Leiden and Other Collections in the Netherlands* (Leiden: Leiden University Press, 1980), 456–58.

Such clear-cut categories do not of course always hold for the manifestations of Arabic in South and Southeast Asian sources, and books were written in ways that defied neat categorization. And yet keeping in mind such multiple modes of production helps us to imagine the great breadth and depth of Arabic's incorporation into the languages and literary cultures of Tamil-, Javanese-, and Malay-speaking Muslims. Although my emphasis is on the Arabicized—not Arabic per se—literary and cultural production of these communities, the broader horizons of Arabic's impact on these regions must remain in sight, as should the notion that Arabic and Arabicized materials were part of the same cultural repository.

Arabic and the Literary Cultures of Javanese-, Malay-, and Tamil-Speaking Muslims

Arabic impacted the literary cultures of Javanese, Malay, and Tamil in particular, localized ways. In Javanese, a large vocabulary from Arabic, including a rich religious terminology, entered the language and often was no longer recognizable as borrowed. Other phrases and terms were viewed by authors as deserving special attention, interpretation or translation. This popular tendency to translate directly from Arabic into Javanese in the body of the text—a kind of "internal translation"—enhanced memorization of important religious concepts and contributed to proficiency in a transregional Muslim vocabulary.

It is not only direct translation that is encountered often. In addition, we find a tendency to give special attention to words or phrases by way of interpretation or commentary. In the 1884 *Serat Samud*, the opening lines of Muhammad's letter inviting Samud to a debate are inscribed thusly:

> Wit ing surat bismillahi rahmani rakimi ika.
>
> (The letter opens with [the traditional greeting] bismillahi rahmani rakimi [from A. "in the name of God the compassionate, the merciful"])[11]

This is directly followed by:

> Tegesé miwiti ingong
> Anebut naming suksma
> Ingkang murahing dunya

11. *Serat Samud*, Pura Pakualaman Library, Yogyakarta, 1884, MS. PP St. 80, c. 1, v. 9.

Nora nana kéwan luput
Tembé asih ning akérat

(This means I begin
By speaking the name of God
Who is merciful in this world
Toward all living creatures
[And] compassionate in the next world)

The Javanese author expands on the literal meaning in Arabic of this oft-used phrase. Elsewhere, when Samud asks for the meaning of *makripat* he is told:

Déné teges ing makripat
Iku apan angwruhi
Marang ing Sanghyang Wisésa
Kalimputan aningali
Mring kawulané yekti

(Makripat means
Coming to know [or seeing]
Almighty God
Being encompassed [by Him] seeing
One's true self.)[12]

Rather than provide a strict translation that would entail using a single, "equivalent" Javanese word for *makripat*, we find a Javanized form of the word (from A. *ma'rifa*) accompanied by a definition. For some listeners—perhaps those with more extensive Islamic education—such phrases or concepts deriving from Arabic would have been familiar; for others—as witnessed by the care taken in the text to translate and offer commentary—this must have presented new or superficially familiar terrain.

Sometimes translation from Arabic was incomplete, pointing to how phrases were broken up when out of context and perhaps no longer understood as meaningful Arabic phrases. Samud's own name—Samud Ibnu Salam in its full Javanese form—was at times shortened to Samud Ibnu. Since *ibnu* (A. *ibn*, *bin*) means "son of" in Arabic, it should conventionally be followed by another name, that of a person's father. The name Samud Ibnu makes no

12. Ibid., c. 6, v. 52.

sense in an Arabic context, but in Javanese the author or scribe treated it as a shortened version of the full name, perhaps as a nickname (J. *julukan*), a typical way of addressing people in Java where complete proper names are almost never used in daily life.

A similar instance is found in the Prophet's explanation of the Arabic-derived term *sirat al-mustakim* (A. *al-ṣirāt al-mustaqīm*), the straight path, or bridge. This Qur'anic term has been interpreted as a bridge stretching over hell that all traverse on the Day of Judgment, falling into the flames or passing successfully to reach paradise. In Java the word *wot* (bridge) has been attached to this phrase, so that it became *wot siratul mustakim*. The bridge is, according to tradition, thinner than one seventh of a hair and sharp as a blade. The use of *wot*—a repetition of the bridge (*sirat*) imagery that could be viewed as redundant—signals a wholesale acceptance, but not literal understanding, of the Arabic phrase, or an attempt to make certain the imagery is conveyed to a Javanese audience.

After the Prophet answers Samud's question about the navel of the earth as *Betal Mukadas*, he goes on to describe it as the site of Judgment where each person will be assessed on *kiyamat* (Judgment Day) based upon their deeds. Then each must approach the risky bridge and try to cross it. Instead of using the entire Arabic phrase along with the Javanese addition of yet another word for "bridge"—*wot sirat al-mustakim*—Muhammad refers to it as *wot siratal*, literally "bridge of the path (or bridge) of," leaving a reader familiar with the Arabic hanging figuratively in midair as if from the bridge itself.

The Prophet adds most of the conventional details—that the bridge is thinner than hair, sharper than a sword—all of this likely to appeal to listeners familiar with the trope.[13] However, examining it as a translation of an Arabic religious concept, we see that it was not complete—and indeed did not have to be—in order to serve its purpose.

The incorporation of Arabic was certainly not limited to single words and phrases. Pijper discussed the use of Qur'anic quotations in the Malay text and, noting their frequent "corruption," assumed they were cited from memory.[14] The result was a form of Arabic that drew more heavily on sound—the way words were heard by a Malay ear—than on accurate spelling, as may be expected in the context of a predominantly oral literary culture. Also, frequent Qur'anic recitations in which Arabic was heard but not necessarily seen by many meant that attempts to recapture it in writing had to be made via aural memory.

13. Ibid., c. 10, v. 5.

14. Guillaume Frederic Pijper, *Het boek der duizend vragen* (Leiden: E. J. Brill, 1924), 82.

A similar phenomenon—although direct citation is much less frequent—is evident in Javanese. When Samud asks about the number of religions that are followed by men and *jinns*, the Prophet replies with an Arabic quotation (Arabic in italics):

Kang muni sajroning Kuran
Inaldinangindallahé
Islamu ing tegesé ira
Satuhu ning agama
Mungguh ing Allah puniku
Amuhung Islam kéwala

(As it says in the Qur'an
Inaldinangindallahe
Islamu this means
The true religion
Of Allah
Is but Islam alone.)[15]

The actual Qur'anic citation above (based on Qur'an 3:19) is not a precise rendering of the original. It adds the typical Javanese nasalization and does not reproduce the Arabic in an exact manner, although it is quite close. Having immediate access to a translation as presented here is helpful in deciphering the meaning. Nevertheless it is apparent that in Arabic the line reads: "the religion (A. *ad-dīn*) [of] Allah [is] Islam," very similar to its rendering in Javanese. The Arabic *dīn* (religion) prefixed by the definite article *al*, refers to *the* religion, Islam. The forcefulness of the term is amplified in Javanese by using *satuhu* (truly, truth), *amuhung* (only), and *kéwala* (only, nothing but). In this brief example it is not just single Arabic words or phrases that are included verbatim in the Javanese text, then translated, but a statement claiming Qur'anic authority is inserted, embedded in the text, and translated.

A significant example is found in the Javanese rendering of the profession of faith. Immediately following the reply about Islam as the true religion, Samud asks what the word Islam, in fact, means. The reply is that the meaning of Islam (or becoming, being Muslim) is saying the *sadat* (A. *shahāda*, from the verb "to see," "to bear witness"). Then the Prophet explains what one must say (Javanese in italics):

15. The examples in this section are drawn from *Serat Samud*. 1884. MS. PP St. 80, c. 1, v. 34.

Ashadu ala *prituwin*
Ilaha ilalah *lawan*
Ashadu ana *lan manèh*
Mukamadarrasul Allah
Sun naksèni tan ana
Pangéran lyaning Hyang Agung
Mukamad utusan ing Hyang

The profession of faith, the two most sacred sentences attesting to the oneness of God and to Muhammad being His messenger, appears in Arabic but is interspersed with Javanese (in italics):

I bear witness [that there is] no *and also*
God but Allah *and*
I bear witness *in addition*
Muhammad is God's messenger.

This is the Arabic affirmation within which—even before reaching the translated portion—the author inserts some Javanese words to parse the two sentences that compose the *sadat*, so that it makes more sense to the listener and is more readily memorized. Again, due to its uttermost importance, special care is taken that it be clearly understood not just in its general meaning but also in the specifics of each segment.

The translation into Javanese follows, using the same divisions of meaning:

I bear witness there is no
God but Hyang Agung
Muhammad [is] Hyang's messenger.

The translation is accurate, with an interesting variation: the word Allah is not used for God in the Javanese rendering, which rather employs two Javanese terms: *Pangéran*, meaning God, Lord, also a royal title, and *Hyang* or *Hyang Agung*, a title often reserved for local or Hindu deities.

The significant influence of Arabic on Malay language and literature has been considered at length in chapter 5 and therefore I only briefly reiterate the main points of that discussion. Arabic had a profound influence on Malay and its literary culture. A large vocabulary from Arabic was adapted into Malay, and genres like *kitab* and *hikayat* became highly popular. Reading texts from the nineteenth century and earlier, one finds many commonly used Arabic expressions and citations, often left untranslated. This pattern suggests or assumes a level of familiarity with Arabic that is not found in similar works written in Javanese or Tamil.

I return once again to van Ronkel, who studied an additional and significant dimension of Arabic's influence on the Malay language, which he discussed in his pioneering study "On the Influence of Arabic Syntax on Malay."[16] It is not enough, van Ronkel argued, to examine how Arabic vocabulary has changed Malay: in order to better understand the impact of the contact between the two languages on Malay, we must also look beyond vocabulary to its deeper syntactical structures, which were so significantly shaped by Arabic.

How texts were translated from Arabic into Malay provides the key evidence for what van Ronkel saw as a systematized translation method, through which various works, whether theological or more narrative in form, employed the same syntactical constructions to convey Arabic prepositions, gender, tense, and plural markers in Malay. Although translations existed in several forms (interlinear, partial, Malay text with some Arabic citations), translation of specific Arabic constructions was consistently followed, creating uniform usage that deeply influenced Malay grammar and syntax.[17]

For example, van Ronkel found that the Arabic preposition *bi* was consistently translated as Malay *dengan*. Thus when writing the phrase *dengan nama* (rather than the grammatically conventional *atas nama*), Malays were borrowing the Arabic phrase *bi ism* (in the name of). The Malay term *setengah orang* (literally, "half a person" or "half the people," meaning "many people") derives from Arabic *ba'd al-nas*.[18] In some cases there is an intrinsic similarity in the way both languages use a preposition or other grammatical marker. In most cases, however, the Arabic form was foreign to Malay and adopted in an attempt to imitate the Arabic as precisely as possible in translation.

The question of Arabic in the 1572 Tamil *One Thousand Questions* is especially significant, considering that it is one of the earliest Muslim literary works extant in Tamil. Many Arabic words appear in the text, often somewhat modified because of constraints of script and pronunciation. This work most likely provided a model for later authors who looked to it for an example of how, and to what degree, they might incorporate Arabic into their writing. Whereas in Javanese many Arabic words or phrases were translated

16. I have used the Indonesian translation of this work, originally published in Dutch in 1899. Ph. S. van Ronkel, *Mengenai Pengaruh Tatakalimat Arab Terhadap Tatakalimat Melayu*, trans. A. Ikram (Jakarta: Bhratara, 1977). Originally published as "Over de Invloed der Arabische syntaxis op de Maleische," *Tijdschrift voor Indische Taal- Land- en Volkenkunde* 41 (1899): 498–528.

17. Ibid., 15–16.

18. These examples appear in ibid., 25 and 37, respectively.

or interpreted within the text, and in Malay some were translated while most were not, the Tamil text includes no such "internal translation." A phrase paralleling Javanese *tegesipun* or Malay *artinya*, conveying "this means" and creating a bridge between Arabic and the language of the text, is nowhere to be found. When Arabic is interwoven into the text, most often in the form of single words, it resides side by side with the Tamil with no apparent distinction or clarification.

It is perhaps this seemingly more smooth blending of the two languages that at first gives the impression that the Tamil text has a much smaller Arabic component than the others. And yet a closer examination shows that this is not the case. To offer just several examples, the following religious terminology—in a Tamilized form of the Arabic—appears time and again: *iculām*, *tīn* (Islam), *imān* (faith), *tuniyā* (this world), *kiyāmattu* (Day of Judgment), *nūr* (light), *napi* (prophet), and *kāpir* (infidel).

Looking once more to the example of the confession of faith, as was done for Javanese and Malay, we find it appears several times, either in its complete form in Arabic without translation, or mentioned as the *kalimā* without further detail. For example, the angels, standing in rows, are described as endlessly reciting *lā ilāha illallāhi muhammatu ṟacūlullā*; Ibnu Salam, when embracing Islam, is said to have recited the *kalimā* along with his seven hundred followers.[19]

An exception to the tendency toward untranslatability in the text can be found in a verse in which Muhammad describes events on the Day of Judgment, when he will be awakened from his grave to lead all of the others rising from their places of burial. The Prophet says: "God will then grant me *uyir* / I will rise to *hayat* / and praise God."[20] The Tamil word *uyir* means life, life's breath, as does the Arabic *ḥayāt*. In this case the use of the two different words in such close proximity and within a clear context of meaning offers a type of "inbuilt" translation, introducing the Arabic term while paralleling the Tamil.

Since the *One Thousand Questions* is an early example of Muslim writing in Tamil, it was likely to have inspired writers of subsequent periods. Discussing the later, undated Tamil Muslim text *Tamīmaṉcāri Mālai*, Shulman notes the impressive "infiltration of Arabic, Persian and Urdu words into the Tamil text," finding it more striking than the reverse trend, the use

19. *AM*, v. 254 for the angels; v. 1052 for the conversion.

20. *Iṟaivaṉ aṉṟu eṉakku uyir nalkuvāṉ / ēviya hayātiṉuṭaṉē yāṉ eḻuntuvantu / ēkaṉaippu kaḻuvēnē.* *AM*, v. 1002.

of non-Muslim Tamil terminology to convey Muslim concepts.[21] A case that is more explicitly linked by tradition to the *One Thousand Questions* is that of Umāṟuppulavar and his famous *Cīṟā*, written a century later in the mid seventeenth century. Many of the miracles only hinted at in the *One Thousand Questions* were elaborated at length in the *Cīṟā*, some expanded to fill entire chapters; much of the same Arabic terminology used in the *One Thousand Questions* was incorporated into the writing of the later text; and Umāṟu, author of this most prominent of Tamil Muslim literary works, is known as a direct descendent of Vaṇṇaparimaḷappulavar.[22]

Defying Translation

Despite the somewhat different approaches to incorporating Arabic and employing translation within the texts, in all three languages certain words defied translation. There is much room for speculation as to why certain Arabic words were adapted into these languages while others were rendered in the local language, but it is likely that some words expressed concepts novel to the society into which they were introduced, so word and idea were accepted together. A certain power associated with the incomprehensible can also explain words left untranslated. This includes both the idea that words can effect change and alter reality regardless of their semantic meaning, and the notion that foreign concepts subordinate local ones through the retention of the foreign terminology. The Arabic word *munāfiq* that appeared as such, untranslated in the Malay, Tamil, and Javanese texts, offers an example.

The *munāfiqūn*—mentioned over three dozen times in the Qur'an—were residents of Medina in the seventh century who ostensibly converted to Islam but did not adhere to the Prophet and his new religion. Officially Muslim but in fact ridiculing and disobeying the Prophet, he found them a threat and a nuisance. Commonly translated into English as "hypocrites," the term in the Qur'an is stronger and has a wider semantic range. In sura 63 the munāfiqūn are described as liars, obstructers, ignoramuses, enemies, arrogant, and deviant. They were clearly dissenters within the *umma*, the emerging Muslim community, refusing to fight at the Prophet's side and deserving of hellfire.

In contrast to the mostly general terms in which the munāfiqūn are referred to in the Qur'an, later Islamic literature in Arabic tended to ascribe the term to specific persons and groups and used the word in a sense that came

21. Shulman, "Muslim Popular Literature in Tamil: The Tamīmaṉcāri Mālai," in *Islam in Asia*, ed. Y. Friedmann, 1:174–207 (Jerusalem: Magnes, 1984), 207, n. 114.

22. *AM*, Introduction, p. 3.

closer to "hypocrite." Still, the best English approximation of the term may be "dissenter," dissent being possible both in private and public, carrying the connotation of religious schism.[23]

In the *One Thousand Questions* tellings discussed, this group, referred to as *munapik*, are mentioned as a category of people who are surely destined for hell. In all three languages a question arises as to their nature, and the same reply is offered by the Prophet: a hypocrite is outwardly Muslim but inwardly an infidel (*kapir*, from A. *kāfir*, another untranslated term). Clearly, even many centuries after the historical munāfiqūn disappointed and betrayed the Prophet, this category—or anyone resembling its members—still connoted deceit and hypocrisy, and was portrayed in the most negative light. The torments they will suffer were vividly depicted in *One Thousand Questions* tellings. But why was a Tamil, Malay, or Javanese word not used to name this group?

It may well be that certain terms remain untranslated because they are so deeply embedded in a particular historical and cultural event that their mention arouses an entire set of images and reactions that would no longer be accessible in translation. This phenomenon of the untranslatability of certain words or terms is related in turn to the notion of "prior text" as discussed by Becker: the ways in which thoughts, writing, and speech derive from, or draw upon, texts that are shared by members of a particular culture and that evoke resonant memories.[24] Many Muslims are familiar with important Qur'anic passages and scenes, of which the citations on the munāfiqūn are examples. The scenes of the Prophet's conflicts with the munāfiqūn or their approaching doom would not be evoked in the same manner in the minds of Javanese listeners familiar with the Qur'an if a (more neutral) Javanese word would substitute for the Arabic. The importance of conveying the full weight of the original term was in part due to the fact that the text dealt with conversion and was likely discussed with the recently converted, for whom it was crucial to understand that their acceptance of Islam must be not in appearance only, but total.[25]

23. A. Brockett, "Al-Munāfiqūn," *Encyclopaedia of Islam*, 2d ed., ed. P. Bearman et al. (Leiden: Brill, 2010), 7:561.

24. A. L. Becker, *Beyond Translation: Essays Toward a Modern Philology* (Ann Arbor: University of Michigan Press, 1995), 285–93.

25. This point is driven home in a powerful way in the Tamil text (*AM*, vv. 633–35.). After the usual punishments the muṉāpik will suffer are depicted (fire, hunger, thirst, cold), they are subjected to a particular punishment which fits their crime: as they beg for water, they see lightning and clouds, and hear thunder brought by God. Rain is near, they think, relieved. Then the rain

The second explanation is more culturally specific: the notion of religious hypocrisy or dissent, of believing inwardly in one thing but posing externally as another, was foreign to the three local cultures before the arrival of Islamic notions of faith. Earlier belief systems in the Archipelago included indigenous systems, in addition to Hindu and Buddhist traditions that had acquired a local character. Similarly, in the Tamil region, that which is today referred to as Hinduism, as well as worship of local warrior gods, goddesses, and saints, prevailed at the time the text was composed. The absence of a word describing a religious hypocrite can thus be seen as an example of a silence within Javanese, Malay, and Tamil, as "every human language is a way that people have developed of orienting themselves to each other and to nature, and each is a different equation, in Ortega's terms, between utterance and silence." The strict Judeo-Islamic notion of a single, clearly defined belief that must be followed exclusively and must not conflict with appearances or words was not a component of these earlier and concurrent traditions, and therefore a word conveying the charged significance of *munapik* was unlikely to exist. We see here that "the immense difficulty of translation . . . is a matter of saying in a language precisely what that language passes over in silence,"[26] and for that reason translation may at times be impossible.

Leaving words like *munāfiq*, *kāfir* (infidel), *nabī* (prophet), *qiyāma* (Judgment Day), and others untranslated (although their spelling and pronunciation were somewhat modified) contributed to the creation of a transregional, standardized Islamic vocabulary across South and Southeast Asian Muslim societies. Such standardization, along with the common use of titles, epithets, and stories, in turn helped shape a religion-based community that was itself translocal. It allowed Muslims from places distant from the Muslim "heartland," like Java, to take part in and belong to the life of a global community that was defined, in part, by its adherence to the Arabic language.

In light of the tendency to leave certain words untranslated, it is tempting to suggest a typology of words that continued to be used in Arabic rather than be translated into the local languages. Following the "munapik paradigm," there would be a host of terms that could be expected to remain untranslated within the texts. The situation, however, is far from consistent: many words

falls, a red, burning hot rain of fire. Watching it they are "like a deer that runs at a mirage." The rain pours, immersing them in it. Guilty of proclaiming one thing and believing another the muṉāpik must suffer the consequences by experiencing the gap between what is outwardly true (rain, water; claiming to be Muslim) and Truth (fire; Islam).

26. Becker, *Beyond Translation*, 290 and 285, respectively.

that fit into the munapik category of novelty, forcefulness, and linkage to prior texts did in fact appear in translation. Not only were they translated, but, as in the case of using Tamil *maṟai* for the Qur'an or Javanese *hyang* for Allah, they were expressed through the use of religious concepts belonging to a different belief system.

A clear example is found in the case of the terminology for paradise and hell, both key concepts in Muslim thought that play a significant role in a variety of texts. Many of the teachings and warnings regarding life in this world in fact focus on the prospect of residing in either hell or paradise in the future. In the case of such central concepts an adoption of Arabic terminology that would powerfully enhance the depictions impressed upon the faithful might be expected. However, in the Tamil, Malay, and Javanese *One Thousand Questions* tellings, the older, Sanskritic terms *swarga* (paradise) and *naraka* (hell) are employed exclusively and consistently.

Notions of swarga and naraka in non-Islamic texts differ markedly from their employment within a Muslim context. Swarga was the world of the gods and demi-gods who enjoyed lives of pleasures before yet other rebirths; naraka, often depicted as a netherworld of suffering, was teeming with demons and other creatures and was, yet again, a temporary stop in the cycle of reincarnation. In contrast, in Muslim teachings, these two realms came to signify the two mutually exclusive, eternal fates for the good and the evil. This prospect meant that the terms swarga and naraka assumed new, dramatically loaded meanings with the transition to Islam.

Keeping old terminology within the context of a new system—religious or otherwise—carries the risk of misunderstanding, of continuing to attach previous meanings to a word altered by a new doctrine. Creating a neologism or bringing in foreign, and sacred, vocabulary—as was often done with Arabic—allows for a distancing from old ideas and a more detached introduction of the new. The break with the past is not necessarily smooth but is more radical.

The cases of Javanese, Tamil, and Malay are interesting precisely because of an inconsistency, a combination of terminology and metaphors that does not fully relinquish the old for the new. For every case where an Arabic word entered these languages and remained untranslated, there is a counterexample of a term associated with earlier (or concurrent) beliefs, seemingly without anxiety about possible confusion and blurring of definitions. In some texts, like the Javanese *Babad Jaka Tingkir*, explicit mention is made of how names of categories of learned religious persons of an earlier age were exchanged with the new, rising Islamic names. The change in roles and attitudes was reflected in a shift in terminology.[27] But in much of the literature terminologies of old and new seem to blend effortlessly without authorial comment.

Such "inconsistency," and the use of combinations of new and old terminology throughout a drawn-out, gradual, and uneven process of religious transformation seems reasonable and predictable. Yet for comparison, we might look to the geographically near yet very different case of conversion to Christianity in the Philippines. By the time the Spanish Church had arrived in the Philippine islands in the late sixteenth century, it had gained much experience from activities of conversion and translation in the Americas. There, during an earlier period, it had made attempts to translate the scripture into local languages for the benefit of the newly converted. The translation of crucial terminology—"God" being a central example—into Quechua or other indigenous languages resulted in a great confusion of categories, an imposition of prior notions of divinity onto the Catholic system. Years of such trial and error and many frustrations in the American "laboratory" convinced the Church's establishment that certain words must remain untranslatable.

Arriving in the Philippines with the conviction that certain crucial terms should remain in Latin within prayers and scripture that would be translated into the locally spoken Tagalog, the Church could create a neat and consistent dichotomy in which some words were translated while others defied translation. This made for a translation texture much different from that found in communities converting to Islam in the same region.[28] The divergence can be explained by the fundamental difference between Catholicism with its hierarchical structure, its Vatican, pope, and priesthood, and Islam, which lacks a similar structure. The Catholic religious hierarchy was reflected in a linguistic hierarchy in which Latin—expressing that which was assumed to be inexpressible in the local language—subordinated Tagalog. For Islamizing societies no such clear-cut division took hold. The difference can also be explained largely by the disparity between conversion to the religion of a Western colonizing power and the gradual spread of a new religion that lacked the backing of military and technological force. The important point, however, is that the Philippine/Tagalog example is instructive in highlighting the complexities and challenges inherent in the study of translation

27. Nancy K. Florida, *Writing the Past, Inscribing the Future: History as Prophecy in Colonial Java* (Durham: Duke University Press, 1995), 155.

28. The Spanish policies had many unintended results, as when "misinterpretation" of the foreign terminology by Tagalogs occurred, but the ideal and the mechanism to enforce it were in place. See Vicente L. Rafael, *Contracting Colonialism: Translation and Christianity in Tagalog Society under Early Spanish Rule* (Durham: Duke University Press, 1993).

patterns in the case of Islamic writings in the region. This complexity is brought out by noting how—even at the end of the nineteenth century, long after conversion began—Javanese and Malay authors still employed old Sanskritic terms alongside Arabic terms to express central Islamic notions, defying simple, easily definable translation patterns.

A Cosmopolitan Script

The adoption of the Arabic script by Muslim communities in South and Southeast Asia to write their own languages was of paramount importance to the emergence of an Arabic cosmopolis in these regions. It was a critical aspect of contact with Arabic, one that transformed local languages and defined them anew. By no means only a technical shift, changing a script entails far-reaching cultural implications. Becker has observed in the context of transliterating Burmese into Latin script "that writing systems . . . are among the deepest metaphors in a language, that they resonate richly throughout a culture, and so for us to substitute one technology of writing for another is not a neutral act, a mere notational variation. It means to re-imagine language itself."[29] Writing in the cosmopolitan Arabic script was an act of reimagining and reformulating the languages of Malay-, Javanese- and Tamil-speaking Muslims.

In some instances, like Persian, the Arabic script replaced an earlier form of writing. Malay was written in local scripts that were gradually overshadowed by Arabic writing until they all but disappeared. In many other cases—of which both Tamil and Javanese are examples—an older script continued to be used alongside the new Arabic script. Whether Arabic script came to be used exclusively or not, a shift from a prior writing system is always significant. Scripts are embedded in particular cultures and histories, and are often associated with creation narratives, mystical calculations, and educational and social practices. Many of these are lost or transformed with changes in script. With the adoption of the Arabic script by communities in the cosmopolis, older writing traditions were lost or marginalized while a certain degree of standardization was achieved: as the cross-regional use of untranslated Arabic terms gave rise to a shared religious vocabulary, so the use of a common script across cultural and geographical distance contributed to the consolidation of an orthographically unified religious community.

The adoption of the Arabic script, wholesale or in part, by Muslim speakers of Tamil, Javanese, and Malay, constituted a pivotal element of their liter-

29. Becker, *Beyond Translation*, 234.

ary cultures and translation practices. The script adopted in all three cases was somewhat modified by using existing Arabic letters with diacritics for the purpose of expressing the particular sounds of each language.[30] However, just as was the case for other dimensions of translation, in matters of the script too there was no uniform path that was exclusively followed.

For Tamil the language known as Arwi or, more fully, as *lisānul-Arwī* (A. "the Arwi tongue") or *Araputtamil̲* (T. "Arabic-Tamil") refers to Tamil written in Arabic script and, by some accounts, also to the spoken language of Tamil Muslims, incorporating many Arabic words not used by non-Muslim speakers.[31] The Arabic alphabet was modified to incorporate Tamil consonants and vowels not present in Arabic by adding diacritical dots to existing letters. The vast majority of texts were accompanied by vowel marks, to enhance understanding. Arwi began developing around the end of the seventeenth century, and thus somewhat later than Muslim literature written in Tamil script. It's "golden age" occurred in the mid to late nineteenth century, when several important works were composed, and the establishment of a printing press in Kilakkarai contributed further to the publishing and distribution of arwi books.[32]

Shu'ayb notes several reasons for the development of arwi, one of which has explicitly to do with translation: according to him "Tamil words and other non-Arabic words lack the capacity to convey the full significance of the Islamic Arabic terms with deep religious, spiritual connotations and significance, like Allah, rasūl, imān. . . ."[33] Although such words could be written in the Tamil script, there was a high probability that doing so would cause a distortion in pronunciation and therefore in understanding their meaning because of the large discrepancy between Arabic sounds and the available

30. The question of script returns us to the discussion of the use of Arabic vs. other languages for reading and reciting the Qur'an. In this context the choice of script and issues of modification proved no simple matter. Reciting translated Qur'anic verses from memory was itself debatable; but possessing a written translation posed a more serious challenge, raising the question of whether the Qur'an could possibly be written down in letters other than the Arabic ones. This in turn was tied to the larger issue of whether the Qur'an (and therefore the Arabic script) was created or eternal. The latter question presented not only theological problems but orthographical difficulties as well, since some Arabic letters had no exact counterparts in other languages, raising concerns of mispronunciation followed by potential misunderstanding. See Tibawi, "Is the Qur'an Translatable?" 16.

31. I refer to it here first and foremost as a script. See note 13 in chapter 4.

32. Torsten Tschacher, *Islam in Tamil Nadu: Varia*, Südasienwissenschaftliche Arbeitsblätter (Halle: Institut für Indologie und Südasienwissenschaften der Martin Luther Universität Halle-Wittenberg, 2001), 59.

33. Shu'ayb 'Alim, *Arabic, Arwi and Persian in Sarandib and Tamil Nadu*, 88.

Tamil letters. In addition, Muslims of both genders typically learned to read the Qur'an in Arabic while many—especially women—could not read the Tamil script. Since they did not speak Arabic, religious education was imparted in Tamil. The use of arwi promoted literacy by allowing Muslims to read and write their mother tongue while also preserving the correct spelling and pronunciation of important religious vocabulary in Arabic.

Arwi was used to compose works of many kinds: creed, mysticism, jurisprudence, hadith, medicine, astronomy, yoga, architecture, biographies, satire, travelogues, and fictional novels. It was widely used among Muslims in both southeast and southwest India and in all parts of Sri Lanka from the seventeenth century through the early twentieth.[34]

Malay written in Arabic script is known as jawi, with which it has been written since at least the sixteenth century. Until recently Malay was thought to have adopted writing primarily through the Arabic script, as the earliest extant texts in Malay—including those with pre-Islamic themes like the Ramayana (M. *Hikayat Seri Rama*)—are written in jawi. That assumption was put to rest by Uli Kozok's important 2002 discovery of a fourteenth century Malay manuscript in Sumatra. The work, a book of laws now known as the Tajung Tanah manuscript, is written in a local India-derived script and contains no Arabic loanwords.[35] With the adoption of the new script, as in the case of Tamil, several new letters were created by adding diacritical dots to existing ones in order to adapt the script to Malay peculiarities. The jawi script is not easily read, especially since the Arabic custom of refraining from the use of vowel marks was followed by Malay scribes.[36]

When Christian missionaries came to the area of present-day Malaysia in the early nineteenth century, jawi ruled the pages not only of literary and religious works but also of Malay newspapers and magazines. However, when the *peranakan* (locally born descendents of Chinese immigrants) began setting up their own newspapers influenced by the missionaries' tendencies toward the Latin script and their own interests, they published Malay written in Latin script (*rumi*). The jawi alphabet was at the center of a struggle between Muslim Malays, who saw its use as an expression of their identity, while the missionaries and peranakan thought it was "too Muslim," a script that might not reach the other ethnic groups in the region. Therefore, for many years,

34. Ibid., 88–89, on arwi literacy; 93 and 105, on the types of works.

35. An even older form of Old Malay, written in a Pallava-type script, is found on inscriptions in Sumatra. Uli Kozok, *The Tanjung Tanah Code of Law: The Oldest Extant Malay Manuscript* (Cambridge: St Catharine's College and the University Press, 2004).

36. Theodore G. T. Pigeaud, *Literature of Java*, 3 vols. (The Hague: Martinus Nijhoff, 1967–1970), 1:25–26.

until the rumi script became standard in the mid-twentieth century, both alphabets were used.

A further note on jawi is warranted, since the name conveys meanings that transcended the script alone, connoting the locale and peoples of Southeast Asia, especially Muslims. *Bahasa Jawi*, the "Jawi language" was used to refer to Malay. According to al-Attas in his study of Islam in Malay history and culture, by the sixteenth century and likely earlier Malay had changed from a language of seamen and markets into a major vehicle for the spread of Islam all over the Archipelago, infused with much Arabic and Persian vocabulary.[37] Somewhat later, and clearly by the mid-nineteenth century, Malay had become an important language in Mecca, second only to Arabic.[38] Despite this fact, and despite Malay people and Malay lands or kingdoms (*orang Melayu* and *negeri Melayu*, respectively) being mentioned in sixteenth- and seventeenth-century Malay texts, almost nowhere are references made to the Malay language (*bahasa Melayu*). In most cases when the language is mentioned it is referred to as *bahasa Jawi*, thus conflating the names of the language and its writing system, the modified Arabic script. This may suggest a case in which language identity was linked with the particular script—an Arabic script, connoting Islam and sacredness—more than with other forms of identity such as geography and cultural community. In modern Malay and Indonesian the verb *menjawikan* means literally "to render into jawi" and more broadly "to translate into Malay."[39]

In the case of Javanese, the modification of the Arabic script was similar to that employed for Malay, with the creation of new letters by adding diacritical dots to existing forms, although the richer vocalism of Javanese required the application of vowel marks in order to prevent equivocality. The script popularized in Muslim communities all over Java was referred to as *pégon*, a term suggesting wryness, obliquity, or odd sound. In some cases, despite the risk of misunderstanding, texts written in pégon were left unvocalized, partly

37. Syed Muhammad Naguib al-Attas, *Islam dalam Sejarah dan Kebudayaan Melayu* (Kuala Lumpur: Universiti Kebangsaan Malaysia, 1972).

38. Martin van Bruinessen, *Kitab Kuning, Pesantren dan Tarekat: Tradisi-Tradisi Islam Di Indonesia* (Bandung: Mizan, 1995), 41.

39. *Jāwī* was a wide-ranging term that the Arabs used interchangeably for the entire region, its diverse peoples, and its most widely spoken language. For a history of the term and its use going back to the thirteenth century, see Michael F. Laffan, "Finding Java: Muslim Nomenclature of Insular Southeast Asia from Srivijaya to Snouck Hurgronje," in *Southeast Asia and the Middle East: Islam, Movement and the Long Durée*, ed. Eric Tagliacozzo (Singapore: National University of Singapore, 2009), 17–64.

or entirely without vowel marks, and were then referred to as *gundhul* (hairless, bald).

The history of the Arabic script on Java is far from definitive, leaving open questions about how and why pégon was selectively adopted. In the fifteenth century the Indian-derived Javanese script had been current for many centuries and was reasonably well adapted to the language. Although the Arabic script was introduced at an early stage of Java's gradual Islamization, some of the oldest, sixteenth-century Islamic Javanese manuscripts are written in the Javanese script. Pigeaud attributed this fact—one he found remarkable—to two possible explanations. The first is a high prestige of pre-Islamic Javanese culture that continued to exert an influence on scribes writing in the Islamic period. The second had to do with practical issues related to writing technologies; palm leaves were used on Java as writing material, and the many dots and short lines used in Arabic script were difficult to inscribe on their fibrous surface. Palm leaf manuscripts with Arabic script are virtually nonexistent.[40]

The use of palm leaves for writing continued well into the Islamic period—and the early twentieth century—especially in East Java and Madura. Even with the introduction of paper, when the difficulty of palm leaf inscription was eliminated, the use of the Javanese script did not cease and continued concurrently with the use of pégon.

In their Arabic-script versions all three languages—Tamil, Malay, and Javanese—added diacritical marks to existing letters to modify and broaden the possibilities of the original Arabic alphabet. In addition, the Indian-Muslim sequence of the Arabic letters was employed by each. In this altered sequence the places of the letters *ha* and *waw* were exchanged.[41] Furthermore, the insertion of an additional letter (combining existing ones) before the final letter *ya*—referred to by Shu'ayb as *lām 'alif hamza*—resulted in the arwi script having 29 rather than 28 Arabic letters. This addition was common in Tamil and Sri Lankan Muslim texts as well as in such works written in Burma, Thailand, the Philippines, and some parts of China.[42] Interestingly, the additional letter was included in the jawi script but not in pégon.

For all three languages the use of Arabic script allowed for easier translation in the sense that texts translated using the Arabic script could retain important Arabic vocabulary, titles, and names in a manner closely resembling or identical with the original. In Venuti's terms this allowed for a more

40. Pigeaud, *Literature of Java*, 1:27.

41. This sequence was also adopted for Turkish and Persian. The latter may have been the source for the change in the Indian subcontinent and beyond.

42. Shu'ayb 'Alim, *Arabic, Arwi and Persian in Sarandib and Tamil Nadu*, 96–97.

"foreignizing" translation, one keeping the flavor, atmosphere, or sounds of the source language, but it also paved the way for these foreign elements to rapidly become familiar.[43]

With the great significance accorded by Muslims to the Arabic alphabet, employing its script meant that the languages of Javanese, Tamil, and Malay Muslims became infused with religious authority and sanctity and that their texts were considered sacred objects. Thurston, in his 1909 *Castes and Tribes of Southern India*, discussed the use of arwi and stated that "A book so written or printed [i.e., in arwi] is called a *kitab*, rather than its Tamil equivalent *pustakam*, and is considered sacred. It commands almost the same respect as the Koran itself, in regard to which it has been commanded 'touch not with unclean hands.' A book of a religious nature, written or printed in Tamil characters, may be left on the ground, but a *kitab* of even secular character will always be placed on a *rihal* or seat, and, when it falls to the ground, it is kissed and raised to the forehead."[44]

Despite the similarities in the adoption of the script for all three languages, the cases of Tamil and Javanese pose common, intriguing questions irrelevant for Malay, due to the continuing use of a prior script alongside the modified Arabic writing in the production and translation of Muslim literature. In the case of Malay, over the course of time the Arabic script subordinated earlier, indigenous forms of writing. However, if future findings bring to light texts written in local scripts other than jawi during the past several centuries, it may well be possible to apply similar considerations of competing and complementing scripts to the study of Malay literary history.

What were the reasons for writing the vernacular in more than one script, and what was the significance of doing so? Answers to these questions are rarely addressed explicitly in the texts. Writing of the origins of the manuscript traditions of the Archipelago, Jones distinguished two coherent and consistent writing traditions, stemming from two cultures: A Hinduized one, bringing with it a script and writing on palm leaves, finding fertile soil in central and east Java and Bali; and an Islamic one, from Western Asia,

43. Lawrence Venuti, ed., *The Translation Studies Reader* (London and New York: Routledge, 2000), 11–14.

44. Edgar Thurston, *Castes and Tribes of Southern India*, 7 vols. (Madras: Government Press, 1909), 4:206. Cummings documents a similar sentiment of veneration toward objects containing the Arabic script in his discussion of Islamization in seventeenth century Makassar (South Sulawesi), where "uttering Arabic and possessing spiritually potent religious manuscripts were the dominant practices shaping Islam's spread, reception and structure. . . ." W. Cummings, "Scripting Islamization: Arabic Texts in Early Modern Makassar," *Ethnohistory* 48.8 (2001): 559.

bringing Arabic script and the tradition of writing on paper. Jones suggested that the choice of writing materials was based on cultural influence more than practical considerations.[45] Similarly, Pigeaud argued that, with some exceptions, there was a general division on Java by which Islamic religious literature was written in pégon, whereas "secular texts" of all kinds were written in the Javanese script. He connected this division to the dichotomies—such as genealogies of the left and the right—commonly used for various classifications on Java.[46]

In the context of the textual repositories of central Java, this argument is problematic. Although Pigeaud claimed that the nineteenth century "cultural renaissance" in Solo returned the Javanese script very much to the foreground all over Java, resulting in a decline of pégon, the *One Thousand Questions* in Javanese—clearly classifiable as Islamic religious literature—appeared in Javanese script as early as the late seventeenth or early eighteenth century. Many other religious texts were inscribed in Javanese script before, and in the early part of, the nineteenth century. The continuing adherence to the Javanese script by Muslim authors and scribes goes beyond a secular/religious division (anachronistic in its own right) or technological practicalities, drawing on long-held assumptions and convictions related to the practice and meanings of writing.

The perception of script as potent on Java dates back to the influence of early translations of Sanskrit texts concerning the *aksaras* (syllables, letters) and the all-powerful creative force of the *sabdas* (sounds). Old Javanese works present an early prototype of ideas that were to be incorporated into later Javanese texts, including those with a clear Islamic character. Texts on the Javanese alphabet, its history, and its many usages—prosaic as well as mystical—abound. A well-known example is found in the *Kridhaksara* texts telling the story of the creation of the Javanese alphabet by king Aji Saka, and go on to offer a mapping of the letters on the human body. In these texts it is clearly the Javanese script that is presented as possessing a unique character. And yet the Arabic script, coming with Islam, was imbued with authority and piety. How then was the importance of the Javanese script reconciled with the supremacy of a recently arrived and radically different script?

45. Russell Jones, "The Origins of the Malay Manuscript Tradition," in *Cultural Contacts and Textual Interpretation*, ed. C. D. Grijns and S. O. Robson, VKI, vol. 115 (Dordrecht and Cinnaminson: Foris Publications, 1986), 121–43.

46. Pigeaud, *Literature of Java*, 1:27. The family trees of Javanese rulers often portrayed a dual genealogy: on the right-hand side it stretched back to nabi Adam, and on the left hand side to the Hindu gods.

Since both scripts continued to be used and neither held complete sway in literary production, and since Islamic traditions did not counter but rather reinforced ideas about the centrality of writing, one way to consider the question is through exploring the creative combinations of the Javanese and Arabic letters within the literary tradition. These may be seen either as compromises between two potent scripts, or as ways of enhancing even further the power of the letters and their effects.

For example, within the *One Thousand Questions* written in Javanese script, Samud asks the Prophet about the revered letters (J. *aksara*) and their number, never stating explicitly which particular letters he is curious about. The reply, mapping the letters in *Kridhaksara*-style onto the human body while also connecting them with the days of the week, the five daily prayers, and the various prophets, concerns Arabic letters. Thus the Arabic letter *jim* is mapped onto the nose and the letter *hamza* (J. *ambyah*) on the soles of the feet.[47] As is often the case the letter *alif*—first in Arabic's sequence and initial in God's name—receives special attention and interpretation.[48] The text uses the words *aksara*, *sastra* (S. *akśara*, *śāstra*), and *hurup* (A. *ḥurūf*) alternately to refer to the Arabic letters. Although *alif* is mentioned also in the Malay and Tamil texts, the wider theme of the alphabet and its connections to time, history, ritual, and the physical body features only in the Javanese *One Thousand Questions* and underscores a preoccupation with the relationship of writing to the world. A further example of a combined use of the scripts appears in manuscripts written using them both, in which the scribe alternates between Javanese and pégon or Arabic. Manuscripts of this type are often written primarily in Javanese script, with particular words—like God's name—repeatedly appearing in Arabic script. In such cases it is clear that certain sacred names or expressions—perhaps considered untranslatable—were retained in Arabic, according a powerful presence to such terms. In other instances the pattern is inconsistent and more difficult to explain, yet nonetheless a mixture of scripts is employed.

An additional method used by Javanese scribes constituted a mirror image of adopting Arabic script with diacritical marks: adding such marks to existing Javanese letters to indicate foreign, usually Arabic sounds. Thus, for example, a Javanese *pa* with three dots above it would be read as Arabic *fa*, converting the Javanese pronunciation of *kapir* into the more Arabic-sounding *kafir* (infidel). This method further complicated the scriptural scene on Java

47. *Serat Suluk Samud Ibnu Salam*, Museum Sonobudoyo Library, Yogyakarta, 1898, MS. MSB P173a, c. 42, v. 12–c. 44, v. 20.
48. Ibid., c. 44, v. 20–c. 44, v. 23.

by introducing yet another innovative possibility of merging Arabic and Javanese writing.[49]

Just as it is difficult to postulate a clear division in the Javanese literature of the Islamic period by categorizing certain works according to script choice, there appears similarly to be no real dividing line between Islamic literature in Tamil or arwi when it comes to ideas and authors.[50] Why then the use of arwi in addition to the Tamil script? Beyond the significance of Arabic script as such, common to Muslim societies, in the case of Tamil there are certain identity issues, two aspects of which in particular seem to have played a major role. First, arwi added a considerable cultural dimension to a Muslim community that was in the minority and helped preserve that community's distinct social identity and religious character. Shu'ayb may have overstated the role of arwi when he wrote that "it is the testimony of history that, had it not been for *lisānul-Arwī*, Muslims in Sarandib and Tamil Nadu would probably have been swept away by rival cultural currents, as the Muslims constituted a mere seven percent of the total population,"[51] yet the assertion that arwi contributed significantly to a sense of Tamil-Muslim identity within the larger society is valid. The second aspect of this question—relevant to the nineteenth and early twentieth centuries—is related to the British colonial presence in the Tamil region. The notion that Tamil-speaking Muslims were not "proper" Muslims was common among the British and some Urdu-speaking Muslims, and it may have given the Tamil Muslim community an additional incentive to emphasize their close connection with Arabia and the Arabic language by producing arwi works.[52]

49. Interestingly, in the context of pointing to various similarities between Tamil and Javanese conceptions of script and language, in Tamil a similar method is followed. Several letters were added to the alphabet to indicate Sanskrit sounds (for example *ha*, *kṣa*), and dots are sometimes added to existing letters to express Arabic sounds. In both languages these diacritical marks are by no means used universally, and more often than not Arabic sounds are approximated by Tamil or Javanese letters.

50. Tschacher, *Islam in Tamil Nadu*, 61.

51. Shu'ayb 'Alim, *Arabic, Arwi and Persian in Sarandib and Tamil Nadu*, 91–92. The figure of 7 percent is from the Sri Lankan census of 1981.

52. Tschacher, *Islam in Tamil Nadu*, 59. In a preliminary finding on the differentiated use of script, Tschacher notes that in the nineteenth and twentieth centuries Arabic script was used mainly for religious prose works with a demotic character, while long narrative poems, literary productions of a more elite character, were typically printed using Tamil script. Torsten Tschacher, "Circulating Islam: Understanding Convergence and Divergence in the Islamic Traditions of Ma'bar and Nusantara," in *Islamic Connections: Muslim Societies in South and Southeast Asia*, ed. R. Michael Feener and Terenjit Sevea (Singapore: ISEAS, 2009), 54–55.

At another level, however, Tamil Muslims placed strong emphasis on their mother tongue and held its long literary history and tradition in high esteem. Even while arguing strongly for the superiority of adopting the Arabic script for Tamil, Shu'ayb stresses the purity and beauty of Tamil and the way in which arwi writing retained all the basic forms of the finest spoken and grammatical Tamil.[53] For many authors, writing in Tamil script meant one more link of continuity with a great tradition as they employed and reformulated Tamil genres, conventions, and styles for the creation of their Islamic works.

A common appreciation for the local language—whether Tamil or Javanese—should not be underestimated. In both cultures literary language and the local script used to write it were highly valued. In contrast, Ali Asani's discussion of literary works produced in Sindh between the early eighteenth and the mid nineteenth centuries paints a different picture. Asani states that in Sindh and north India the intelligentsia regarded only Persian and Arabic as appropriate for literature. The poetry produced was remarkable for drawing all of its symbols and metaphors from the "unseen and un-experienced sights, sounds and smells of Persia and central Asia," while completely rejecting Indian life and landscape as poetic resources.[54] North Indian vernaculars were thus viewed as unfit for literature and Indian life as inappropriate inspiration for creative works. When compared with Tamil and Javanese conceptions, a sharp contrast emerges in terms of attitudes toward local language, its legitimate use for literary purposes, and the localization of this literature within the region's physical and cultural landscapes. Retaining the scripts for Javanese and Tamil was one aspect of a reverence toward the local that did not diminish with the adoption of new beliefs and cosmopolitan literary forms.

Discussing the way Sanskrit was written in multiple scripts across the Sanskrit cosmopolis (and noting that Kālidāsa could have written the opening words of the *Raghuvaṃśa* in Javanese, Thai, or Sinhala script), Pollock writes that "perhaps no better sign than the graphic sign itself shows how clearly one could be in the Sanskrit cosmopolis and simultaneously remain at home."[55] As the examples of Tamil and Javanese suggest, these words ring true for many South and Southeast Asian Muslims in the Arabic cosmopolis

53. Shu'ayb 'Alim, *Arabic, Arwi and Persian in Sarandib and Tamil Nadu*, 89.

54. Ali Asani, "At the Crossroads of Indic and Iranian Civilizations: Sindhi Literary Culture," in *Literary Cultures in History: Reconstructions from South Asia*, ed. Sheldon Pollock (Berkeley and Los Angeles: University of California Press, 2003), 627.

55. Sheldon Pollock, *The Language of the Gods in the World of Men: Sanskrit, Culture, and Power in Premodern India* (Berkeley and Los Angeles: University of California Press, 2006), 274.

who composed and read Islamic works—many of which, like the *One Thousand Questions*, were shared amongst them, in their own local scripts. These writing traditions may at times have stood in tension with the use of Arabic script—as was likely the case when early scripts used for writing Malay were gradually abandoned, along with the associations and memories they carried. However, in many instances the use of two scripts seems to have been complementary and to have enabled a diverse field of literary production.

The employment of Arabic script in Tamil, Malay, and Javanese significantly enhanced other aspects of translation. Its use allowed for an easier and accurate rendering of important Arabic terminology; it sustained—as far as possible considering the vastly different sound systems—a correct pronunciation of Arabic words, thus decreasing the chance of misunderstanding and error; and it bestowed upon these South and Southeast Asian languages a presence that echoed that of the most sacred of languages, placing them on a par with many other Islamic languages and making their texts, including translated works, into revered objects.

The most important element of writing these languages using Arabic script had to do with the potential, and indeed inevitable, change that it enabled and facilitated in each language. Far from being only a technical—or even religious—maneuver, the use of a new script was bound to open up new possibilities, some expected, others surprising. The adoption of a new script was akin to translation in the guise of transliteration: it meant a change in the sequence of the letters, their number, and, perhaps most strikingly, the directionality of writing the language—from right to left rather then left to right, as had been previously done. Adopting a new script also meant including new letters, sounds, and modes of expression in one's own language, a process that is in itself a form of translation. This conversion of a familiar language into something novel—a new version of itself—points very concretely to a pivotal moment of change.

In another sense the adoption of Arabic signaled a defiance or rejection of translation. As with certain words or phrases that were left untranslated and consistently maintained in their Arabic form (like *kapir* or *munapik*), writing their own languages in the cosmopolitan Arabic script was a way for Muslims to insist on a connection to the foundational and irreplaceable language of Islam. Scripts, often viewed as technical devices in the service of meaning, are in fact sites of power: religious, social, and political. Writing in Arabic script infused Javanese, Malay, and Tamil with the power of a cosmopolitan, expanding, and divinely inspired civilization.

Employing a script considered cosmopolitan and potent for the writing of local languages in distant lands is neither an uncomplicated nor monolithic act. I would like to suggest that at the very moment that the Arabic script was conferring a certain aura of sanctity on South and Southeast Asian languages, that same Arabic script was itself being vernacularized: that in its contact with the local, the mundane, the immediate, it was changed and "normalized." And thus Arabic both consecrated the local language *and* was secularized in the process, at least when its script came to be used widely for nonreligious writings.[56]

The Arabic script constituted a key site of contact between the cosmopolitan Arabic and the vernacular languages that came to be written in it. Other overlapping and parallel contact zones flourished, as discussed throughout this chapter, in translated works, adapted genres, idiomatic phrases, Qur'anic citations, titles, names, rituals, and daily speech. For many of its users, Arabic was not only a religious or literary language. It was the revered language of the Qur'an and prayer used also for contemporary reflection and exchange. It was capable of offering inspiration, comfort, and courage, as evident from the following lines depicting the youth of Aceh under unrelenting Dutch siege, written by Snouck Hurgronje in 1901:

> The correspondence [among the youth] is carried out in Malay, mingled with Arabic expressions, or else entirely in Arabic, and the questions the young scholars ask each other in their hiding places in the mountains, and the books they borrow from each other serve to prove that science is not abandoned by them even there . . .[57]

Examining the roles and modes of Arabic in South and Southeast Asia is a complex and vast task that remains far from finished. Yet there is no doubt that Arabic—at many levels and in various forms—emerged as an integral element of Islamic culture in these regions. It was studied and revered and used to compose many kinds of works, ranging from the sacred to the philosophical

56. Although my focus here has been on Arabic within a cosmopolitan, transregional sphere prior to the emergence of nation states, its importance remained great also in the era of nationalist struggles and state formation. Especially for Indonesia and Malaysia, with their Muslim majorities, the question of how ideas about Islam and Arabic played out in the choice and development of national languages is fascinating. For brief but suggestive comments in this direction, see Michael F. Laffan, *Islamic Nationhood and Colonial Indonesia: The Umma Below the Winds* (London and New York: Routledge Curzon, 2003), 236–38.

57. Translated and cited in van Ronkel, ed., *Supplement to the Catalogue of the Arabic Manuscripts Preserved in the Museum of the Batavia Society of Arts and Sciences*, ii.

to the mundane. In addition to being employed as such, Arabic also figured as a prominent force that was to transform the languages of Muslim communities across these regions. Arabic was a unifying and standardizing force across the cosmopolis, while the local, Arabicized forms of language used by Muslims of different regions were manifestations or variations of that authoritative, cosmopolitan language.

7

Conversion to Islam and the *Book of One Thousand Questions*

As a fundamental component of the Arabic cosmopolis, Arabic, in its multiple appearances and trajectories, was closely tied to conversion to Islam. The dissemination, translation, and adaptation of Arabic sources went hand in hand with an ongoing Islamization in South and Southeast Asia. Just as the spread of Arabic beyond Arabia was a complicated and at times elusive endeavor, so the phenomenon of conversion is not easily defined and summarized, embodying as it does social, cultural, political and economic aspects as well as personal, spiritual, and psychological dimensions. Conversion can take place in the private and public spheres, and, in its temporal dimension, it has been viewed both as a gradual process and a one-time transformative event.

Possible causes or incentives for conversion to Islam have long been debated, yielding multiple perspectives. For example, Dale cited sixteenth-century evidence from Kerala suggesting that Indians converted to Islam to escape rigid caste boundaries;[1] Levtzion argued that trade and credit opportunities among the Hausa of Nigeria depended on one's allegiance to Islam, creating a strong economic incentive;[2] Khan discussed the performance of miracles as a way to attract followers to Islam in different regions of India;[3]

1. Stephen F. Dale, "Trade, Conversion, and the Growth of the Islamic Community in Kerala," in *Religious Conversion in India: Modes, Motivations, and Meanings*, ed. Rowena Robinson and Sathianathan Clarke (Oxford: Oxford University Press, 2003), 60.
2. Nehemia Levtzion, "Toward a Comparative Study of Islamization," in *Conversion to Islam*, ed. Nehemia Levtzion (New York and London: Holmes and Meier, 1979), 15.
3. Dominique-Sila Khan, "Diverting the Ganges: The Nizari Ismaili Model of Conversion in South Asia," in *Religious Conversion in India*, ed. Robinson and Clarke, 37.

and Eaton attributed an accelerated pace of Islamization in the seventeenth and eighteenth centuries in eastern Bengal to Mughal land policies.[4] Dutton, in pointing to the shifting nature of understandings of conversion, noted that although in early accounts dreams played an important role, most modern theories stress material benefits gained, or harm avoided, as justifying the decision to convert.[5]

Various methodologies have been employed in the study of conversion, in attempts to discern when, where, and how individuals and communities turned to Islam and how such change affected their lives. Archeological and architectural findings have proven important, including the location, design, and function of early tombstones, mosques, holy shrines, and pilgrimage sites.[6] Anthropological studies of Muslim communities in the present and attempts to record their historical traditions regarding Islamization have also been significant, as have analyses of accounts by travelers like Ibn Baṭṭūṭa and Tomé Pires, who visited societies in the process of conversion. Naming practices have been suggested as a key to tracing conversion patterns in particular societies.[7]

Assessing the history of conversion through written accounts of those who experienced or witnessed it in the past would have been enlightening. However, in his pioneering essay "Toward a Comparative Study of Islamization," Levtzion noted that because historiography developed only gradually with the establishment of the new religion and the rise of a class of literati, an absence of contemporary local Islamic sources for the earliest period of the spread of Islam is a problem common to all parts of the Muslim world.[8] Data from later periods, too, does not always lend itself to the drawing of firm conclusions. For example, Peter Hardy, in studying the development of ideas about conversion to Islam in India over time, noted that conversion was little

4. Richard Eaton, "Who Are the Bengal Muslims? Conversion and Islamization in Bengal," in *Religious Conversion in India*, ed. Robinson and Clarke, 84.

5. Yasin Dutton, "Conversion to Islam: The Qur'anic Paradigm," *Religious Conversion: Contemporary Practices and Controversies*, ed. Christopher Lamb and Darrol M. Bryant (London and New York: Cassell, 1999), 161.

6. Mehrdad Shokoohy, *Muslim Architecture of South India: The Sultanate of Ma'bar and the Traditions of Maritime Settlers on the Malabar and Coromandel Coasts* (*Tamil Nadu, Kerala and Goa*) (London: Routledge, 2003).

7. Richard W. Bulliet, *Conversion to Islam in the Medieval Period* (Cambridge and London: Harvard University Press, 1979).

8. Levtzion, "Toward a Comparative Study of Islamization," 2.

mentioned before the twentieth century, when it became a major focus of the unfolding debates leading to British India's partition along religious lines.[9]

One thing that is clear, despite all the still open questions regarding conversion to Islam in the Arabic cosmopolis, is that the process was far from simple, linear, or uniform. This complexity is reflected also in the narrative traditions that recall, recount, and explain the processes of localized conversion. In this chapter my emphasis, within the necessarily variegated and nuanced big picture, is on the ways in which conversion to Islam was represented in the *Book of One Thousand Questions* and additional sources in Javanese, Malay, and Tamil, and the claims—both discursive and intuitive—regarding the adoption of a new religion put forth through such literature.

The gap between local and outside views of conversion processes was often significant, as the cases of India and Indonesia exemplify. Local perceptions of conversion will be addressed below. As for early European observers, they commonly asserted that the conversion to Islam of the inhabitants of India and Indonesia was flawed and incomplete.[10] The religion practiced in these regions, according to such accounts, was an unauthentic, distorted, diluted form of Islam that did not live up to its supposed standards in Arabia and to the ideal religion portrayed in textual sources. Islam was often described as a "thin veneer" overlaying the older, local religious ideas and practices that preceded it. This view—based in large part on observations revealing a fluid and open belief system rather than a highly codified and exclusive one—implied a population that was at best naïve and at worst hypocritical or unable to distinguish right from wrong. A classic example is found in Sir Thomas Stamford Raffles's influential work, *The History of Java*. In it he wrote that Islam "has taken but little root in the hearts of the Javans." Discussing the role of Arabic, he claimed that "the Javan language owes little or nothing to the Arabic. . . . The language, as well as the ancient institutions of the country, have been but little affected by the conversion. The Javan language was

9. Peter Hardy, "Modern European and Muslim Explanations of Conversion to Islam in South Asia: A Preliminary Survey of the Literature," in *Conversion to Islam*, ed. Nehemia Levtzion (New York: Holmes and Meier, 1979), 88.

10. In an article first published in 1985, Roff pointedly remarked on a later manifestation of a similar phenomenon: "There seems to have been an extraordinary desire on the part of Western social science observers to diminish, conceptually, the place and role of the religion and culture of Islam, now and in the past, in Southeast Asian societies." William R. Roff, *Studies on Islam and Society in Southeast Asia* (Singapore: National University of Singapore, 2009), 3. Recent scholarship by Azra, Hadler, Feener, Florida, Laffan, Millie, Ricklefs, Roff, Tagliacozzo and others has done much to address this problem.

abundantly copious before the introduction of Arabic literature, and had few or no deficiencies to be supplied."[11] Almost a century earlier Valentijn wrote of the Muslims in the Moluccas that they were "the most ignorant and least trained in the principles of their religion and know very little of the content of the Koran."[12]

Such perceptions, as well as other, more nuanced ones, were related in turn to a fascination with origins: what was the source of a particular form of Islam, and from where did it arrive? A hierarchy that posited (visible) Arab influence as the most authentic and more highly considered than other influences (Persian, Turkish, and for Indonesia, Indian) played a role in determining who may be a "good Muslim." In this context both South Indian and Indonesian Islam was perceived negatively. In India, seeing Muslims live and work in highly segregated social strata reminiscent of the caste system, visit "Hindu" shrines to ask for blessings, dress as their non-Muslim neighbors, and follow many of the same rituals created the impression that they were ignorant of their own religion; in Java ongoing ancestor and spirit worship, the many Hindu-Buddhist monuments dotting the landscape, and the popular shadow puppet performances recounting Mahabharata tales contributed to a similar view. But, as several scholars have noted, the religious world of the seventeenth to nineteenth centuries in these regions was much less fixed and limited than the one imagined by contemporary Europeans. It was, as some observers remarked, a site of unusual tolerance and exchange.[13] In addition, many of the links to Arabic and Arabian Islam that did exist were obscured, hidden from European view in religious books, educational institutions of traditional learning, guru-disciple lineages, trade and family contacts.

The diverse meanings assigned to conversion and its aftermath and the

11. Thomas Stamford Raffles, *The History of Java in Two Volumes with Maps and Plates*, 2 vols. (1817; London and New York: Oxford in Asia Historical Reprints, Oxford University Press, 1965), 2:4 and 1:371.

12. Cited in A. Karel Steenbrink, *Dutch Colonialism and Indonesian Islam: Contacts and Conflicts, 1596–1950*, trans. C. Steenbrink and H. Jansen (Amsterdam: Rodopi, 1993), 39. The view of Islam as an artificial veneer which, consequently, should not pose a political and security threat to European rule conflicted with coexisting notions of Islam as a dangerous, treacherous, and threatening element in nineteenth-century colonial India and Java. For a literary exploration of this anxiety, see Louis Couperus, *The Hidden Force*, ed. E. M. Beekman, trans. Alexander Teixeira de Mattos (Amherst: University of Massachusetts Press, 1985).

13. Susan Bayly, *Saints, Goddesses and Kings: Muslims and Christians in South Indian Society, 1700–1900* (Cambridge: Cambridge University Press, 1989); Richard M. Eaton, *The Rise of Islam and the Bengal Frontier, 1204–1760* (New Delhi: Oxford University Press, 2000); Merle Calvin Ricklefs, "Six Centuries of Islamization in Java," in *Conversion to Islam*, ed. Nehemia Levtzion (New York and London: Holmes and Meier, 1979).

multiple perspectives through which it has been viewed and studied suggest it should be best analyzed in a specific context, with the contours of its particular study explicitly stated. In the Arabic cosmopolis of South and Southeast Asia processes of conversion to Islam were central and, at an early stage, were the driving cause of the cosmopolis's emergence and expansion. Conversion did not "just happen" in the Arabic cosmopolis, nor was it limited as a force to the religious or political spheres: it inspired a remarkable creative output whose products brought increasing numbers of people into contact with Islam and its traditions. Among such creative and influential works were those that recounted conversions to Islam in various periods and places.

Such textual sources, often based on oral narratives, offer a glimpse of a community's understanding of its own past: how and why it embraced Islam. In these accounts, attitudes and beliefs tend to appear in condensed form, making such stories, at the very least, rich sources for studying how conversion was imagined and represented to successive generations. Some scholars have treated such "local myths" with suspicion, deeming them fantastic tales that can reveal little if anything of historical developments.[14] Others have heavily relied on them to explain particular features of local Islamic expression. T. W Arnold, for example, in his 1896 *The Preaching of Islam: A History of the Propagation of the Muslim Faith*, claimed that Islam spread largely due to peaceful missionary efforts. Determined persuasion, often against all odds, coupled with untiring energy and an employment of "superior intelligence and civilization" allowed its missionaries to achieve great success, according to this narrative. Arnold reached his conclusions based in large part on the many local conversion stories he collected, especially those depicting the deeds and charisma of Sufi saints.[15] In the following discussion I take the view that conversion narratives should neither be discarded as fantasy nor uncritically embraced but rather explored for the variety of perspectives and insights their study offers.

Within a discussion of narratives recounting earlier conversions, I focus first and foremost on the *One Thousand Questions* as a little-explored source for the study of conceptions about, and representations of, conversion to Islam among Tamil, Malay, and, in particular, Javanese Muslims. I examine how the *One Thousand Questions* tellings portray conversion during the Prophet's

14. C. C. Berg, "Javanese Historiography: A Synopsis of Its Evolution," in *Historians of South East Asia*, ed. D. G. E. Hall (London: Oxford University Press, 1961), 22.
15. T. W. Arnold, *The Preaching of Islam: A History of the Propagation of the Muslim Faith* (1896; Lahore: Sh. Muhammad Ashraf, 1961), 369; see esp. chapter 12 (367–412), "The Spread of Islam in the Malay Archipelago."

time and what they reveal about later, local notions of conversion, especially when read side by side with additional important conversion narratives from across the Arabic cosmopolis. Studying various narratives of conversion is important to understanding the representation of a process that was heterogeneous, long, and very complex. It allows us to follow this process as it related to changing societies grounded in particular cultural, linguistic, and historical circumstances.[16] The purpose is not so much to try and salvage definitive historical details from a text like the *One Thousand Questions* but to understand how the distant developments portrayed in it were remembered, shaping later notions of the past as well as contemporary identities. Another goal is to further the discussion about the interconnectedness of conversion and translation.

Translation is, in itself, a form of conversion. I have examined how Javanese, Malay, and Tamil were converted, or translated into new forms of themselves through their contact with Arabic and, along with it, Islam's religious and literary legacies. Religious conversion gave rise to translation endeavors, and the products of these in turn encouraged further conversion. Exploring the ways conversion was depicted and justified when the *One Thousand Questions* was translated into Malay, Tamil, and Javanese highlights the complex relationships between translation, conversion to Islam, and the later, literary representations of that conversion.

Representations of Conversion in One Thousand Questions *Tellings*

The *One Thousand Questions* narrates a conversion in seventh-century Arabia, set in the early days of Islam, when the Prophet persuaded many to embrace his new religion. One such encounter and its outcome, as represented in the story, evokes an atmosphere of openness to change and of intellectual and religious engagement of the highest order. Above all, the encounter points

16. In the locales under consideration, Southeast India and Java, as well as the larger regions of which they are a part, conversion to Christianity was often occurring simultaneously with, or consecutively to, conversion to Islam. Few comparative studies of these processes have been attempted, although such a perspective may shed light on both forms of conversion. For South India see Bayly, *Saints, Goddesses and Kings*, and H. Bjerrum, "Muslim Literature in Tamil," *The Moslem World* 15 (1925): 115–18. For Southeast Asia see Anthony Reid, "Islamization and Christianization in Southeast Asia: The Critical Phase, 1550–1650," in *Southeast Asia in the Early Modern Era*, ed. Anthony Reid (Ithaca: Cornell University Press, 1993), 151–79, and, most recently, Merle Calvin Ricklefs, *Polarising Javanese Society: Islamic and Other Visions (C. 1830–1930)* (Singapore: National University of Singapore Press), 105–25.

to the Prophet's supreme, irresistible Truth. The Javanese, Malay, and Tamil tellings replicate much of this early depiction by recounting the old story, and especially by retaining the Prophet's role within it, thus setting the successful conversion in an early and authentic historical context.

However, in the retellings of the *One Thousand Questions* many centuries after the events depicted in its narrative, in communities distant from the birthplace of Islam, we also encounter a different story: the translated tellings still present their audiences with the tale of an early conversion that was facilitated long ago by the Prophet himself, but, as that story absorbed elements more specific to the receiving cultures, it became also a commentary on local notions of conversion, suggesting through the winding path of questions and replies preceding its climactic embrace of Islam what a particular culture (or author/sect within it), at a particular historical moment, viewed as the crucial elements of belief and practice justifying a religious transformation.

It is here that the tension between studying an imported story depicting a foreign past, such as the *One Thousand Questions*, and reading it as expressing local perceptions is, at least partially, resolved. An emphasis on details added and omitted in translation—what Becker, citing Ortega y Gasset, called the "deficiencies and exuberances" apparent in any form of language use[17]—brings out the particularities of how the story was told differently as it traveled and calls for an interpretation of such difference. Reading a narrative comparatively across languages and time allows for that added value of particularity to shine through.

Considering conversion during the Prophet's time, as depicted in the *One Thousand Questions*, it appears as an uncomplicated matter.[18] In the Latin translation of 1143, based on an early Arabic telling, the ritual simplicity of the affair is notable. After Muhammad tells Ibnu Salam that on the Last Day the dead reside between paradise and hell, Ibnu Salam declares that the Prophet has won him over and asks to be received as a professor of his religion. Then, with his pronouncement of the shahāda, the book ends. In the Arabic *Kitāb Masā'il* the final lines are similar, with Muhammad offering the same reply about the dead, Abdullah reciting the shahāda and then proclaiming his faith in paradise, hell, and the Final Hour.[19]

17. A. L. Becker, *Beyond Translation: Essays Toward a Modern Philology* (Ann Arbor: University of Michigan Press, 1995), 231–32.

18. A similar simplicity of ritual in early conversions across the Middle East and North Africa is discussed in Bulliet, *Conversion to Islam in the Medieval Period*, 10.

19. *Kitāb Masā'il Sayyidī 'Abdallāh Bin Salām Lin-Nabī* (Cairo: Al-Yusufiya, ca. 1920), 15.

The ending variously changes in later Arabic tellings. Some contain a speech by Ibnu Salam in which he goes through the main points of the new faith. There is also the addition that Muhammad gives him the new name 'Abdullah and that he becomes one of the greatest *ṣaḥāba*, or companions of the Prophet.[20]

In the later Tamil, Malay, and Javanese tellings only a short list of conversion scene elements appear. The single most important among them is the recitation of the shahāda. Whether Ibnu Salam is told to recite it in Arabic or in Javanese, whether it is elaborated word for word in Arabic, in translation, or both, or whether it is only mentioned referentially, reciting it is an ever-present obligation the convert must fulfill. This is by no means a unique feature in conversion depictions but rather has been central to them since early on, including those accounts specifically pertaining to Ibnu Salam's early biographical notes in Arabic.[21] Another recurring element is the awe expressed by Ibnu Salam at the ability of the Prophet to answer so many questions, on so many matters, correctly, a feat that has brought about the conviction that he must be a true prophet, providing the rationale for conversion.

Conferring a new name on the convert is another element common to the conversion scene in those tellings in which Abdullah Ibnu Salam was not the protagonist's name from the start. When only named Samud throughout the text, he receives the full name Abdullah Ibnu Salam at the end; when named Samud Ibnu Salam throughout, the Arab name Abdullah—meaning "God's servant," also the name of the Prophet's father—is given to him at conversion. The Muslim custom of giving a convert a new name is common also to Judaism and Christianity, signifying a new birth and a new life—and an erasing of a former identity—within the adopted religion. In the case of Samud not only the new name but also the old one may be significant to the discussion of conversion.

Although the origin of the name Samud, as well as the reason for its selection for the protagonist in Javanese and Malay texts, is uncertain, it may well be related to the Qur'anic tribe Thamūd. Indeed, in some Javanese manuscripts written in pégon, a script that incorporates the Arabic letter *thā*, the

20. Guillaume Frederic Pijper, *Het boek der duizend vragen* (Leiden: E. J. Brill, 1924), 52–53. Pijper does not mention what, in this case, was the previous name of the Jewish leader, but in the 1143 manuscript he has a Hebrew name—Abdia iben Salon (H. Ovadia ben Shalom?), and so the change may have been from that name to a (very similar in sound and meaning) Arabic one.

21. Wensinck cites hadith reports of Ibnu Salam's recitation of the shahāda in front of the Jews as acknowledgment of his conversion to Islam as evidence for the very early use of the shahāda by converts. Arent Jan Wensinck, *The Muslim Creed* (1932; Cambridge: Cambridge University Press, 1995), 33.

name appears as Thamūd rather than the Javanized form Samud. The prosperous tribe was one of evil, sinful people who did not heed the warning of Ṣāliḥ, the prophet sent to divert them from their path of idol worship, slave ownership, and disregard for the poor. The members of Thamūd were offered many opportunities to repent and mend their ways. Interestingly, these included their asking questions and requesting proof of Ṣāliḥ, who replied with exceeding impatience because of their dishonesty and false promises. Finally, when it was clear they would not heed his words, God brought upon them a violent earthquake that decimated their fields, homes, and lives.[22]

Samud of the *One Thousand Questions* may well be linked by several underlying associations with the Qur'anic Thamūd. He appears quite different in character, yet similarities both in theme and in the text's ultimate message are apparent: Samud is initially non-Muslim, one who might potentially accept the true faith but has not yet done so; he and his followers may be associated in the minds of those who hear his name with a distrustful and skeptical people; he questions the Prophet repeatedly, requesting wisdom as proof of his Truth, and is not quickly persuaded; the oneness of God is central to the unfolding debate and the crux of his decision to convert, as expressed in his uttering the shahāda, proclaiming Allah as the only God; the meeting between him and Muhammad is preordained, destined to happen, as Ṣāliḥ was destined to approach the Thamūd, asking that they repent. Finally, the Qur'anic warning reminding readers of the Thamūd's rejection of their prophet and their resulting fate—"Thamūd denied their Lord. Gone are the people of Thamūd" (Qur'an 11:68)—was transformed in the *One Thousand Questions* into a different, reverse kind of reminder, invoking in its audience a recollection of Samud's acceptance of Islam and its fruitful outcome.

It is very likely that conversion scenes in the *One Thousand Questions*, while reflecting early traditions, also incorporated views and assumptions about conversion that were prevalent during the time of translating and transmitting the texts. These views, in turn, represent particular angles on conversion within Muslim societies with diverse perspectives and affiliations. In order to contextualize and assess particular representations of conversion, it is instructive to examine conversion scenes within the Tamil, Malay, and Javanese tellings of the *One Thousand Questions* and to compare them with other representations of conversion from their respective regions' literary cultures.

In Tamil, when the Prophet completes his final answer to Ibnu Salam, one addressing heaven, hell, and the Day of Judgment, he recounts how he

22. Qur'an 11:60–67. Kholilah Marhiyanto, *Kisah Teladan 25 Nabi dan Rasul* (Surabaya: Arkola, 1995), 60–78.

himself previously received the replies to Ibnu Salam's questions from God by way of Jipuṟayīl. Then he adds, in a summary of all he had spoken:

Truth is truth
A lie is a lie.
They cannot be combined into one,
Like paddy and weeds in the field.
[Mixing] meanness with sweet truth
Is akin to bitter sugarcane.
(*AM*, v. 1042)

After this assertion, the final canto of the story, in which the conversion of Ibnu Salam and his followers is depicted, begins:

Aptullā speaks:
God is one.
We stood in the thick darkness of *kupir*
You spoke truth and good about *maṟai*.
You are the guru.
There are many religions
You've conquered them all.
O faultless *napī*
Teacher of *tīn*
Our hearts are full of light
Like rain [coming down] on a tree
Your hands grant
O king.
(*AM*, v. 1043)

There are several powerful motifs in this brief verse: the first is Ibnu Salam's admission of God's oneness, central to Islam, with which he opens his speech. Then comes the metaphor of going from the darkness of infidelity (T. *kupir*, from A. *kufr*) to the light of Islam. Maṟai, the Tamil word for veda, which can also mean "secret, mystery" and which was used throughout the text to refer to the Qur'an, appears somewhat ambiguously here and reaffirms the specifically Tamil characteristics of the Jew and the Prophet in this telling. In this word and others is found a microcosm of the combinations and alternatives offered by the use of Tamil and Arabic, as Muhammad is addressed as both prophet (A. *nabī*) and guru, teacher of maṟai and of tīn (A. *dīn*, the Religion, Islam). Finally, the Prophet is likened to rain falling on a tree, giver of life, growth, and prosperity, a common and appropriate simile in the Tamil region where the monsoon rains fall after months of dryness and heat.

Ibnu Salam then goes on to describe Muhammad's greatness, to glorify the beauty of his city, and to praise the Prophet for showing him and his people the right path. He acknowledges that the Prophet gave answers to all one thousand questions he posed and uses the phrase "we *saw* and believed"—perhaps in deference to the shahāda—before bowing down and touching Muhammad's feet.[23] Then comes his explicit request to become a Muslim:

> To Man's sanctuary he prayed,
> Touching His feet.
> Aptullā spoke:
> O great prophet of Allah
> Victorious one
> With the seven hundred who joined me
> At this time
> To the faith glowing with great virtue
> Accept me,
> He said.[24]

Before Muhammad can reply to this request, Ibnu Salam interjects again, seemingly unable to refrain from more praise and wonder at the Prophet's ability to answer his questions, numerous and diverse as they were:

> The planets, the sun, the moon
> Paradise, the eight atmospheres, the size of God's throne
> The seven skies, Mount Kopukā,
> The mountains, the lakes,
> The horned beast, the netherworld, the seven hells,
> Of all these wonders that I questioned
> You spoke.
> Muhammad! King of truth![25]

23. *AM*, v. 1049. The Arabic word *shahāda* derives from the Arabic root which means "to see," "to bear witness."

24. *AM*, v. 1050. The Tamil literally reads "give me your reply" (rather than acceptance), which is in line with the entire prior debate in which Abdullah was requesting answers from the Prophet. The word *aṟam*, translated here as "virtue," which could also be translated as "moral conduct," "law," "religious path," and more, is the Tamil translation of Sanskrit *dharma*. "Faith" here translates Arabic *imān*.

25. *AM*, v. 1051. There is an obscure word in the list of topics, after the seven hells are mentioned.

In a second direct request Ibnu Salam then asks the Prophet to "cause him to be in a condition of tīn."[26] With his hand held by Muhammad's two beautiful palms he recites the profession of faith (T. *kalimā*) along with his seven hundred followers, and all "come into a relationship with Islam." I present here a literal and somewhat awkward translation of the Tamil, that could even more literally be rendered as "in Islam their contact became" or "in Islam they arrived, came near, united," so as to emphasize the nuances of this particular portrayal of conversion. There is no single verb that captures it but rather a series of expressions. An additional phrasing appears in the following stanza when the poet, speaking of the events unfolding, says the Jews had *iculāmil ottaṉarkaḷ*, that is "adapted to Islam," "consented to Islam" or "were just like Muslims" (*AM*, v. 1053). The depiction then continues with everyone rejoicing, speaking of the great event taking place, and celebrating it with a feast and prayer.

Ibnu Salam and his followers are then briefly described as faithful believers (T. *mūminkaḷ*) as they hold prayer beads, extol God, and recite the Muslim prayers, worshipping at Muhammad's lotus feet. After acknowledging their debt to him they ask to take leave and return to their land (T. *Kaipar*), for which he grants them permission. The text ends with the journey home—depicted in a single verse—on which those who realized the Prophet's truth convinced others to follow them in professing the faith.

This depiction underscores several elements: the profession of faith is not spelled out but only mentioned by name, referentially; part of accepting Islam involves touching the Prophet, holding his hands, and worshipping at his feet, pointing to physical contact as a means to tap his special powers; ritual elements—congregational prayer, holding the *tacupīku* beads (used to recount God's names), the feast—are significant, as the converts join a community that rejoices with them; Muhammad is praised repeatedly for his wisdom and potency; there is a stress on Ibnu Salam's followers converting with him, only to convert yet others on the way home, thus multiplying the number of conversions in time and space; finally, we find no single term for embracing the new faith, although the word "Islam," not often used throughout the Tamil *Book of One Thousand Questions*, appears in several expressions that capture the moment of change.

This conversion story differs from many others told in the Tamil region and beyond due to its spatial dimensions. In it the converter, Muhammad, remains in place while those wishing to convert approach him, with the potential converts often depicted as having traveled a great distance. In many

26. *Tīṉ nilaiyil ākkum eṉavē*, *AM*, v. 1052.

popular accounts, conversely, a teacher or holy man is said to have come from afar to introduce the local population to Islam.

Conversion Narratives: A Comparative Perspective

This trope of travel is central to the biography of a key Tamil converting figure, Shāhūl Hamītu, who passed away just before the Tamil *Āyira Macalā* was composed. His father, said to have come from Baghdad to northern India, where he married a local woman, was a descendant of the famed Muḥyīuddīn 'Abdul Qādir al-Jīlānī (1077–1166). The story of Shāhūl Hamītu incorporates many elements common to Tamil accounts of the conceptions, births, and childhoods of holy men, including a dream his mother had anticipating his arrival, miracles he performed while still in the womb, and the visit by several prophets hours after his birth. Born in 1504, Shāhūl Hamītu was destined to "instill Islam and *ilmu tasawuf* (mysticism) and *ilmu tauhīd* (the unity of Allah) in the Indian subcontinent and the adjoining countries."[27]

His life continued in the trajectory of one who was bound to become a great teacher and saint. He cured the sick while still a young child, recited the entire Qur'an by the age of eight, and subdued fierce tigers with the gaze of his eyes. As he grew older he set upon a quest for mystical knowledge, studying with great masters. He traveled widely, going all the way to Khorasan, Istanbul, Baghdad, and Mecca, converting thieves and kings alike. On his return trip from Jeddah to India he boarded a ship to Kerala, from where he eventually reached Tamil Nadu and traveled among its towns. In Tanjore the Hindu king, after Shāhūl Hamītu saved him from an evil spell, granted him land in Nagore, along the southern Coromandel coast, where he remained for the rest of his life and where his shrine still stands.

Shāhūl Hamītu is known as a crucial figure in the history of the propagation of Islam in the region, and his miraculous deeds are recounted in many epics and poems. As an agent of conversion he is remembered both as a highly knowledgeable teacher—master of Qur'an, hadith, and mystical Qādirī thought—as well as one who could cure the sick, feed the hungry, grant wishes, and change misery into peace. There are elements in the stories about him that closely resemble those that appear in tales of Hindu saints of the same region—like the ever-filling food bowl, meeting sages in a mountain cave—and he is known to have performed specific miracles to aid those who were neither Muslims nor potential converts. For example, once several

27. Shaik Hasan Sahib S. A Qadhiri, *The Divine Light of Nagore* (Nagore: Habeen and Fahira Publishers, 1998), 5–9. The summary below draws on Qadhiri, 10–43.

of his followers, overcome by hunger, are said to have slaughtered and eaten a bull from one of the Hindu temples. The temple-goers complained to Shāhūl Hamītu, who collected the bull's bones and performed a miracle that brought the bull back to life.[28]

Other examples of such saints abound. The narrative frames stressed in these biographies are those of mobility and travel—the saint either coming from distant places or going to them—in order to spread Muslim faith, practice, and learning. The Sufi tendencies of these men, performing miraculous deeds, living in the jungle, encountering other mystics, and distancing themselves from the householder's life, are central to their portrayal. In these respects the Tamil *One Thousand Questions*, although incorporating many local elements, differs from typical conversion stories. Although it does refer to miracles performed in the past and to the Prophet's exceptional powers, its stress on a single, static site—centered on the teacher—for the entire conversion process and its clear delineation of Muslim and non-Muslim practices, make for a story that offers a certain alternative to popular images of conversion.

In Javanese historiography as well the Samud narratives represent a non-dominant strain addressing the topic of conversion to Islam, one that is significant in offering an alternative "version of conversion." This alternative narrates conversion as a discursive, peaceful, and effective process, highlighting persuasion and devotion as the major elements that affect the decision to embrace Islam. This dimension can be gleaned by examining a conversion scene from a Javanese *Book of One Thousand Questions* that is in many ways typical of other tellings in this language, then turning for comparison to the dominant tradition of the *wali sanga*, the nine "saints" credited with introducing Islam to Java.

The conversion scene I address appears in an 1823 Javanese *One Thousand Questions* fragment inscribed in Surakarta.[29] Samud asks the Prophet to be his witness, or allow him to bear witness, that he is acknowledging

28. Shāhul Hamītu died in 1570 and has been viewed, down to the present, as a source of blessings and power to Muslims and non-Muslims alike. Not only did his miracles extend to neighboring communities, but he is also famed for having once saved a Dutch ship that was on its way from Nagore to Batavia, an incident that is retold in J. M. Cāli, *Tamiḻakattu Tarkākkaḷ* (Madras: Nur Patippakam, 1981), 34.

29. *Samud* fragment in *Para Nabi Nerangaken Bab Rijal Saha Sanès-Sanèsipun*, Karaton Surakarta Library, Surakarta, 1823 [?], MS. KS 339.1. See Nancy K. Florida, *Javanese Literature in Surakarta Manuscripts*, vol. 2: *Manuscripts of the Mangkunagaran Palace* (Ithaca: Cornell University Press, 2000), 192.

Muhammad's religion, without mentioning Islam as such (Samud fragment, 65). Muhammad responds to Samud's claim by praising God, saying *alhamdullilah*, in a Javanese version of the Arabic. He blesses Samud and asks him to repeat the confession of faith that is then recited, first in Arabic, then in Javanese. Samud's followers, here referred to as *sabat*—the title bestowed on the Prophet's companions—"follow in Islam" (J. *tumut Islam*).

The archangel Jabarail then tells the Prophet to acknowledge Samud for all time, in this world and the next, and the Prophet does so. The Javanese verb used by Jabarail, *ngaku*, can mean not simply to acknowledge in a general sense but to acknowledge, recognize, or adopt a person as one's relative, and this is likely what Jabarail is proposing here.[30] Incorporating this familial element adds a dimension of great depth to the conversion because Samud would not only be converting to Islam but, in doing so, would enter the Prophet's closest circle of kin as a revered elder. The genealogy of the protagonist—and by extension of the story—would thus become the most authentic possible not only for passing down the Prophet's words but for doing so via a man who—due to his great learning and authority—became a revered figure even for Muhammad.

Abdullah, Samud's new name which is also the name of Muhammad's father who died before Muhammad was born, is symbolic in this context. It presents Samud at story's end as replacing Muhammad's biological father—whom he never knew—connecting the Prophet and the converted Jewish leader in the closest of ties. It also symbolizes the process through which Judaism preceded Islam, "gave birth" to it, and inspired it. Ultimately, however, Islam prevailed and Muhammad was recognized as the final prophet. This outcome is echoed in several *One Thousand Questions* texts in the question about the son who is stronger than his father—a son who is born of a father whom he is later able to overcome—as Muhammad overcomes Samud in the debate.[31] This motive—of acknowledging Samud as father to the Prophet—appears only in Javanese tellings where the name change (from Samud to Abdullah) also consistently appears and is most pronounced.

The text notes yet again that Samud's companions all became Muslim (J. *samya Islam sedaya*) and that all were in awe of Muhammad for answering

30. In this case the Javanese would mean, literally, "it is fitting O Messenger that Samud / you acknowledge, adopt as a father," thus telling the Prophet to view Samud as his father, or elder, from this day on.

31. The reply is that iron—extracted from stone—can crush the stone when made into a tool. Interestingly in this example the son overcomes the father by force.

the questions. The companions then return home to their land, which is not indicated by name. No mention is made of Abdullah leaving with them, nor of their spreading their new faith to others.

This description of conversion thus far is similar to those found in other Javanese *One Thousand Questions* tellings, stressing as it does Samud's acceptance of Muhammad's teachings and the Prophet's acceptance of the new convert. The depiction is brief yet quite powerful. Samud's decision is based entirely on conviction, seemingly free of social, economic, or political motivations, portrayed as complete, whole-hearted, pure. Serving as the background against which this *One Thousand Questions* portrayal of conversion must be examined are the more dominant, pervasive Javanese stories that narrate early conversion to Islam.

There is no doubt that the most popular, well-known, and oft-cited stories depicting and explaining Java's conversion are those pertaining to the lives and deeds of the *wali sanga*, the nine "saints" said to have introduced Islam to Java and to have overseen the initial stages of the conversion of its population. Since the sources on the walis are vast, only select elements are highlighted here; these are meant, first and foremost, to point to additional Javanese literary traditions of conversion to Islam besides the *One Thousand Questions*, traditions whose dissemination has been quite remarkable. In many cases they too, like the *One Thousand Questions* tellings, were composed—at least in written form—during a period when the conversion of Java to Islam was largely accomplished, a fact that affected their tone and emphases.

The wali accounts do not always explicitly or implicitly connect conversion in Arabia to conversion on Java, as the *One Thousand Questions* does, but rather focus on the specific challenges and successes of converting Java to Islam. And yet, such links to Arabia do occasionally occur, and they are significant for the authority they bestow on a Javanese wali. The *Serat Walisana*, an undated manuscript copied in the Pakualam court of Yogyakarta that combines histories of the walis with many other moral tales, depicts the walis gathered after the Friday prayers when a bundle suddenly appears, containing a garment and a letter from the Prophet.[32] The letter instructs Sunan Kalijaga to wear the garment in this world and the next, as a sign of inheriting the Prophet's role. The Javanese reads *mengko sira genti ingsun*—"you shall be my successor"—and corresponds to the Arabic meaning of the title *khalīfa*, used by the Prophet's early successors and by subsequent Muslim rulers. The Prophet thus personally designates a Javanese successor for himself.

32. *Serat Walisana*, Pura Pakualaman Library, Yogyakarta, MS. PP Pi. 32.

The importance of genealogy—biological or symbolic—for Islamic traditions is again witnessed here. As Samud in the *One Thousand Questions* was acknowledged by Muhammad (and proclaimed as his father), so Sunan Kalijaga was granted the status of khalīfah by the Prophet himself. He is destined to continue Muhammad's role and mission—conversion being central to them—in the Javanese context. The texts accord both leaders unquestionable legitimacy.

The wali corpus is made up of multiple stories. The walis, whose narratives echo with others in South and Southeast Asia, were active during the fifteenth and sixteenth centuries as teachers, healers, and miracle workers who, sometimes coming from afar and sometimes of local descent, lived in different parts of Java and introduced the population to Islamic beliefs and institutions. Although usually referred to as the *wali sanga*—the nine walis—traditions of their number and identity vary by region, period, and affiliation. Their tolerance toward pre- or non-Islamic Javanese culture and their attempts to curb the spread of pantheistic teachings are two central elements of their hagiographies.

Accounts of the walis and their attitudes are far from monolithic. Nevertheless, with some exceptions, the walis are depicted as having accepted the continuing practice of such earlier traditions as the *wayang* shadow puppet theater and gamelan music. Furthermore, they are even sometimes credited with introducing to Java, or inventing, some of the "most Javanese" cultural elements, like the local tellings of the Ramayana or the *macapat* verse forms. Such attributions suggest that the walis are remembered as supporting a form of Islam that recognized and respected prior tradition in the belief that more adherents would be gained if they were not forced to leave behind older ways. Tendencies toward openness, flexibility, and the acceptance of local customs, common to Sufi teachers elsewhere, were evident in their leadership.

Depictions so far examined suggest the walis followed a strategy of propagating Islam by peaceful means, notably education and persuasion, similar to the core elements of the conversion process appearing in the *One Thousand Questions*. However, this was not the only trajectory of their actions. As recounted in Javanese chronicles, two major struggles were at hand for Islamic leaders on Java. The first was directed outward, in an effort to strengthen the hold of Islam where it had already taken root and to extend it further on Java. Majapahit, the last Hindu-Buddhist kingdom on Java, was attacked by disciples of Sunan Ampèl and Sunan Giri. Demak, the most important Islamic state on Java's north coast in the early sixteenth century, where the walis are said to have earlier collectively erected a mosque aligned with the mosque at Mecca, conquered the Hindu-Buddhist kingdom at Kediri with additional conquests reaching major ports and many inland areas of East Java.[33] Gresik, on Java's coast, a major international trading center in the fifteenth century, became also an important center of Islam when Sunan Giri established his headquarters nearby.[34] These examples, and others, point to the participation of the walis, their descendents, and followers in the political and military campaigns that were involved in establishing Islam on Java.

The second struggle was internal, involving conflicts over power amongst the walis. The latter focused on how far to accommodate local traditions and, above all, on the types of knowledge to be revealed to the masses. It is for a struggle surrounding this issue that their internal rivalries are best known.

At the center of the controversy stood the figure of Sèh Siti Jenar. This well-known and ambiguously regarded wali's biography has been compared with that of al-Ḥallāj, the famous martyr executed in tenth-century Baghdad for the perceived heresy of proclaiming himself one with God.[35] According to some tellings of this story Siti Jenar was sentenced to death by the council of walis for teaching secret religious doctrines to the uninitiated that included what may be interpreted as a similar heresy. The conflict did not surround the essence of the teachings but rather centered on the other walis' claim that access to them by the unqualified would have serious moral, social, and political ramifications. The Siti Jenar episode is important in suggesting that—as one would expect with regard to such a complicated process—not all conversion efforts on Java came about in a peaceful, conciliatory manner. It adds a dimension of danger, threat, struggle, and aggression to a story that is often imagined as lacking such elements.[36]

The account addresses not a context where Muslims come as foreigners to convert a local population by force but rather the execution of a religious figure by his co-religionists through which a violent element within the tradition is openly acknowledged and widely recounted to this day. Whereas the foreign element of conversion on Java is usually represented as peaceful, associated with trade and traveling mystics, the wali stories combine both peaceful and violent trends and in this may be most persuasive. Social, doctrinal, and political issues emerge in these tales, underscoring the perceived danger

33. Merle Calvin Ricklefs, *A History of Modern Indonesia since C. 1200*, 3d ed. (Basingstoke: Palgrave, 2001), 37.

34. Ibid. Sunan Giri founded a line of spiritual teachers that lasted until 1680, the only wali who had successors to his authority.

35. On Siti Jenar's popularity and for a telling of the story from Banjar, see Steenbrink, *Beberapa Aspek Tentang Islam di Indonesia Abad Ke-19*, 198.

36. For the causes for such perceptions see Ricklefs, *A History of Modern Indonesia since C. 1200*, 12–13.

of chaos, misunderstanding, and neglect of ritual and social-religious practices if Siti Jenar were allowed to have his way.

Does Javanese literature offer alternative depictions of conversion that differ from the way the very popular—and mostly positive—hagiographies of the walis relate the process, stories that will convey some of the more tumultuous elements found in the Siti Jenar episode? It certainly does. It offers evidence for the existence of differing viewpoints on conversion complementing the traditions of the walis, alternatives which depict a more aggressive and competitive process. In the text translated as *An Early Javanese Code of Muslim Ethics*, partaking in "holy war" (J. *perang sabil*) is presented as an obligation; the *Babad Tanah Jawi* depicts the majority's acceptance of Islam and the minority's subsequent flight to the mountains; the 1873 *Babad Kedhiri* depicts the destruction of ancient books under Islam; the late nineteenth-century *Serat Dermagandhul* rejects Islam as foreign to Java, forced upon the island's inhabitants through violent means.[37]

The *Serat Pandhita Raib* narratives, inscribed in Surakarta in 1792, also narrate an alternative to peaceful conversion that is closely associated with the story of Samud.[38] Pandhita Raib was a teacher of Judaism and powerful warrior in the country of Kebar who lured already converted kings away from Islam. The story relates the Prophet's struggle against, and eventual victory over, Pandhita Raib. As Ibnu Salam was known in many tellings of the *One Thousand Questions* to have come to meet the Prophet from this same land (A. *Khaybar*), an important Jewish center in seventh-century Arabia, this story of competition and war between Muhammad and a Jewish leader from that locale offers a different perspective on—and a different resolution to—the theme at the heart of the Samud texts.

This episode and others, deriving ultimately from Arabic or Persian sources, depict an explicitly non-peaceful way communities were converted during the time of the Prophet. The Jewish element and Khaybar as a site of conflict and confrontation strengthen the impression that, when posed side

37. See, respectively G. W. J. Drewes, *An Early Javanese Code of Muslim Ethics*, Bibliotheca Indonesica, vol. 18 (The Hague: Martinus Nijhoff, 1978), 17; Sapardi Djoko Damono and Sonya Sondakh, eds., *Babad Tanah Jawi: Mitologi, Legenda, Folklor, dan Kisah Raja-Raja Jawa* (Jakarta: Amanah-Lontar, 2004), 1:115, on Islam's takeover in Java; Ricklefs, *Polarising Javanese Society*, 185, on the burning of books, and G. W. J. Drewes, "The Struggle between Javanism and Islam as Illustrated in the Serat Dermagandul," *BKI* 122.3 (1966): 309–65 on the rejection of Islam as foreign. Additional, non-wali accounts of political instability and warfare are discussed in Nancy J. Smith- Hefner, "A Social History of Language Change in Highland East Java," *Journal of Asian Studies* 48.2 (1989): 260.

38. *Serat Pandhita Raib*, Mangkunagaran Library, Surakarta, 1792, copied 1842, MS. MN 297.

by side with the Samud story, these Javanized narratives offer an alternative to thinking about the process and meaning of conversion to Islam, both during the Prophet's time and, much later, on Java.

The Javanese One Thousand Questions *and the Wali Traditions*

Returning to the Samud fragment, we have seen that it contains many of the elements typical of Javanese *One Thousand Questions* tellings depicting conversion to Islam, such as, for example, Samud's recital of the confession of faith and his acquiring a new name. Above all it is typical of this textual tradition in the way it narrates conversion as peaceful, facilitated by respect, conviction, and persuasion. However, this particular telling is also linked to the more dominant—and not necessarily peaceful—traditions by its genealogy of transmission. Although this is a non-representative instance within the *One Thousand Questions* tradition, it is worth delving into precisely because the connection between the different traditions of conversion allows for a more complicated assessment of both.

What is unique about the 1823 Samud fragment is the way it ties in to a larger narrative of Javanese conversion traditions, highlighting some ambiguities about the process that other tellings do not make evident. Although many Javanese works do not mention their genealogy of transmission, names of authors, and translators or places of inscription, this text, which does incorporate certain identifying details, allows a glimpse into possible readings of the *One Thousand Questions* as a Javanese conversion story.

This telling of the Samud story explicitly connects the *One Thousand Questions* to the more dominant Javanese conversion narratives of the walis. The link is achieved by its attribution to Makedum Rahmat, otherwise known as Radèn Rahmat or Sunan Ampèl, who is said to have "Javanized" it, making it accessible to a local audience.[39] Radèn Rahmat is remembered as a central figure in the conversion of Java to Islam in the fifteenth century. The text reads:

> This rendering in Javanese of the parable
> The Samud Ibnu Salam
> Accordingly has as its beginning
> Makedum Rahmat

39. Radèn Rahmat's title *makedum* (A. *makhdūm*) is the same as that possessed by Mullāmiyā Cayitu Makutum, the scholar who provided Vaṇṇaparimaḷappulavar with materials for composing his Tamil *One Thousand Questions.*

Who settled in Ngampèl Gadhing
As for his settling
This was by the will of his forebears
And so this was copied
With the permission of Champa's king
Thus came it to be

For granted surpassing knowledge
Was Sunan Rahmat of Ngampèl Denta
Greater than all his peers
And so he who requested this
Was Lord Sunan Rahmat
Who dwelled in Ngampèl Denta
Was permitted by his father
And having been permitted by his father
Then set forth on his voyage to the island of Java
To become a principal saint.
(Samud fragment, 66)

Contextualizing this passage and Sunan Ampèl's role in it deserves some elaboration, which is best accomplished by turning to the *Babad Tanah Jawi* corpus. This chronicle, which exists in multiple tellings, recounts Javanese history from the days of Adam to the eighteenth-century kings of Mataram, including the transition from Hindu-Buddhist rule to the rise of Islamic states on Java. Although its earliest known tellings were written long after the events depicted, it provides a glimpse—at the very least—of certain ways in which the spread of Islam on Java was remembered.[40]

According to the 1874 Meinsma edition of the *Babad Tanah Jawi*, Radèn Rahmat was the son of Ibrahim Asmarakandi (of Samarkand in central Asia) and Dewi Candrawulan, the princess of Champa. Ibrahim convinced Champa's king and all his people to embrace Islam.[41] Radèn Rahmat's aunt from

40. Babad (literally "to clear the forest") is a genre of Javanese history-writing. There are numerous copies of the *Babad* in Javanese literature collections.

41. J. J. Ras, ed., *Babad Tanah Djawi: De prozaversie van Ngabehi Kertapradja voor het eerst uitgegeven door J. J. Meinsma* (Dordrecht: Foris Publications, 1987), 18. Unless noted otherwise, the following summary of Radèn Rahmat's biography is based on R. Sofwan, H. Wasit, and H. Mundiri, *Islamisasi di Jawa: Walisongo, Penyebar Islam di Jawa Menurut Penuturan Babad* (Yogyakarta: Pustaka Pelajar, 2000), 35–58, and A. Rahimsyah, *Biografi dan Legenda Wali Sanga dan Para Ulama Penerus Perjuangannya* (Surabaya: Penerbit Indah, 1997), 59–68.

Champa married Prabu Brawijaya, the king of Majapahit, the last Hindu-Buddhist kingdom on Java. Radèn Rahmat was given permission by his father to travel to Java with his brother and cousin to visit his aunt. Upon arrival he was granted land in Ngampèl Denta, a seaside region of Majapahit's capital Surabaya, in eastern Java, and married a Javanese woman, the sister of the future Sunan Kalijaga.[42] His first deed was to erect a mosque, then a *pesantren*, that developed into a center for the propagation of Islam. He came to be known by the honorific *sunan* (Sunan Ampèl, for his dwelling place) and was considered a wali.

Sunan Ampèl was allowed to propagate Islam peacefully all over the Majapahit lands, although his uncle by marriage, King Brawijaya, did not himself wish to convert. After the death of Sheikh Maulana Malik Ibrahim, traditionally considered eldest among the walis, he became the leader of Javanese Muslims.

In the Javanese Samud story, the "Javanization" of which is credited to Sunan Ampèl, key elements of this history appear in the brief lines toward the text's conclusion: Sunan Ampèl is mentioned initially by his title *makdum*, then as *sunan*; his familial connection as son of the king of Champa is stressed, as is his asking permission to journey to Java; the land he was granted on the island, the site known as Ngampèl Denta or Ngampèl Gadhing, is mentioned three times, emphasizing the locale as crucial to his biography, the place from which he began his endeavors as a teacher and propagator of Islam. Although conversion is not explicitly discussed, Sunan Ampèl is depicted as having noble ancestors, as possessing superior knowledge (J. *ngèlmi kang linuwih*, often referring to esoteric knowledge), and finally, as one whose voyage to Java culminated in his becoming a prominent wali, leader, and guru for the emerging Muslim community of East Java.

It is intriguing, and in some ways fitting, that the Samud story be associated with such a figure. Sunan Ampèl, of royal foreign lineage but with familial ties to a great Javanese kingdom that would soon fall to the forces of the new faith, is often depicted as a major figure in bringing Islam to Java. He is portrayed as an important religious scholar, second leader and elder of the walis whose deeds encompassed converting, teaching, and the erection of mosques and *pesantren* at a time when these were new to Java, making the Surabaya region the first on the island to convert. These actions, as well as sending out messengers to other areas and his marriage to a daughter of the local elite, were all strategies in the peaceful introduction of the new religion. The way the association is made in the text between Sunan Ampèl and the

42. Ras, ed., *Babad Tanah Djawi*, 20.

Samud story, especially through the use of the words *ngibarat* (metaphor, parable) and *teladha* (example, model), points to the dialogue between Ibnu Salam and the Prophet—with its elements of persuasion, inspiration, and devotion—as a desired model for the activities of Sunan Ampèl and others on Java.[43]

But the association is neither this simple nor exemplary. Just as Islam's spread on Java was a complicated and multifaceted process, so Sunan Ampèl's story itself is more complex than it first appears. Among his many deeds was the acceptance as close disciple of Radèn Patah, son of Brawijaya by his second wife and the man who would attack Majapahit, bringing about the demise of his own father, Sunan Ampèl's uncle.[44] Radèn Patah would come to rule Demak, the first Muslim kingdom on Java. The close relationship between the two men points to an ambiguity regarding the atmosphere and attitudes in this early conversion stage as understood by Javanese writers of history. Radèn Patah refused to pay homage to King Brawijaya on the grounds that it was improper for a Muslim to bow to an infidel.[45] This act of defiance was followed by a revolt in which he and his brother led all local Muslims in an attack on Majapahit. Brawijaya, who wished to see his son one more time, did so and then disappeared in a flash of light and a thundering sound. The last Hindu-Buddhist kingdom on Java had fallen and Sunan Ampèl then proclaimed Radèn Patah as heir to the throne.[46]

Radèn Patah is remembered both as an important figure in the Islamic history of Java and as one who brought about the death or vanishing of his own father, betraying the land's supreme ruler, the king, and destroying a kingdom that, although weakening gradually by the late fifteenth or early sixteenth century when it collapsed, had a grand past closely associated with a Javanese age of power and influence. Sunan Ampèl's close ties to him—as guru, family elder, and supporter of his rule—complicated the notion that this early bearer of Islam to Java represented peaceful means alone.

Acknowledging this ambivalence, I suggest that connecting Sunan Ampèl with the story of Samud and the Prophet is significant to thinking about images of conversion on Java and their relationship to elements of tolerance. Crediting the introduction of the Javanese *One Thousand Questions* to Radèn

43. The word *teladha* appears immediately after the passage cited above, referring to the text (or manuscript) and its owner: "The one possessing this example is a man of Palembang by the name pun Sabarodin." Samud fragment, 66.

44. Ras, ed., *Babad Tanah Djawi*, 22; Rahimsyah, *Biografi dan Legenda Wali Sanga dan Para Ulama Penerus Perjuangannya*, 73–75.

45. Ras, ed., *Babad Tanah Djawi*, 29.

46. Ibid., 30.

Rahmat connected an ancient story of conversion to Islam in an atmosphere of persuasion to a well-known local figure who followed the same path. It suggested a parallel between early conversions in Arabia and initial conversion on Java. Such links made the story relevant and credible, echoing with familiar traditions. Its genealogy stretched from the Prophet Muhammad through a Javanese wali to the present of its audience.

These episodes that stress the personalities and strategies of both the king and the wali on Java as well as the Prophet and Jewish leader in Arabia are necessarily part of a larger picture. The wider frame of a narrative as grand as the conversion of Java or Arabia includes instances of violence, coercion, and struggles for political and economic domination. As the process of conversion in the Prophet's time is known to have entailed military campaigns and elements of aggression, so no doubt did the spread of Islam on Java and elsewhere in the region take many forms. By linking the stories of Sunan Ampèl and Samud, the Javanese author may have wished to stress Sunan Ampèl's early career of persuasion and tolerance. The connection, however, rather than point to that initial stage alone, underscores the ambiguities of conversion and the various and contradictory personalities involved and strategies entailed.

When considering representations of conversion to Islam in Javanese, the question of course arises as to who is, and is not, represented in surviving chronicles, most of which were written long after the initial stages of the process. Even through the obscuring filter of time and selective sources, the ambiguity regarding the means and attitudes involved in conversion is clear, an ambiguity suggested in the biography of Sunan Ampèl, who began his proselytizing career under the wings of his non-Muslim uncle the king, and continued it by supporting that same king's heir who refused to bow to his infidel father.

The link made in a single example of the Javanese *One Thousand Questions* between this important Javanese wali and the Samud story echoes with many of the events that shaped Islam's beginnings on Java: the mid-fifteenth century fall of Majapahit to internal, Muslim-Javanese forces was a turning point of immense importance in Javanese history; memories of flight and destruction have survived despite the dominant tradition's allegiance to Islam; and memories of the walis' power struggles amongst themselves and execution of a member of their council were formative in shaping the tone and tendencies of Javanese Islam. It may well be that the emphasis on a peaceful process of conversion is the result of developments that occurred much later than actual events and of ideologies that favored such a version. Without detracting from the importance of the violent events and dynamics depicted in some chronicles, it is significant that a major theme of recollections of the conversion of Java is its gradual and to a large extent peaceful character. I have suggested that the inclusion of the Samud story among depictions of Javanese conversions offers a particular perspective on the matter that is also in line with many others in Javanese literature. Its link to Sunan Ampèl, with his acceptance by Brawijaya and the freedom he had to convert, build mosques, and teach, created within its own tale of persuasion an echo of an episode imagined as one of openness, dialogue, and tolerance in Java—one central to remembered conversions—and tied this episode to one of a similar nature and magnitude during the Prophet's time.

Associating a wali with Samud's tale is an exception within the *One Thousand Questions* corpus in Javanese. However, in the background is not an attribution of the text's additional manuscripts to sources other than the walis but rather an almost complete silence regarding the arrival of the Samud story to Java. Therefore, this particular telling opens a window to the critically important realm of textual and religious genealogy, often obscured by the typical anonymity of authors and transmitters of such texts. The walis' association to the *One Thousand Questions* corpus is significant, above all, in inviting reflection as to how the different traditions of conversion to Islam do and do not relate to one another, and what each conveys about history, especially how the past is remembered, contested, and retold.

Malay Conversion Narratives in South and Southeast Asia

In a mode similar to the Javanese, Malay *One Thousand Questions* tellings do not widely vary in the way Ibnu Salam's conversion is depicted. In the *Hikayat Seribu Masalah* Abdullah's final question to the Prophet concerns the prophets' ages, the reply to which ends with Muhammad's own age, sixty-three.[47] Abdullah then acknowledges that his heart is now "clear" (M. *terang hati*), realizing God's oneness and Muhammad as His messenger. He kisses the Prophet and tells him he will "enter the Muslim religion" (M. *masuk agama Islam*) along with his seven hundred followers. The term employed for conversion is common and implies one's entry into a new domain of action and beliefs, a stepping out of the old and *into* the new. This may well be modeled on the phrase appearing in sura 110 of the Qur'an depicting the multitudes entering God's faith after Islam's victory (A. *yadkhulūna fī dīni Allāh*). Abdullah and his followers are then taught the profession of faith (M. *kalimat syahadat*) and all recite it in Arabic along with several additional, untranslated Arabic verses. Then the Prophet teaches them to recite a verse in praise of

47. Muhammad did indeed live to be sixty-three (570–622). This reply suggests that the dialogue and conversion are taking place not long before the Prophet's death.

God. The number of followers—seven hundred—is mentioned several times, as if to stress the large number of Jews that have been persuaded by Muhammad. Abdullah returns home to Khaybar, and several among his followers, who also return, are said to "bring along" the Prophet's religion, signifying their contribution to further dissemination of the faith.

An additional conversion portrayed within the main conversion story of this Malay *One Thousand Questions* is worthy of note. In a section discussing the calamities to be imposed by Dajjal, the "Anti-Christ," Muhammad tells Abdullah of four worldly safe havens that Dajjal is incapable of destroying. When the believers gather in these places—Mecca, Medina, Jerusalem, and Mt. Sinai—Jesus (M. *nabi Isa*) will descend to their aid. Dajjal will be defeated and the believers freed (*HSM*, 76). Muhammad continues his reply to Abdullah, unprompted. He tells of his grandchild, the *imam mahdi* who will then emerge and will be surrounded by Jesus and all Muslims, together praying and praising God.[48] The mahdi shall be crowned king and "all Muslim communities will be strong" (*HSM*, 76). The hypocrites (M. *munafik*) gather from all directions and convert to Islam. Three days later the mahdi will die and will be buried, followed by the disaster of Yajuj and Majuj's arrival on earth. The mahdi's appearance provides an interlude of hope and strength between two great periods of upheaval. And indeed, his role is traditionally to reveal himself in times of distress and need. What I wish to stress here, however, is how an additional conversion finds its way into the story.

The munafik, as discussed, were the group most resistant to true acceptance of Islam, as they feigned conversion but at heart were nonbelievers. Confronting them proved a difficult struggle even for the Prophet. As portrayed here, only someone of the mahdi's caliber could persuade them to become true Muslims. Within the ongoing dialogue between Abdullah and Muhammad and the recurring references to the munafik and their future torments in hell, this anecdote suggests that even they—the worst of the Prophet's enemies—posses the potential to repent and choose the right path through conversion. This anecdote sends a message and provides an example to Abdullah and his followers as they continue listening to the Prophet, on the way to their own transformative decision.

Many other conversion stories have circulated in the Malay-speaking world. Jones summarized Malay literary representations related to the spread

48. The imam mahdi (A. *imām mahdī*) is a redeemer/Messiah who will come to earth before the Last Day.

of Islam, citing accounts from 1300 to 1600.[49] In most of these accounts the coming of Islam is associated directly with the conversion of local rulers, unlike the case of the Majapahit king of Java. The convert is an existing ruler rather than a Muslim usurper or foreign conqueror: religion changed, not the state or its ruler. In these stories conversion agents tend to come from afar, often from Mecca or Baghdad. The Prophet appears in several instances, either in person or via a dream or vision. For example, in a fifteenth-century account from Malacca, the ruler has a dream in which Muhammad arrives by ship and orders him to recite the shahāda. The king awakens to discover that he has been circumcised and converts along with his people. The Qur'an too was significant to conversions, even when not literally understood. In an account from Ternate, where Islam was introduced as early as 1500, a Javanese merchant reads the Qur'an to the people, and they sense a new, magical force in the book, leading them to grow interested in learning to understand it.[50] Many of these elements, like the encounter with the Prophet, the awe at his words, the initial conversion of a ruler or leader followed by his people, the role of the supernatural or divine, the recitation of Arabic verses and especially the shahāda, are common to these stories and the *One Thousand Questions*. They suggest that these were among the fundamental building blocks of how conversion was understood and narrated in the Malay world.

The depiction of abrupt conversions under the influence of powerful events are similar to wider trends apparent in Islamic hagiography, complementing and contradicting historical evidence of a gradual process. In this respect too we find a connection to the *One Thousand Questions* that can be read both as an "instant" conversion occurring after a single debate between Ibnu Salam and the Prophet or as a drawn out, ongoing process of acquiring knowledge and serving a guru.

A remarkable 1897 Malay manuscript from Sri Lanka testifies further to the persistence of circulating conversion narratives within the Arabic cosmopolis of South and Southeast Asia. The *Hikayat Tuan Gusti*, narrated in Malay written in jawi script on South Asian soil not far from the site where, according to Arab traditions, Adam is said to have fallen from the heavens to earth, recounts the biography of one of the nine Javanese walis, Sunan Giri, employing it to retell the story of Java's Islamization. In these combined attributes the *Hikayat* attests to complex and protracted transmission

49. Russell Jones, "Ten Conversion Myths from Indonesia," in *Conversion to Islam*, ed. Nehemia Levtzion (New York and London: Holmes and Meier, 1979), 133–58.
50. Ibid., 136–37, 152.

patterns that have resulted in interconnected images and echoes of earlier conversions.[51]

The *Hikayat Tuan Gusti* may well represent the farthest limits of the circulation in manuscript form of the wali tales. Sunan Giri (ascribed the honorific Javanese titles *radèn* and *gusti* as well as the Malay *tuan* throughout) is portrayed as the son of the Arabian sheikh Muḥīddīn. The sheikh, by virtue of his powers of intercession, averted a calamity about to befall the kingdom of Palembang and in return was given the king's daughter in marriage. He later returned to Arabia, and the princess, who had converted to Islam, died in childbirth. Palembang's king feared his infant grandson, whose face glowed like the full moon, and put him in a basket on the river (in a motif familiar from the biblical story of Moses as well as the Javanese chronicles of the Prophet's uncle Ménak). Thus sent away, the grandson was found and raised by a wealthy merchant woman. The boy grew into a man exhibiting many of the characteristics typical of the walis and other Muslim saints: travelling widely, interceding on behalf of the needy, performing miracles, marrying a local princess, and propagating Islam.

The portrayal of Sunan Giri as the son of sheikh Muḥīddīn is suggestive. The "original" Muḥīddīn (A. *Muḥyīuddīn*, "reviver of religion") was of course Ibn al-'Arabī (d. 1240), but the epithet is also widely associated, as mentioned, with the greatest of all Muslim saints, 'Abdul Qādir al-Jīlānī. Although several of the walis are said to have had foreign, and most notably Arab, fathers or ancestors, the intimate connection in this telling between Sunan Giri and a figure of such supreme importance in Muslim history and culture is striking. In addition, as a descendent of sheikh Muḥīddīn, himself a great preacher of Islam, Sunan Giri's genealogy stretches back to the Prophet Muhammad, as was the case for Shāhūl Hamītu, also valorized as the sheikh's descendent. The appearance of this motif in a Sri Lankan manuscript may reflect its Javanese source, as Javanese biographies of the sheikh circulated in Central Java and were especially popular in the western part of the island. In that region the tradition of reciting the sheikh's deeds in Sundanese, still popular today, was based on at least two sources: an Arabic translation of a Persian book written in Ahmadabad and dating to the fourteenth century, and the Sundanese *Layang Seh* manuscripts.[52] Portraying Sunan Giri as sheikh Muḥīddīn's

51. The discussion below is based on Subidara Mursid, *Hikayat Tuan Gusti*, 1897. Hussainmiya Collection, Department of National Archives, Colombo. Microfilm reel 182. The author self-identifies as a retiree of the Ceylon Rifle Regiment.

52. Abdul Qadir al-Jaelani, *Celebration of the Desires through the Narration of the Deeds (Manaqib) of the Crown of Saints and the Conviving Beacon among Allah's Beloved Friends*, trans. Julian Millie (Queenscliff: Joseph Helmi, 2003), 11.

son may also be attributed to close contacts between the Malay and Tamil-Muslim communities in Sri Lanka, as the sheikh was a central focus of devotion among Tamil Muslims in south India and Sri Lanka, and the subject of a wide array of Tamil literary works since at least the seventeenth century.[53] According to localized hagiographical traditions, sheikh Muḥīddīn traveled to places like Tamil Nadu, Sri Lanka, and Java during his many years of wandering and asceticism before returning to Baghdad at the age of forty, in which case he could have fathered Sunan Giri along the way.

The *Hikayat Tuan Gusti* stresses several conversion elements repeatedly while remaining silent on others. The erection of mosques, prayer (both communal and individual), the recital of the shahāda, and the complete shunning of idolatry are consistently upheld. The latter in particular is highlighted when the narrative opens with an idol worshipped by the Palembang king falling to the ground and shattering, signifying the false god's impotence and an approaching doom for the nonbelievers. Throughout the *Hikayat* different communities encountered by Sunan Giri and his representatives are reminded to refrain from resorting to idolatry. This tendency is reminiscent of one encountered in the Tamil *One Thousand Questions*, where Muslims are warned of worshipping idols of stone and copper as God, and it may reflect the author's concerns in late nineteenth-century Buddhist-majority Sri Lanka projected on an earlier, imagined Java. The belief in, or devotion to, the Prophet is also emphasized (M. *beriman kepada nabi kita Muhammad*), as is the adoption of a new name upon conversion. For example, when the Palembang princess Dewi Aranadani converts before marrying the sheikh, she is bestowed the name Siti Jini.

War, violence, and a threat toward those who refuse to convert are significant in this telling. For instance, when the great infidel king of Kartasuru (likely Kartasura) sends a messenger to demand that Sunan Giri pay him tribute, the messenger is told to convert but refuses, only to be humiliated and sent back. The king is furious, gathers many allies and a large army and charges at Giri. The Sunan calls upon God for help and a great swarm of bees appears, attacking the approaching forces. After the king is killed, Sunan Giri announces that any enemy caught should be bound but not put to death unless refusing to accept Islam. The people of Kartasuru joyfully agree to convert and return to their land along with two hundred teachers, leaders,

53. Susan Elizabeth Schomburg, "'Reviving Religion': The Qādirī Sufi Order, Popular Devotion to Sufi Saint Muḥyīuddīn 'Abdul Qādir al-Gīlanī, and Processes of 'Islamization' in Tamil Nadu and Sri Lanka" (Ph.D. diss., Harvard University, 2003). On pages 375–463 Schomburg discusses no less than fourteen Tamil genres in which works on the saint were composed.

and muezzins from Giri, who will teach them the five pillars of Islam, how to build mosques, and how to recite the shahāda. The *Hikayat* contains several such episodes, all portraying an acceptance of Islam after military defeat and under circumstances of significant threat.

An anxiety about the possibility of a reversal of faith—of converts reverting to old ways—is palpable in the *Hikayat*. In several instances audiences made up of those who had converted under the influence (spiritual or military) of Sunan Giri are reminded not to go back on their commitment. This is true for both kings and their subjects, as when the king, ministers, and people of Majapahit listen to Sunan Giri's confidante, Sunan Panji, preach at the mosque on Friday, warning them not to forget or forsake Islam, after which they promise to remain loyal to the new religion. This sense of doubt or insecurity regarding the depth of the conversion process is perhaps related to the imposed acceptance of Islam as depicted in the *Hikayat* or, once again, a reflection of the Muslim community's sense of vulnerability living as a minority within Sri Lankan society.

The genealogy of the *Hikayat* is unknown. Some of its elements are very similar to those appearing in Javanese tellings of Sunan Giri's biography. Interestingly, and despite its popularity amongst the Malays of Sri Lanka, its narrative is not traceable to any known Malay literary work from across Southeast Asia.[54] Whether this manuscript exemplar is a copy of an older text, brought to Sri Lanka in the early eighteenth century by Javanese exiles, or whether it was introduced there in later years, its presence and content are suggestive of an ongoing circulation of conversion narratives in the Arabic cosmopolis and their susceptibility to contemporary and differentiated reinterpretation.

The One Thousand Questions *and Conversion to Islam*

An analysis of depictions of conversion to Islam in *One Thousand Questions* tellings in Javanese, Tamil, and Malay, as well as alternative portrayals of conversion in literary sources in these languages, shows that the *One Thousand Questions* exhibits some elements that are common to other, widely circulated stories. In some ways, however, the *One Thousand Questions* differs from these traditions. In all three languages most conversion stories revolve around travel—at least insofar as the teacher comes from elsewhere—and miraculous deeds, as well as the establishment by converters of certain religious institu-

54. B. A. Hussainmiya, *Orang Rejimen: The Malays of the Ceylon Rifle Regiment* (Bangi: Universiti Kebangsaan Malaysia, 1990), 137.

tions. Boundaries between Muslim and non-Muslim practices are often not clearly defined. In these respects the *One Thousand Questions* offers an alternative, complementary way to think about the conversion process: some mobility is involved, although by the disciple rather than the teacher, who remains in one place. The entire debate—analogous to a conversion process, whether swift or gradual—takes place in a static environment and is centered on the exhibition of persuasive knowledge. Through this body of knowledge, it is often explicated how Muslims do differ from others and why they should. Beyond reflecting a much older tradition of conversion in Arabia, South and Southeast Asian tellings of the *One Thousand Questions* point to an enduring relevance of this particular story for perceptions of conversion, despite the distance in space and time.

The translation and dissemination of such a text in its localized forms was a sign of Islam's successful incorporation on these distant shores. Eaton concluded his book on Islamization in Bengal by saying that "what made Islam in Bengal not only historically successful but a continuing vital social reality has been its capacity to adapt to the land and the culture of its people, even while transforming both."[55] These words ring equally true for the broader regions of the Arabic cosmopolis, as the transmission of texts like the *One Thousand Questions* transformed the religious landscapes while being localized into particular circumstances of language, culture, and conversion histories.

It is intriguing—in the context of the eighteenth- and nineteenth-century Malay-Indonesian world, and earlier for South India—to ask how the *One Thousand Questions* addressed people who were not potential converts but Muslims. Although the *One Thousand Questions* could certainly have been used to introduce new converts to Islam, the majority of its audience was probably already Muslim, perhaps for several generations, when encountering the story. What did a story about conversion aim to highlight under such circumstances?

The *One Thousand Questions* certainly had a didactic purpose. Both for newly converted Muslims wishing to understand more of their people's history and faith, and for those living in long-converted communities, the text offered a starting point for discussion and debate on a wide array of topics and terminology. Consequently it could always be approached anew and did not lose its relevance. Related to these didactic aims was the presentation of a hierarchy of authority through the story, highlighting teachers and religious scholars as the providers of answers to queries stemming both from

55. Richard M. Eaton, *The Rise of Islam and the Bengal Frontier, 1204–1760* (New Delhi: Oxford University Press, 2000), 315.

everyday situations and from deep philosophical meditations arising in the context of religious life. Although the Prophet himself was no longer present to provide guidance to contemporary audiences, the institution of guru and disciple, known in India and the Archipelago in pre-Islamic times (S. *guru-śiṣya*), remained indispensible once Islam was adopted, and it was reinforced further by influential networks of foreign and local *'ulamā*. The *One Thousand Questions* stresses the irreplaceable relationship between a disciple and his teacher, without which true knowledge cannot be attained.

But assigning only a didactic purpose to the *One Thousand Questions* within processes of conversion and the strengthening of Muslim belief across the Arabic cosmopolis is too narrow a role: the work had an impact on linguistic change and on the extent to which popular stories of prophets circulated; it offered guidance, restated the justifications for becoming or remaining a practicing Muslim, and propagated a model of embracing Islam by persuasion; in addition, it enhanced community-building by supplying a complex web of intertextual sources in the local language to which people could relate, and which tied them to the broader cosmopolis in their part of the world and, beyond it, to the universal *umma*. All these roles—effected and enhanced by the translation of this and similar texts—contributed to a process of ongoing Islamization.

In regions where the *One Thousand Questions* and similar texts circulated, processes of translation and religious conversion were strongly intertwined. Conversion to Islam meant, in part, the translation of stories from Arabic or Persian into Tamil, Malay, and Javanese. Connected, overlapping stories like those depicting episodes from the Prophet's lifetime, the lives of his companions and successors, and the deeds of Muslim leaders and holy men in the coastal towns of Tamil Nadu or mountainous Javanese villages were copied, translated, recited, performed, and listened to, enhancing Islamization. Such translations introduced those who became Muslim or who were potential converts to the terminology, beliefs, stories, and rituals of a new religion, expressed in their own familiar idiom. Although the rituals and beliefs underpinning conversion were portrayed to a large degree, as discussed earlier, in rather standardized, conventional tropes across languages and genres, it was their translation into these diverse arenas—fluid, creative, and localized translations—that guaranteed their relevance and resonance.

The questions of what is a "faithful" translation and what constitutes a "true" (or "faith-full") conversion can be seen as closely linked as well. Both prioritize fidelity, and a certain absoluteness that is often utopian. Two examples raised earlier provide a metaphor for considering their relationship. The word for hypocrite, munafik (or munapik), never translated from Arabic and transmitted as such into Javanese, Malay, and Tamil, defines a category of people who claimed to convert but in fact remained infidels. Their example suggests that the external—the words and deeds of the hypocrites as outwardly expressed—is insignificant, while only the internal true faith counts. On the other hand, the utterance of the shahāda, appearing time and again in conversion scenes, was sufficient to turn one into a Muslim even when untranslated and potentially unintelligible to the reciter. This instance, conversely, points to the external—a public recitation of Arabic phrases—as crucial, whereas internal beliefs or conviction remain hidden and elusive.

Somewhere between these two clear-cut paths (in conviction or speech) is the kind of ambivalence emerging from the *Hikayat Tuan Gusti*, a narrative that translated and transmitted the experience of Javanese conversion to South Asia, in which new converts to Islam, perceived as still wavering among deeds, words, and new and old beliefs, were admonished to remain Muslim. In the final lines of the *Hikayat*, Sunan Giri is preaching at the mosque on Friday and, once again, reminding his audience not to forget to recite the shahāda, to pray five times a day, recite the Qur'an, and refrain from evil doing and from eating forbidden foods. The list goes on until, for the first time in the *Hikayat* and directly before its closing lines, he speaks of the Day of Judgment, the threat of hell, and the promise of paradise. This section (reminiscent of the Tamil *One Thousand Questions*' final section) is laced with untranslated Arabic terms (*ḥarām*, *mu'min*, *yaum al-qiyāma*, *'amal*, *yātīm*), indicating a Muslim ethos pervading the story, one that nonetheless requires repeated reinforcement. Here conversion and its stakes are projected on Java long ago, but in the translated text's closing lines also echo for contemporary listeners in Sri Lanka engaging with the story and its message. Both conversion and translation, in their transformative powers, contradictions, and complexities, lie along the continuums of explicit and implicit, expressive and silent, hidden and revealed that these examples suggest.

8

A Jew on Java, a Model Malay Rabbi, and a Tamil Torah Scholar

Representations of Abdullah Ibnu Salam and the Prophet in the *Book of One Thousand Questions*

In contrast to many regions of the Middle East, where Jewish communities existed during the Prophet's time and throughout the centuries following his death, the Tamil region of South India and the Indonesian-Malay world lacked such populations. An absence of "real" Jews or their marginal position in a society, however, does not preclude the presence of attitudes, sentiments, and perceptions related to them, as the cases of Indonesia and other countries have shown. A Jewish presence, whether real or symbolic, has been important to the formulation of various agendas and identities. In particular, the Jew has tended to epitomize an "Other," a figure possessing a largely imagined amalgam of traits and attitudes against which Muslims could negotiate and define their own individual and communal selves. It is therefore worth exploring how authors retelling the story of the Jewish leader Abdullah Ibnu Salam's encounter with the Prophet portrayed him, and asking what images, of Ibnu Salam and his people, were projected through the texts by authors—and to audiences—to whom Jews were known from other textual sources alone, most notably from their mention in the Qur'an.[1] Muhammad's portrayal in

1. This particular discussion cannot be generalized across the Arabic cosmopolis, as there were longstanding Jewish communities in some regions, most notably in Malabar. Even so, Jews, when present, formed a miniscule minority in most periods and places discussed in this study.

the *One Thousand Questions* in Javanese, Malay, and Tamil is also revealing, especially in his role as supreme guru, as is the depiction of his relationship with Ibnu Salam as his disciple. The special bond and commitment between guru and disciple, culturally important in pre-Islamic times in these regions and reinforced by Muslim models of teaching and learning, is central to this inquiry.

Early Sources on Ibnu Salam

The story of a Jew by the name of Ibnu Salam meeting the Prophet Muhammad and converting to Islam goes back to some of the earliest recorded Muslim traditions extant. These are tied to the theme of asking questions as a test of true prophethood, and are also related to prophecies of Muhammad's eventual arrival, which according to Muslim sources appear explicitly in the Jewish scripture. Ibnu Salam's appearance in older sources helps contextualize the image and significance of the man and the encounter.

The earliest authoritative source narrating the story of Ibnu Salam is Ibn Isḥāq's *Sīrat Rasūl Allāh*, known also as *Al-Sīrat al-Nabawīyya*, composed in Arabia in the eighth century and reworked in the following century by Ibn Hishām. It is the latter's version that has survived to the present, while only fragments of the earlier—and much fuller—text survive. Ibn Hishām relates that Jewish rabbis used to annoy the Prophet with confusing questions, so as to confound the truth with falsity. Qur'anic verses would descend in response to these questions of theirs, though some of the questions came from the Muslims themselves.[2] This passage accords the Jews a remarkable position, as partly dictating through their questions the content of the Qur'an. It also portrays the questioning as an attempt to confuse and entrap, a tendency that is linked to other characteristics with which Jews are typically endowed in these traditions. Ibn Hishām then lists the names of rabbis from the different Jewish clans or tribes who participated, at one time or another, in such questioning of the Prophet. The last rabbi mentioned from amongst the Banū Qaynuqā' is 'Abdullah bin Salām bin Ḥārith, who was the community's rabbi and most learned man.[3] His name was al-Ḥusayn, but the Prophet renamed him 'Abdullah after he embraced Islam. Two elements that remain significant in future tellings are found here: Ibnu Salam is portrayed as an important and wise leader of his people, and he receives a new name upon conversion.

2. 'Abdul Mālik Ibn Hishām, *Al-Sīrat al-Nabawīyya*, ed. Muṣṭfā al-Saqqā, Ibrahīm al-Ibyari, and 'Abd al-Ḥafiz Shalabi, 2 vols. (Cairo: Maktabat wa-Maṭba'at al-Bābī al-Ḥalabī, 1955), 1:513.
3. Ibid., 1:516.

How the conversion actually took place was related to the author by one of 'Abdullah's family members. 'Abdullah is said to have known right away, upon hearing the description of the Prophet, his name, and the time of his arrival, that he was the Awaited One. The news of Muhammad's arrival in Medina came when 'Abdullah, then still known as al-Ḥusayn, was working at the top of a palm tree and his aunt Khālida was sitting below. Hearing the news he cried "God is Great" and his aunt, confused, retorted that even had Musa himself arrived at that moment he would not have made more of a fuss. Al-Ḥusayn then explained to her that the Prophet is indeed Moses' brother, a follower of the same religion, and sent to them with the same mission.[4] Noteworthy here are the readiness of a Jewish rabbi to accept Muhammad as fulfilling a prophecy given to the Jews, and Muhammad's intimate relationship with the figure of Moses, tying him immediately to the heart of Jewish tradition.

Al-Ḥusayn descended from the tree. In describing his conversion briefly he tells of immediately approaching the Messenger and becoming a Muslim (A. *aslamtu*), then returning home and ordering his family to do the same.[5] It is a description omitting any details of what the ritual of this conversion consisted of, but it appears to have been a quick and simple affair. As the head of the family, the newly converted and newly named 'Abdullah ordered his family to follow him in accepting Islam, a hint of the seven hundred followers who would convert along with him in later versions of this account. The final section of this narrative, as recorded in the Sīra, is significant in its portrayal of the Jews as a community, elements of which are echoed in later tellings. 'Abdullah conceals his conversion from the Jews, goes to the Prophet, and tells him the Jews are a nation of liars. He asks to hide in the Prophet's house while the Prophet asks the Jews about 'Abdullah's position among them, without mentioning his conversion. He fears that if they know he has converted they will slander him. The Prophet agrees and asks the Jews about 'Abdullah, and they reply that he is their rabbi, chief, and a learned man. 'Abdullah then emerges and asks his people to acknowledge Muhammad, who has been named and described in the Torah (A. *tawrāh* or *tawrāt*). Hearing this, the Jews immediately accuse him of lying. Reminding the Prophet of his prediction, 'Abdullah again proclaims them as a community of traitors, liars, and evildoers (A. *ahlu ghadrin wa kadhibin wafujūr*).[6]

4. Ibid., 1:516–17.
5. Ibid., 1:517.
6. Ibid.

Although not all mention of Jews in the Sīra is negative, it is so in the majority of cases. Jews are consistently portrayed in various episodes as liars, as corrupt and deceitful people, often equated with the despised hypocrites. They should not be trusted; they are envious that God has sent the seal of the prophets to the Arabs rather than to them; they should never be taken as close, intimate friends. 'Abdullah himself, beyond his conversion scene, is mentioned as one who reveals the treachery of the Jews and brings it to light, in the scene of the adulterous man and woman mentioned in chapter 2.

The accounts by Ibn Hishām consistently appeared anew in hadith collections recounting the deeds and sayings of the Prophet. Ibnu Salam became the token Jewish convert, exemplifying through his story the logic inherent in Jewish conversion. This was a logic that, according to Muslim sources, followed the tenets of Judaism's own sacred scripture. At the same time, the repetition of the story—as opposed to mention of many such cases—underscored the Jewish resistance to Muhammad, the antagonisms between the Jews and the emerging Muslim community during the Prophet's time, and the relative uniqueness of Ibnu Salam's experience.

With time the Ibnu Salam tradition began acquiring an element central to the *One Thousand Questions* that is not found in Ibn Hishām's account: the questioning of the Prophet. According to the late ninth-century Ṣaḥīḥ al-Bukhārī hadith collection, 'Abdullah, upon hearing of the Prophet's arrival, approached him and asked about three things that only a prophet is assumed to know. The questions were: What is the first sign of the last hour? What is the first thing the inhabitants of paradise shall eat? And what makes a boy look like his father or his mother? The Prophet replied that—just as in the *One Thousand Questions*—the archangel Jibrīl has just informed him of the answers. Hearing the answers, Ibnu Salam converted on the spot, professing his faith in Allah and His messenger.[7]

The theme of the Jews posing questions to the Prophet and requesting proof of his prophecy appears already in the Qur'an, as discussed in chapter 2.[8] Also noted already was the way a Jewish convert to Islam, mentioned in the Qur'an, has been taken to refer to Ibnu Salam, the protagonist of the

7. Muhammad Muhsin Khan, *Miracles of the Prophet Muhammad: Adapted from Introduction to Ṣaḥīḥ al-Bukhārī* (New Delhi: Taj, 1982), 24–25.

8. An early tradition mentions three questions that the Jews of Medina encouraged the Jews of Mecca to pose to Muhammad, as a test of his prophecy. These are mentioned in Qur'an 17:87 (about the Spirit), 18:8 (about the cave dwellers), and 18:82 (about the "two-horned one"). Not only the Jews demanded such proofs, so did the infidels. See, for example Qur'an 6:7, 6:50, 17:92–93, 8:32 (for the infidels), and 3:179 and 4:152 (for the Jews). Christians too are depicted as arguing with Muhammad over certain points, see 3:54.

One Thousand Questions. This is further testimony to the importance of his figure in this tradition and to the significance accorded to this particular conversion story. The incorporation of questions into ʿAbdullah's encounter with Muhammad is likely a combination of the earlier conversion story and the accounts of questioning, doubting Jews, and it was further elaborated in subsequent centuries until ʿAbdullah was said to have asked the Prophet no fewer than one thousand questions.

The consistent appearance of Ibnu Salam's account in the collected hadith of eminent Muslim scholars raises the question of why it was so significant. I have noted the way in which it presented a Muslim perspective on the rationale for Jews to embrace Islam and how it highlighted the rarity of this occurrence, as it was not accompanied by similar stories portraying other converts. Consideration of the historical expectations and struggles between Jews and Muslims in the Prophet's time, and the sometimes violent means employed against Jewish communities, certainly highlights this story of a peaceful, voluntary conversion as a particularly powerful tale. That it was then retold, transmitted, and expanded on in so many languages is even more remarkable.

On Judaism, Leadership, and Conversion: Related Narratives

Recounting earlier traditions of the encounter between Muhammad and the Jewish leader Ibnu Salam and examining their links to the *One Thousand Questions* is important for contextualizing this story within a long history, one that began centuries before it was translated in South and Southeast Asia. Central to this context is the crucial importance of transmission genealogies (A. *isnād*) in Islam, especially as related to the authoritative and sacred words and deeds of the Prophet, a genre to which this account belongs.

In addition to the tradition of early depictions of Ibnu Salam, the story has been inspired by, and has also inspired, other, related stories. It is not unique in its general parameters but rather belongs to a broader genre addressing the relationship between Judaism, leadership, and conversion. One story that may have in part inspired the way the Ibnu Salam episode was narrated—especially as we know it from the *One Thousand Questions*—is the account of the encounters between King Solomon and the Queen of Sheba. First mentioned briefly in the Jewish Bible, it was later developed by scriptural commentators into a full-fledged tale of persuasion, love, and religious transformation.[9] The

9. The encounter is mentioned in 1 Kings 10:1–3: "The queen of Sheba heard of Solomon's fame through the name of the Lord, and she came to test him with hard questions. . . . Solomon had

similarities between the narratives are quite striking: King Solomon, ruling in Jerusalem, was known to be the leader of his people and the wisest of men. The queen, herself the ruler of a powerful kingdom in Africa, had heard of his greatness and, upon receiving a letter of invitation, went to his city. There she asked him many questions—most of them riddle-like—as a test of his knowledge and spirituality. The queen was convinced by Solomon's words about God, albeit more gradually than Abdullah. She and the king fell in love, for the queen felt a strong attraction to him and to his wisdom. Arriving back in her country she told her people of the One God, and they followed her in conversion to Judaism.[10] The story of Solomon and the queen appears also in the Qur'an, where she accepts the king's faith (although Islam is not explicitly mentioned) after he proves his powers to her.[11] This episode was elaborated in Ibn Isḥāq's Sīra, probably drawing on Jewish sources like the one mentioned above.

In these sources, and especially the Jewish source, many elements familiar from the Ibnu Salam narrative appear: the meeting of two important religious, and also political, leaders;[12] the letter of invitation to a debate, which appears in many of the later Ibnu Salam accounts; the love and admiration that develops within the relationship; and of course the dialogue of questions and answers, which serves to prove that one contender possesses knowledge and divine inspiration that cannot be outdone. One of the questions the queen asks the king—about a place on earth that has seen the light of day only once—appears as such in Arabic, Malay, and Tamil *One Thousand Questions* tellings.[13] The major difference between the stories lies in their directionality: whereas the Queen of Sheba follows a Jewish leader and converts to his faith, 'Abdullah, a Jewish leader himself, follows a Muslim prophet and embraces Islam. Despite this difference, the similarities draw attention to a pool of motifs and stories, many of them appearing in Jewish literature and

answers for all her questions; there was nothing that the king did not know, [nothing] to which he could not give her an answer" (*JPS Tanakh trans.*).

10. A sample of such Jewish traditions appears in Louis Ginzberg, *The Legends of the Jews*, vol. 4: *From Joshua to Esther* (Baltimore: Johns Hopkins University, 1998), 142–49.

11. Solomon is mentioned in seven suras of the Qur'an, two of which also mention the queen of Sheba: 27:15–44 and 34:12–20.

12. According to tradition the queen was a follower of Manichaeanism; see Gordon Darnell Newby, *The Making of the Last Prophet: A Reconstruction of the Earliest Biography of Muhammad* (Columbia: University of South Carolina Press, 1989), 164. Solomon says of her: "Her false gods have led her astray, for she comes from an unbelieving nation" (Qur'an 27:43).

13. The answer is the bottom of the Red Sea, revealed when Moses split it open to allow the Israelites to escape Pharaoh's army.

incorporated into Muslim sources, which came to be shared across the two religious traditions.

More directly linked to the Ibnu Salam episode in terms of region and, no less important, directionality of conversion, is a tradition from Afghanistan. When Ibn Baṭṭūṭa visited Kabul in the fourteenth century, he found it inhabited by the Afghans, a "powerful and violent people" from Persia, who believed they were descended from the house of Israel, from the family of Saul, the first king.[14] Originally residing on Mt. Solomon in Syria, they migrated to Kandahar, some making their way into India and assisting Maḥmūd of Ghizna in his first conquests there.

A local historian and author, Ibn Shāh 'Alam, who put this history in writing in his *Khulāṣat al-Ansāb*, told Ibn Baṭṭūṭa that his ancestors, upon hearing in Kandahar of Muhammad's teachings, sent a deputation to him in Arabia to inquire whether or not he was the last prophet mentioned in "the law and the gospels." Upon being assured that he was, the entire nation accepted the Muslim faith at once.

Although Lee, the nineteenth-century translator and editor of Ibn Baṭṭūṭa's travelogue, believed this tradition to be largely a fable, the strong similarities between this tradition and that of Ibnu Salam point to the popularity of this circulating model, which emphasized the doubts and questions arising with regard to Muhammad's Truth, conversion by persuasion, a leader or representative of a people initially convinced, then followed by the community, and the importance of direct contact with the Prophet. Clearly, the *One Thousand Questions* fits into a larger paradigm that crossed religious and geographical lines. The images of Ibnu Salam and his people as portrayed in the Tamil, Malay, and Javanese traditions of the *One Thousand Questions* were elements of this larger picture.

Depicting Ibnu Salam and Judaism in Javanese, Tamil, and Malay

In the three languages Ibnu Salam is, generally, depicted in very positive terms, most often in the opening section of the texts. For example, in Ja-

14. Samuel Lee, ed., *The Travels of Ibn Baṭṭūṭa: Translated from the Abridged Arabic Manuscript Copies Preserved in the Public Library of Cambridge with Notes Illustrative of the History, Geography, Botany, Antiquities Etc. Occuring Throughout the Work* (London: Oriental Translation Committee, 1829), 99. Also appearing in the same translation series is the *Tareki Afghan*, Ni'mat Allāh's seventeenth-century Persian-language history of the Afghans, who claim descent from the Jews. Ni'mat Allāh, *Tareki Afghan*, trans. Bernhard Dorn (London: Oriental Translation Committee, 1829–36).

vanese tellings the Jewish leader is given the titles of "sage-king" (J. *sang raja pandhita*) and "guru," and his powers are described as exceedingly great (J. *saktinipun kalangkung*). Some Malay tellings employ only the title "scholar" or "sage" (M. *pandita*) when depicting Ibnu Salam, while others elaborate further and refer to him also as a "pious, learned man" (A. *'ālim*) and "chief" (M. *penghulu*), one who is versed in the Torah, the Psalms, and the Gospels and can interpret them all. In the Tamil *One Thousand Questions*, which generally tends to be more elaborate and descriptive, he is depicted throughout as learned and wise, knower of the Vedas, an ascetic, a faultless man. Such positive, respectful terminology employed in the portrayal of the Jewish leader was rooted in the earliest Arabic traditions, which proclaimed him to have been a learned rabbi and chief of his people. Such portrayals serve the purpose of strengthening the message that Ibnu Salam was a worthy opponent. His broad knowledge and intimate understanding of the scriptures made his acceptance of the Prophet's words all the more persuasive.

The image is not, however, entirely positive. In one instance Ibnu Salam is referred to in Tamil as *aṟapiṉiṉ kāpir*—"infidel of Arabia"—and in a Javanese telling he is twice mentioned as being the guru of the infidels (J. *gurunė wong kapir*).[15] But these attributes pale in comparison to the positive aspects, which appear consistently in the different tellings. In addition, the distinction between Ibnu Salam, the individual and leader, and the Jews as a people had to be upheld since he was considered an exception.[16] The episode appearing at story's end in many hadith, in which Ibnu Salam was afraid of the Jews' reaction to his conversion and asked for assistance and protection from the Prophet, while also attempting to prove the Jews' deceptive and untruthful character, is highly unusual in the tellings discussed here, where the negative Jewish response to conversion is generally absent. The questioning is, at a fundamental level, a test. And yet the deceitful nature of the Jews, attempting to prove Muhammad wrong, constantly doubting him and trying to catch him in a mistake, does not come across as a prominent feature. On the contrary, in all the tellings discussed, Ibnu Salam—and sometimes his followers—graciously accept the prophet's words and acknowledge their truth.

Several Malay tellings bring out an additional facet of the Jews' portrayal as a community. Ibnu Salam announces to his people that he has received a letter from the "seal of the prophets," whose coming had been prophesied in

15. *AM*, v. 281, and *Samud*, Perpustakaan Nasional Republik Indonesia, Jakarta, MS. PNRI Br. 504, respectively.

16. However, Muhammad refers to the Jews collectively as "experts in the scriptures" and a people "revered in the world" in Tamil. *AM*, v. 70.

the Torah. He repeatedly invokes the name of Moses to convince the Jews of the authenticity of the new Prophet. The Jews remain doubtful and ask him how they may know for certain that they should leave their religion behind. They are described as *masygul di dalam hati*, sad in their hearts, confused, despairing. Ibnu Salam then invokes the solution of asking the Prophet one thousand questions as a test, and the Jews all agree that if he is convinced they will follow suit (*HSM*, 20–21). Here, although the Jews are presented as doubtful and initially disbelieving, their leader is able to convince them that a test by questioning will provide the desired proof. The Jews are not depicted as evil or cunning so much as perplexed and open to persuasion.

The terminologies and definitions for "Jews" and "Judaism" employed in the different *One Thousand Questions* tellings are also significant. The Arabic-derived term *yahudi*, appearing in the Qur'an, is used in Malay and Javanese. The Tamil word for Jews—*cūtar*—may derive less directly from Arabic (from Judah?). Its definition in nineteenth- and twentieth-century dictionaries reveals an interesting and perhaps telling phenomenon: the word *cūtar* refers to gamblers, deceitful people, deriving from *cūtu*, a Sanskritic name of a dice game.[17] The other definition is "bards, singers." Whether either of these definitions—and especially the former—is related to an attitude toward the Jews remains an open question. Also intriguing in thinking about how Jews were collectively imagined and understood is the phenomenon in several Javanese *One Thousand Questions* tellings of what appears as a conflation of Jews with Christians. In the 1884 *Serat Samud* from Yogyakarta, Muhammad's letter is explicitly addressed, no less than three times, to the *yahudi nasarani* (Jews [and] Christians).[18] This combination may have referred to Jews *and* Christians while also addressing them as a single group—that is, they were seen as both conflated and separate.[19]

It is difficult to deduce a clear conclusion from the appearance of this terminology in Javanese, but it is noteworthy that the conflation does not ap-

17. "Cologne on-Line Tamil Lexicon." 2003 edition. http://webapps.uni-koeln.de/tamil/.
18. *Serat Samud*, Pura Pakualaman Library, Yogyakarta, 1884, MS. PP St. 80, c. 11, vv. 48–49.
19. This type of conflation is not only a thing of the past. In an illustration accompanying a retelling of the early hadith about Ibnu Salam meeting the Prophet and converting that appeared in the Indonesian magazine *Al-Kisah*, the Jew (I. *yahudi*) Ibnu Salam is depicted wearing the garments of a Catholic priest, and his face resembles that of Jesus in the popular imagination, long haired and bearded. In the text itself he is described as a pastor or priest (I. *pendeta*) and as teaching in a church (I. *gereja*). "Kuda Kecil Yang Menjadi Hamba Allah," *Al-Kisah*, September 2007, 50–53.

pear, to the best of my knowledge, in Arabic and Malay tellings of the story.[20] Whether it represents a purposeful conflation of non-Muslims belonging to "the people of the book," a misunderstanding of the distinctions between the religions, or a vision of Muhammad preaching to both peoples is impossible to determine, largely because definitions of what it meant to be Jewish or Christian—in the eyes of a Javanese author—are rare in the texts. An exception is found in the undated *Samud*, where Ibnu Salam, described as the guru of Jews and Christians (J. *guru ning wong yahudi lan ning srani*), a man of exceptional powers, introduces himself to the Prophet as follows:

> Yes my name is Samud
> I am Ibnu Salam
>
> Indeed I follow
> The religion of the prophet Abraham
> Of the descendents of Jacob
> Who are exalted
> Granted an authority in reading
> The Torah scripture
> By Him who sent
> The prophets bearing it [to] me
> Indeed that which is
> Followed by all Jews
> And Christians.[21]

In this brief segment Ibnu Salam defines his own religion, whose scripture, in the concluding lines, applies to both Jews and Christians. He traces his faith to the prophet Abraham (as do Muslims) and to his grandson Jacob. The Torah is presented as the supreme scripture, followed by adherents of Judaism and Christianity alike. In this instance the text's audience is provided with a glimpse of what members of these faiths are assumed to believe.

20. Van Ronkel notes a Malay tale in which a question and answer dialogue, similar in many of its themes to the one depicted in the *One Thousand Questions*, takes place between the sheikh Ibn Yazīd al-Bustamī and Rubhān, a Christian monk. Van Ronkel views this as a displacement of the scene from a Jewish sphere to a Christian one, but no conflation is involved. The debate takes place in a church, and following it Rubhān and five hundred monks convert to Islam. Ph. S. van Ronkel, "Malay Tales about Conversion of Jews and Christians to Muhammedanism," *Acta Orientalia* 10 (1932): 62–65.

21. *Samud*, Perpustakaan Nasional Republik Indonesia, Jakarta, MS. PNRI Br. 504, p. 212.

Ibnu Salam's place of origin in the different *One Thousand Questions* traditions also offers an indication of his identity. In many Arabic tellings Ibnu Salam is from Khaybar, a settlement that had a large and prosperous Jewish community in the seventh century. In the Tamil telling he hails from Khaybar (T. *Kaipar*) as well, and is mentioned many times as "king of Kaipar," "the wise man from Kaipar," and "Kaipar's protector," and the city itself is depicted as one that "flows with light of precious stones."[22] In Malay tellings Ibnu Salam is also a leader of Khaybar. In Javanese tellings, however, a wider range of possibilities emerges in regard to Ibnu Salam's place of origin, implying a more broadly defined identity for the story's protagonist and more flexibility on the part of the author. In some Javanese tellings Ibnu Salam concedes only that he is coming from "my land, my kingdom" (J. *saking nagari amba*), without supplying any details, geographical or otherwise. Occasionally, as in the 1898 *Serat Suluk Samud Ibnu Salam*, nothing at all is mentioned about his origins, not even his Jewish affiliation. An interesting option chosen by some writers for his homeland—both in tellings in which he is Jewish and in those he is not—is the land of Rum.

Rum, referring in the narrow sense to Turkey or the lands of the Ottoman Empire, has a special place in Javanese works. Although the term may connote the historical region of the Eastern Roman Empire or Byzantium, which finally gave way to the Ottoman Turks with the fall of Constantinople in 1453, and whose empire would survive into the twentieth century, in Javanese literature it often refers to a Muslim domain, shrouded in mystery and glory. It is a distant land of kings and warriors, representing Muslim authority and dominance. Significantly, it is sometimes depicted as the land of origin of the first humans to ever have settled on Java, thus marking the Javanese as direct descendents of the people of Rum. Depicting Samud Ibnu Salam and his followers as coming from Rum—especially when imagined as a faraway, unknown Muslim locale—distances the story from an immediate Jewish-Muslim context. It may also be that designating Rum as Ibnu Salam's home resonated with the audience, as it stressed his arrival from afar, his transformative journey to meet the Prophet long and arduous, yet worthy of its hurdles.

The distancing of Ibnu Salam from his "natural" home of Khaybar in Javanese tellings is only one way in which his biography was transformed. As discussed, in some tellings he is no longer depicted as Jewish, a portrayal that is in many ways easier to explain than that of a Jewish and Javanese Ibnu Salam. For instance, in the 1898 *Serat Suluk Samud Ibnu Salam*, the clearest

22. See for example *AM*, vv. 1027, 663, 205, and 191 respectively.

example of this trend, there is no mention of Samud's Jewish identity, of his place of origin, his leadership within a community, or his desire or decision to convert to Islam. Since there was no Jewish community to speak of in Java or its vicinity, the questions of Muslim-Jewish relations remained to a large extent issues raised in the Qur'an and other sources, but not issues relevant to everyday life, including those of conversion, competition, and inter-religious dynamics. As Javanese authors and translators adapted other stories to local concerns and models, the *One Thousand Questions* too shed this seemingly unnecessary element yet continued to be told in a way that was considered locally appropriate.

The tellings that did depict Ibnu Salam as Jewish, in Javanese, Tamil, and Malay, remained more "faithful" to the story as it appears in the hadith literature and in Arabic works. Motivations for this tendency included preserving a strong link to Arabic traditions, including the canon of Muhammad's deeds, and following their conventionalized, formulaic manner, as well as allowing the story to remain more firmly grounded in the Prophet's time. By so doing, important elements of the story were retained, among them the victory of the Prophet over an opponent, the emphasis on persuasion, and the ongoing connection with complementary knowledge about the Jews available in the Qur'an and hadith. Indeed, the absence of "real Jews" in Java, in much of the Malay world, or in the Tamil region did not preclude the existence of deeply rooted perceptions and images of which they are a focus. As Siegel argues, an absence of Jews in Indonesia has not led to a lack of anti-Semitism, but, on the contrary, in some ways such a lack makes holding on to negative perceptions all the more likely, as they cannot be countered by living experience, personal ties, and familiarity.[23] Ibnu Salam's story is, in this sense, but an element in the larger cultural picture addressing prior, as well as contemporary, Jewish-Muslim relations. This picture includes not only the Qur'an and hadith in Arabic or translation but also a variety of other texts.

Jews and Judaism in Additional Sources

Alternatives to the peaceful conversion process depicted in the *One Thousand Questions* are found in, for example, the Javanese Pandhita Raib and Raja Kandak narratives.[24] Malay tellings of these narratives exist as well. In the Malay *Hikayat Raja Khaybar* once again, the king of Khaybar, in this case

23. James Siegel, "Kiblat and the Mediatic Jew," *Indonesia* 69 (2000): 9–42.

24. On the *Serat Pandhita Raib* see Ronit Ricci, "The Ambiguous Figure of the Jew in Javanese Literature," *Indonesia and the Malay World* 38.3 (2010): 403–17.

not a Jew but not yet a Muslim either, fights the Prophet's Muslim army and is defeated. His daughter Ṣafiyya marries Muhammad and converts, paving the way for all of Khaybar's residents to do the same.[25] Another circulating story, appearing in early Arabic sources and translated from that language, is relevant to the discussion both in the more general sense of depicting the Jews and more specifically in its relationship to conversion. It recounts how a Jewish man captured a doe that had recently given birth. Muhammad, who came across the doe and heard her pleas, agreed to remain as hostage with the wicked Jew while she nursed her young. The fawns refused to nurse when they heard of the Prophet's plight and returned, along with their mother, to release him. Overwhelmed by the sight of the returning doe with her young, the Jew embraced Islam on the spot. This miraculous tale is cited in many classical Arabic sources, is at the center of a very popular contemporary Egyptian ballad, and is the focus of a beloved Acehnese poem.[26] Additional tellings are likely circulating in the Archipelago. Two points are significant here: the image that emerges is one of the Jew as greedy, voracious, untrustworthy, cunning, and cruel, while the Prophet, on the contrary, is noble, humble, courageous, and willing to sacrifice himself for the good of another of God's creatures. In addition, the narrative highlights once again the Prophet's ability to persuade—here with his actions—and to overwhelm a Jew into conversion.

Among the most popular of tales bringing to the fore Jewish traditions that have been adapted within Islam, rather than a strict image of the Jews, are the traditions known in Arabic as *hadith Isrāʾīliyāt* (I. *hadis Israiliya*), or Judaica. In his early biography of the Prophet, Ibn Isḥāq drew extensively on this body of stories concerning, and usually derived from, Jewish and Christian sources. In the latter contexts the literary sources for Isrāʾīliyāt were haggadic and midrashic treatises explicating Jewish scripture. One effect of their use by Ibn Isḥāq was to link his Sīra and the Qur'an to previous scripture through these stories, fostering the claim that Islam was the heir to Judaism and Christianity.[27] They include narratives regarded as historical, serving to complement the information provided in the scriptures, particularly regarding the prophets; edifying narratives placed within the chronological framework of "the period of the ancient Israelites"; and fables allegedly, and

25. *Hikayat Raja Khaybar*, MS. PNRI W81, listed in T. E. Behrend, ed., *Katalog Induk Naskah-Naskah Nusantara: Perpustakaan Nasional Republik Indonesia* (Jakarta: Yayasan Obor Indonesia, 1998), 329.

26. In Arabic sources a Bedouin, rather than a Jew, often captures the doe. On these sources and the Egyptian ballad, see Kamal Abdel-Malek, *Muhammad in the Modern Egyptian Popular Ballad* (Leiden: E. J. Brill, 1995), 69–71.

27. Newby, *The Making of the Last Prophet*, 3.

sometimes actually, borrowed from Jewish sources. In the Archipelago and South India such stories have been, and remain, very popular, and they have been widely incorporated into the Islamic literary sphere. Many accounts of the lives of the prophets appear in Javanese, Tamil, and Malay, emerging from the often brief facts appearing in the Hebrew scriptures and the New Testament, elaborated on in Jewish and Christian sources, and embellished further by Muslim scholars and storytellers.

The narrative of Ibnu Salam's question and answer dialogue with the Prophet thus did not occur in isolation. Although it may be quite unusual in its consistently positive portrayal of the Jewish leader and in its denial of overt conflict, it forms an element in a much larger, longstanding tradition of engaging with and imagining Jews and Judaism. The way Jews figure in these narratives reveals something not only about how Jews were perceived or imagined in premodern Indonesia and India, but also about how Javanese, Malay, and Tamil Muslims telling these stories understood their own community and history. The narrative of early Islam was told, in part, through emphasizing the Jew as the "other" against whom Muslims could be portrayed and their identity defined. In line with the human tendency to view oneself in relation to other individuals or groups by highlighting similarities and above all differences and distinctions, the appearance of a Jew as enemy, cunning opponent, or wise competitor contributed to Muslims' ability to shape their own story in a meaningful way. In these narratives Jews and Judaism symbolized, ultimately, what Islam had left behind as it moved forward with its final Prophet and its new convictions, toward the formation of a new community and an adoption of a new history. This is especially evident when we consider that the accounts in some of the texts, including the *One Thousand Questions*, represent struggles over the acceptance of Islam as ultimate Truth, as well as differing perspectives on the path to conversion. These struggles and the questions that accompanied them surely must have resonated across the Arabic cosmopolis, where conversion to Islam was a process taking place over several centuries, and continuing still to this day.

Diverse Depictions of the Prophet

Depictions of the Prophet Muhammad, Ibnu Salam's counterpart and teacher within the dialogue, are part of a rich and complex tradition as well. The Prophet Muhammad has been loved and venerated across the Muslim world for the past fourteen centuries. Countless works celebrate his birth, life events, and death, his sayings and deeds. Interpretations of these range from the strictly historical and theological to the mystical, and have been told, sung, and written down in diverse languages. The Prophet has been at the center of devotional cults and practices. Here I concern myself specifically with the depiction of Muhammad within the Ibnu Salam tradition and especially in the Tamil, Malay, and Javanese *One Thousand Questions* tellings.

Returning for a moment to Ibn Hishām's Arabic Sīra, where the conversion of Ibnu Salam is briefly narrated, no description whatsoever of the Prophet appears. He is mentioned only as arriving in Medina, agreeing to Ibnu Salam's request that he house him, and asking the Jews about him as their leader.[28] In the 1143 Latin edition of the *One Thousand Questions*, based on an early Arabic telling, Muhammad is depicted as sitting with his companions in Yathrib when Jibrīl comes with a message that four important Jews are on their way to him, to ask for proof of his prophecy. Muhammad gives their names and describes their appearance to the astonishment of all present. The greatest among them is Abdia iben Salon (an approximate Hebrew equivalent to 'Abdullah Ibnu Salam). Greetings between the Jews and the Prophet are described and Iben Salon introduces himself as the leader who has come with one hundred questions.[29] In later Arabic tellings Muhammad is depicted as the initiator of contact with the Jews of Khaybar—rather than hearing they are on their way to him—when he sends them a letter dictated by Jibrīl. Here too none of his external characteristics are mentioned. Within the text the Prophet is defined by his ability to answer all questions and by the deep respect granted him by his opponent.

In Tamil the *One Thousand Questions* frequently and poetically depicts various attributes of the Prophet. One aspect of such descriptions, already discussed, has to do with the invocation of many miracles performed by the Prophet which, although only briefly hinted at in the text, create an entire image for those familiar with the stories. They arouse emotions and recreate scenarios of deed and speech for the listener.

Throughout the *One Thousand Questions*' verses, references to history and social context, interwoven with the Prophet's biography, repeatedly and emphatically stress the Prophet's attitudes, actions, and powers. He is portrayed as a follower of good, faith flowing from his heart, destroyer of darkness; as "the prophet known as *kapīpu* (A. *ḥabīb*, beloved)" to whom all kings pay tribute; the Prophet who lived in Mecca and moved to Medina, who showed others the true way of Islam; he was "related to all mankind, the life of everything"; the *gurunabi* ("guru and prophet," "guru among prophets") from the Kuraishi family, versed in the Qur'an (T. *maṟai, vētam*), wise, compassionate,

28. 'Abdul Mālik Ibn Hishām, *Al-Sīrat al-Nabawīyya*, 1:517.

29. Guillaume Frederic Pijper, *Het boek der duizend vragen* (Leiden: E. J. Brill, 1924), 41.

patient in advocating new ideas; one "who is like lightning to his enemies," remover of suffering. On their way to meet him the Jews are described as passing through many places, where "everywhere crowds of people spoke of the Prophet, praising his qualities"; he is the *napī* who obtained imperishable fame, known by the Sanskrit epithet *Cintāmaṇi* (wish-granting gem). He was the one who drank milk from Alimā's breasts; who reached God's throne (T. *aṟush*), noblest of messengers, destroyer of evil, victor in battle, courageous like a tiger. Clearly, such depictions, and others, incorporate Muhammad's actions and abilities as a young child, warrior, teacher, reformer, and, above all, God's messenger, and present them in a tangible and moving way.

A third aspect of Muhammad's portrayal in the Tamil telling brings forth his more physical characteristics, although these may relate to his spiritual powers and are often indistinct from them. His physicality reminds the audience that he was indeed a mortal—as the early accounts mention he always insisted he was—but also attributes to his nature elements that transcend the human and resonate with depictions of Hindu gods. Time and again he is described as "he whose exalted body emitted the fragrance of musk"; he is often mentioned as having the rain cloud as parasol, or as the king bearing the heavy rain cloud, both reminiscent of portrayals of the god Viṣṇu. Other attributes of his that are conventionally associated with the gods include his lotus feet, which do not touch the ground, and his adornment by an ever-fragrant garland. He is also "the one who is like dawn at the time when the cock calls," whose face is like a perfect lotus, shining like the sun and moon. Muhammad is said to be the "giver of *amṛta*," the nectar of immortality, and to possess shoulders that are like Mount Mandāra, referring to the mythical mountain used by gods and demons to churn the sea of milk in their attempt to gain the coveted nectar. In addition, the Prophet is presented as "the medicine [of the world]," in a hint of Buddhist teachings that saw the Buddha as the world's physician and the Dharma as its healing potion.

Such physical attributes of the Prophet add a strong element of sensuality to his character, with scents, color, flavor, and light all coming together to form an image of a luminous and handsome prophet of mythical proportions. Elements from local traditions depicting gods and saints contribute prominently to this image that conjures a very Tamil Muhammad.

In Malay tellings, where the language tends to be more straightforward and less poetic than either the Tamil or Javanese, it comes as no surprise that the Prophet's depiction too is limited and brief.[30] The text relates the time, place, and something of the etiquette of the meeting between the Prophet

30. Examples in this section are drawn from *HSM*.

and Ibnu Salam, setting it in the historical and cultural context of the Prophet's life. The debate is said to have taken place on a Sunday in Medina. Ibnu Salam first kisses the Prophet's feet, then he and his seven hundred followers praise the Prophet and show their respect. The Prophet welcomes Ibnu Salam, who then explains the reason for his coming, and the Prophet replies that, God willing, he will answer all of the questions posed to him. Immediately before the dialogue begins Jibrail and Mikail, the two archangels, descend and sit on Muhammad's left and right.

This short introduction situates the characters in a very particular context and also orients the audience to the stage in the Prophet's life during which the event takes place, stressing the respect shown to him by members of a rival religion even before the debate begins. It emphasizes that the angels played a crucial part in the outcome of the question and answer session, representing God's ongoing support of His Prophet, and ensuring his success.

Arabic blessings are consistently appended to Muhammad's name in the text, framing it in sanctity. Most often *salla llahu 'alayhi wa salam* (from A. "May Allah bless Him and grant Him peace") is employed. Although this is a conventional practice in Arabic writings when referring to the Prophet, it stands out in the context of the comparison of *One Thousand Questions* tellings as it does not appear at all in Tamil and Javanese. Once more it brings to the fore the heavy stress on Arabic in Malay literature. Throughout the dialogue Ibnu Salam addresses the Prophet as Muhammad. The narrator describing the replies then consistently refers to the Prophet as *rasulullah*, God's messenger, beginning every reply with "thus spoke the messenger of God." In response to each answer Ibnu Salam acknowledges the truth of Muhammad's words, himself using the messenger epithet (M. *sidiq ya rasulullah*). Thus the Prophet's name and his role as messenger and prophet appear several times with each question and reply, with the effect of reproducing and amplifying the name and role throughout the dialogue. Although this Malay telling, as is typical, does not expand on the Prophet's character or physicality, there are several additional epithets used sparingly throughout to refer to him. These include "the Prophet of the end of Time" (M. from A., *nabi akhir zaman*), "seal of the prophets" (M. from A., *khatamun nabi*), and "head, chief among all prophets" (M. *penghulu segala nabi*). In the final lines he is addressed by Ibnu Salam as *junjungan*, a Malay term employed for the Prophet, translating approximately as "revered one." The strong influence of Arabic and the adopted formulas exclude imaginative depictions of Muhammad from the text but ground it in traditional Muslim writing, with which it echoes at every turn through its terminology and structure.

The Prophet's strength shines through here not via beautiful metaphors as in Tamil, but first and foremost by means of the comprehensiveness of his replies and Ibnu Salam's consistent acceptance and acknowledgement of them, through ongoing reminders of his unique position in relation to God and of his ability to bring about the conversion. A final tribute to Muhammad is paid in the closing lines, in which a warning appears: the author reminds the audience that it should not make light of anything appearing in this book. Whosoever does so "is rebellious toward Allah and His messenger" (*HSM*, 87). This statement—the final words in the text—further stresses the relationship between Muhammad and God, and encompasses both of them within a single category.

Javanese tellings portray the Prophet in a similar vein. In the 1884 Pakualam *Serat Samud*, for example, a brief contextualizing section places the story within the Prophet's lifetime. It gives his name, Muhammad, states that he was Prophet and Messenger of God (using a form of Arabic *rasūl* directly followed by a Javanese translation, *utusan ning suksma*), reveals that he was the son of Abdullah, living first in Mecca and then in Medina, and that he was appointed God's deputy on earth. In this extremely condensed biographical note we learn the basic, most crucial facts: the Prophet's name, familial origin, place of birth and death, and his relationship to God and role among men. In this telling, when Samud arrives for the debate, the Prophet is surrounded by many companions. He and Samud greet each other, and then Muhammad astonishes Samud by telling him he knows his name and his intention in coming, and even the exact number of questions he plans to ask. This anecdote clearly places Muhammad in a superior position even before the dialogue begins by pointing to his insight, clarity of mind, wisdom, and divine inspiration. Samud enters the encounter already filled with admiration and awe.

The most common forms of address for Muhammad throughout the text are *kangjeng nabi* and *kangjeng rasul*, both combining the Javanese honorific title *kangjeng* with the Arabic terms for prophet and messenger. This both endears the Prophet in the eyes of the Javanese audience and reaffirms the use of translocal Arabic terminology. Javanese speech levels, with *krama inggil* verbs used for the Prophet's speech (J. *ngandika*) and lower forms used for Samud (J. *matur*), emphasize the status difference between the two. When the Prophet replies to Samud's questions, he sometimes addresses him directly, in a conversational manner. Samud is often depicted as showing great esteem (J. *abekti*) or paying homage to the Prophet (J. *awot sekar*) as he presents his queries and acknowledges the Prophet's words. As in the Malay telling, he admits to the truth and relevance of Muhammad's message by repeatedly using phrases such as *leres andika tuan* ("true are the words of my Lord"). Occasionally he pays the Prophet further compliments, expressing his admiration, as when he tells him that "vast is your knowledge / many are my questions, none [find you] unaware."[31]

The final section of the text invokes the blessing of the Prophet for all those who take part in the production of the book or attend to its message. As in the Malay, the Prophet is barely depicted throughout in terms of his physical presence, and his personality and presence are projected via the sheer volume of questions and topics that he proves able to tackle successfully throughout the dialogue with Samud.

These various depictions of the Prophet in Tamil, Malay, and Javanese attest to the ways in which each corresponds with the more general trends of how the story is told in a particular language. In Tamil Muhammad is more richly and elaborately described than in the other languages, and a stress is put on the physical and sensual aspects of description. Malay and Javanese present Muhammad in quite similar ways, yet there are differences: in Malay—as is consistently the case—Arabic phrases and terms play a large role in references to the Prophet, whereas in Javanese—also typically—we find more combinations of Arabic and Javanese and translations of the former into the latter. Malay offers the most formulaic depiction, probably closest to the Arabic and Persian sources, through which Muhammad's relationship to God is highlighted. Although this relationship is important in the Javanese tellings, they also stress Muhammad's insight and mystical tendencies, in accordance with a broader inclination toward mysticism in Javanese culture. The tellings in all three languages, through the scope of the answers provided by the Prophet, provide a powerful image of him as wise, knowledgeable, and divinely inspired.

The Prophet as Guru

The special bond connecting guru and disciple—exemplified in the relationship between Ibnu Salam and Muhammad—has a long history in both South and Southeast Asia. Whether known as a relationship between *guru* and *śiṣya* (Sanskrit), *murshid* and *murīd* (Arabic), *pīr* and *murīd* (Persian), or *kyai* and *santri* (Javanese), such a relationship has been considered crucial for the personal, intellectual, and spiritual development of the disciple. Although such ties varied according to time, place, and religious tradition, their core elements were a commitment on the part of the teacher to help the disciple

31. *Serat Samud*, 1884, MS. PP St. 80, c. 5.

progress on the path to knowledge, and the latter's absolute dedication and devotion to the master. In the *One Thousand Questions* Muhammad, apart from his roles as Prophet and Messenger, appears as the ultimate guru, instructing, chiding, and initiating.

Writing of nineteenth-century Java, Steenbrink lists five types of gurus active at the time.[32] These categories—often overlapping—included the teacher of Qur'anic recitation (J. *guru ngaji Koran*), whose task was to instruct his pupils in the Arabic alphabet, the five pillars of Islam, prayer, and Qur'anic recitation; and teachers in the pesantren religious schools (called *guru kitab* or *kyai*), located mostly in the countryside, where Arabic grammar, Islamic law, theology, and Qur'anic recitation were primary topics. The disciples (J. *santri*) often worked their guru's rice fields and did other chores in his household. Such teachers all across the Netherlands East Indies were exempt from forced labor. The third group were the *guru tarékat*, often the same educators teaching at pesantren, who initiated disciples into the teachings of a particular Sufi order. Whereas one often studied the *kitab* with several teachers, the relationship with a *guru tarékat* was close and exclusive, at least as long as a disciple was in residence or in conversation with a particular guru. The fourth category consisted of teachers of esoteric, supernatural knowledge (J. *guru ilmu gaib*), who often sold amulets and charms, taught secret incantations, and otherwise dealt with the supernatural realm. These forms of knowledge were often propagated by pesantren and tarékat gurus but were also considered by many to be un-Islamic. Finally, there were the wandering gurus, divided into two groups: Arabs or Javanese searching for potential pilgrims, who also gave religious sermons, sold charms, and the like, and local teachers still following the ancient practice of wandering from cave to cave or mountain to mountain with a select entourage of disciples, performing ascetic practices and living away from society.

The teacher–disciple model found in the *One Thousand Questions*, especially considering that such gurus and disciples were not new to Java in the nineteenth century, most closely resembles that of the guru tarékat and his followers. Javanese tellings—like those from other traditions—are not tied explicitly to a particular Sufi order, yet the model itself seems to hold true: Ibnu Salam and the Prophet appear in a close and intense relationship; it is exclusive in the sense that no other teacher is mentioned and that Ibnu Salam emerges from the debate transformed, Muhammad having brought that transformation about through his instruction; although there is no initiation

32. The following is based on A. Karel Steenbrink, *Beberapa Aspek Tentang Islam di Indonesia Abad Ke-19* (Jakarta: Bulan Bintang, 1984), 152–53.

into a particular order, the much broader and more significant initiation into the Islamic faith is depicted; and the teachings include a combination of Qur'anic references, Arabic, rituals, and worship matters that were often part of the curriculum taught by a guru tarékat, as well as the additional more mystical and abstract elements that such a teacher would have taught. No less important are the genealogies appearing in *One Thousand Questions* tellings through which Muhammad traces his ancestry, as a *silsilah* ("pedigree," "lineage") of gurus—going back to the founder—was a crucial element of every tarékat.[33] Ibnu Salam's attainment of knowledge from the Prophet himself and the conferring of this knowledge to his people signifies the founding of a new line of transmission and points to Muhammad as the first Sufi guru.

And so, at least for nineteenth-century *One Thousand Questions* tellings—for which era supporting historical evidence of the importance of the tarékat on Java is available—it is likely that this model inspired their writing and perhaps also partially explains their popularity. In his analysis of the guru–disciple relationship within Javanese tarékat during this period, Kartodirdjo writes that, as far as the disciples were concerned, the guru was understood to be Allah's deputy on earth. A complete obedience to him was indispensable, and intimacy in the relationship with him was crucial for the transmission of esoteric knowledge.[34] If this level of dedication to a teacher was expected and practiced in the case of various Javanese gurus, such would be all the more true in the case of the Guru, Muhammad. Surely there was no better-proven candidate for the title of Allah's deputy than he, "seal of the prophets" and God's emissary. And indeed *One Thousand Questions* texts emphasize the crucial importance of gaining knowledge and inspiration directly from one's guru. The repetitive acknowledgement of the truth of his replies by Ibnu Salam and his conviction in embracing Islam signal the complete obedience and devotion stressed by Kartodirdjo as the hallmarks of this type of bond.

Similar, long-held traditions of the guru–disciple relationship are known from South India, where Sufi orders, and especially the Qadiriya, were popular. In the Tamil *One Thousand Questions* Ibnu Salam refers to Muhammad as *gurunabi* and consistently addresses him with respect and admiration. This attitude is quite mutual in this telling (although clearly Muhammad is the more

33. Muhammad's genealogies mentioned in these *One Thousand Questions* tellings were those of ancestors, not gurus, but they provide a genealogical model nonetheless: *Serat Suluk Samud Ibnu Salam*, Museum Sonobudoyo Library, Yogyakarta, 1898, transcribed 1932, MS. MSB P173a., c. 75, v. 8–c. 77, v. 14; *Serat Samud*, 1884, MS. PP St. 80, c. 20, vv. 8–14. Both lists begin with Adam and end with Muhammad.

34. Kartodirdjo, *The Peasants' Revolt of Banten in 1888*, VKI, vol. 50 (The Hague: Martinus Nijhoff, 1966), 159.

revered one), as the Prophet often complements Ibnu Salam for his wisdom and learning. In this way the Prophet exhibits his generosity and confidence, showing respect toward a leader of a rival religion who here appears as his disciple. Certain sections in the text are explicit in pointing to the awe Ibnu Salam feels toward Muhammad and his message, expressed by means of the former's inability to speak, or his frank acknowledgement that Muhammad's Truth is supreme to all he has previously known.

When Ibnu Salam arrives to meet Muhammad, the Prophet is surrounded by his companions and disciples in a scene reminiscent of depictions of an Indian guru. The Jews' arrival is described thus:

> Entering Medina
> In the street by the palace
> Aputullā and the Jews
> Were like a bee about to fall into honey.
> At the entrance to the mosque
> He saw the one whose face was lovelier than a ruby.[35]

Ibnu Salam and his people are likened to a bee about to sink into, and consume, the sweet honey of the Prophet's words, providing energy, insight, and life. The Prophet is described in terms implying radiance and beauty, glowing like a precious stone. The verb used for "saw" (T. *tericittār*, from Sanskrit *dṛś*) means not only to see in the narrow sense but to obtain an auspicious sight (S. *darśan*) and is the term for witnessing the sight of a god. Ibnu Salam is drawn to Muhammad at this moment not so much for his intellect or even inspiration but through a strong attraction of the senses. This too is a mark of the type of relationship to develop between guru and follower, going beyond intellect and doctrine to encompass the whole of the disciple's being.

The portrayal of Muhammad's role as teacher and prophet in the various conversion scenes suggests that his personal or symbolic presence was important in conveying a convincing message in the name of Islam. Many *One Thousand Questions* tellings incorporate the very old and related notion that Muhammad's appearance in the world was predicted already in the Torah, putting forward the claim that accepting and adopting him as a teacher, and consequently embracing Islam as his disciples, was a natural and necessary step for the Jews.[36]

35. *AM*, v. 45. The word for "mosque" is not the Arabic *masjid* but the Tamil *paḷi*.
36. On these traditions, see Arendt Jan Wensinck, *Muhammad and the Jews of Medina*, trans. Wolfgang Behn (1908; Freiburg: Klaus Schwarz, 1975), 39–44.

This claim is found across languages. In Malay tellings Abdullah speaks to the Jews and seems convinced by receiving the letter from Muhammad that he is the true Prophet, whom Moses had described to his people, mentioning several important details including the name Muhammad, and the fact that he will be an Arab of the Quraysh clan. He tells the Jews that Moses declared that once the awaited Prophet arrives "we shall leave our religion and our books too shall we destroy." When the Jews express doubt, Abdullah mentions Moses' authority three times, in addition to using his own scholarly clout to convince them that the true Prophet was indeed nearby (*HSM*, 20). In a very similar scene in the Tamil *One Thousand Questions*, Abdullah tells the Jews of the letter and reminds them that Moses had in the past predicted Muhammad's future coming, claiming this prophecy appeared in the three scriptures that preceded the Qur'an: the Torah, the Psalms, and Gospels. He then notes, in a detail that appears also in Malay, that "what is forbidden (*ḥarām*) to us is permitted (*ḥalāl*) to them" and vice versa, concluding that, now that Muhammad has made his appearance, the earlier three holy books are no longer relevant and their rulings are no longer binding (*AM*, vv. 27–29).

The 1884 Javanese *Serat Samud* from the Pakualam collection contains a very similar motif. Samud tells his people of the prophet mentioned in the Torèt (but Moses is not invoked) and how the rules of conduct and ritual are about to change.[37] Upon meeting Muhammad he repeats that "the Torèt speaks of signs of Muhammad's coming as God's messenger, the seal of the prophets, whose faith will be followed all over the world by men and animals."[38] In several instances throughout the text the Torèt is the standard by which Samud explicitly measures the accuracy of Muhammad's replies, and states that they are true because they are consistent with passages in it. For example, for this reason he agrees with Muhammad's version of the story of Adam's creation and pardon and the sequence of creation in which jinns were created first, then angels, and lastly Man.[39] Tellings of the story in all three languages state that Ibnu Salam selected his questions from the Torah, making that scripture both the source of the queries and test for Muhammad, as well as the foundation of his legitimacy and ability to reply.

37. *Serat Samud*, 1884, MS. PP St. 80, c. 1. The Torèt prophecy is also related in the Samud Leiden manuscript (MS. LOr 4001), indicating an early acquaintance with this motif in Java.
38. *Serat Samud*, 1884, MS. PP St 80, c. 1, v. 26.
39. Ibid., c. 4, v. 39 and c. 5, v. 93 respectively. In the same telling (c. 12, v. 50) Muhammad also claims that his name and the names of his people and grandson, appear in the Torèt.

The idea that Muhammad was in fact to be expected and awaited by Jewish communities, who would recognize him by the signs portended in their scripture, deepened the sense that Ibnu Salam's commitment toward the Prophet in *One Thousand Questions* tellings reaffirmed the anticipated outcome of such a meeting, whereas historically the Jews—according to this interpretation—misunderstood or rejected the signs. This ambiguity touches upon the notion of *taḥrīf*, the deliberate corruption by the Jews of God's words as revealed in the Torah. Such accusations appear in the Qur'an and were probably a reaction to the Jews' unwillingness to accept the Qur'anic statement that Muhammad and his prophecy were indeed mentioned in the Torah.[40] Since, to Muslim eyes, the Prophet's mention was obvious, the People of the Book were thought to have obscured such references through misinterpretation. In the early Arabic accounts of the Jewish convert 'Abdullah Bin Salām, the scene of punishing a Jewish couple who committed adultery—with the rabbi putting his hand over the Torah portion that demanded they be stoned, and Ibnu Salam pushing away his hand to reveal the true commandment—is cited as a Jewish attempt at taḥrīf.

The intention of the *One Thousand Questions* is, in this sense, to correct a crucial mistake made by most Jews of Arabia—and their descendents—and to write a history in which the Jews fulfilled their true calling when the last prophet arrived, by acknowledging his predicted appearance in their own sacred scripture and accepting his teachings as Truth. The teaching method presented in Malay and Tamil *One Thousand Questions* tellings strengthens this impression further, as Muhammad is consistently given the answers to Ibnu Salam's questions by Jibrail, in a manner reminiscent of the revelation of Qur'anic verses. This powerful image states anew the Prophet's divine connection and—according to the text's logic—provides additional proof and incentive for the Jews to view him as a truly inspired prophet.

Further related to the Prophet's role as teacher is the question of who possesses the authority to place words in the Prophet's mouth. In *masalah* texts that present a guru and disciple, husband and wife, or any other pair in dialogue, controversy may arise among scholars or audiences regarding the accuracy of the teachings being presented. However, in those cases, less is at stake, since the teachings of a particular school or period may always be seen as irrelevant by those outside the particular context. The words of Muhammad,

40. The various elements of taḥrīf, including, for example, concealing the truth, hiding parts of the Book, and substituting words, are listed in Camilla Adang, *Muslim Writers on Judaism and the Hebrew Bible from Ibn Rabban to Ibn Hazm* (Leiden: E. J. Brill, 1996.), 223. Taḥrīf was taken to be of two types: a distortion of a biblical text and a distortion of its sense.

however, have been considered timeless and fundamentally true by Muslims throughout the centuries that have passed since his death. By presenting the Prophet as the propagator of certain ideas—whatever these may consist of in the different *One Thousand Questions* tellings—the stakes are raised in the sense that the texts can become divisive and criticism of them more pronounced. Concurrent with these potential problems is the fact that citations of the Prophet's words are strongly linked to the hadith tradition, which began as an oral recounting of what Muhammad said on various occasions, and was later compiled in many written collections. Numerous hadith and their lines of transmission throughout the centuries were contested—considered controversial or false—and attempts were made to distinguish the reliable from the doubtful. Even so, full agreement on which hadith are authentic is not always attainable.

The practice of representing the Prophet's words, developed from early hadith literature, was expanded to represent the sayings of other important religious figures. For example, Asani writes of the *malfūẓāt* oral discourses, a category of Persian-language South Asian Sufi literature which originated as records of the actual words, sayings, and actions of Sufi masters made by their disciples. Influenced in style by the hadith, their purpose was to evoke the personal presence of the Sufi master. As oral texts recorded in writing, "they straddled the boundary between text and speech."[41]

The *One Thousand Questions* tellings present versions of the Prophet's words encompassing many topics, some of which—like Indian practices depicted in the Tamil telling—were unknown to the historic Muhammad of the seventh century. They are attempts to legitimize certain beliefs and ideas, some rather traditional and accepted and others less so, by expressing them through the speech of the indisputable founder of Islam. The way in which Muhammad is cited in the *One Thousand Questions* is reminiscent of Asani's description above in that it too falls somewhere between the assumed actual speech of the Prophet and an authoritative, hadith-like compilation that recounts for Muslims of later centuries the words spoken by their Prophet. Such citation can be highly controversial.

Examined from a strictly historical perspective, Muhammad's spoken words in *One Thousand Questions* tellings were clearly later, and so less authentic, than the very early accounts. Muhammad as teacher and prophet was redefined, through the *One Thousand Questions*, in time and place. The citation

41. Ali Asani, "At the Crossroads of Indic and Iranian Civilizations: Sindhi Literary Culture," in *Literary Cultures in History: Reconstructions from South Asia*, ed. Sheldon Pollock (Berkeley and Los Angeles: University of California Press, 2003), 612–46, at 619.

of his opinions under such circumstances, without the necessary transmission genealogy, was potentially an issue to be contested, and was in some ways considered quite radical, at least since the reforms of the nineteenth century. Hamid cites Dimyati, an Indonesian scholar, who claimed many of the Prophet's words in the Malay *Kitab Seribu Masa'il* were distorted and fabricated and, since they appear neither in the Qur'an nor hadith, represent borrowings of "foreign mythology."[42] Similar accusations have been leveled in the twentieth century against Vaṇṇapparimaḷappulavar and his Tamil *One Thousand Questions*, especially with regard to the Prophet's discussion of the female body as he describes women's punishments in hell.[43] Despite such claims, the appearance of the Prophet, and his speaking at great length to such a variety of topics with wisdom and clarity, certainly added to the story's potency as a means for increasing devotion.

The Prophet and the Jew: Portrayals across the Arabic Cosmopolis

The figures of both the Jew Ibnu Salam and the Prophet Muhammad as portrayed in these texts provide insight into the ways Jewish-Muslim relations in their formative period were represented throughout the Arabic cosmopolis, and into the ongoing echoes of these representations through time. As for Jewish communities, although they were traditionally absent from the social landscape of the Indonesian-Malay world and the Tamil land of southeast India, and Jews were rarely encountered across these regions, they consistently appeared in religious and literary sources and played important roles in depictions of early Islam in Javanese, Tamil, and Malay. Despite a physical absence, their image—at times negative but often complex and ambiguous—was certainly present. The *One Thousand Questions* opens a window onto the multifaceted perceptions of Jews across these Muslim societies. The role of the Prophet Muhammad as he appears in Tamil, Malay, and Javanese *One Thousand Questions* tellings, especially his role as the ultimate guru, was likely modeled on the relationships between guru and disciple within Sufi orders, although not exclusive to them, known from pre-Islamic times in both India and Indonesia. As such he is presented as forming a bond of intimacy, knowledge, and initiation with his disciple Ibnu Salam.

42. Dimyati, "Analisa Kitab Seribu Masalah dan Hubungannya dengan Bidang Keimanan" (M.A. thesis, IKIP Yogyakarta, 1975), 117. Cited in Ismail Hamid, *The Malay Islamic Hikayat*, Monograph Institut Bahasa Kesusastraan dan Kebudayaan Melayu (Kuala Lumpur: Universiti Kebangsaan Malaysia, 1983), 198–99.
43. Takkalai M. S. Basheer, personal communication, Madras, 2003.

The dynamic between these two figures is more complex than it first appears. Ibnu Salam, himself a respected and worthy religious scholar, relinquishes that role to become a pupil. Then, in the Javanese *Sèh Ngabdulsalam* tellings from the turn of the twentieth century, he regains his status as teacher, this time not as a Jewish scholar but a Javanese guru. The Prophet, on the other hand, begins the debate as a teacher and remains one, but, through his replies, his gained authority, and his initiation of Ibnu Salam into Islam, he *replaces* Ibnu Salam as the leading religious figure of the Jewish community. The changing roles and commitments are reflected in part in the use of a wide array of terminologies for the status and skills possessed by teachers—guru, 'alim, pundit, messenger, ascetic, sheikh—representing different traditions of learning and leadership.

Although his prophethood was denied by many Jewish communities, Muhammad in this version of the past conquers the Jews with his wisdom and irresistible truth, while Ibnu Salam is directed to correct the historical mistake of his people. Rather than ignore the Qur'anic dictum of Muhammad's appearance in the Torah or discredit it with false interpretation, Ibnu Salam fully embraces the earlier, sacred prophecies fortelling the Prophet's appearance and his call to all people to embrace a new faith. Speaking to the Jews, he explicitly mentions and employs these scriptural references to convince his community to engage in dialogue with Muhammad, a dialogue that will end in acknowledgment that the Torah prophecy was accurate, and that conversion was the inevitably correct choice.

Part Three *Conclusion*

9

The Arabic Cosmopolis of South and Southeast Asia

How did societies in transition, undergoing a profound change such as Islamization, gradually amass for themselves the textual sources allowing an engagement with, and commitment to, a history only recently adopted? How did translators and authors assemble for their audiences pieces of this long, initially foreign history, in which these audiences would eventually come to be included and could begin calling their own? In this final chapter, I want to broaden the discussion of these questions well beyond the single corpus of the *One Thousand Questions*. Expanding on the notion of the Arabic cosmopolis of South and Southeast Asia, to which linguistic and literary components were central, and maintaining an emphasis on the importance and interdependence of the processes of translation and conversion, I explore the way communities went about the formation of a new literary and religious repository that was richly interconnected both with a distant past and with a local present.

Prior Texts

Becker's notion of "prior text" will be central to my discussion. Becker writes that "all that we know has an agenda, an aggregate of remembered and half-remembered prior texts, which are there to be evoked." Almost everything we utter comes to us already in the form of words, "already languaged," and with a history.[1] Although misunderstanding and a lack of common prior texts can occur in any communication, the broad cultural memories evoked by words and phrases are more likely to be shared by people speaking the same language and living within a particular society. An outsider may have difficulty grasping the allusions and connections to prior texts and memories, cultivated from a young age, and often subtle and unspoken. The question I address in this chapter is how does a society, in the face of such a significant change as the conversion to a new religion, address the absence of prior text and memory, which are both so important in creating and maintaining a shared identity? If prior texts are, by definition, old and familiar, the challenge of assembling them to fill a void for a society transformed by conversion would seem daunting. How are texts newly created for this purpose, and how are they established so that they, in turn, come to figure as prior texts? More specifically, I consider how this process took shape in Javanese, Malay, and Tamil communities that converted to Islam and, initially, lacked the relevant prior texts and cultural memories, which only gradually evolve. I explore the mechanisms and strategies that were developed in connection with such processes, and that resulted in the rich and vast repositories of Muslim texts that have since been accumulated in these regions.

Becker writes that "everything one says has a history, and hence is, in part, a quotation. Everything anyone says is also partly new, too."[2] As is the case for individual speech, so it is for literary expression. New prior texts are created in two ways, not always distinct: (1) the reformulation of old texts; and (2) the creation of new ones, often through translation.

Just as speaking entails adjusting old language to new situations, changing circumstances entail re-presenting familiar stories or their frames in a new light. In the case of Javanese and Tamil especially, literary production long preceded the adoption of Islam, and there was no lack of textual models and literary vocabulary to draw on to reformulate texts anew. The well-known tale of Prince Aji Saka illustrates this point. Although depicted as hailing from India and introducing various aspects of Indian civilization to Java, including music, poetry, and, in many accounts, a writing system, Aji Saka's story was eventually infused with new meaning. In some tellings he traveled to Mecca and met there with the Prophet Muhammad. He received a new etymology for his name, derived from Arabic, traveled with the Prophet's companions, and the twenty new Javanese letters he created were interpreted

1. A. L. Becker, *Beyond Translation: Essays Toward a Modern Philology* (Ann Arbor: University of Michigan Press, 1995), 286–87.
2. Ibid., 286.

as God's twenty attributes. However, in a version recounted to the anthropologist Robert Heffner in the 1970s in the mountainous Tengger region of East Java, an area where an ancient, non-Muslim tradition was still practiced, Aji Saka's standing appeared to be diminishing. The story ended abruptly after Muhammad had called Aji Saka back to Mecca to report on his activities and the boat in which he sailed became stuck in a motionless, windless sea. Concerning this disappearance of Aji Saka, along with everything he signified about Javanese culture, and the symbolism of his disappearance for the Tengger, struggling to affirm their identity in a time of revitalized Islam, Hefner comments: "There is here no conversion by the sword, but the benign if deliberate neglect of a collective memory. The culture hero does not die; he and his truth fade away."[3]

The path to creating prior texts by using familiar stories and characters to introduce new ideas and narratives is not limited to a wholesale adoption of texts. It is also evident in subtler changes that occur on a smaller scale when particular words change their meaning, or new titles are bestowed on old rulers or teachers, as when yogis or rishis become sheiks, etymologies shift and places acquire new names, creating novel physical and mental geographies. This all suggests that "languaging," as Becker claims, is an endless social process of orienting and reorienting to a constantly changing environment, for which Javanese employs the term *jarwa dhosok* (literally "pressing old texts into the present situation").[4]

The acquisition—usually via translation—of new stories provides a second way in which previously unknown materials become prior texts and are adapted to their changed circumstances. Despite the problems inherent in pointing to a moment of "true" beginnings within a literary culture, Pollock argues that such instances do on occasion occur. Ideas and forms are used in a creatively novel way, marking a point of departure from what was previously known.[5] This is at times the case with works that are newly translated into a language or when such foreign works provide inspiration for introducing new themes and literary models. New stories are often presented in localized form so that they seem less foreign. This is an immense task. The first and major localization is achieved by the use of the familiar language and idiom, which immediately makes texts sound similar to that which is already known. Other

3. Robert W. Hefner, *Hindu Javanese: Tengger Tradition and Islam* (Princeton: Princeton University Press, 1985), 137.

4. Becker, *Beyond Translation*, 288.

5. Sheldon Pollock, "Literary History, Indian History, World History," *Social Scientist* 23.10–12 (1995): 112–42.

common strategies include relocating scenes within local landscapes and customs, as when the Tamil Kaipar is depicted surrounded by lush rice fields, or the Javanese Ibnu Salam performs the customary *sembah* in deference to Muhammad. Through such processes, new texts, in time, will themselves become prior texts.

Through places, flora, fauna, food, music, dress, and other local phenomena, the new text needs to have certain ties with a known past or present so that audiences may relate to it. When the nine walis credited with converting Java are associated with Javanese musical instruments, for example, an element of prior text—evoking sound, or a certain sensibility—is inserted into the story. The frequent use of epithets for Muhammad, discussed in chapter 4, is an additional example of how new information and meaning is infused through an already familiar convention.

Let us consider the *One Thousand Questions* in terms of its tellings becoming prior texts. When an unfamiliar religion is introduced to a society, as with Islam, a body of newly created and fashioned prior texts must eventually cover a range of great scope. No single text can attain that goal and therefore an entire textual spectrum is produced with multiple topics, stories, and meanings. However, some such works—such as the *One Thousand Questions*—strive to cover a wide territory. They present a combination of reworked older notions, language use, and literary conventions with new notions coming from Islam. The *One Thousand Questions* no doubt helped establish prior text on several levels by introducing much Arabic, Islamic stories, history and genealogies, geography and cosmogony, even as it connected with local literary conventions.

The notion of a body of prior texts is closely linked to that of intertextuality. By the latter I refer to the ways in which texts are interconnected, whether explicitly through mention of other titles, narratives, or episodes or, more implicitly, through subtle thematic and stylistic ties. Intertextuality is by definition related to prior texts in that the links between literary works are based on mentionings of, or reflection about, texts already in existence. A text like the *One Thousand Questions*, drawing as it does on the prior texts of scriptures, hadith, and *kisah* literature, as well as legal and mystical treatises, is highly intertextual. As it traveled and was translated into the languages of converted communities, it, too, came to be understood as an important prior text.

Prior texts and intertextual links are elements figuring within a larger project to create a new history, one which would in part succeed older ways of imagining and understanding the past. In the early stages of conversion to Islam and throughout subsequent generations, Muslims living in India and Indonesia invested great effort, time, and ingenuity into gradually assembling the pieces of a long history—with its origins in Arabia—which led to their own familiar present. The *One Thousand Questions* participated in this project in several ways, one of which was by conveying an explicit interest in literary sources, writing, and transmission, creating a kind of branching out across time and space that can be imagined as a map of linked literary roads, crossings, and signals.

The prior texts most often mentioned in *One Thousand Questions* tellings across languages are the four scriptures. Three of them, Torèt, Sabur, and Injil, retain their Arabic titles and recall the literature and history of the pre-Islamic past that is nonetheless incorporated into the Islamic canon with the understanding that the Qur'an is the seal of the scriptures and their ultimate perfection. Interestingly, in the context of discussions of alphabet mysticism in Javanese *One Thousand Questions* tellings, different words for "letters"—adopted from Arabic and Sanskrit—are used interchangeably for the same purpose, implying that the profound acts of writing and inscribing, representing creativity and creation, are not necessarily bound by a particular alphabet or semantic code.

The mention across languages of the *lawḥ*, the board or slate upon which all past and future events are inscribed, provides another example of the critical importance of writing and its presentation as a link between human and divine actions. Also relevant is the appearance of the two angels that sit on every person's shoulders, recording in writing their good and bad deeds, their fate determined with every passing minute by means of the documentation produced. In the Tamil *One Thousand Questions* this motif is elaborated, as Ibnu Salam asks the Prophet to explain in detail about the pen and ink used. Muhammad replies that the angels' tongues are the pens, their hearts the book, their saliva—sweet as fruit—is the ink, emerging from the ink-bottle of their throats (*AM*, vv. 179–80). The benefits of contact with the text—through writing, inscribing, listening, reading, or possessing it—are also highlighted, whether in the opening lines (in Tamil) or in closing (as is often true for Javanese and Malay tellings), promising a blessed future to those who internalize its message. The appearance of a *One Thousand Questions* telling within a multi-text volume, as happens quite often in Javanese, means creating a connection—both figuratively and concretely—with neighboring and distant texts.

All these instances unfolded within the larger framework not only of the Arabic cosmopolis of South and Southeast Asia, where Muslims read and listened to *One Thousand Questions* tellings in their own languages, but also in the context of a global Muslim culture that greatly emphasized the power of language: Allah's creative powers were condensed in and expressed through the single imperative *kun*, and His words were recorded for all future generations in the Qur'an. It is these fundamental beliefs in the power of words that in large part gave rise to, and sustained, the ideals and practices in the linguistic and literary spheres that developed among Tamil, Javanese, and Malay Muslims.

Beyond a general emphasis on themes of writing, telling, recording, reading, and transmitting, the *One Thousand Questions* contains instances of more specific forms of intertextuality and uses of prior texts. Central among them is the "number questions" sequence in which Abdullah Ibnu Salam asks the Prophet what is one, not two . . . what is two, not three . . . going from one to thirty; he then continues in the same vein, proceeding by tens and asking what is thirty, not forty . . . what is forty, not fifty . . . continuing all the way to one hundred.[6] These number questions, in various forms, appear in early Arabic *One Thousand Questions* tellings, in the twelfth-century Latin translation, and in other languages, including Tamil and Malay. The questions in the latter two languages are almost identical. When they do differ it is mostly in detail, style, or emphasis, not theme.[7] The replies to the "number questions" in Tamil and Malay—thirty-seven in all—offer a brief mapping of several domains, which in turn gain their own references from additional textual sources. The themes addressed include God's unity, cosmology, cosmogony, histories of the prophets, and a Muslim understanding of time. The latter two topics occupy the prominent positions within this condensed presentation of Islam.

There are seventeen questions—almost half of the total number—addressing the lives and deeds of the prophets: for example, the number nine stands for the number of times God revealed himself to Musa; eleven are Yusuf's brothers; Musa was born on the twenty-second of the month of Ramadan, while on its twenty seventh day Yunus was swallowed by the fish. The brief presentation of these prophets offers the kernel of their life story—Yunus and the fish, Idris ascending to the sky—as popularly known and as elaborated in the much longer, detailed, and popular renditions of the prophets' biographies.

6. This question is highly reminiscent of the Hebrew Song *Eḥad Mi Yode'a* ("Who Knows What is One?"), appearing toward the end of the Passover Haggadah, and it is only one among several major haggadic elements incorporated into the *Book of One Thousand Questions*. The Haggadah—the text read on the eve of Passover recounting the Israelite's exodus from Egypt—is framed by a set of questions that the child—who is young and inexperienced and can be likened to the disciple Ibnu Salam—asks his parent, who is an elder, teacher, authority figure, like the Prophet; the transformative journey from slavery to freedom can be likened to the one from Judaism to Islam; and there are additional thematic and structural similarities.

7. A similar series of questions, going from one to fourteen, appears in a Malay narrative that depicts the conversion of five hundred monks to Islam. Ph. S. van Ronkel, "Malay Tales about conversion of Jews and Christians to Muhammedanism," *Acta Orientalia* 10 (1932): 56–66, at 64.

Addressing Muslim notions of time occurs through, for example, the replies on the number five (number of daily prayers), six (days of creation), seven (days of the week), twelve (months of the year), and, most notably, the various days of the month of Ramadan on which auspicious events occurred: the fifteenth (Muhammad received the Qur'an), the twentieth (Daud received Psalms), the twenty-first (Sulayman received his ring), the twenty-second (Musa's birth), the twenty-third (Isa received the Gospel), the twenty-fifth (Musa crossed the Red Sea, escaping Pharaoh's army), the twenty-sixth (the Torah was revealed to Musa), and the thirtieth (God spoke to Musa).

Various dimensions of time are incorporated into these replies, from the divisions of a single day to the days of the week and the annual cycle of months, to a larger sacred history condensed into the holy month of Ramadan, during which so many events significant to Muslim history are said to have occurred. The first theme—that of the prophets' lives—is linked to notions of time through the days of Ramadan, with Musa providing the most pronounced connection. Audiences attentive to this list of questions and answers receive an abbreviated introduction to their prophets, the structures of time that guide Muslim lives, and to the way the two are intertwined in the ritual and moral observances of the fasting month.

Other matters are addressed only briefly in this series of questions, yet together the "number questions" and their replies strengthen the impression that for the reader/listener an entire picture emerges, its details ranging from the four holy scriptures to the punishment of one hundred blows inflicted on those who commit adultery. In their intertextual drawing on Qur'anic verses, the canonical tradition, and Islamic law, the "number questions" present a web of meanings and associations in which history and memory play major roles. The connections made between the days of the Ramadan and so many central events and figures collapse the boundaries between past and present and draw the listener closer to a past of mythical proportions, with which he can now more strongly identify. The "number questions" are a "mini-guide" of sorts or, even more pertinently, a condensed *Book of One Thousand Questions* in which the important facets covered in the text as a whole are put forth in abbreviated form, appropriate for both new converts and long-practicing Muslims.

The *One Thousand Questions* includes many additional instances of linking together past and present, familiar and foreign. It presents not only the ongoing dialogue between Muhammad and Ibnu Salam but an entire set of figurative dialogues among prior texts and contemporary events, overlapping and interacting, connecting and diverging in sometimes subtle and sometimes explicit ways.

The letter from the Prophet inviting Ibnu Salam to a debate in the *One Thousand Questions'* opening scene is a case in point. Well-known traditions in Arabic tell of letters sent out by Muhammad to kings and leaders of his era, calling them to Islam. Among them were those addressed to Heraclius, the Byzantine Emperor, to the governor of Bahrain, and to the king of Persia. The letters, always conveyed by messengers, began with the *bismillah* greeting and with mention of the Prophet as sender—as did the letter to Ibnu Salam—and invited the leaders to accept Islam, promising rewards if they did and hardship if they refused.[8] In early Arabic renditions of the *One Thousand Questions* this element did not yet appear. Rather, Muhammad sits with his companions in Yathrib as Jibrīl comes with a message that four important Jews are on their way to him, to ask for proof of his prophethood. The greatest among them is named Abdia iben Salon. Muhammad already knows their names and physical appearance and sends 'Alī to meet them. The Jews are astonished when 'Alī addresses them by their names. In this telling the Jews are already secretly admiring Muhammad and so come to him. Abdia then introduces himself as an emissary for the Jews, coming to ask one hundred questions based on the Law, which he has in writing.[9]

Many details are introduced in later Arabic tellings. Two important motives are that Muhammad is the first to initiate contact with the Jews of Khaybar and that he does so by sending them a letter dictated by Jibrīl.[10] Thus these later additions likely combine the tradition of letters sent out to various leaders (among whom Ibnu Salam is included) and the canonical story of Ibnu Salam's conversion to Islam. The additions—Muhammad initiating the contact and sending a letter—appear also in *One Thousand Questions* tellings in Tamil, Malay, and Javanese, as well as in the Arabic manuscript from Batavia.

In Tamil Jipuṟayīl arrives as Muhammad is sitting with his companions and tells him to write a letter to the wise Ipuṉu Calām.[11] Muhammad immediately asks that the scribe Cātu Ipuṉu Ukkācu be summoned so that the letter, dictated by Jipuṟayīl, can be inscribed by him, and Ukkācu comes swiftly "like an arrow hurled from a bow" (*AM*, v. 14).

8. Muhammad ibn 'Abd Allah al-Khaṭīb Tibrīzī, *Mishkāt Al-Maṣābiḥ*, trans. James D. Robson, 4 vols. (Lahore: Sh. Muhammad Ashraf, 1963), 3:832–33.

9. Guillaume Frederic Pijper, *Het boek der duizend vragen* (Leiden: E. J. Brill, 1924), 41. The number one hundred resonates with the above mentioned "number questions" that go from one to one hundred, and may have been the kernel which was later expanded to one thousand.

10. *Kitāb Masā'il Sayyidī 'Abdallāh Bin Salām Lin-Nabī* (Cairo: Al-Yusufiya, ca. 1920), 1.

11. The word for letter, *ōlai*, literally "palm leaf,"' indicates the material dimension of letter-writing at the time.

The letter is then dictated by the Prophet, who has already received its content from the archangel:

First write: *picumillākiṟ ṟakumāṉiṟ ṟakīm*
The words of God's messenger are written
I am Muhammad
I [teach] God's exalted way
In this world, to all.
All will be blessed
Those who take the right path—that of the mustakīm, steadfast in it
Will gain prophet and heaven
Listen to my words and you will succeed.
(*AM*, v. 17)

Going on to describe God's greatness and Muhammad's position, the scribe completes the letter, defined as a "message of peace." He then hurries to deliver it, arriving in Kaipar as the letter "in his hand brings light, like the moon shining and removing darkness" (*AM*, v. 22). Reaching Ibnu Salam, he gives him the invitation. The scene is described as follows:

He took the letter from the messenger, telling of truth
The handsome Aputullā wonders:
Which is your town? Which is your land? Who has sent you?
And the messenger explained the purpose.[12]

12. *AM*, v. 23. This verse echoes with a very early—and well-known—poem, "What He Said," of the Tamil caṅkam age (circa 1st–3rd centuries AD) in which a man speaks to his beloved, asking similarly about her origins, her identity:

What could my mother be
to yours? What kin is my father
to yours anyway? And how
did you and I meet ever?
But in love our hearts are as red
earth and pouring rain:
mingled
beyond parting.

Cempulappeyaṉīrār, *Kuṟuntokai* 40, in A. K. Ramanujan, trans. and ed., *Poems of Love and War* (New York: Columbia University Press, 1985), 37. This poem recounts how a man and a woman, unrelated and from different places, came together, becoming inseparable. In a reminiscent fashion Ibnu Salam wonders where the messenger—who carries the fateful letter that will bring

In Malay tellings the scene is quite similar. After Muhammad has migrated to Medina, Jibrail arrives by his side, following God's command. He tells the Prophet he has been commanded to send a letter to a learned Jew in Khaybar by the name of Abdullah Ibnu Salam, who is well versed in the Torah, Gospels, and Psalms and in their interpretation. Muhammad then asks what should be written in the letter and who shall write it. This latter question may be a subtle reference to Muhammad's well-known illiteracy. Jibrail tells him to call the *qāḍī* Sa'id, who then writes it as dictated by the angel. This brief letter too begins with the *bismillah*, introduces Muhammad as Prophet and Messenger and—citing in Arabic—announces that the righteous shall be blessed. The text then relates that the letter is delivered to Ibnu Salam in Khaybar but not by whom, nor does any detail of the delivery encounter appear. In both Tamil and Malay, Ibnu Salam's speech to the Jews elaborates on the content of the letter and gives the impression that he had prior knowledge of the Prophet and the events about to unfold, stemming from the above-mentioned prophecies in the Torah, of which he was very much aware.

According to the Batavia *One Thousand Questions* manuscript, written in Arabic and dating from the eighteenth century, after Muhammad received God's revelation, all people were summoned to the faith except the Jews and Christians. Then the Prophet wrote a letter similar in content to those already mentioned, dictated to him by Jibrīl, and in turn by him to his scribe, Sa'd bin Abī Wakkās. Once again, in this telling from the region, all the elements appear: the Prophet's initiative, the same scribe serving him, and the brief content of the letter.[13]

The passages discussed thus far recount traditions concerning letters sent by the Prophet during his lifetime. However, even many centuries after his death, the motif of a letter received from the Prophet was kept alive in the Muslim world. Already noted is the case of the Javanese *Serat Walisana*, which tells of a letter from the Prophet descending miraculously and determining Muhammad's Javanese successor. Other, more transregional letters appeared as well, attesting to the persistence of this theme.

A "last testament of the Prophet" (J. *serat wasiat*) also circulated in nineteenth-century Java.[14] Written in simple Arabic and then translated into

him into an inseparable bond with the Prophet—is from, and how did this joining—destined to be one of love and devotion—come to be.

13. There seem to be two major traditions regarding the actual writing of the letter, one which depicts 'Alī as writing it, while the other consistently mentions Sa'd bin Abī Wakkās as scribe.

14. Sartono Kartodirdjo, *The Peasants' Revolt of Banten in 1888*, VKI, vol. 50 (The Hague: Martinus Nijhoff, 1966), 167.

Malay, it originated in Islam's centers in Arabia and contained a message from Muhammad, transmitted via Abdullah, the guardian of his tomb. The message was revealed in a dream and depicted a dialogue between Muhammad and God in which the Prophet requested divine intervention on behalf of all Muslims, listed moral and sinful behaviors, and warned of the approach of the Final Judgment. The letter circulated widely in West Java in 1884, with a similar one appearing in 1891. This latter document was copied by hand and also printed for wider dissemination in Singapore and Penang.

Such letters were not a new phenomenon. The well-known Dutch scholar and colonial administrator Snouck Hurgronje claimed that such letters had been circulating for at least a century or two, brought back by those returning from Mecca. They expressed religious and political aspirations, employing the letter motif that was long known but responding to changing circumstances. For example, the prophecies of approaching *kiyamat* were related to the rise of messianic movements in Mecca, Java, and elsewhere toward the end of the nineteenth century. These in turn were tied to the strengthening of colonial regimes over largely Muslim-populated regions, and, in the case of Java, they aroused fear, suspicion, and dissatisfaction within the Dutch administration, which tried different means to decrease or eliminate the letters' impact. The circulation of such letters was known also in British India at the time.[15]

Although letters received from the Prophet in eras long postdating his historical lifetime may in some respects seem to comprise a very different category from the earlier letters sent during his lifetime, there is in fact no inherent contradiction in the importance granted them within an Islamic worldview. Such later letters from Muhammad are related to the much broader belief in the Prophet's powers of intercession on behalf of believers of subsequent generations. It is therefore not difficult to situate the letters from Muhammad received by the walis, as well as those circulating in nineteenth-century India, Singapore, and Indonesia, within these traditions of an ongoing, living presence of the Prophet.

What would it have meant to hear about such a letter from the Prophet? Although it remains uncertain how familiar the earlier traditions were to particular individuals or communities, it is clear that mention of letters from Muhammad—addressed to kings, potential converts, and subsequent generations of Muslims—appearing in the canonical hadith collections, law books, and local literary works, were a powerful and consistent thread within the Muslim imagination. Considering not only the early hadith traditions but

15. A. Karel Steenbrink, *Beberapa Aspek Tentang Islam di Indonesia Abad Ke-19* (Jakarta: Bulan Bintang, 1984), 254–67.

also the *One Thousand Questions* itself in light of late nineteenth-century developments points to how such a text—translated and adapted, initially foreign—becomes a prior text, in the light of which contemporary events may be assessed and understood.

The two examples, the "number questions" and the Prophet's letter, highlight how the story told in the *One Thousand Questions* was connected in multiple ways to other, prior textual (and, most likely oral) sources, providing their audiences with important links to a larger cultural landscape and to a sense of the depth and richness of their shared history. In both cases the bonds of time and space were loosened so that this shared history—with the Prophet as its axis—became more accessible to contemporary Muslims in distant lands.

The *One Thousand Questions* not only reached outward, toward broader, translocal Muslim frames of reference, but was, in some ways, also inwardly directed, moving toward the local and the culturally specific. This tendency is seen clearly in an instance from Javanese literature. Many of the themes appearing in the *Serat Samud* tellings are common to Javano-Islamic literature of the eighteenth to early twentieth centuries. Much of the mystical speculation and structural elements it contains can be found in similar or identical forms in other poems and prose works. These include, for example, the use of analogies, classification systems, alphabet mysticism, God's oneness, and His relation to creation. In this sense the narrative serves predominantly as a way to enhance the authority of the teachings, by presenting them as the Prophet's own words. This is especially the case when details of the older tellings—having to do with Samud's Jewish identity, the setting of his meeting with the Prophet, and his conversion—are diminished or missing. Samud's story may then still echo with an important translated work, but it also becomes one more *suluk* in a vast Javanese repository.

In line with this trend there are sections in the Javanese tellings that clearly connect with other texts, external to the *One Thousand Questions* and concurrently popular on Java. One such thematic example, which has no correlative in the Arabic, Tamil, and Malay tellings and represents an example of a specifically Javanese intertextuality, will suffice to make the point. The themes of human conception and gestation and their relationship to Muslim notions of cosmogony appear within Samud's repertoire of questions in several Javanese *One Thousand Questions* tellings, including the 1898 *Serat Suluk Samud Ibnu Salam* and the 1884 *Serat Samud*. In the *Serat Samud* the discussion of the months of pregnancy comes after a long outline of the descent of the *rahsa* (secret, semen) through the human male body until it enters the woman, the receptacle for it (J. *wadhah*), the site where the embryo is formed.

Samud then asks for the names of the different forms in the womb (J. *wujud*) during gestation, followed by a question about the reality or essence of the body (J. *kakékaté ingkang jisim*) developing in utero, about its changing nature with the passing months. The reply addresses the nine months of pregnancy, assigning a name to each.[16] (It is noteworthy, especially when compared with other texts that address this topic, that the names for the gestation months or forms—all in Arabic or derived from it—appear as such, without commentary or translation.)

This section is followed by a discussion of God's *titipan* (gift, deposit) in the form of the senses to the developing human in the womb. When the baby is ready to be born, his body complete, he faces a great door as he emits a sun-like light. It does not take long and the baby emerges, his eyes and ears closed. The *takbir*, a recounting of God's greatness, is recited. The text then moves on to a discussion of a mapping of the Arabic letters on the human body. A very similar sequence and details are found in the *Serat Suluk Samud Ibnu Salam*, including the forms in the womb, the nature of the developing fetus, God's gifts, the birth scene, and the mapping of Arabic letters on the body.[17] Neither offers any elaboration on the terms related to gestation or a translation of their meaning into Javanese.

A corresponding reference to this theme in Javanese literature can be found in at least two texts. The first is the *Serat Niti Mani*, a modern Javanese prose treatise on procreation, sexuality, and asceticism, which "connects eroticism with the indigenous kind of mystic Muslim speculations."[18] The work, composed by R.M.H. Sugonda, a son of Mangkunagara IV and himself the Bupati of Pasuruhan between 1887 and 1903, was written in 1886 and revised in 1892.[19] It is reminiscent of the *One Thousand Questions* in that it is written as a dialogue between *Juru Patanya* ("the one asking questions") and *Sang Murwèng-gita* ("respected author of the song") and covers many topics. The relevant *Niti Mani* section is preceded by a description of conception. The question then follows: what happens next? The reply is an explanation of the names and meanings of the seven spheres (J., from A. *alam*) and the seven grades, or stages, of emanation (J., from A. *martabat*) by way of the pregnancy

16. *Serat Samud*, Pura Pakualaman Library, Yogyakarta, 1884, MS. PP St. 80, c. 17. vv. 30–34.

17. *Serat Suluk Samud Ibnu Salam*, Museum Sonobudoyo Library, Yogyakarta, 1898, MS. MSB 173a, c. 38, vv. 22–23.

18. Theodore G. T. Pigeaud, *Literature of Java*, 3 vols. (The Hague: Martinus Nijhoff, 1967–70), 1:274.

19. Nancy K. Florida, *Javanese Literature in Surakarta Manuscripts*, vol. 2: *Manuscripts of the Mangkunagaran Palace* (Ithaca: Cornell University Press, 1993), 448–49. The work was first published in Surakarta in 1908 by Albert Rusche and Co. I cite the 1919 edition of this publication.

months. A similar interest is apparent here to that in the *One Thousand Questions* regarding the gestation process, the development of the new human in the womb, and the relationship between that creation and development and an Islamic conceptualization of creation, space, and time via a presentation, however condensed, of the teachings about the spheres. But, whereas the *One Thousand Questions* tellings only briefly mention Arabic terms without translation or commentary upon their significance, the *Niti Mani* explicitly locates the seven months within a coherent sphere of meaning.

The seven months are correlated with the seven worlds, or spheres, and the seven "grades of being," so central to Javano-Islamic mystical teachings.[20] In addition, the meaning of each grade in Arabic is then explained in Javanese. For example, the first month is equated with *alam akadiyat* (from A. *aḥadiyya*, the initial stage of nondifferentiation), "rendered in Arabic as *la takyun*" (A. *la ta'ayyun*). The Arabic is further explained to refer to an embryo who "has no attributes as of yet" (J. *dèrèng sanyata ing kahananipun*). These attributes emerge gradually until by the end of the seventh month the fetus is a complete human (J. *sampurna ing manungsa*) who is ready to be born into the world (J. *alam donya*).[21]

This reply is then followed by an additional elaboration on the theme, presented as an ancient, local allegory (J. *pralambang*) attributed to the Javanese sages of old. This time the pregnancy months are linked to a list of analogies, responding to the same question of the fetus's nature with every passing month. Taking the first month as an example again, the embryo is likened to a "flower in the sky," which is then elaborated to mean "like pollen of a flower scattered in the air," conjuring the image of subtle, almost invisible particles that have no coherent form or attributes.[22]

A second source besides the *Niti Mani* where this theme is found is the *Serat Kridhaksara*, a treatise on the origins and meaning of the Javanese alphabet, especially pertaining to its writing on the human body. It is some-

20. Here, probably because the months resonate with the *martabat*, it takes only seven—rather than nine—months for the fetus to be ready for birth. Harya Sugonda, *Niti Mani* (Surakarta: Albert Rusche and Co., 1919), 92.

21. Sugonda, *Niti Mani*, 90–92. The translation of the Arabic terminology is based on P. J. Zoetmulder, *Pantheism and Monism in Javanese Suluk Literature: Islamic and Indian Mysticism in an Indonesian Setting*, trans. Merle Calvin Ricklefs (Leiden: KITLV, 1995), xv and 138.

22. Sugonda, *Niti Mani*, 92. It is noteworthy that both Arabic and Javanese terminology receive an interpretation/translation via the word *tegesipun*, "this means." The concept *alam akadiyat* is described as being translated into Arabic (*ing tembung Arab binasakaken*), literally "put into language, presented as a saying," while the depiction for the first month, presented in Javanese, is analogized, likened to (J. *dipunupamakaken*). This raises the question of the relationship between these (often overlapping) processes of definition, translation, and analogy.

times attributed to Aji Saka and said to have been adapted from Kawi into modern Javanese in the mid nineteenth century, providing an example of a reformulated prior text.[23]

In this work, as in the *One Thousand Questions* and *Niti Mani*, the theme of gestation appears. As in *Niti Mani* the seven months of pregnancy are related to the seven spheres, using mostly the same sequence and names.[24] The text goes further than any of those so far discussed in its elaboration of these themes, with an additional interpretation of the letters (this time the Javanese characters) offered, followed by a revelation of the condition of the human while in utero, using approximate sketches, said to be based on the opinions of Islamic scholars (J. *bangsa ulama*). The developing fetus is described and its *wujud* for each month compared to a letter and number, with an accompanying sketch. Here analogy is employed (for example, in the first month the fetus resembles a tadpole) along with these additional elements.[25]

It is clear that both the *Niti Mani* and *Serat Kridhaksara* elaborate more than does the *One Thousand Questions* on the theme of gestation and its relationship to Muslim terminologies of creation and world order. The *One Thousand Questions* tellings discussed do not mention the seven spheres or grades of being, do not include analogies of any kind to portray fetal development, and, perhaps most strikingly in view of their tendency to offer commentary and interpretation, do not translate or explain the significance of the names and forms of the passing pregnancy months. Nevertheless, the appearance of this topic within Javanese *One Thousand Questions* tellings connects them with a prevalent local tradition. This tradition was attributed in part to pre-Islamic times (a Kawi work by Ajisaka) and was adapted to contemporary circumstances (mapping Arabic, rather than Javanese, letters on the body). Its unique appearance in the Javanese *One Thousand Questions* is an instance of how this transregional story also put down deep local roots. It provides an example of both how a prior, non-Islamic Javanese text was reshaped and incorporated into a widely known Islamic work *and* of how this work—the *One Thousand*

23. T. E. Behrend, ed., *Katalog Induk Naskah-Naskah Nusantara: Museum Sonobudoyo Yogyakarta* (Jakarta: Jembatan, 1990), 489–90. I cite the transliterated version of the anonymous *Serat Kridhaksara*, Museum Sonobudoyo Library, Yogyakarta. MS. MSB P93.

24. *Serat Kridhaksara*, Museum Sonobudoyo Library, Yogyakarta, MS. MSB P93, pp. 8–9.

25. The tadpole in this analogy is likened to the god Viṣṇu, one of whose incarnations was the fish, pointing to the pre-Islamic in this work. The sketches are simple and crude and, since the original Javanese manuscript has been lost, it is unfortunately impossible to know how similar its sketches were to this copy, made in the twentieth century. *Serat Kridhaksara*. MS. MSB P93, 14–17.

Questions—was interconnected with other specifically Javanese texts through common references, allusions, and themes.

I have looked at the notions of prior texts and intertextuality and how their employment by authors and translators contributed to the shaping of a multilayered, interconnected Islamic literary world, presenting audiences with repeated mention of certain ideas, characters, and themes that both tied them to their local community and to a wider, translocal community possessing a common history. In these concluding pages I examine more closely the contours of the latter, larger Islamic sphere which emerged in South India, the Archipelago, and beyond, and broaden the discussion of how language, literature, and writing—and ideas about them—contributed to the shaping and ongoing vitality of the Arabic cosmopolis.

Literary Networks and the Arabic Cosmopolis

I began this book by introducing the notion of "literary networks" as an important addition to the familiar scholarly discussions of the networks of trade, scholarship, politics, and travel in the Muslim world. Literary networks, however symbolically, connected Muslims from different places and cultures. My thinking about these networks has centered on the ways in which language and literature, often via translation, participated in creating, forging, and sustaining such networks across both time and space.

Pollock's work on the Sanskrit cosmopolis of South and Southeast Asia provides an inspiring model for considering the idea of a later, Arabic cosmopolis that emerged in parts of the same regions, existing side by side with, overlapping with, and at times inheriting the Sanskrit one. Although the emphases of Pollock's work differ from mine, and although the dissimilarities between the Sanskrit and Arabic cosmopoleis are significant, the comparison between the roles and histories of Sanskrit and Arabic across similar geographical terrain has important implications for our understanding of these regions' diverse and complex histories, the ways in which languages, religions, and power structures wax and wane, and the roles of literature in large, transformative processes.

Throughout this book I have closely examined the formation of Malay, Tamil, and Javanese literary cultures not as profoundly novel but as reconstituted in various ways following the encounter with Islamic and Arabic culture, fitting the model of "cosmopolitan vernacularism."[26] Having laid out

26. Sheldon Pollock, "The Cosmopolitan Vernacular," *The Journal of Asian Studies* 57.1 (1998): 6–13, at 6–8.

evidence for the consolidation of an Arabic cosmopolis in these regions of South and Southeast Asia, I return briefly to a discussion of how it differed from, resembled, and overlapped with the Sanskrit cosmopolis.

A major difference between the Sanskrit cosmopolis and the Arabic one is in their links to religion, as the Arabic cosmopolis's coming into being and its consolidation corresponded to an ongoing process of Islamization. The translocality, dignity, and authority of Arabic were fundamentally linked to its role as the language of God and His Prophet. Another difference or variation in my account is that the bulk of my analysis was not limited to Arabic but rather focused on the broader Arabicized cultures of several Muslim communities. Thus I am not comparing, as Pollock did, a strictly cosmopolitan age with a vernacular one. Arabic and Arabicized literature are part of the same continuum and represent both a more recent cosmopolitan stage in South and Southeast Asia, when compared with Sanskrit, and a force that transformed vernaculars already endowed with literary traditions before Islamization.

Despite the differences, there are notable similarities. As Sanskrit became the major vehicle for expressing royal will, Sanskrit learning itself evolved into an essential component of power, with the figure of the learned king firmly established.[27] Similarly in Java, Sultan Agung, the seventeenth-century monarch who perhaps best of all represents the synthesizing of Javanese and Islamic identities, was a pious follower of Islam in whose time important Arabicized works were composed, while concurrently, in Banten, King Pangeran Ratu corresponded with Islamic scholars in Arabia and studied difficult Sufi works.[28] The figure of Ibnu Salam himself highlights the centrality of a learned man who is both a religious authority on the scriptures and a leader of his people.

Perhaps most importantly, in the cases of both Sanskrit and Arabic, it was the circulation of the texts written in these languages within a particular region that produced the cosmopolis as a cultural political space. In the case of Sanskrit, courtly epics, histories, and grammatical textbooks were studied across the Sanskrit world, regulating norms of literary production over a vast area.[29] Across the Arabic cosmopolis treatises on law, mysticism, grammar, and ritual were studied and read in Arabic along with the corresponding Arabicized literature that produced multiple echoes of the cosmopolitan language.

27. Sheldon Pollock, *The Language of the Gods in the World of Men: Sanskrit, Culture, and Power in Premodern India* (Berkeley and Los Angeles: University of California Press, 2006), 166.
28. Merle Calvin Ricklefs, *Mystic Synthesis in Java: A History of Islamization from the Fourteenth to the Early Nineteenth Centuries* (Norwalk: EastBridge, 2006), 33–52.
29. Pollock, *The Language of the Gods in the World of Men*, 255.

These echoes, in their multiplicity, are comparable to the regional variations apparent among Indian languages negotiating with the dominant cosmopolitan literary idiom of Sanskrit during the shift to the vernacular era in South Asia. Often, as in the cases of *meykkīrtti* or *maṇippiravāḷam*, the complex combinations created in cosmopolitan-vernacular idioms were embodied in the terms or titles used themselves, epitomizing the cultural and political shifts. And just as the critical vocabulary of literary and linguistic analysis in the Sanskrit cosmopolis came to be deeply colored by Sanskrit (as when Sanskrit *kāvya* was localized as Tamil *kāppiyam* and as Javanese *kakawin*),[30] much of that critical vocabulary during a later period was colored by Arabic literary traditions. Terms like *serat*, *syair*, *kitab*, *hikayat*, *masalah*, *suluk*, and *tafsir* were widely and consistently employed in the Arabic cosmopolis.

It is intriguing to examine not just the differences and similarities between the Sanskrit and Arabic comopoleis but also the thread of continuity that connects them. Addressing a culture central to my inquiry, Pollock asserts that "Javanese offers a paradigm case for the appropriations, negotiations, and compromises achieved by a cosmopolitan-vernacular literary culture. And it bears close comparison to the cultures of southern India in respect to language, philologization, literary form and style, and, most unexpectedly, the localized and allegorized representations of political power and its geocultural expositions."[31] An unsuspecting reader might assume these lines were written about the Arabicized cosmopolitan-vernacular idiom of an Islamized Java. And, indeed, the many "appropriations, negotiations, and compromises" that characterized the interactions of Arabic and its manifestations within the literary worlds of Muslims in the region played a major role in creating and sustaining literary networks within a sphere of shared idioms, ideas, and stories. Examples of Arabic's dissemination, many of which have been mentioned, abound.

Arabic infuses both Islamic texts and everyday speech, especially in Javanese and Malay. This includes the language of both the sacred and the ordinary, such as daily greetings, the names of the days of the week, and personal names. Arabic's influence on grammatical structures—often via interlinear translation—is evident, as is its impact on poetics and literary genres. All three languages discussed here adopted modified forms of the Arabic script, used for translated as well as original writings. An important feature of the cosmopolis, this orthographic transformation allowed Muslims in diverse

30. Ibid., 384–85.
31. Ibid., 388.

locales to experience their own languages in the shared, religiously charged form of Arabic.

The literary networks that crisscrossed the Arabic cosmopolis of South and Southeast Asia were determined and defined not solely by the use of a certain "amount" of Arabic but also by the type of works disseminated and the extent of that dissemination. Islamic theological, grammatical, and moral works were conveyed in local languages, as were the deeds and adventures of early Muslim warriors and kings. A popular example of the latter is found in the many volumes depicting the life of Amir Hamza, one of the Prophet's uncles, in Javanese and Malay. Tales of the Prophet's companions and previous prophets—those leading up to Muhammad—were widespread. The stories narrating the life of Muhammad himself were of course pivotal to such literary networks. Central episodes from his biography—his birth, ascent to the heavens, splitting of the moon, and his death—became cornerstones in an early history shared by all who followed his path, no matter their mother tongue.

Literary works were not only translated and adapted into regional languages; there is evidence of single textual sources being written in more than one of the region's languages. Complex combinations were created: for example, some Tamil poets composed multilingual verses comprised of Arabic, Persian, and Urdu, in addition to Tamil. A book on Islamic medicine, inscribed in 1807 and currently in the Indonesian National Library, was written in four languages as well: Javanese, Persian, Tamil, and Arabic.[32] Such multiple language volumes were an additional contribution to bridging linguistic gaps between Muslims from different communities, and they enhanced the creation of shared repositories of knowledge. The shared use of Arabic script in such collections traversed and blurred the boundaries between languages and between the cosmopolitan and vernacular. If we imagine a map of the literary networks across which texts, stories, and ideas were carried between and among different people and places in South and Southeast Asia, citations *from* and above all *in* Arabic might appear as sites along the routes of transmission and circulation. Citing familiar Qur'anic passages, carefully transmitted words of the Prophet, or legal injunctions created symbolic sites of exchange, acceptance, and recognition for Muslims of diverse backgrounds.

Beyond the realm of manuscripts and books, Arabic script was to be found in the Archipelago above all on tombstones, as noted in the Introduction,

32. Takya Shu'ayb 'Alim, *Arabic, Arwi and Persian in Sarandib and Tamil Nadu* (Madras: Imāmul 'Arūs Trust, 1993), 105–6.

with the earliest instance in Java dating from the fourteenth century.[33] In the Tamil region, Arabic epitaphs in Kayalpattinam, dating from the fifteenth century, record names and Hijri death dates. Some include sections of religious texts, genealogies, and occupations like *qāḍī* (judge), *amīr* (military title), and *tājir* (learned merchant), employing the Arabic titles of the kind routinely adopted by rulers, members of the nobility, and literary figures in both Southern India and the Archipelago.[34]

Educational institutions played a major role in fostering a sense of shared identity within the cosmopolis. In religious educational centers Arabic and its branches of learning—grammar, syntax, jurisprudence, Qur'anic exegesis, hadith—were routinely taught to new generations of pupils. Madrasas in South India and pesantren on Java and Sumatra provided a similar structure for learning—from the very basics of Arabic to highly specialized knowledge—and for bonding with Islamic scholars and other members of the community. From their ranks emerged the religious officials, leaders, and teachers who would in turn train and inform their own disciples.

Religious teachers often traveled in a quest to disseminate their knowledge and religious convictions to others, expanding the geographical and cultural limits of the cosmopolis. The *Sejarah Melayu* (*Malay Annals*) relates that Tamil Muslim teachers were influential in the Malay regions in the fifteenth century. The *Annals* also claim—as does the *Hikayat Raja-Raja Pasai* (*Book of the Pasai Kings*)—that the apostles of Islam reached Malay shores from the Coromandel coast.[35] Shu'ayb discusses at length the deeds of 'Umar Wali, an eighteenth century Tamil "saint" who spent years in the forests of Sumatra, propagating Islam;[36] Bayly mentions a Tamil *pīr* from Vetalai who, while meditating in a Sumatran jungle, encountered and overcame a fierce elephant. In gratitude the sultan granted him his daughter in marriage and nominated him as successor to the Acehnese sultanate;[37] Javanese nobles and their retinues, exiled to Sri Lanka from the eighteenth century onwards, brought with them—if not in written then certainly in oral form—stories and

33. Ricklefs, *Mystic Synthesis in Java*, 12.

34. On the Kayalpattinam tombstones, see Mehrdad Shokoohy, *Muslim Architecture of South India: The Sultanate of Ma'bar and the Traditions of Maritime Settlers on the Malabar and Coromandel Coasts* (*Tamil Nadu, Kerala and Goa*) (London: Routledge, 2003), 275–90.

35. Stuart Robson, "Java at the Crossroads," *BKI* 137 (1981): 259–92, at 262.

36. Shu'ayb 'Alim, *Arabic, Arwi and Persian in Sarandib and Tamil Nadu*, 502.

37. Susan Bayly, "Islam and State Power in Pre-Colonial South India," in *India and Indonesia During the Ancien Regime*, ed. P. J. Marshall and R. van Niel (Leiden: E. J. Brill, 1989), 143–64, at 155.

traditions which were eventually shared with other Muslims on the island.[38] Although the historical accuracy of some of these accounts cannot always be determined with certainty, such traditions attest to a sustained memory of participation in promoting networks of Arabicized language, literature, and learning that connected Muslims across the region.

In discussing such connections, the wide-ranging spiritual and intellectual networks of the Sufis must be mentioned. Individual masters, and to an even greater extent the various schools of mysticism that coalesced into Sufi orders, linked widely scattered communities with shared literatures and spiritual genealogies.[39] Similar stories relating the tolerance of Sufi masters toward non-Islamic forms of worship, their powers of healing, their supernatural perceptions, and their generosity toward the poor circulate in different regions, and they strengthen the impression that these figures played a central role in introducing local populations to aspects of Islam that are broadly shared among them, including a reverence toward "saints" and an emphasis on hagiographic literature.[40]

Although the Muslim communities I discuss no doubt had a strong sense of attachment to their particular locales, there were also ways in which a sense of place or space transcended the local, reaching toward the wider region and beyond its horizons. A shared notion of sacred space (differing from that found in Western Asia or North India) is evident in the architectural resemblances among the fifteenth-century Great Mosque of Demak, the eighteenth-century Selo mosque in Yogyakarta, the mosques of South India including those of Kayalpattinam and the Malabar coast (from the fourteenth century onwards), as well as the eighteenth-century Kampong Laut mosque in Kelantan, Malaysia.[41]

In a way parallel to that which I noted for Islamic literature, through which a distant and foreign history gradually became familiar by way of translation and prior texts, within the sacred space of the mosques attempts were sometimes made to introduce and recreate a faraway geography of great importance and sanctity for the local, often recently converted faithful. For example, the three-lobed *maḥārib* (pl. of *miḥrāb*, niche in a wall indicating the

38. B. A. Hussainmiya, *Orang Rejimen: The Malays of the Ceylon Rifle Regiment* (Bangi: Universiti Kebangsaan Malaysia, 1990), 38–42.

39. Richard M. Eaton, *The Rise of Islam and the Bengal Frontier, 1204–1760* (New Delhi: Oxford University Press, 2000), 28.

40. Anthony H. Johns, "Sufism as a Category in Indonesian Literature," *JSEAH* 2 (1961): 10–23; J. M. Cāli, *Tamiḻakattu Tarkākkaḷ* (Madras: Nūr Patippakam, 1981).

41. Shokoohy, *Muslim Architecture of South India*, 249.

direction of prayer) of the mosques in Madura and Kayalpattinam, of a type uncommon in India, are modeled on the miḥrāb in Jerusalem's Dome of the Rock.[42] A related, even more remarkable instance is found in Kudus, on Java's northern coast. The sole place in Java to adopt an Arabic name, it bears that of Islam's third most sacred city, Jerusalem (A. *al-Quds*).

The town's mosque, erected in the sixteenth century by Sunan Kudus, is known to this day as *Mesjid al-Aqsa*, named for Jerusalem's ancient mosque built on the Temple Mount, where Muhammad is believed to have passed on his Night Journey to the heavens. The mosque's foundational charter, inscribed in Arabic and said to have been brought from Jerusalem by Sunan Kudus himself, may be interpreted as drawing a parallel between this leader in an Islamizing Java and King David, the biblical unifier of Jerusalem.[43]

In Java localization through site names was apparently uncommon, but in this case a distant, sacred city and its holy mosque were erected anew in Java, mapping a center of Islamic piety and sanctity upon it. Sunan Kudus's journey to Jerusalem represented a venture into a larger Islamic world. It resulted in the enrichment and authentication of the Arabic cosmopolis he set out from, linking it explicitly to the historical heartland while declaring its own centrality. The Kudus inscription attests to a political role accorded to Arabic within the cosmopolis, as it was chosen, without the more typical translation act, to legitimize the ruler of a new Islamic center likely modeled on Jerusalem, ruled and rebuilt at the time by another leader of an expanding Islamic power, Suleiman the Magnificent.

Another case in point is the account of the famed Sunan Kalijaga orienting Java's first mosque (b. 1479, Demak) and the mosque in Mecca toward one another, which figures in many Javanese chronicles. It too attests to important notions of space, directionality of power within the Muslim world, and the claims made by members of the cosmopolis regarding their place and role within and beyond it as sanctified histories and geographies were adopted as their own.[44]

Taken together, such textual accounts, inscriptions, and epitaphs attest to the many ways in which Arabic and Arabicized language participated in the creation of new understandings of space, community, and authority. And so,

42. Ibid., 55, 91.

43. On the Kudus mosque and inscription, see Claude Guillot and Ludvik Kalus, "Kota Yerusalem di Jawa dan Mesjidnya Al-Aqsa: Piagam Pembangunan Mesjid Kudus Bertahun 956h/1549m," in *Inskripsi Islam Tertua di Indonesia* (Jakarta: Kepustakaan Populer Gramedia / EFEO, 2008), 101–32. In Islam, King David is known as a prophet, nabi Da'ud.

44. For a depiction of the Demak episode see the anonymous, nineteenth-century *Serat Walisana*, Pura Pakualaman Library, Yogyakarta, MS. PP Pi 32, p. 129.

despite the many differences that continued to exist among Muslim communities of various origins within the cosmopolis, they also shared a great deal. Central to translocal ties were a reverence towards, and certain familiarity with, Arabic language and terminology, Arabic's textual world, and religious figures representing Islam, all of which fostered a common bond. The sheer volume and scope of Arabic and Arabicized materials in the region is testimony to their centrality.

Shifting Cosmopolitanisms

These regions of South and Southeast Asia—as a part of a larger Muslim world and as an area with its own networks and characteristics—were not in any way static. On the contrary, they were constantly shifting, both internally and in relation to other regions of this global sphere. A textual corpus like the *One Thousand Questions* allows us to examine how agendas were set differently for different Muslim communities while, concurrently, a certain process of standardization was taking place, shaping shared perceptions and allegiances. For example, in some ways Muslims of the Tamil region and of Turkey in the sixteenth century surely belonged to a single global community. And yet in a text from one—the Tamil *One Thousand Questions*—a strong condemnation of homosexuality appears, whereas in a text from the other—a catechism manual (*ilm-i-hal*) in Ottoman Turkish—it is mentioned matter-of-factly as common practice.[45]

Other issues and stories, which do appear in the *One Thousand Questions* consistently across languages, indicate a standardizing impulse: the centrality of the prophets, rituals such as the five daily prayers and the fast, the descriptions of hell and paradise, and the like underscore elements which were considered as representing a translocal understanding of Islam's history and beliefs.

Not only was the Arabic cosmopolis of South and Southeast Asia shifting according to the specifics of time and place, but it was also never a singular entity in the region: overlapping, waxing, and waning cosmopolitan worlds existed and were not mutually exclusive. Some, like the Sanskrit cosmopolis analyzed by Pollock, had language as a central component. Persian is another case in point. As the result of a constant interaction between the literary matrices of India with those of Iran, Afghanistan, and Central Asia, Persian gradually emerged as the vehicle of rule, poetry, and administration in north

45. The catechism, *Mukkadime*, is one of the earliest known in Ottoman Turkish and dates from the fifteenth century (Tijana Krstic, personal communication 2005).

India, recognized as the language of politics and cultural accomplishment in nearly the whole of the subcontinent.[46] As I have shown, this linguistic and cultural influence was deeply felt in the Tamil region and beyond, with important textual sources—including the *One Thousand Questions*—translated from Persian into Tamil and Malay.

Other cosmopoleis, like the Arabic one or the Buddhist one studied by Anne Monius, were centered around religion, with language playing a greater or lesser role, depending on the circumstances. In her study of the *Maṇimēkalai*, a sixth-century Tamil-Buddhist narrative, Monius notes the recurring appearance of the goddess in subsequent centuries in a variety of languages and literary forms throughout Southeast Asia. Referring more specifically to southeast India and the Archipelago, she states that "a longstanding relationship among various monastic establishments in the Tamil port city of Nagapattinam . . . and the Sailendra kings of Java and Sumatra can be traced to at least the early eleventh century reign of the Cola king, Rajaraja I."[47] This provides clear evidence of a Buddhist cosmopolitan sphere, formed largely in the same region as the Sanskrit and Muslim-Arabic spheres, and of the importance of the literary element within it. A key example of how the Islamic cosmopolitan sphere of South and Southeast Asia and its literary networks connected and overlapped with the Arabian world is found in the history of the Hadrami diaspora. Its networks based on trade, writing, and kinship have long traversed the broad regions discussed throughout this book.[48]

A Return to the Story

The *Book of One Thousand Questions* traveled, changed, and prevailed over at least three centuries in South and Southeast Asia. What can it teach us?

In previous chapters I examined in detail how the particular language in which a story is told shapes its telling. In turn, the question arises of how the story itself shapes both the language and tradition in which it is told, and

46. Muzaffar Alam, *Languages of Political Islam: India—1200–1800* (London: C. Hurst, 2003), 121.

47. Anne E. Monius, *Imagining a Place for Buddhism: Literary Culture and Religious Community in Tamil-Speaking South India* (Oxford: Oxford University Press, 2001), 112.

48. On the Hadrami networks, see Engseng Ho, *The Graves of Tarim: Genealogy and Mobility across the Indian Ocean* (Berkeley and Los Angeles: California University Press, 2006). The *Book of One Thousand Questions* was certainly known in Yemen, the Hadrami homeland. For a description of a seventeenth-century manuscript from that region, see J. J. Witkam, ed., *Catalogue of Arabic Manuscripts in the Library of the University of Leiden and Other Collections in the Netherlands, Fascicule 4* (Leiden: E. J. Brill, 1986), 396.

the culture's understanding of the past. Like the human embryo depicted in the Javanese *Niti Mani*, which changes and takes form with every passing month, the *One Thousand Questions*—and many other texts—have over time developed and changed into their present form, embodying a powerful creative force.

Reading the *Book of One Thousand Questions*—in a way a literary network in its own right—reveals various kinds of interactions. There are those, as in the cases of Javanese and Malay, between the different tellings and copies of the story that make up the extended corpus in each language. These provide evidence of changes over time in a local community, and of diverse interpretations by speakers of the same language who reside in different places or belong to particular schools of thought.

Connections across languages are highlighted through common usage of words and phrases, common themes raised and addressed in the dialogue between Ibnu Salam and the Prophet, and a shared narrative frame and structure. In the *One Thousand Questions* tellings I examined, such similarities are especially evident in the comparison between Malay and Tamil tellings, which likely hark back to a common Persian source or even contact between Tamil and Malay traders or travelers visiting each others' lands.

Javanese tellings, which are quite markedly different, may have derived directly from an Arabic source or may be adaptations from Malay. It is likely that the line of transmission for the story was not really a straight line at all. Rather, it is probable that different tellings—in Persian, Tamil, Malay, Javanese, and Arabic—circulated concurrently in the region, perhaps at times crossing paths, giving rise to further changes and reinterpretations.

In addition to the links within and beyond language and place are the temporal links that define the story's regional histories. Almost three and a half centuries separate the composition of the Tamil text (1572) and the most recent copies, from the early twentieth century, preserved in Malay and Javanese. These years span fundamental changes in the region, among which the domination by colonial European powers over local political and economic systems is no doubt pivotal. I have noted, for example, that the rise of the *Sèh Ngabdulsalam* texts on Java at around the turn of the twentieth century—in which Ibnu Salam appears as teacher rather than disciple—corresponds with a decline (or cessation) of production of the older Samud story, attesting, perhaps, to the declining relevance of the previous story in a radically transforming cultural setting facing the challenges of modernity.

These different types of links that establish a literary network—whether of a single story, a corpus, or a combination of texts—create a kind of meta-intertextuality that extends across distances both great and small. The distance need not be geographical; many worlds can exist in one place at one time, as when Muslim and non-Muslim Tamils shared sacred pilgrimage sites and derived inspiration from texts using similar literary conventions but calling upon different divine powers for mercy. The distance can also be physically or temporally vast, as when Ibnu Salam's tale of conversion was recounted in different languages and during different centuries in India and Java. All such connections, in their multiple dimensions, are part of the creation and continuity of a shared cosmopolis of ideas, beliefs, idioms, and stories.

Having considered how a body of prior texts is created and the degree to which prior texts from Muslim sources were incorporated into the *One Thousand Questions*, one is compelled to ask whether the *One Thousand Questions* itself became a prior text, to be relied on for conversation and writing that would evoke familiar associations and memories. In his beautiful essay on the many Ramayana traditions of India, A. K. Ramanujan discussed how the Rama story ramifies throughout Indian culture. Not confined to the textual or even devotional sphere, it has found its way into lullabies, children's games, and many idiomatic expressions.[49] In the case of the *One Thousand Questions*, it is harder to make such a confident claim about where and how it figures in the cultural landscape, because the vast repository of topics that makes it such a fitting candidate as a prior text is not unique to it and appears—most often in partial form—in many other texts as well. Nevertheless, we may look to the "number questions" and the many miracles mentioned in the *Āyira Macalā* as kernels developed in later works. For example, the Tamil biography of the Prophet, Umaṟuppulavar's *Cīṟāppurāṇam*, written over a century after the *One Thousand Questions* by a descendent of its author, elaborates on many of the miracles only hinted at in the Prophet's *One Thousand Questions* epithets. The wide use of Arabic in other, later Tamil Muslim works may well have been inspired by Vaṇṇapparimaḷappulavar's pioneering Arabicized style.[50]

Considering not only the early hadith traditions about letters by the Prophet but also the *One Thousand Questions* itself in view of late nineteenth-century developments on Java and beliefs about the Prophet's intercessionary

49. A. K. Ramanujan, "Three Hundred Ramayanas: Five Examples and Three Thoughts on Translation," in *Many Ramayanas: The Diversity of a Narrative Tradition in South Asia*, ed. Paula Richman (Berkeley and Los Angeles: University of California Press, 1991), 22–48, at 35.

50. Examples include the *Tamīmaṇcāri Mālai* and Kacimpulavar's *Tiruppukaḻ*; see, respectively, David Shulman, "Muslim Popular Literature in Tamil: The Tamīmaṇcari Mālai," in *Islam in Asia*, ed. Y. Friedmann (Jerusalem: Magnes, 1984), 1:174–207, at 204, and David Shulman, "Tamil Praises of the Prophet: Kacimpulavar's Tiruppukaḻ," *Jerusalem Studies in Arabic and Islam* 27 (2002): 6.

powers points to how such a text—translated and adapted, initially foreign—becomes a potential prior text, in the light of which contemporary events may be assessed and understood. Accumulated textual layers resound with one another, shaping subsequent memories and understandings of the past.

The *One Thousand Questions* is also a component of, and resonates with, a larger literature of questions and answers, including the institution of the issuance of *fatwa*s by religious authorities, popular books in dialogue format offering advice on various issues, contemporary internet sites like Islam Q&A and Ask-Imam.com,[51] and perhaps even an idiomatic Javanese expression like "don't be like a Jew," alluding to one who asks too many questions.[52]

* * *

Throughout this book I have suggested thinking of translation and conversion as mutually constitutive processes. The significance of translation and conversion, as well as the interactions between them, was most evident when I considered the notion of prior texts, the creation of new histories for Muslim communities, and the wider contours of literary networks and their role in the Arabic cosmopolis in the region. A crucial element in the spread of Islam, and thus the creation of a translocal Islamic sphere, was translation—of texts, ideas, and stories—as well as the more subtle reconstitution of local languages infused by Arabic, by which they were "converted" into new forms of themselves. Through translation, communities gradually created, adopted, and accumulated the cultural resources that made memories of an Islamic past and a lived Islamic present possible.

As individuals and communities embraced Islam, the need arose for additional and ever larger translation projects, broadening the range of textual sources available to include many fields of Islamic learning and literature. Initially foreign histories combined and merged with local ones through joint genealogies and the localization of past events in familiar landscapes. Such works echoed with both the distant and the familiar, gradually blurring the lines between them, enhancing profound shifts in identity, social life, and political structures. Thus conversion to Islam and translation reinforced one another in multiple ways within the Arabic cosmopolis of South and Southeast Asia, itself a part of an even larger and more diverse Islamic global sphere. The cosmopolis's literary networks, along with its networks of trade and travel, contributed significantly to the shaping and vitality of Muslim

51. http://www.islam-qa.com/ and http://www.islam.tc/ask-imam/.
52. Wasim Bilal, personal communication, 2003.

life, which was rooted both in the universal community of believers and in the very local, specific manifestations of belief and practice.

The *Book of One Thousand Questions* teaches us much about these processes and their historical developments. It also demonstrates to us the importance of continuing to question, to debate, and to retell the stories that truly matter.

Bibliography

The Book of One Thousand Questions *in Arabic, Javanese, Malay, and Tamil*

ARABIC

Kitāb Masā'il Sayyidī 'Abdallāh Bin Salām Lin-Nabī. Cairo: Al-Yusufiya, ca. 1920.

JAVANESE

Samud. Perpustakaan Nasional Republik Indonesia, Jakarta. MS. PNRI KBG 434.

Samud. Perpustakaan Nasional Republik Indonesia, Jakarta. MS. PNRI KBG 413.

Samud. Perpustakaan Nasional Republik Indonesia, Jakarta, MS. PNRI Br. 504.

Samud. Leiden Oriental Manuscripts Collection, MS. LOr 4001.

Samud fragment in *Para Nabi Nerangaken Bab Rijal Saha Sanès-Sanèsipun*. Karaton Surakarta Library, Surakarta, 1823 [?]. MS. KS 339.1.

Sèh Ngabdulsalam in *Suluk Warna-Warni*. Fakultas Sastra Universitas Indonesia, Jakarta, 1930s. MS. FSUI PW 128.

Sèh Samud. Fakultas Sastra Universitas Indonesia, Jakarta, 1901. MS. FSUI PW 56.

Serat Samud. Pura Pakualaman Library, Yogyakarta, 1884. MS. PP St. 80.
Serat Samud. Fakultas Sastra Universitas Indonesia, Jakarta. MS. FSUI CI 109.
Serat Samud. Fakultas Sastra Universitas Indonesia, Jakarta. MS. FSUI CI 110.
Serat Suluk Samud. Museum Sonobudoyo Library, Yogyakarta, 1835. MS. MSB P 207.
Serat Suluk Samud Ibnu Salam. Museum Sonobudoyo Library, Yogyakarta, 1898, transcribed 1932. MS. MSB P173a.
Soeloek Sheh Ngabdoelsalam. Edited by Sastrawiryana. Surakarta: Albert Rusche and Co., 1913.
Suluk Sèh Ngabdulsalam. Fakultas Sastra Universitas Indonesia, Jakarta, 1901. MS. FSUI PW 56.
Suluk Sèh Ngabdulsalam. Museum Sonobudoyo Library, Yogyakarta, 1898. MS. MSB P184.
Suluk Sèh Ngabdulsalam in Kempalan Serat Piwulang. Museum Sonobudoyo Library, Yogyakarta, 1917. MS. MSB P 121.

MALAY

Hikayat Seribu Masa'il. Perpustakaan Nasional Republik Indonesia, Jakarta, 1757. MS. PNRI ML 200.
Hikayat Seribu Masa'il. Perpustakaan Nasional Republik Indonesia, Jakarta. MS. PNRI W 82.
Hikayat Seribu Masa'il. Perpustakaan Nasional Republik Indonesia, Jakarta. MS. PNRI W 83.
Hikayat Seribu Masa'il. Perpustakaan Nasional Republik Indonesia, Jakarta. MS. PNRI W 82.
Hikayat Seribu Masalah. Edited by Edwar Djamaris. Jakarta: Pusat Pembinaan dan Pengembangan Bahasa Departemen Pendidikan dan Kebudayaan, 1994.
Kitab Seribu Masa'il. Perpustakaan Nasional Republik Indonesia, Jakarta, 1910. MS. PNRI ML 442.

TAMIL

Vaṇṇapparimaḷappulavar. *Āyira Macalā.* 1572. Edited by M. Saiyitu Muhammatu "Hasan." Madras: M. Itrīs Maraikkāyar/Millat Publishers. 1984.

Additional Primary Sources and Secondary Sources

Abdel-Malek, Kamal. *Muhammad in the Modern Egyptian Popular Ballad.* Leiden: E. J. Brill, 1995.

Abu Amar, Imron H. *Sunan Kalijaga Kadilangu Kudus.* Kudus, Indonesia: Menara Kudus, 1992.

Adam, Ahmat B. *The Vernacular Press and the Emergence of Modern Indonesian Consciousness.* Ithaca: Cornell University Press, 1995.

Adang, Camilla. *Muslim Writers on Judaism and the Hebrew Bible from Ibn Rabban to Ibn Hazm.* Leiden: E. J. Brill, 1996.

Affifi, A. E. *The Mystical Philosophy of Muhyiddin Ibn 'Arabi.* Cambridge: Cambridge University Press, 1939.

Ahmad, Mohammad Inayat. *The Authenticated Miracles of Mohammad.* New Delhi: Award Publishing, 1982.

Alam, Muzaffar. *Languages of Political Islam: India—1200–1800.* London: C. Hurst, 2003.

Umaimah. Muhammad Ali. *Kisah-Kisah Para Nabi.* 2002. Yogyakarta: Mitra Pustaka, 2003.

al-Allusi, A. *Arab Islam di Indonesia dan India.* Translated by H. Basyrahil. Jakarta: Gema Insani Press, 1992.

al-Attas, Syed Muhammad Naguib. *Raniri and the Wujudiyyah of 17th Century Acheh.* Monographs of the Malaysian Branch of the Royal Asiatic Society. Singapore: Malaysia Printers, 1966.

Amisena, Harya Surya. *Serat Kadis Serta Mikrad.* Pura Pakualaman Library, Yogyakarta. MS. PP Is. 9.

Andaya, Leonard. "Aceh's Contribution to Standards of Malayness." *Archipel* 61 (2001): 29–68.

Arasaratnam, Sinnappah., ed. *Francois Valentijn's Description of Ceylon.* London: Hakluyt Society, 1978.

———. *Islamic Merchant Communities of the Indian Subcontinent in Southeast Asia.* Kuala Lumpur: Universiti Malaya, 1989.

———. "The Chulia Muslim Merchants in Southeast Asia, 1650–1800." In *Merchant Networks in the Early Modern World,* edited by Sanjay Subrahmanyam, 159–77. Aldershot: Variorum, 1996.

———. "Coromandel's Bay of Bengal Trade, 1740–1800: A Study of Continuities and Change." In *Commerce and Culture in the Bay of Bengal, 1500–1800,* edited by Om Prakash and Denys Lombard, 307–28. New Delhi: Manohar, Indian Council of Historical Research, 1999.

Arberry, A. J., ed. *A Second Supplementary Hand-List of the Muhammadan Manuscripts in the University and Colleges of Cambridge.* Cambridge: Cambridge University Press, 1952.

Armstrong, Karen. *Muhammad.* Oxford: Felicity Bryan, 1993.

Arnold, T. W. *The Preaching of Islam: A History of the Propagation of the Muslim Faith.* 1896. Lahore: Sh. Muhammad Ashraf, 1961.

Arps, Bernard. *Tembang in Two Traditions: Performance and Interpretation of Javanese Literature.* London: School of Oriental and African Studies, 1992.

Asani, Ali. "At the Crossroads of Indic and Iranian Civilizations: Sindhi Literary Culture." In *Literary Cultures in History: Reconstructions from South Asia,* edited by Sheldon Pollock, 612–46. Berkeley and Los Angeles: University of California Press, 2003.

Asani, Ali S., and Kamal Abdel-Malek, with the collaboration of Annemarie Schimmel. *Celebrating Muhammad: Images of the Prophet in Popular Muslim Poetry.* Columbia: University of South Carolina Press, 1995.

al-Attas, Syed Hussain. "On the Need for an Historical Study of Malaysian Islamization." *JSEAH* 4.1 (1963): 68–81.

al-Attas, Syed Muhammad Naguib. *Raniri and the Wujudiyyah of 17th Century Acheh.* Monographs of the Malaysian Branch of the Royal Asiatic Society. Singapore: Malaysia Printers, 1966.

———. *Islam dalam Sejarah dan Kebudayaan Melayu.* Kuala Lumpur: Universiti Kebangsaan Malaysia Press, 1972.

———. *The Oldest Known Malay Manuscript: A 16th Century Malay Translation of the 'Aqa'id of Al-Nasafi.* Kuala Lumpur: University of Malaya Press, 1988.

Azra, Azyumardi. "A Hadhrami Religious Scholar in Indonesia: Sayyid 'Uthman." In *Hadhrami Traders, Scholars and Statesmen in the Indian Ocean, 1750s–1960s,* edited by Ulrike Freitag and William G. Clarence-Smith, 249–63. Leiden: E. J. Brill, 1997.

———. *Jaringan Ulama: Timur Tengah dan Kepulauan Nusantara Abad XVII dan XVIII.* Bandung: Mizan, 1999.

———. "Opposition to Sufism in the East Indies in the Seventeenth and Eighteenth Centuries." In *Islamic Mysticism Contested: Thirteen Centuries of Controversies and Polemics,* edited by Frederick De Jong and Bernd Radtke, 655–86. Leiden: E. J. Brill, 1999.

———. "Networks of the Ulama in the Haramayn: Connections in the Indian Ocean Region." *Studia Islamika* 8.2 (2001): 83–120.

Basheer, Takkalai M. S. " Iculāmiya Ṅāṉam: Oru Viḷakkam." In *Meyṅāṉāmirtam,* 1–15. Madras: Tilshat, 2001.

Bassnett, Susan, and Andre Lefevere, eds. *Translation, History and Culture.* London: Pinter, 1990.

Bayan Budiman. Pura Pakualaman Library, Yogyakarta. MS. PP St. 16.

Bayly, Susan. "Islam and State Power in Pre-Colonial South India." In *India and Indonesia During the Ancien Regime,* edited by P. J. Marshall and R. van Niel, 143–64. Leiden: E. J. Brill, 1989.

———. *Saints, Goddesses and Kings: Muslims and Christians in South Indian Society, 1700–1900.* Cambridge: Cambridge University Press, 1989.

Becker, A. L. *Beyond Translation: Essays Toward a Modern Philology.* Ann Arbor: University of Michigan Press, 1995.

———. "Giving Distance Its Due (on 'Mutual Translatability')." In *Proceedings from the Annual Meeting of the Berkeley Linguistics Society,* edited by L. C. Bilmes, A. Liang, and W. S. Ostapirat, 1–15. Berkeley: Berkeley Linguistics Society, 1995.

Behari, Benkey. *Sufis, Mystics and Yogis of India.* 1962. Bombay: Bharatiya Vidya Bhavan, 1991.

Behrend, T. E., ed. *Katalog Induk Naskah-Naskah Nusantara: Museum Sonobudoyo Yogyakarta.* Jakarta: Jembatan, 1990.

———, ed. *Katalog Induk Naskah-Naskah Nusantara: Perpustakaan Nasional Republik Indonesia.* Jakarta: Yayasan Obor Indonesia, 1998.

Behrend, T. E., and Titik Pudjiastutu, eds. *Katalog Induk Naskah Naskah Nusantara: Fakultas Sastra Universitas Indonesia.* Jakarta: Yayasan Obor Indonesia/École Française D'Extrême Orient, 1997.

Benda, H. J. "Christian Snouck Hurgronje and the Foundation of Dutch Islamic Policy in Indonesia." *Journal of Modern History* 30 (1958): 338–47.

Berg, C. C. "Javanese Historiography: A Synopsis of Its Evolution." In *Historians of South East Asia,* edited by D. G. E. Hall, 13–23. London: Oxford University Press, 1961.

———. "The Javanese Picture of the Past." In *An Introduction to Indonesian Historiography,* edited by Mohammad Ali Soedjatmoko, G. J. Resnik, and G. McT. Kahin, 87–117. Ithaca: Cornell University Press, 1965.

Bhattacharya, Bhaswati. "The Chulia Merchants of Southern Coromandel in the Eighteenth Century: A Case for Continuity." In *Commerce and Culture in the Bay of Bengal, 1500–1800,* edited by Om Prakash and Denys Lombard, 285–305. New Delhi: Manohar, Indian Council of Historical Research, 1999.

Bin Ismail, Ibrahim. "Newbold's Malay Manuscripts in India." *Kekal Abadi* 5.1 (1986): 5–8.

Bjerrum, H. "Muslim Literature in Tamil." *The Moslem World* 15 (1925): 115–18.

Bobzin, Hartmut. *Der Koran im Zeitalter der Reformation*. Stuttgart: Steiner, 1995.

Braginsky, Vladimir. *The Heritage of Traditional Malay Literature: A Historical Survey of Genres, Writings and Literary Views*. Singapore: ISEAS, 2004.

Brakel, L. F. *Hikayat Muhammad Hanafiyyah: A Medieval Muslim-Malay Romance*. The Hague: Martinus Nijhoff, 1975.

Breckenridge, Carol A., Homi K. Bhaba, Sheldon Pollock, and Dipesh Chakrabarty, eds. *Cosmopolitanism*. Durham and London: Duke University Press, 2002.

Brockett, A. "Al-Munāfiqūn." In *Encyclopaedia of Islam*, 2d ed., edited by P. Bearman, Th. Bianquis, C. E. Bosworth, E. van Donzel, and W. P. Heinrichs, 7:561. Leiden and Boston: E. J. Brill, 2010.

Browne, Edward G., ed. *A Hand List of the Muhammadan Manuscripts, Including All Those Written in the Arabic Character, Preserved in the Library of the University of Cambridge*. Cambridge: Cambridge University Press, 1900.

———, ed. *A Supplementary Hand-List of the Muhammadan Manuscripts, Including All Those Written in the Arabic Character, Preserved in the Libraries of the University and Colleges of Cambridge*. Cambridge: Cambridge University Press, 1922.

Bruinessen, Martin van. *Tarekat Naqsyabandiyah di Indonesia*. Bandung: Mizan, 1992.

———. "Origins and Development of the Sufi Orders (Tarékat) in Southeast Asia." *Studia Islamika* 1.1 (1994): 1–23.

———. "Pesantren and Kitab Kuning: Maintenance and Continuation of a Tradition of Religious Learning." In *Texts from the Islands: Oral and Written Traditions of Indonesia and the Malay World*, edited by Wolfgang Marschall, 121–45. Berne: University of Berne, Institute of Ethnology, 1994.

———. *Kitab Kuning, Pesantren dan Tarekat: Tradisi-Tradisi Islam di Indonesia*. Bandung: Mizan, 1995.

———. "Controversies and Polemics Involving the Sufi Orders in Twentieth Century Indonesia." In *Islamic Mysticism Contested: Thirteen Centuries of Controversies and Polemics*, edited by Frederick De Jong and Bernd Radtke, 705–28. Leiden: E. J. Brill, 1999.

Bryant, Darrol M., and Christopher Lamb. "Conversion: Contours of Controversy and Commitment in a Plural World." In *Religious Conversion: Contemporary Practices and Controversies*, edited by Christopher Lamb and Darrol M. Bryant, 1–19. London and New York: Cassell, 1999.

Bulliet, Richard W. *Conversion to Islam in the Medieval Period.* Cambridge, Mass.: Harvard University Press, 1979.

Burnett, Charles. "Arabic into Latin in Twelfth Century Spain: The Works of Hermann of Carinthia." *Mittellateinisches Jahrbuch* 13 (1978): 100–34.

Cāhipu, K. E. S. Cultāṉ. *Nākūr Nātar.* Nākūr: Mīrāṉ Patippakam, 2002.

Cāli, J. M. *Tamiḻakattu Tarkākkaḷ.* Madras: Nūr Patippakam, 1981.

Campbell, Stuart. "Indonesian/Malay." In *Encyclopaedia of Arabic Language and Linguistics*, edited by Kees Versteegh et al., 2:340–45. Leiden: E. J. Brill, 2007.

Cattar. *Maṇimēkalai: The Dancer with the Magic Bowl.* Translated by Alain Daniélou. New Delhi: Penguin, 1993.

Christomy, Tommy. "Shattariyyah Tradition in West Java: The Case of Pamijahan." *Studia Islamika* 8.2 (2001): 55–82.

Coedes, George. *The Indianized States of Southeast Asia.* Edited by Walter F. Vella. Translated by Sue Brown Cowing. Honolulu: University of Hawai'i Press, 1968.

Coenders, H., ed. *Kramers vertaalwoordenboek Nederlands-Engels.* Amsterdam: Bona Ventura, 1996.

cook, miriam, and Bruce B. Lawrence, "Introduction." In *Muslim Networks from Hajj to Hip Hop,* edited by miriam cook and Bruce B. Lawrence, 1–29. Chapel Hill: University of North Carolina Press, 2005.

Couperus, Louis. *The Hidden Force.* 1900. Edited with an introduction by E. M. Beekman. Translated by Alexander Teixeira de Mattos. Amherst: University of Massachusetts Press, 1985.

Cowan, J. M., ed. *Arabic-English Dictionary: The Hans Wehr Dictionary of Modern Written Arabic.* Ithaca: Spoken Languages Services, 1999.

Cummings, W. "Scripting Islamization: Arabic Texts in Early Modern Makassar." *Ethnohistory* 48.8 (2001): 559–86.

Daiber, H. "Masā'il wa-Ajwiba." *Encyclopaedia of Islam,* 2d ed., edited by P. Bearman et al., 6:636. Leiden and Boston: E. J. Brill, 2010.

Dale, Stephen F. "Trade, Conversion, and the Growth of the Islamic Community in Kerala." In *Religious Conversion in India: Modes, Motivations, and Meanings,* edited by Rowena Robinson, and Sathianathan Clarke, 54–74. Oxford: Oxford University Press, 2003.

d'Alverny, Marie-Therese. "Translations and Translators." In *Renaissance and Renewal in the Twelfth Century,* edited by R. L. Benson, G. Constable, and C. D. Lanham, 421–60. Cambridge, Mass.: Harvard University Press, 1982.

Damono, Sapardi Djoko, and Sonya Sondakh, eds. *Babad Tanah Jawi: Mitologi, Legenda, Folklor, dan Kisah Raja-Raja Jawa*, vol. 1. Jakarta: Amanah-Lontar, 2004.

Davis, N. *The Errors of Mohammedanism Exposed or, a Dialogue between the Arabian Prophet and a Jew*. Malta: G. Muir, 1847.

Day, Anthony. "Islam and Literature in Southeast Asia: Some Pre-Modern, Mainly Javanese Perspectives." In *Islam in Southeast Asia*, edited by M. B. Hooker, 130–60. Leiden: E. J. Brill, 1983.

Devy, Ganesh. "Translation and Literary History: An Indian View." In *Post-Colonial Translation: Theory and Practice*, edited by Susan Bassnett and Harish Trivedi, 182–88. London: Routledge, 1999.

Dharwadker, Vinay. "A. K. Ramanujan's Theory and Practice of Translation." In *Post-Colonial Translation: Theory and Practice*, edited by Susan Bassnett and Harish Trivedi, 114–40. London: Routledge, 1999.

Drewes, G. W. J. "The Struggle between Javanism and Islam as Illustrated in the Serat Dermagandul." *BKI* 122.3 (1966): 309–65.

———. "New Light on the Coming of Islam to Indonesia?" *BKI* 124.4 (1968): 433–59.

———, ed. *The Admonitions of Seh Bari: A Sixteenth Century Javanese Muslim Text Attributed to the Saint of Bonang, Re-Edited and Translated with an Introduction*. The Hague: Martinus Nijhoff, 1969.

———. *Directions for Travellers on the Mystic Path: Zakariyyā' al-Anṣārī's "Kitāb Fatḥ al-Raḥmān" and Its Indonesian Adaptations*. VKI, vol. 81. The Hague: Martinus Nijhoff, 1977.

———. *An Early Javanese Code of Muslim Ethics*. Bibliotheca Indonesica, vol. 18. The Hague: Martinus Nijhoff, 1978.

———. "Javanese Versions of the 'Questions of 'Abdallah B. Salam.'" *BKI* 142 (1986): 325–27.

———. "Nur al-Din al-Raniri's Charge of Heresy against Hamzah and Shamsuddin from an International Point of View." In *Cultural Contact and Textual Interpretation*, edited by C. D. Grijns and S. O. Robson, 54–59. Dordrecht: Foris, 1986.

———. "The Story of Dewi Maleka." *BKI* 142 (1986): 327–29.

Drewes, G. W. J., and L. F. Brakel. *The Poems of Hamzah Fansuri*. Leiden: KITLV, 1986.

Dunn, R. E. *The Adventures of Ibn Battuta*. London and Sydney: Croom Helm, 1986.

Dutton, Yasin. "Conversion to Islam: The Qur'anic Paradigm." In *Religious Conversion: Contemporary Practices and Controversies*, edited by Chris-

topher Lamb and Darrol M. Bryant, 151–65. London and New York: Cassell, 1999.
Eaton, Richard M. *Sufis of Bijapur*. Princeton: Princeton University Press, 1978.
———. *Islamic History as Global History*. Washington, D.C.: American Historical Association, 1990.
———. *The Rise of Islam and the Bengal Frontier, 1204–1760*. 1993. New Delhi: Oxford University Press, 2000.
———. "Who Are the Bengal Muslims? Conversion and Islamization in Bengal." In *Religious Conversion in India: Modes, Motivations, and Meanings,* edited by Rowena Robinson and Sathianathan Clarke, 75–97. Oxford: Oxford University Press, 2003.
Echols, John, and Hassan Shadily. *An Indonesian-English Dictionary*. 3d ed., 1961. Ithaca: Cornell University Press, 1994.
Eickelman, Dale F. "The Study of Islam in Local Contexts." *Contributions to Asian Studies* 17 (1982): 1–15.
Ernst, Carl W. "Persecution and Circumspection in Shattari Sufism." In *Islamic Mysticism Contested: Thirteen Centuries of Controversies and Polemics,* edited by Frederick De Jong and Bernd Radtke, 416–35. Leiden: E. J. Brill, 1999.
Fathurahman, Oman, and Holil Munawar, eds. *Catalogue of Aceh Manuscripts: Ali Hasjmy Collection*. Tokyo: C-DATS, 2007.
Feener, R. Michael. "A Re-Examination of the Place of al-Ḥallāj in the Development of Southeast Asian Islam." *BKI* 154.4 (1998): 571–92.
———. "Introduction: Issues and Ideologies in the Study of Regional Muslim Cultures." In *Islamic Connections: Muslim Societies in South and Southeast Asia,* edited by R. Michael Feener and Terenjit Sevea, xiii–xxiii. Singapore: ISEAS, 2009.
Feener, R. Michael, and Michael F. Laffan, "Sufi Scents across the Indian Ocean: Yemeni Hagiography and the Eastern History of Southeast Asian Islam." *Archipel* 70 (2005): 185–208.
Fikri, Ali. *Jejak-Jejak Para Nabi*. Translated by Wafa Tholhatul Choir. Yogyakarta: Mitra Pustaka, 2003.
Florida, Nancy K. *Javanese Literature in Surakarta Manuscripts,* vol. 1: *Introduction and Manuscripts of the Karaton Surakarta.* Ithaca: Cornell University Press, 1993.
———. *Writing the Past, Inscribing the Future: History as Prophecy in Colonial Java*. Durham: Duke University Press, 1995.
———. "Writing Traditions in Colonial Java: The Question of Islam." In

Cultures of Scholarship, edited by S. C. Humphreyes, 187–217. Ann Arbor: University of Michigan Press, 1997.

———. *Javanese Literature in Surakarta Manuscripts*, vol. 2: *Manuscripts of the Mangkunagaran Palace*. Ithaca: Cornell University Press, 2000.

Freedman, Rich. "Rubies and Coral: The Lapidary Crafting of Language in Kerala." *The Journal of Asian Studies* 57.1 (1998): 38–65.

Friederich, R., and L. W. C. van den Berg, eds. *Codicum Arabicum in Bibliotheca Societatis Artium et Scientiarum Quae Bataviae Floret Asservatorum Catalogum*. Batavia: Bruining et Wijt and M. Nijhoff, 1873.

Friedmann, Y. "Qiṣṣat Shakarwatī Farmāḍ: A Tradition Concerning the Introduction of Islam to Malabar." *Israel Oriental Studies* 5 (1975): 233–58.

Gaur, Albertine. "Bartholomäus Ziegenbalg's *Verzeichnis der Malabarischen Bücher*." *JRAS* 3/4 (October 1967): 63-95.

Gallop, Annabel Teh, and Bernard Arps. *Golden Letters: Writing Traditions of Indonesia / Surat Emas: Budaya Tulis di Indonesia*. London: The British Library, 1991.

Genette, Gerard. *Paratexts: Thresholds of Interpretation*. 1987. Translated by Jane E. Lewin. Cambridge: Cambridge University Press, 1997.

Germann, Wilhelm. "Ziegenbalgs Bibliotheca Malabarica" (part 1). *Missionsnachrichten der Ostindischen Missionsanstalt zu Halle* 32.1 (1880): 1-20.

Gibson, Walter M. *The Prison of Weltevreden; and a Glance at the East Indian Archipelago*. New York: J. C. Riker, 1855.

Ginzberg, Louis. *The Legends of the Jews*, vol. 4: *From Joshua to Esther*. 1913. Baltimore: Johns Hopkins University Press, 1998.

Goitein, S. D. "Banū Isrā'īl." *Encyclopaedia of Islam*, 2d ed., edited by P. Bearman et al., 1:1020. Leiden and Boston: E. J. Brill, 2010.

Goldziher, Ignaz. *Introduction to Islamic Theology and Law*. 1910. Translated by Andras Hamori and Ruth Hamori. Princeton: Princeton University Press, 1981.

———. *Muslim Studies*. Translated by C. R. Barber and S. M. Stern. 2 vols. 1889–90. Chicago: Aldine, 1971.

Gomez, Luis O. "Observations on the Role of the Gaṇḍavyūha in the Design of Barabudur." In *Barabudur: History and Significance of a Buddhist Monument*, edited by Luis O. Gomez, 173–94. Berkeley and Los Angeles: University of California Press, 1981.

Gonda, J. *Sanskrit in Indonesia*. Nagpur: International Academy of Indian Culture, 1952.

Grijns, C. D., and Stuart Robson, eds. *Cultural Contact and Textual Interpretation*. Dordrecht: Foris, 1986.

Guillaume, A. *The Life of Muhammad: A Translation of Isḥāq's "Sīrat Rasūl Allāh."* London: Oxford University Press, 1955.

Guillot, Claude. "Banten and the Bay of Bengal During the Sixteenth and Seventeenth Centuries." In *Commerce and Culture in the Bay of Bengal, 1500–1800,* edited by Om Prakash and Denys Lombard, 163–82. New Delhi: Manohar, Indian Council of Historical Research, 1999.

Guillot, Claude, and Ludvik Kalus. "Kota Yerusalem di Jawa dan Mesjidnya Al-Aqsa: Piagam Pembangunan Mesjid Kudus Bertahun 956h/1549m." In *Inskripsi Islam Tertua di Indonesia,* 101–32. Jakarta: Kepustakaan Populer Gramedia / EFEO, 2008.

———. *Les Monuments Funéraires et L'histoire du Sultanat de Pasai à Sumatra.* Paris: Archipel, 2008.

Hagen, Gottfried. "Translations and Translators in a Multilingual Society: A Case Study of Persian-Ottoman Translations, Late Fifteenth Century to Early Seventeenth Century." *Eurasian Studies* 2.1 (2003): 95–134.

Hall, D. G. E. "Looking at Southeast Asian History." *The Journal of Asian Studies* 19.3 (1960): 243–53.

Halperin, David J. "The Ibn Ṣayyād Traditions and the Legend of al-Dajjāl." *Journal of the American Oriental Society* 96.2 (1976): 213–25.

Hamid, Ismail. *The Malay Islamic Hikayat.* Monograph Institut Bahasa Kesusastraan dan Kebudayaan Melayu. Kuala Lumpur: Universiti Kebangsaan Malaysia, 1983.

Hardy, Peter. "Modern European and Muslim Explanations of Conversion to Islam in South Asia: A Preliminary Survey of the Literature." In *Conversion to Islam,* edited by Nehemia Levtzion, 68–99. New York: Holmes and Meier, 1979.

Hart, Priya. *Guru.* Tel Aviv: Mapa, 2006.

Haskins, Charles Homer. *The Renaissance of the Twelfth Century.* Cambridge, Mass.: Harvard University Press, 1927.

Hefner, Robert W. *Hindu Javanese: Tengger Tradition and Islam.* Princeton: Princeton University Press, 1985.

Hidayat, Rachmat Taufiq. *Khazanah Istilah Al-Quran.* 6th ed. Bandung: Mizan, 1996.

Hirschfeld, H. "Historical and Legendary Controversies between Mohammed and the Rabbis." *The Jewish Quarterly Review* 10 (1897): 100–16.

Ho, Engseng. *The Graves of Tarim: Genealogy and Mobility across the Indian Ocean.* Berkeley and Los Angeles: University of California Press, 2006.

Hodgeson, M. G. *The Venture of Islam.* 3 vols., vol. 2. Chicago: University of Chicago Press, 1974.

Hooykaas, C. *The Old-Javanese Ramayana Kakawin with Special Reference to the Problem of Interpolation in Kakawins*. The Hague: M. Nijhoff, 1955.

Horovitz, J. "'Abd Allāh B. Salām." *Encyclopaedia of Islam*, 2d ed., edited by P. Bearman et al., 1:52. Leiden and Boston: E. J. Brill, 2010.

Houben, Vincent J. H. *Kraton and Kumpeni: Surakarta and Yogyakarta, 1830–1870*. Leiden: KITLV, 1994.

Howard, Joseph H., ed. *Malay Manuscripts: A Bibliographical Guide*. Kuala Lumpur: University of Malaya Library, 1966.

Huen, P. Lim Pui, ed. *The Malay World of Southeast Asia: A Select Cultural Bibliography*. Singapore: Institute of Southeast Asian Studies, 1986.

Hunter, Thomas. "The Poetics of Grammar in the Javano-Balinese Tradition." In *The Poetics of Grammar and the Metaphysics of Sound and Sign*, edited by Sergio LaPorta and David Shulman, 271–304. Jerusalem: Magnus, 2007.

———. "Translation in a World of Diglossia." Unpublished paper, 2009.

Hunter, W. W. *The Indian Musalman*. 1871. New Delhi: Rupa and Co., 2002.

Hurgronje, Snouck C. *The Achehnese*. Translated by A. W. S. O'Sullivan. 2 vols. Leiden: E. J. Brill, 1906.

———. *Muhammedanism*. New York: Putnam, 1916.

———. *Mekka in the Latter Part of the Nineteenth Century*. Het Mekkaansche Feest, 1880. Translated by J. H. Monahan, 1931. Reprint ed., Leiden: E. J. Brill, 1970.

Hussainmiya, B. A. *Lost Cousins: The Malays of Sri Lanka*. Bangi: Universiti Kebangsaan Malaysia, 1987.

———. *Orang Rejimen: The Malays of the Ceylon Rifle Regiment*. Bangi: Universiti Kebangsaan Malaysia, 1990.

Ibn Hishām, 'Abdul Mālik. *Al-Sīrat al-Nabawīyya*. 1936. Edited by Muṣṭafā al-Saqqā, Ibrāhīm al-Ibyāri, and 'Abd al-Ḥafīẓ Shalabi. 2d ed. Cairo: Maktabat wa-Maṭba'at, 1955.

Ikram, Achadiati. *Hikayat Sri Rama*. Jakarta: Universitas Indonesia, 1980.

Ilakkuvanar, S. *Tolkappiyam (in English) with Critical Studies*. Madurai: Kural Neri Publishing, 1964.

al-Jaelani, Abdul Qadir. *Celebration of the Desires through the Narration of the Deeds (Manaqib) of the Crown of Saints and the Conviving Beacon among Allah's Beloved Friends*. Translated by Julian Millie. Queenscliff, Australia: Joseph Helmi, 2003.

Johns, Anthony H. "Muslim Mystics and Historical Writing." In *Historians of South East Asia*, edited by D. G. E. Hall, 37–49. London: Oxford University Press, 1961.

———. "Sufism as a Category in Indonesian Literature." *JSEAH* 2 (1961): 10–23.

———. *The Gift Addressed to the Spirit of the Prophet*. Canberra: Australian National University, 1965.

———. "From Buddhism to Islam: An Interpretation of the Javanese Literature of the Transition." *Comparative Studies in Society and History* 9.1 (1966): 40–50.

———. "Islam in the Malay World." In *Islam in Asia,* edited by R. Israeli and A. Johns, 115–61. Jerusalem: Magnes, 1984.

———. "Sufism in Southeast Asia: Reflections and Reconsiderations." *JSEAS* 26.1 (1995): 169–83.

Jones, Russell. "Ten Conversion Myths from Indonesia." In *Conversion to Islam,* edited by Nehemia Levtzion, 129–58. New York and London: Holmes and Meier, 1979.

———. "The Origins of the Malay Manuscript Tradition." In *Cultural Contacts and Textual Interpretation,* edited by C. D. Grijns and S. O. Robson, 121-43. VKI, vol. 115. Dordrecht and Cinnaminson: Foris Publications, 1986.

———, ed. *Loan Words in Indonesian and Malay*. Jakarta: KITLV, 2008.

Juynboll, H. H. *Catalogus van de Maleische en Sundaneesche handschriften der Leidesche Universiteits-Bibliotheek*. Leiden: E. J. Brill, 1899.

Kahane, R. "Unique Patterns of Indonesian Islam." In *Islam in Asia*. edited by R. Israeli and A. Johns 2:162-88. Jerusalem: Magnes, 1984.

Kalabadzi, Abu Bakar M. *Ajaran-Ajaran Sufi*. 1985. Translated by Nasir Yusuf. Bandung: Pustaka, 1995.

Kartodirdjo, Sartono. *Indonesian Historiography*. Yogyakarta: Kanisius, 2001.

———. *The Peasants' Revolt of Banten in 1888*. VKI, vol. 50. The Hague: Martinus Nijhoff, 1966.

Katalog Manuskrip Melayu di Singapura. Kuala Lumpur: Perpustakaan Negara Malaysia, 1993.

Katalog Manuskrip Melayu Mikrofom. Kuala Lumpur: Perpustakaan Negara Malaysia, 1989.

Katalog Manuskrip Melayu Mikrofom Tambahan Pertama. Kuala Lumpur: Perpustakaan Negara Malaysia, 1998.

Kempers, A. *Cultural Relations between India and Java*. Calcutta: University of Calcutta Press, 1937.

Kern, H. *Ramayana Kakawin, Oudjavaansch Heldendicht*. The Hague, 1900.

Khan, Dominique-Sila. "Diverting the Ganges: The Nizari Ismaili Model of Conversion in South Asia." In *Religious Conversion in India: Modes,*

Motivations, and Meanings, edited by Rowema Robinson and Sathianathan Clarke, 29–53. Oxford: Oxford University Press, 2003.

Khan, Muhammad Muhsin. *Miracles of the Prophet Muhammad: Adapted from Introduction to Ṣaḥīḥ al-Bukhārī.* New Delhi: Taj, 1982.

Knappert, Jan. *Malay Myths and Legends.* Kuala Lumpur: Heinemann Educational Books, 1980.

Knysh, Alexander D. *Ibn ʿArabī in the Later Islamic Tradition.* Albany: State University of New York Press, 1999.

Koentjaraningrat. "Javanese Terms for God and Supernatural Beings and the Idea of Power." In *Man, Meaning, and History: Essays in Honour of H. G. Schulte Nordholt,* edited by R. Schefold, J. W. Schoorl, and J. Tennekes, 286–92. The Hague: Martinus Nijhoff, 1980.

Kokan, Muhammad Yousuf. *Arabic and Persian in Carnatic, 1710–1960.* Madras: Ameera, 1974.

The Koran. Translated by N. J. Dawood. London: Penguin, 1956.

Kozok, Uli. *The Tanjung Tanah Code of Law: The Oldest Extant Malay Manuscript.* Cambridge: St. Catharine's College and the University Press, 2004.

Kritzeck, James. *Peter the Venerable and Islam.* Princeton: Princeton University Press, 1964.

"Kuda Kecil Yang Menjadi Hamba Allah." *Al-Kisah,* September 2007: 50–53.

Laffan, Michael F. *Islamic Nationhood and Colonial Indonesia: The Umma Below the Winds.* London and New York: Routledge Curzon, 2003.

———. "Finding Java: Muslim Nomenclature of Insular Southeast Asia from Srivijaya to Snouck Hurgronje." In *Southeast Asia and the Middle East: Islam, Movement and the Long Durée,* edited by Eric Tagliacozzo, 17–64. Singapore: National University of Singapore Press, 2009.

Lawrence, Bruce B. "Islam in South Asia." In *The Oxford Encyclopaedia of the Modern Islamic World,* edited by John Esposito, 2:278–84. New York: Oxford University Press, 1995.

Lee, Samuel, ed. *The Travels of Ibn Baṭṭūṭa: Translated from the Abridged Arabic Manuscript Copies Preserved in the Public Library of Cambridge with Notes Illustrative of the History, Geography, Botany, Antiquities Etc. Occurring Throughout the Work.* London: Oriental Translation Committee, 1829.

Lefevere, Andre. *Translation, Rewriting, and the Manipulation of Literary Fame.* London: Routledge, 1992.

Leigh, Barbara. "Design Motifs in Aceh: Indian and Islamic Influences." In *The Malay-Islamic World of Sumatra: Studies in Polities and Culture,* edited by J. Maxwell, 3–33. Monash: Monash University Press, 1982.

Levtzion, Nehemia. "Toward a Comparative Study of Islamization." In *Conversion to Islam,* edited by Nehemia Levtzion, 1–23. New York and London: Holmes and Meier, 1979.

Lindsay, Jennifer, R. M. Soetanto, and Alan Feinstein, eds. *Kraton Yogyakarta.* Jakarta: Yayasan Obor Indonesia, 1994.

Lombard, Denys. "The Indian World as Seen from Acheh in the Seventeenth Century." In *Commerce and Culture in the Bay of Bengal, 1500–1800,* edited by Om Prakash and Denys Lombard, 183–96. New Delhi: Manohar, Indian Council of Historical Research, 1999.

Loth, Otto, ed. *A Catalogue of the Arabic Manuscripts in the Library of the India Office.* London: Stephen Austin and Sons, 1877.

Mabbett, I. W. "The 'Indianization' of Southeast Asia: Reflections on the Historical Sources." *JSEAS* 3.2 (1977): 143–61.

Maier, Henk. *We Are Playing Relatives: A Survey of Malay Writing.* Leiden: KITLV, 2004.

Marcinkowski, M. Ismail. "Persian Presence in Southeast Asia." *Encyclopaedia Iranica Online. July 20, 2004.* Available at www.iranicaonline.org.

———. "Shi'ites in Southeast Asia." *Encyclopaedia Iranica Online.* July 20, 2003. Available at www.iranicaonline.org.

Marhiyanto, Kholilah. *Kisah Teladan 25 Nabi dan Rasul.* Surabaya: Arkola, 1995.

Marrison, G. E. "The Coming of Islam to the East Indies." *JMBRAS* 24.1 (1951): 28–37.

———. "Persian Influences in Malay Life (1280–1650)." *JMBRAS* 27.1 (1955): 52–69.

Marsden, William. *The History of Sumatra, containing an Account of the Government, Laws, Customs and Manners of the Native Inhabitants, with a Description of the Natural Productions, and a Relation of the Ancient Political State of That Island.* London: Printed for the author and sold by T. Payne and son, 1784.

Mat Piah, Harun, Ismail Hamid, Siti Hawa Salleh, Abu Hassan Sham, Abdul Rahman Kaeh, and Jamillah Haji Ahmad. *Traditional Malay Literature.* Translated by Harry Aveling. 2d ed. Kuala Lumpur: Dewan Bahasa dan Pustaka, 2002.

McPherson, Kenneth. *The Indian Ocean: A History of People and the Sea.* New Delhi: Oxford University Press, 1993.

Meglio, R. R. di. "Arab Trade with Indonesia and the Malay Peninsula from the 8th to the 16th Century." In *Islam and the Trade of Asia,* edited by D. S. Richards, 105–36. Oxford: Bruno Cassirer and University of Pennsylvania Press, 1970.

Meilink-Roelofsz, M. A. P. "Trade and Islam in the Malay-Indonesian Archipelago Prior to the Arrival of the Europeans." In *Islam and the Trade of Asia,* edited by D. S. Richards, 137–58. Oxford: Bruno Cassirer, and Philadelphia: University of Pennsylvania Press, 1970.

Menocal, Maria Rosa. *The Arabic Role in Medieval Literary History: A Forgotten Heritage.* Edited by Edward Peters. Philadelphia: University of Pennsylvania Press, 1987.

Metcalf, Barbara Daly. *Perfecting Women: Maulana Ashraf Ali Thanawi's "Bihishti Zewar": A Partial Translation with Commentary.* Berkeley and Los Angeles: University of California Press, 1990.

———, ed. *Islam in South Asia in Practice.* Princeton: Princeton University Press, 2009.

Moestopo, Moehamad Habib. *Kebudayaan Islam di Jawa Timur: Kajian Beberapa Unsur Budaya Masa Peralihan.* Yogyakarta: Jendela, 2001.

Monius, Anne E. *Imagining a Place for Buddhism: Literary Culture and Religious Community in Tamil-Speaking South India.* Oxford: Oxford University Press, 2001.

Muchlis, A. *Dari Walisongo Hingga Sunan Bungkul.* Surabaya: Penerbit SIC, 1996.

Muhammad, Pīr. *Meyṅānappāṭalkaḷ.* Takkalai: Añcuvaṉṉam Pīr Muhammatiyyā Muslim Association, 1995.

Mursid, Subidara. *Hikayat Tuan Gusti.* 1897. Hussainmiya Collection, Department of National Archives, Colombo, Sri Lanka. Microfilm reel 182.

Muslim, Imām. *Ṣaḥīḥ Muslim: Being Traditions of the Sayings and Doings of the Prophet Muhammad as Narrated by His Companions and Compiled under the Title Al-Jāmi al-Ṣaḥīḥ by Imam Muslim.* Translated by Abdul Hamid Siddiqi. 4 vols. New Delhi: Kitab Bhavan, 1977.

Nainar, S. Muhammad Husayn. *Arab Geographers' Knowledge of Southern India.* Madras: University of Madras, 1942.

Narayan, V. "The Ramayana and Its Muslim Interpreters." In *Questioning Ramayanas,* edited by Paula Richman, 265–81. New Delhi: Oxford University Press, 2000.

———. "Religious Vocabulary and Regional Identity: A Study of the Tamil *Cīṟappurāṇam.*" In *Beyond Turk and Hindu,* edited by D. Gilmartin and B. Lawrence, 74–97. Gainesville: University of Florida Press, 2001.

Newby, Gordon Darnell. *The Making of the Last Prophet: A Reconstruction of the Earliest Biography of Muhammad.* Columbia: University of South Carolina Press, 1989.

Ni'mat Allāh. *Tareki Afghan.* Translated by Bernhard Dorn. London: Oriental Translation Committee, 1829–36.

Noer, Kautsar Azhari. *Ibn al-'Arabi: Wahdat al-Wujud dalam Perdebatan.* Jakarta: Paramadina, 1995.

Pearson, M. N. "Conversion in South-East Asia: Evidence from the Portuguese Records." In *The World of the Indian Ocean, 1500–1800: Studies in Economic, Social and Cultural History,* edited by M. N. Pearson, 53–70. Aldershot and Burlington: Ashgate/Variorum, 2005.

———. "Littoral Society: The Case for the Coast." In *The World of the Indian Ocean, 1500–1800: Studies in Economic, Social and Cultural History,* edited by M. N. Pearson, 1–8. Aldershot and Burlington: Ashgate/Variorum, 2005.

Pedersen, J. "Ādam." *Encyclopaedia of Islam,* 2d ed., edited by P. Bearman et al., 1:176. Leiden and Boston: E. J. Brill, 2010.

Peterson, Indira Viswanathan. "Lives of the Wandering Singers: Pilgrimage and Poetry in Tamil Saivite Hagiography." *History of Religions* 22.4 (1983): 338–60.

Pigeaud, Theodore G. T. *Literature of Java.* 3 vols. The Hague: Martinus Nijhoff, 1967–70.

Pigeaud, Theodore G. T., and H. J. de Graaf. *Islamic States in Java, 1500–1700.* VKI, vol. 70. The Hague: Martinus Nijhoff, 1976.

Pijnappel, J. *Maleisch-Hollandsch woordenboek.* 3d ed. Amsterdam: Frederik Muller, 1884.

Pijper, Guillaume Frederic. *Het boek der duizend vragen.* Leiden: E. J. Brill, 1924.

Pillai, Somasundaram J. M. *Two Thousand Years of Tamil Literature: An Anthology with Studies and Translations.* Madras: J. M. Somasundaram Pillai, 1959.

Pistor-Hatam, A. "The Art of Translation: Rewriting Persian Texts from the Seljuks to the Ottomans." In *XII Congress of the Comite International d'Études Pre-Ottomanes et Ottomanes,* 305–16. Prague: Academy of Sciences of the Czech Republic Oriental Institute, 1996.

Poerbatjaraka, R. M. Ng., and Tardjan Hadidjaja. *Kapustakaan Djawa.* Jakarta: Djambatan, 1952.

Poerbatjaraka, R. M. Ng., P. Voorhoeve, and C. Hooykaas. *Indonesische handschriften.* Bandung: A. C. Nix and Co., 1950.

Poerwadarminta, W. J. S. *Javaans-Javaans woordenboek.* Groningen and Batavia: J. B. Wolters, 1937.

Poerwokoesoemo, Soedarisman. *Kadipatèn Pakualaman.* Yogyakarta: Gadjah Mada University Press, 1985.

Pollock, Sheldon. "Literary History, Indian History, World History." *Social Scientist* 23.10–12 (1995): 112–42.

———. "The Sanskrit Cosmopolis, 300–1300 AD: Transculturation, Vernacularization, and the Question of Ideology." In *Ideology and the Status of Sanskrit,* edited by J. Houben, 198–247. Leiden and New York: E. J. Brill, 1995.

———. "Philology, Literature, Translation." In *Translating, Translations, Translators from India to the West,* edited by Enrica Garzilli, 111–29. Cambridge, Mass.: Harvard University Press, 1996.

———. "The Cosmopolitan Vernacular." *The Journal of Asian Studies* 57.1 (1998): 6–13.

———. "Introduction." In *Literary Cultures in History: Reconstructions from South Asia,* edited by Sheldon Pollock, 1–36. Berkeley and Los Angeles: University of California Press, 2003.

———. *The Language of the Gods in the World of Men: Sanskrit, Culture, and Power in Premodern India.* Berkeley and Los Angeles: University of California Press, 2006.

Prange, Sebastian R. "Like Banners on the Sea: Muslim Trade Networks and Islamization in Malabar and Maritime Southeast Asia." In *Islamic Connections: Muslim Societies in South and Southeast Asia,* edited by R. Michael Feener and Terenjit Sevea, 25–47. Singapore: ISEAS, 2009.

Qadhiri, Shaik Hasan Sahib S. A. *The Divine Light of Nagore.* 1980. Nagore: Habeen and Fahira Publishers, 1998.

Qazi, M. A. *A Concise Dictionary of Islamic Terms.* Delhi: Noor Publishing House, 1989.

Al-Qur'an dan Terjemahannya. Bandung: Diponegoro, 2000.

Rafael, Vicente L. *Contracting Colonialism: Translation and Christianity in Tagalog Society under Early Spanish Rule.* 1988. Durham: Duke University Press, 1993.

Raffles, Thomas Stamford. *The History of Java in Two Volumes with Maps and Plates.* 1817. 2 vols. London and New York: Oxford in Asia Historical Reprints, Oxford University Press, 1965.

Rahimsyah, A. *Biografi dan Legenda Wali Sanga dan Para Ulama Penerus Perjuangannya.* Surabaya: Penerbit Indah, 1997.

Rahman, Fazlur. "Translating the Qur'an." *Religion and Literature* 20.1 (1988): 23–30.

Ramakrishnan, S., ed. *Kriyāviṉ Taṟkālat Tamiḻ Akarāti Tamiḻ-Tamiḻ Āṅkilam.* Madras: Cre-A, 1992.

Ramanujan, A. K. *Speaking of Siva.* New Delhi: Penguin, 1973.

———. *Poems of Love and War.* New York: Columbia University Press, 1985.

———. "On Translating a Tamil Poem." In *The Art of Translation: Voices from the Field,* edited by R. Warren, 47–63. Boston: Northeastern University Press, 1989.

———. "Three Hundred Ramayanas: Five Examples and Three Thoughts on Translation." In *Many Ramayanas: The Diversity of a Narrative Tradition in South Asia,* edited by Paula Richman, 22–48. Berkeley and Los Angeles: University of California Press, 1991.

———. *Hymns for the Drowning: Poems for Visnu by Nāmmaḻvār.* 1981. New Delhi: Penguin, 1993.

Rao, M., S. Pande, and B. Misra. *India's Cultural Relations with Southeast Asia.* Delhi: Sharada Publishing House, 1996.

Ras, J. J., ed. *Babad Tanah Djawi: De prozaversie van Ngabehi Kertapradja voor het eerst uitgegeven door J. J. Meinsma.* Dordrecht: Foris Publications, 1987.

Reid, Anthony. *Southeast Asia in the Age of Commerce, 1450–1680.* 2 vols. New Haven: Yale University Press, 1988.

———. "Islamization and Christianization in Southeast Asia: The Critical Phase, 1550–1650." In *Southeast Asia in the Early Modern Era,* edited by Anthony Reid, 151–79. Ithaca: Cornell University Press, 1993.

Ricci, Ronit. "Translating Conversion in South and Southeast Asia: The Islamic *Book of One Thousand Questions* in Javanese, Tamil and Malay." Ph.D. diss., University of Michigan, 2006.

———. "A Jew on Java, a Tamil Torah Scholar, and a Model Malay Rabbi: Representations of Abdullah Ibnu Salam in the 'Book of One Thousand Questions,'" *JRAS 18*.4 (October 2008): 481–95.

———. "Conversion to Islam on Java and the 'Book of One Thousand Questions,'" *BKI* 165.1 (April 2009): 8–31.

———. "From Jewish Disciple to Muslim Guru: On Literary and Religious Transformations in Late Nineteenth Century Java." In *Islamic Connections: Muslim Societies in South and Southeast Asia,* edited by R. Michael Feener and Terenjit Sevea, 65–85. Singapore: ISEAS, 2009.

"Saving Tamil Muslims from the Torments of Hell." In *Islam in South Asia in Practice*, edited by Barbara Metcalf, 190-200. Princeton: Princeton University Press, 2009.

———. "Islamic Literary Networks in South and Southeast Asia," *Journal of Islamic Studies* 21.1 (January 2010): 1–28.

———. "The Ambiguous Figure of the Jew in Javanese Literature." *Indonesia and the Malay World* 38.3 (2010): 403–17.

———. "On the Untranslatability of 'Translation': Considerations from Java, Indonesia," *Translation Studies* 3:3 (2010) 287–301.

Richman, Paula. *Extraordinary Child: Poems from a South Indian Devotional Genre*. Honolulu: University of Hawai'i Press, 1997.

Ricklefs, Merle Calvin. "Javanese Sources in the Writing of Modern Javanese History." In *Southeast Asian History and Historiography,* edited by C. D. Cowan and O. W. Wolters, 332–44. Ithaca: Cornell University Press, 1976.

———. "Six Centuries of Islamization in Java." In *Conversion to Islam,* edited by Nehemia Levtzion, 100–28. New York and London: Holmes and Meier, 1979.

———. "Islamization in Java: An Overview and Some Philosophical Considerations." In *Islam in Asia,* edited by R. Israeli and A. Johns, 2:11–23. Jerusalem: Magnes, 1984.

———. *The Seen and Unseen Worlds in Java, 1726–1749: History, Literature and Islam in the Court of Pakubuwana II*. Honolulu: University of Hawai'i Press, 1998.

———. "Babad Sangkala and the Javanese Sense of History." *Archipel* 55 (1998): 125–40.

———. *A History of Modern Indonesia since C. 1200*. 1981. 3d ed. Basingstoke: Palgrave, 2001.

———. *Mystic Synthesis in Java: A History of Islamization from the Fourteenth to the Early Nineteenth Centuries*. Norwalk: EastBridge, 2006.

———. *Polarising Javanese Society: Islamic and Other Visions (C. 1830–1930)*. Singapore: National University of Singapore Press, 2007.

Riddell, Peter G. "Religious Links between Hadhramaut and the Malay-Indonesian World, C. 1850 to C. 1950." *Hadhrami Traders, Scholars and Statesmen in the Indian Ocean, 1750s–1960s,* edited by Ulrike Freitag and William G. Clarence-Smith, 217–30. Leiden: E. J. Brill, 1997.

Rinkes, D. A. *Nine Saints of Java*. 1910–13. Translated by H. M. Froger. Kuala Lumpur: Malaysian Sociological Research Institute, 1996.

Riyadi, Slamet. *Ha-Na-Ca-Ra-Ka: Kalahiran, Penyusunan, Fungsi dan Makna*. Yogyakarta: Yayasan Pustaka Nusantara, 1996.

Rizvi, Saiyid Athar Abbas. *A History of Sufism in India*. 2 vols. 1978. New Delhi: Munshiram Manoharlal, 2003.

Robinson, Rowena. "Modes of Conversion to Islam." In *Religious Conversion in India: Modes, Motivations, and Meanings,* edited by Rowena Robinson and Sathianathan Clarke, 23–28. Oxford: Oxford University Press, 2003.

Robson, Stuart. "Java at the Crossroads." *BKI* 137 (1981): 259–92.

———. *The Wedhatama: An English Translation*. Leiden: KITLV, 1990.

Robson, Stuart, and Singgih Wibisono. *Javanese-English Dictionary*. Singapore: Periplus, 2002.
Roff, William R. *Studies on Islam and Society in Southeast Asia*. Singapore: National University of Singapore Press, 2009.
Ronkel, Ph. S. van. *De roman van Amir Hamza*. Leiden: E. J. Brill, 1895.
———. *Mengenai Pengaruh Tatakalimat Arab Terhadap Tatakalimat Melayu*. Translated into Indonesian by A. Ikram. Jakarta: Bhratara, 1977. Originally published as "Over de Invloed der Arabische syntaxis op de Maleische." *Tijdschrift voor Indische Taal- Land- en Volkenkunde* 41 (1899): 498–528.
———. "Over eene oude lijst van Maleische handschriften." *TBG* 42.2 (1900): 309–22.
———. "De oorsprong van het Maleische woord tjoema." *TBG* 46.1 (1903): 71–72.
———. "Over den Oorsprong Van Het Maleische Woord Binara." *TBG* 46.1 (1903): 92–94.
———. "De oorsprong van het Maleische woord bagai." *TBG* 46.2 (1903): 241–42.
———. "De oorsprong van het Maleische woord djodo." *TBG* 46.2 (1903): 128–31.
———. "De oorsprong van het Maleische woord kamandikai." *TBG* 46.5 (1903): 476–77.
———. "De oorsprong van het Maleische woord pawai." *TBG* 46.5 (1903): 469–71.
———. "Tamilwoorden in Maleisch gewaad." *TBG* 46.6 (1903): 532–57.
———. "Over de herkomst van enkele Arabische bastaardwoorden in het Maleich." *TBG* (1904): 189–94.
———. *Catalogus der Maleische Handschriften in het Museum van het Bataviaasch Genootschap van Kunsten en Wetenschappen*. Batavia and The Hague: Albrecht and Co. and Martinus Nijhoff, 1909.
———, ed. *Supplement to the Catalogue of the Arabic Manuscripts Preserved in the Museum of the Batavia Society of Arts and Sciences*. Batavia and The Hague: Albrecht and Co. and Martinus Nijhoff, 1913.
———. *Supplement-Catalogus der Maleische en Minangkabausche handschriften in de Leidsche Universiteits Bibliotheek*. Leiden: E. J. Brill, 1921.
———. "A Tamil Malay Manuscript." *Journal of the Straits Branch of the Royal Asiatic Society* 85 (1922): 29–35.
———. "Malay Tales about Conversion of Jews and Christians to Muhammedanism." *Acta Orientalia* 10 (1932): 56–66.

Rowson, E. K. "Homosexuality in Islamic Law." *Encyclopaedia Iranica,* www.iranicaonline.org. Accessed April 1, 2006.

Sahabdeen, Mohamed A. M. *The Sufi Doctrine in Tamil Literature.* Colombo: Abdul Majeed Mohamed Sahabdeen Foundation, 1986.

Saktimulya, Sri Ratna. "Fungsi Wedana Renggan dalam Sestradisuhul." Masters thesis, Universitas Gadjah Mada, Yogyakarta, 1998.

———, ed. *Katalog Naskah-Naskah Perpustakaan Pura Pakualaman.* Jakarta: Yayasan Obor Indonesia, 2005.

Sarkar, H. B. *Indian Influences on the Literature of Java and Bali.* Calcutta: Greater India Society, 1934.

———. "A Geographical Introduction to Southeast Asia: The Indian Perspective." *BKI* 137 (1981): 293–323.

———. *Cultural Relations between India and Southeast Asian Countries.* New Delhi: Motilal Banarsidas, 1985.

Sastri, N. *South India and Southeast Asia: Studies in Their History and Culture.* Mysore: Geetha Book House, 1977.

Schimmel, Annemarie. *Islamic Literature of India.* Wiesbaden: Otto Harrassowitz, 1973.

———. *Mystical Dimensions of Islam.* Chapel Hill: University of North Carolina Press, 1975.

———. *And Muhammad Is His Messenger: The Veneration of the Prophet in Islamic Piety.* Chapel Hill: University of North Carolina Press, 1985.

Schomburg, Susan Elizabeth. "'Reviving Religion': The Qādirī Sufi Order, Popular Devotion to Sufi Saint Muḥyīuddīn 'Abdul Qādir al-Gīlanī, and Processes of 'Islamization' in Tamil Nadu and Sri Lanka." Ph.D. diss., Harvard University, 2003.

Sears, Laurie Jo. "The Transmission of the Epics from India to Java." In *Wisconsin Papers on Southeast Asia,* 1–44. Madison: Center for Southeast Asian Studies, University of Wisconsin-Madison, 1979.

———. *Shadows of Empire: Colonial Discourse and Javanese Tales.* Durham and London: Duke University Press, 1996.

Serat Kridhaksara. Museum Sonobudoyo Library, Yogyakarta. MS. MSB P93.

Serat Mikrad Nabi Muhammad. Museum Sonobudoyo Library, Yogyakarta, 1920s. MS. MSB I23.

Serat Pandhita Raib. Mangkunagaran Library, Surakarta, 1792, copied 1842. MS. MN 297.

Serat Walisana. Pura Pakualaman Library, Yogyakarta. MS. PP Pi. 32.

Shokoohy, Mehrdad. *Muslim Architecture of South India: The Sultanate of Ma'bar and the Traditions of Maritime Settlers on the Malabar and Coromandel Coasts (Tamil Nadu, Kerala and Goa).* London: Routledge, 2003.

Shu'ayb 'Alim, Takya. *Arabic, Arwi and Persian in Sarandib and Tamil Nadu.* Madras: Imāmul 'Arūs Trust, 1993.

Shulman, David. "Muslim Popular Literature in Tamil: The Tamīmaṉcāri Mālai." In *Islam in Asia,* edited by Y. Friedmann, 1:174–207. Jerusalem: Magnes, 1984.

———. "First Grammarian, First Poet: A South Indian Vision of Cultural Origins." *Indian Economic and Social History Review* 38.4 (2001): 359–61.

———. "Tamil Praises of the Prophet: Kacimpulavar's Tiruppukaḻ." *Jerusalem Studies in Arabic and Islam* 27 (2002): 86-108.

Siegel, James. "Kiblat and the Mediatic Jew." *Indonesia* 69 (2000): 9–42.

Silva, C. R. de. "Muslim Traders in the Indian Ocean in the Sixteenth Century and the Portuguese Impact." In *Muslims of Sri Lanka: Avenues to Antiquity,* edited by M. A. M. Shukri, 147–65. Beruwala: Jamiah Naleemia, 1986.

Simuh. "Gerakan Kaum Shufi." *Prisma* 11 (1985): 72–85.

———. *Sufisme Jawa: Transformasi Tasawuf Islam ke Mistik Jawa.* Yogyakarta: Bentang, 1999.

Simuh, Wasim Bilal, Yusuf Mundzirin, and Mohammad Damami. *Suluk, the Mystical Poetry of Javanese Muslims.* Yogyakarta: IAIN Sunan Kalijaga, 1988–89.

Smith-Hefner, Nancy J. "A Social History of Language Change in Highland East Java." *Journal of Asian Studies* 48.2 (1989): 257–71.

Soebardi. *The Book of Cabolek.* The Hague: Martinus Nijhoff, 1975.

———. "Santri-Religious Elements as Reflected in the Book of Tjentini." *BKI* 127.3 (1971): 331-49.

Soedjatmoko, Mohammad Ali, G. J. Resnik and G. McT. Kahin, eds. *An Introduction to Indonesian Historiography.* Ithaca: Cornell University Press, 1965.

Sofwan, R., H. Wasit, and H. Mundiri. *Islamisasi di Jawa: Walisongo, Penyebar Islam di Jawa, Menurut Penuturan Babad.* Yogyakarta: Pustaka Pelajar, 2000.

Steenbrink, Karel, A. *Beberapa Aspek Tentang Islam di Indonesia Abad Ke-19.* Jakarta: Bulan Bintang, 1984.

———. "Indian Teachers and Their Indonesian Pupils: On Intellectual Relations between India and Indonesia, 1600–1800." In *India and Indonesia During the Ancien Regime,* 129–42. Leiden: E. J. Brill, 1989.

———. *Dutch Colonialism and Indonesian Islam: Contacts and Conflicts, 1596–1950.* Translated by C. Steenbrink and H. Jansen. Amsterdam: Rodopi, 1993.

———. "Opposition to Islamic Mysticism in Nineteenth Century Indonesia."

In *Islamic Mysticism Contested: Thirteen Centuries of Controversies and Polemics,* edited by Frederick De Jong and Bernd Radtke, 687–703. Leiden: E. J. Brill, 1999.

Steiner, George. *After Babel.* 1975. Oxford: Oxford University Press, 1992.

Stutterheim, W. *Rama Legends and Rama Reliefs in Indonesia.* 1924. New Delhi: Abhinav Publications, 1989.

Subrahmanyam, Sanjay. "'Persianization' and 'Mercantilism': Two Themes in Bay of Bengal History, 1400–1700." In *Commerce and Culture in the Bay of Bengal, 1500–1800,* edited by Om Prakash and Denys Lombard, 47–85. New Delhi: Manohar, Indian Council of Historical Research, 1999.

Subramaniam, V. I. "Muslim Literature in Tamil." *Tamil Culture* 4.1 (1955): 73–88.

Sugonda, R. M. Harya. *Niti Mani.* Surakarta: Albert Rusche and Co., 1919.

Syakir Ali, M. *Serat Jaka Semangun: Studi Tentang Pengaruh Bahasa Arab Terhadap Bahasa Jawa.* Yogyakarta: Departemen Pendidikan dan Kebudayaan: Proyek Penelitian dan Pengkajian Kebudayaan Nusantara, 1986.

Talbot, Cynthia. "Inscribing the Other, Inscribing the Self: Hindu-Muslim Identities in Pre-Colonial India." *Comparative Studies in Society and History* 37.4 (1995): 692–722.

Tassy, Garcin de. *Muslim Festivals in India and Other Essays.* 1831–32. Translated by M. Waseem. Delhi: Oxford University Press, 1997.

Teeuw, A. "Translation, Transformation and Indonesian Literary History." In *Cultural Contacts and Textual Interpretation,* edited by C. D. Grijns and S. O. Robson, 190–203. Dordrecht: Foris Publications, 1986.

Thorn, William. *Memoir of the Conquest of Java; with the Subsequent Operations of the British Forces in the Oriental Archipelago. To Which Is Subjoined a Statistical and Historical Sketch of Java; Being the Result of Observations Made in a Tour through the Country, with an Account of Its Dependencies.* London: T. Egerton, Military Library, 1815; rpt., Hong Kong: Periplus, 1993.

Thurston, Edgar. *Castes and Tribes of Southern India.* 7 vols. Madras: Government Press, 1909.

Tibawi, A. L. "Is the Qur'an Translatable?" *The Muslim World* 52 (1962): 4–16.

Tibrīzī, Muhammad ibn 'Abd Allah al-Khaṭīb. *Mishkāt al-Maṣābīḥ.* Translated by James D. Robson. 4 vols. Lahore: Sh. Muhammad Ashraf, 1963.

Tolkāppiyam Poruḷatikāram. Tirunelveli: Caivacittānta Nūlpatippu Kaḻakam, 1977.

Toury, Gideon. *Descriptive Translation Studies and Beyond.* Benjamins Translation Library. Amsterdam and Philadelphia: John Benjamins Publishing Company, 1995.

Trimmingham, J. *The Sufi Orders in Islam*. New York and Oxford: Oxford University Press, 1971.

Tschacher, Torsten. *Islam in Tamil Nadu: Varia*. Südasienwissenschaftliche Arbeitsblätter. Halle: Institut für Indologie und Südasienwissenschaften der Martin Luther Universität Halle-Wittenberg, 2001.

———. "Circulating Islam: Understanding Convergence and Divergence in the Islamic Traditions of Ma'bar and Nusantara." In *Islamic Connections: Muslim Societies in South and Southeast Asia,* edited by R. Michael Feener and Terenjit Sevea, 48–67. Singapore: ISEAS, 2009.

———. "Commenting Translation: Concepts and Practices of Translation in Islamic Tamil Literature." Unpublished paper, 2009.

Tsuchiya, K. "Javanology and the Age of Ranggowarsita: An Introduction to Nineteenth Century Javanese Culture." In *Reading Southeast Asia,* 75–108. Ithaca: Cornell Southeast Asia Program, 1990.

Uwise, M. M., ed. *Tamiḻilakkiya Aṟapuccol Akarāti.* Madurai: Kamaraj University Press, 1983.

———. *Muslim Contribution to Tamil Literature*. Kilakkarai: Fifth International Islamic Tamil Literary Conference, 1990.

Uwise, M. M., and B. M. Ajmalkāṉ. *Islāmiyat Tamiḻ Ilakkiya Varalāṟu.* 4 vols. Maturai: Kāmāracar Palkalai Kaḻakam, 1986–97.

Venkatachari, K. *Maṇipravāḷa Literature of the Śrīvaiṣṇava Ācāryas*. Bombay: Ananthacarya Research Institute, 1978.

Venuti, Lawrence, ed. *The Translation Studies Reader*. London and New York: Routledge, 2000.

Voorhoeve, Petrus, ed. *Handlist of Arabic Manuscripts in the Library of the University of Leiden and Other Collections in the Netherlands.* Leiden: Leiden University Press, 1980.

Vreede, A. C., ed. *Catalogus van de Javaansche en Madoereesche handschriften der Leidsche Universiteits-Bibliotheek*. Leiden: E. J. Brill, 1892.

Wales, H. G. *The Making of Greater India*. London: Bernard Quartich, 1961.

Wensinck, Arent Jan. *Muhammad and the Jews of Medina*. 1908. Translated by Wolfgang Behn. Freiburg: Klaus Schwarz, 1975.

———. *The Ideas of the Western Semites Concerning the Navel of the Earth*. Amsterdam, 1916.

———. *The Muslim Creed*. 1932. Cambridge: Cambridge University Press, 1995.

———. "Lawḥ." *Encyclopaedia of Islam,* 2d ed., edited by P. Bearman et al., 5:698. Leiden and Boston: E. J. Brill, 2010.

Wieringa, E. P. "The Javanese Story of Dewi Maleka: A Transformation of a Persian or Perso-Urdu Tale." *BKI* 150.3 (1994): 584–87.

———. "A Javanese Handbook for Would-Be Husbands: The *Serat Candraning Wanita.*" *JSEAS* 33.3 (2002): 431–49.

———. "Dotting the Dal and Penetrating the Letters: The Javanese Origin of the Syair Seribu Masalah and Its Bantenese Spelling." *BKI* 159.4 (2003): 499–517.

Wieringa, E. P., Joan de Lijster-Streef, and Jan Just Witkam, eds. *Catalogue of Malay and Minangkabau Manuscripts in the Library of Leiden University and Other Collections in the Netherlands,* vol. 1. Leiden: Legatum Warnerianum in Leiden University Library, 1998.

Wink, Andre. *Al-Hind, The Making of the Indo-Islamic World,* vol. 3: *Indo-Muslim Society, 14th–15th centuries.* Leiden: E. J. Brill, 2004.

———. "'*Al-Hind*': India and Indonesia in the Islamic World Economy, C. 700–1800 A.D." In *India and Indonesia During the Ancien Regime,* 33–72. Leiden: E. J. Brill, 1989.

Winslow, M., ed. *A Comprehensive Tamil and English Dictionary.* 1862. New Delhi: Asian Educational Services, 1991.

Winstedt, Richard O. *A History of Classical Malay Literature.* 1940. Kuala Lumpur: Oxford University Press, 1969.

———. *An Unabridged Malay-English Dictionary.* 6th ed. Kuala Lumpur: Marican and Sons, 1967.

———. "Malay Chronicles from Sumatra and Java." In *Historians of South East Asia,* edited by D. G. E. Hall, 24–28. London: Oxford University Press, 1961.

Witkam, J. J., ed. *Catalogue of Arabic Manuscripts in the Library of the University of Leiden and Other Collections in the Netherlands, Fascicule 4.* Leiden: E. J. Brill, 1986.

Yocum, Glenn E. "Maṇikkavācakar's Image of Śiva." *History of Religions* 16.1 (1976): 20–41.

Zaman, Muhammad Qasim. "The Scope and Limits of Islamic Cosmopolitanism and the Discursive Language of the 'Ulama." In *Muslim Networks from Hajj to Hip Hop,* edited by miriam cook and Bruce B. Lawrence, 84–105. Chapel Hill: University of North Carolina Press, 2005.

Zoetmulder, P. J. *Pantheism and Monism in Javanese Suluk Literature: Islamic and Indian Mysticism in an Indonesian Setting.* 1935. Translated by Merle C. Ricklefs. Leiden: KITLV, 1995.

Zulkifli. *Sufism in Java: The Role of the Pesantren in the Maintenance of Sufism in Java.* Leiden: INIS, 2002.

Zvelebil, Kamil. "The Earliest Account of the Tamil Academies." *Indo-Iranian Journal* 15 (1973): 109–35.

Index

said to be corrupted in, 241; "number questions" in, 250; onomatopoeia in, 118, 119–20; particularities of, 116–28; patron acknowledged by, 99; Persian source of, 40, 98, 101, 132, 269; poetic language of, 100, 101; Portuguese context of, 98, 102–3; proverbs incorporated in, 118; as *purāṇam*, 100–101; purposes of, 104; reconstruction of sixteenth-century text, 102; as remnant of pre-Portuguese tradition, 103; repetitive use of vocative in, 121–22; riddles in, 135; self-identifies as *macalā*, 98; sensuality of, 118–19; table of contents of, 101; Tamilizing the text, 121–27; teacher as focus of, 196; title page of, *28*; topics covered in, 101; verses and sections of, 101; on writing as link between human and divine, 249; writing emphasized in, 120–21

Azra, Azyumardi, 97

Babad Jaka Tingkir, 168

Babad Kedhiri, 201

Babad Tanah Jawi, 6, 201, 203–4

al-Bal'ami, 35

Batavia Society of Arts and Sciences, 155–56

Bayly, Susan, 10, 264

bearded books (*kitab jenggotan*), 43

Becker, A. L., 166, 167, 170, 189, 245–46, 247

bhakti hymns, 125

Bibliander, Theodorus, 37

Bibliotheca Malabarica (Ziegenbalg), 102, 102n8

Bidāyat al-Hidāya (al-Ghazāli), 43, 52, 156

Bihishti Zewar (Thanawi), 39

bismillah, 131, 143, 158, 252, 254

Bobzin, Hartmut, 37, 38

Book of One Thousand Questions: Abdullah Ibnu Salam in, 21, 34, 67, 69, 71–72, 75–76, 99–100, 130–31, 149–50, 159–60, 189–95, 197, 201, 207–8, 216–27, 252; on Adam's Peak, 7; in Arabic, 35–37; Batavia MS. Nr. 553, 36, 252, 254; becomes commentary on local notions of conversion, 22; becoming prior texts, 248–60; brief history of, 34–41; closing of, 94, 189–90; continuity between Arabic and other tellings, 39–40; depiction of Ibnu Salam and Judaism in tellings in Javanese, Tamil, and Malay, 222–27; didactic purpose of, 213–14; earlier traditions of encounter of Abdullah Ibnu Salam and the Prophet, 220–22; English translation of, 38, 63; explicit interest in literary sources, writing, and transmission, 249; final question of, 131, 207; on genealogy of Muhammad, 236; guru-disciple model in, 234–41; as imported story depicting foreign past, 189; incorporation of questions into 'Abdullah encounter, 220; as inwardly directed, 256; Islamic rites and traditions introduced by, 70; in Islamization, 213; in Javanese, 39, 40, 47–49, 66–98, 269; Latin translation of 1143, 36–38, 62, 63, 189, 230, 250; as literary network, 269–70; little changed elements in translations of, 33; in Malay, 39, 40–41, 49, 52–55, 129–50, 269; manuscript found in Jakarta, 35–36; Muhammad's words in, 239–41; within multitext volume, 249; as not occurring in isolation, 229; number of questions in, 35, 36, 39, 40, 68, 72; "number questions" sequence, 250–51, 256, 270; as paradigm for examining "Arabic cosmopolis," 4, 20, 23; Persian tellings of, 38–39, 40, 41; print editions in Arabic, 36; Prophet Muhammad in, 20, 34, 67, 71–72, 75–76, 91, 99–100, 131, 189–95, 197, 207–8, 229–42, 252; religious conversion in, 20, 22, 34, 183–215, 242; representations of conversion in, 188–95; roles filled by, 214; roots in Qur'an and hadith literature, 20–21, 34–35; standardization impulse indicated in, 267; in Tamil, 40, 98–128, 269; translation discourse in Javanese, 47–49; translations of, 21, 35–41; Turkish manuscript of, 39; Urdu translations of, 39; what it can teach us, 268–71; wide scope of, 22. See also *Āyira Macalā* (Vaṇṇapparimaḷappulavar); *Samud* corpus; *Seribu Masalah*

Braginsky, Vladimir, 140

Brakel, L. F., 32, 132

Brawijaya, King, 204, 205, 207

Bruinessen, Martin van, 90n41

Brunei, Islamization in, 6

Buddhism, 231, 268

Buginese, 39

Printed and bound by CPI Group (UK) Ltd, Croydon, CR0 4YY

09/06/2025

14685709-0004